LANGUAGE PROCESSING IN SPANISH

LANGUAGE PROCESSING IN SPANISH

Edited by

Manuel Carreiras
Universidad de La Laguna, Spain

José E. García-Albea
Universitat Rovira i Virgili, Spain

Núria Sebastián-Gallés
Universitat de Barcelona, Spain

LEA LAWRENCE ERLBAUM ASSOCIATES, PUBLISHERS
1996   Mahwah, New Jersey

Lawrence Erlbaum Associates, Inc., Publishers
10 Industrial Avenue
Mahwah, New Jersey 07430

cover design by Cheryl Minden

Library of Congress Cataloging-in-Publication Data

Language processing in Spanish / edited by Manuel Carreiras, José E. García-Albea, Núria Sebastián-Gallés.
     p.   cm.
   Includes bibliographical references (p.   ) and index.
   ISBN 0–8058–1721–2 (alk. paper).
   1. Psycholinguistics.   2. Spanish language—Psychological aspects.   I. Carreiras, Manuel.   II. García-Albea, José E.   III. Sebastián-Gallés, Núria.
P37.L368 1995
401'.9'0946—dc20   95-37986
                                                         CIP

Books published by Lawrence Erlbaum Associates are printed on acid-free paper and their bindings are chosen for strength and durability.

Printed in the United States of America
10 9 8 7 6 5 4 3 2 1

CONTENTS

PREFACE

Since the early 1980s, there have been a number of important changes in Spain that bear, among other things, on scientific and academic policies: the number of universities has doubled; research funding has multiplied tenfold, with the creation of graduate scholarships, exchange programs, travel grants, and financial support for laboratory equipment; and the organization of scientific meetings has increased dramatically. Psychology has particularly benefited, as an emerging field that has developed in new university departments and curricula throughout the country. This development has coincided with a general trend within psychology toward the study of the functioning of the cognitive mind. The important role played by psycholinguistics in this enterprise has been reflected in the orientation of a considerable number of Spanish scholars and research groups. A sample of their main contributions to the field is offered in this book. In these introductory remarks, however, we offer a brief account of the process that has made it possible.

The concern about language is not entirely new among Spanish psychologists. On a smaller scale, and from quite different perspectives, the work of Mariano Yela in Madrid—on the factorial dimensions of verbal intelligence—and by Miquel Siguan in Barcelona—on developmental stages in language acquisition and bilingualism—prepared the ground during the late 1960s and the 1970s for the new generation. The changes experienced during the 1980s and 1990s provided opportunities for graduate and postdoctoral training in foreign universities; for establishing contacts and cooperative projects with some of the leading groups in psycholinguistic research all over the world; for attending international conferences; and, at home, for setting up laboratories and starting new projects with an even newer generation of graduate students.

Over these years, we were perhaps overengaged in keeping track of what was happening abroad, trying to absorb new ideas and techniques and test them in our language. Until very recently, we were blind to what was happening within our borders, ignoring the work of our closest fellows. We were trapped in an almost paradoxical situation. It was usually in other countries that we started to meet each other (while visiting foreign research centers or attending international conferences) and to discuss our work on Spanish (sometimes, obligated to speak in a foreign language); at the same time, we also began to meet our compatriots through publications in some of the leading journals in the field. We eventually discovered that exchange and collaboration in psycholinguistics might also be pursued with our next-door neighbors.

An initiative was needed to facilitate communication at home. A

Simposium de Psicolingüística, organized by Manuel Carreiras in Tenerife (April 1993), was an important step in this direction. It is illustrative of the situation just described that the first announcement of the event was made from the University of Oregon, where Carreiras was spending a short sabbatical. Further contacts with José García-Albea and Núria Sebastián-Gallés, at that time visiting at Rutgers University and the University of Pennsylvania respectively, served to consolidate the idea and ensure a certain level of continuity in the collaborative efforts.

The Tenerife Symposium attracted about 30 Spanish-speaking researchers who presented and discussed their work in a friendly and pleasant atmosphere. Everyone was convinced of the necessity of pursuing this kind of meeting periodically, so we planned to hold a symposium every 2 years, progressively opening them to the international community of psycholinguists. The second meeting took place in Tarragona, in April 1995, and was organized by García-Albea. We envisage a third one to be held in Oviedo in 1997, to be organized by Francisco Valle-Arroyo and Fernando Cuetos.

In addition to paving the way for continued interaction, the first symposium was a starting point for collaborative projects between participants, such as the creation of a lexical database for psycholinguistic research in Spanish—a project currently underway, promoted by Sebastián-Gallés, Cuetos, Carreiras and Martí—and the exploitation of a Spanish corpus of speech errors compiled by Del Viso, Igoa, and García-Albea (this corpus is already available). At the first symposium, a decision was also made to compile a set of contributions covering a wide range of topics in psycholinguistics, which was the origin of this book. From the beginning, it was clear to us that this book had to be written in English, to reach the international community and, to a certain extent, to acknowledge our debt to it for what we received during our training years. At the same time, we thought that it was important to incorporate research made on Spanish by Spanish authors, with new, challenging data, into the flow of present concerns about language processing in different languages.

The topics covered by this book range from one end of the spectrum of language-related behavior to the other: speech perception, lexical access in word recognition, relations between phonological and orthographic/visual representations, sentence processing, discourse comprehension, and language production. It goes without saying that the treatment of these topics is far from exhaustive. Nevertheless, each chapter focuses on questions of general interest within its areas, and in most cases they appeal to one or another particular feature of the Spanish language that is relevant to a given question.

Spanish, the third most widely used language in the world, belongs to the family of Romance languages and differs from English in a number of respects. Because English has predominated in psycholinguistic research, contrasting properties of Spanish may help to test the generality of language processing mechanisms and refine their description. The set of contrasting features considered in this book includes the following: acoustical and syllabic transparency (fewer vowels, no ambisyllabicity, no vowel reduction), shallow orthography, a much richer morphology, flexibility in constituent order within the sentence, less variability in intonational contours, and the existence of null pronominal subjects for inflected verbs. There are also interesting contrasts in the frequency of different types of units (syllables, words, phrases) whose impact on language processing are also considered. All in all, one of the main lines of argument throughout this book deals with the tension between universality and variation as a way of characterizing the functioning of our language capacities and processes.

We have organized the book to follow the processing steps from speech perception to language production. The first chapter, by Núria Sebastián-Gallés, focuses on the role played by syllabic and metrical structure in the segmentation of the speech signal that is required for accessing the mental lexicon. She compares results in Spanish and Catalan with the ones obtained by other authors in English and French, establishing a scale of influence for both kinds of variable (syllabic and metrical) that is sensitive to the phonological characteristics of each language.

The second and third chapters move on to visual word recognition and explore different aspects of lexical access through various priming techniques. Rosa Sánchez-Casas (chap. 2) examines the notion of access code in light of search-based and activation models. She questions the validity of structurally defined units (in terms of either phonological or orthographic syllables) and presents evidence, in Spanish and English, showing that access from partial inputs is mainly driven by a restrictivity principle operating on each word according to the statistical distribution of grapheme sequences in the language. José Cañas and María Teresa Bajo (chap. 3) concentrate on studying priming effects on lexical decision under different temporal constraints. They show how these effects can be attributed to either automatic activation processes or expectancy attentional strategies. They also suggest distinguishing these two types of prelexical factors from the kinds of postlexical strategies that are mainly associated with checking and decision routines (once lexical information has been made available).

In chapter 4, Francisco Valle-Arroyo tests dual-route models of reading in Spanish. This is a language with a shallow (transparent) orthography, where grapheme-to-phoneme conversion rules apply unequivocally, contrasting with languages, such as English, that have deep (opaque) orthographies. In spite of the potential advantage of nonlexical routines in Spanish, Valle-Arroyo provides convergent evidence, from children at different reading levels and from adult patients with different types of acquired dyslexia, that supports the availability and efficient use of lexically mediated routines in Spanish readers. The incidence of these routines increases with reading expertise and is particularly manifest in the dissociation pattern between phonological and surface dyslexics.

Reading behavior in a more constrained set of circumstances is also explored by Jesús Alegría in chapter 5. He considers the case of deaf children who receive early training in lip-reading, with the aid of a complementary system of manual gestures known as Cued Speech. Their performance in a variety of experimental tasks shows that these children closely resemble their normally hearing peers, as far as the role played by phonological information is concerned. Alegría advocates generality over differences in input modality, in much the same way as Valle-Arroyo argues for the generality of a dual-route model of reading over orthographic differences between languages. Alegria's is the only chapter that does not make explicit reference to the Spanish language, but the phonological closeness between French and Spanish provides some support for the hypothesis that similar processing mechanisms should be expected for deaf Spanish speakers.

The next two chapters deal with the issue of universality in sentence processing. They are representative of an intense dispute over parsing theories that has been provoked, in large part, by Spanish results. On the one hand, Fernando Cuetos, Don Mitchell, and Martin Corley (chap. 6) present evidence—from corpus studies, questionnaires, and on-line processing—that is difficult to reconcile with classical accounts of parsing based on structural principles. They propose, instead, a tuning model that is sensitive to the statistical prevalence of interpretative analyses, best suited to explain not only crosslanguage differences, but also other kinds of idiosyncratic variation (e.g., developmental and individual differences). On the other hand, Elizabeth Gilboy and Josep Sopena (chap. 7) criticize Cuetos et al.'s conclusions, appealing to the distinction between primary and nonprimary relations among constituents. They propose that the former are processed by universal mechanisms that honor grammatical constraints, whereas the latter are managed by the principles derived by the *construal hypothesis*. Under this hypothesis, preferences among alternative analyses are exposed to structural and nonstructural influences.

Apart from parsing operations (to recover phrase structure), sentence processing also includes mechanisms for establishing coreference relations between meaning-dependent elements (roughly termed *anaphoric expressions*) and their antecedents. In chapter 8, José García-Albea and Sheila Meltzer make use of the contrast between two types of null subject pronominals in Spanish—little pro and big PRO—in order to test the graded influences of linguistic and nonlinguistic factors on antecedent assignment. Through a slightly revised version of the crossmodal priming paradigm, they show that the role of contextual (nonlinguistic) information is constrained by the previous presentation of grammatical information, in agreement with a modular view of syntactic operation. From a different perspective, Manuel Carreiras, Alan Garnham, and Jane Oakhill (chap. 9) also examine the influence of linguistic and nonlinguistic variables on the interpretation of definite pronouns. They are more concerned with discourse comprehension in the light of the *mental models* theoretical approach, mostly using self-paced reading times as the performance measure. Through a long series of experiments, they disentangle a number of factors that clearly influence anaphoric resolution and that can be grouped into two classes, superficial and conceptual, which seem to operate in parallel.

In a further application of the mental models approach, Manuel de Vega (chap. 10) explores different kinds of inference that operate in the comprehension of narratives. He reports a wide range of experimental data that contribute to clarifying the mechanisms underlying the construction of a discourse-specific model to gain coherence from the text, to process spatial information, and to represent interpersonal relations (characters, emotions, goals, and beliefs). At the same time, de Vega analyzes the specific nature of this format of representation by distinguishing it from other kinds of representation, such as propositions, mental images, and schemas.

Finally, in chapter 11, José Manuel Igoa looks at the field of language production, addressing central topics concerning the architecture and functional properties of the corresponding system. He adopts the framework of a staged-level model to scrutinize the relations that may hold between message-level and sentence-level components, on the one hand, and among subcomponents of the latter, on the other. Evidence from spontaneous speech errors and self-repairs in Spanish shows a very limited top–down influence of conceptual processes on sentence formulation, whereas interaction is only allowed within the formulation processes themselves. Igoa also reports evidence from an experimental study in Spanish assessing the effects of lexical activation (semantic vs. phonological priming) on syntactic planning in a picture description task. His results suggest a functional separation of processes driven by meaning and thematic relations from those that are sensitive to word form and positional relations.

As already noted, the chapters included in this book are no more than a sampling of the contributions to psycholinguistic research from a Spanish perspective. Other topics and other highly active researchers have been neglected with no better justification than lack of space. It is worth recognizing here the existence of important lines of research—on, for example, language acquisition, language breakdown, bilingualism, and pragmatics—that have not been fairly represented. We hope that this initiative will serve as an incentive for better and more complete accounts of the progress achieved by Spanish psycholinguistics.

There is a long list of people and institutions that deserve our sincere gratitude. Thanks, first, to all the contributors to this volume, for their willingness to collaborate in the editorial process. We are most grateful to Jacques Mehler and Juan Seguí, who contributed greatly to the Tenerife Symposium and joined us in the early discussions that led to the plan for this book. We also thank some experienced friends who advised and supported us in the early stages: Chuck Clifton, Anne Cutler, Janet Fodor, and Morti Gernsbacher. In addition, we acknowledge a debt to our colleagues at the Universities of La Laguna, Barcelona, and Rovira i Virgili, who helped us to read the chapters, conveyed insightful comments to the authors, and provided support during the production of the book. Our thanks, also, to the staff of Lawrence Erlbaum Associates, in particular to Judith Amsel, Kathleen Dolan, and Chava Reyna Casper for their generous support, patience and understanding. A very special acknowledgement to Patricia Duarte who has taken care of the editing of this book. The Spanish Ministry of Education, the Research Council of the Canary Islands and the Research Council of the Generalitat of Catalunya provided financial support for most of the research and for organizing the symposia that form the basis of this book, we are pleased to acknowledge this support.

Finally, we thank many friends and colleagues, from home and abroad, who have influenced our training and interest in language research over the years. We especially thank our families for their understanding and silent collaboration during the time that we were so deeply engaged in this project. We dedicate this book to all of them.

Manuel Carreiras
Universidad de La Laguna
José E. García-Albea
Universitat Rovira i Virgili
Núria Sebastián-Gallés
Universitat de Barcelona

LIST OF CONTRIBUTORS

Jesús Alegría
Laboratoire Psychologie Experimentale
117 Av. Adolphe Buyl
1050 Bruxelles, Belgium
e-mail: alegria@ulb.ac.be

María Teresa Bajo
Departamento de Psicología
Universidad de Granada
Granada, Spain
e-mail: delagado@ugr.es

José Cañas
Departamento de Psicología
Universidad de Granada
Granada, Spain
e-mail: delagado@ugr.es

Manuel Carreiras
Departamento de Psicología Cognitiva
Universidad de La Laguna
38205 Tenerife, Spain
e-mail: mcarreiras@ull.es

Martin M.B. Corley
Department of Psychology
University of Edinburgh
7 George Square
Edinburgh EN8 9JZ
United Kingdom
e-mail: Martin.Corley@ed.ac.uk

Fernando Cuetos
Departamento de Psicología
Universidad de Oviedo
C/ Aniceto Sela s/n
33005 Oviedo, Spain
e-mail: cmssi2@vmesa.cpd.uniovi.es

Manuel de Vega
Departamento de Psicología Cognitiva
Universidad de La Laguna
38205 Tenerife, Spain
email: mvega@ull.es

José E. García-Albea
Universitat Rovira i Virgili
Departamento de Psicología
Carretera de Valls, s/n
Aptdo 576
43007 Tarragona, Spain
email: jegar@astor.urv.es

Alan Garnham
Experimental Psychology, BIOLS
University of Sussex
Brighton BN1 9QG
United Kingdom
e-mail: alang@epunix.susx.ac.uk

Elizabeth Gilboy
Departament de Psicologia Bàsica
Universitat de Barcelona
Passeig de la Vall d'Hebron, 171
08035 Barcelona, Spain
e-mail: egilboy@psi.ub.es

José Manuel Igoa
Departamento de Psicología
Universidad Autónoma de Madrid
Campus de Cotoblanco
Madrid, Spain
e-mail: jigoa@ccuam3.sdi.uam.es

Sheila Meltzer
Graduate Center of CUNY
33 W. 42 Street
New York, NY 10036
e-mail: sgm@cunyvm.cuny.edu

Don C. Mitchell
Department of Psychology
University of Exeter
Exeter
Devon EX 4QG
United Kingdom
e-mail: D.C.Mitchell@exeter.ac.uk

Jane Oakhill
Experimental Psychology, BIOLS
University of Sussex
Brighton BN1 9QG
United Kingdom
e-mail: janeo@epunix.susx.ac.uk

Rosa M. Sánchez-Casas
Universitat Rovira i Virgili
Departamento de Psicología
Carretera de Valls, s/n
43007 Tarragona, Spain
email: rscp@astor.urv.es

Núria Sebastián-Gallés
Departament de Psicologia Bàsica
Universitat de Barcelona
Passeig de la Vall d'Hebron, 171
08035 Barcelona, Spain
e-mail: nsebastian@psi.ub.es

Josep M. Sopena
Departament de Psicologia Bàsica
Universitat de Barcelona
Passeig de la Vall d'Hebron, 171
08035 Barcelona, Spain
e-mail: jsopena@psi.ub.es

Francisco Valle-Arroyo
Departamento de Psicología
Universidad de Oviedo
c/Aniceto Sela, s/n
33005 Oviedo, Spain

1

Speech Perception in Catalan and Spanish

Núria Sebastián-Gallés
Departament de Psicologia Bàsica
Universitat de Barcelona
Barcelona, Spain

All human beings share the capacity to use language. Therefore, there must be some fundamental functions common to all language users; the basic functioning of both understanding and producing language must be the same for all human beings.

Accordingly, most models of speech perception and acoustic lexical access assume that the primary underlying mechanisms are identical, regardless of the languages speakers and listeners are using. It is obvious that, to a certain extent, this must be the case, but it may also be that, beyond this basic commonality in language processing, there are language-specific routines that impose certain restrictions on the way languages are used. One of the fields where these differences seem to be most important is speech perception. If this were not the case, it would be nonsensical to write a chapter on speech processing in such-and-such a language.

In this chapter, we first present an overview of the state of the art in cross-linguistic studies of speech perception, and then proceed to detail studies in

Spanish and Catalan.

LANGUAGE SPECIFICITY

Language is a biological function. One of the basic concepts of biology is the adaptation of organisms to their environment. Therefore, given a certain genetic endowment, which will determine the limits and landmarks of development of a certain function, the precise form a function (organ) will adopt will depend (partially) on its interactions with the environment. All human beings are born with a genetic endowment that allows them to develop a linguistic capacity. This genetic endowment imposes some limits and restrictions on what can and what cannot be a natural language, the initial capacities of newborns to acquire a language, the sequence and pace of neurological maturation, and other fundamental cornerstones of language development and use.

Until very recently, the general assumption was that these constraints were extremely rigid, and therefore it was not useful to study language-specific properties to understand language processing. However, research conducted in different languages has shown that these differences are quite important, at least in the field of speech perception, for both theoretical and practical reasons.

From a theoretical point of view, two issues are crucial: First, it is important to know to what extent the mechanisms underlying speech perception are different (i.e., language-specific), and to what extent they are common. The second consideration is a developmental one. On the one hand, all human beings can learn any language at birth, and on the other, the only determining factors in developing a certain language and not another are environmental. Thus, knowing how adults process speech (in the stable state) can shed light on the way babies solve the problem of learning a language.

The study of crosslinguistic differences in speech perception is an important domain for many practical reasons, too. Consider the extreme difficulty we have when learning a new language as adults. A superficial analysis of the problems that adult learners suffer as second-language learners shows that strong biological (adaptational) processes took place during the first years of our lives (as, e.g., the work of Werker and colleagues has shown: Werker, Gilbert, Humphreys, & Tees, 1981; Werker & Tees, 1983, 1984). Very young children do not seem to make any effort in learning a new language; this is not only true of the acquisition of new words and syntactic structures, but also of basic mechanisms involved in speech perception. As adults, however, even when we know the words pronounced in a foreign language, we still may not be able to split the continuous sound stream into appropriate words. Being a native speaker of two Romance languages, I have found that my colleagues who are also native speakers of other Romance languages pronounce English very clearly, even clearer than native English speakers. Speakers of other languages, such as German, Russian or Japanese have a very poor pronunciation of English to my Romance ears! This tells us that there must be some specificity in the way languages are pronounced and/or perceived by speakers of different languages.

THE PROCESS OF SPEECH PERCEPTION

Speech perception is a process by which information contained in an acoustic stream is transformed into meaningful words and sentences. We do not discuss here either the complexity of this acoustic stream, or how the very first processes of transforming it into a suitable format for the nervous system are performed. Although no direct evidence is available, we can assume that these processes are universal and, therefore, no language-dependent.

Most classical models of speech perception (though not all; see further on) assume that this acoustic information is organized into sublexical units before the lexicon is accessed. These units are used to contact the lexicon to select the appropriate entry. Two important remarks must be made here. First, although no one model has made this assumption explicitly, this sublexical unit is presumed to be a universal, and therefore all speakers of all languages should make use of the same one. Second, there has been more or less general agreement that this sublexical unit is equivalent to something close to what linguists describe as a *phoneme*. Research performed crosslinguistically indicates that neither of these assumptions is correct.[1]

THE INITIAL WORK: THE IMPORTANCE OF STRUCTURES

As I have said, one of the central problems of speech processing is how the

---

[1]The argument that speakers of different languages use different words can be used to trivialize the issue under discussion. Speakers of different languages must have language-specific lexicons, but the important thing is that, apparently, properties of the sublexical units seem to be dependent on the phonological properties of the languages.

acoustic information makes contact with the lexicon. Two solutions have been proposed. First, acoustic information (almost) directly contacts the lexicon. This approach assumes that there are no intermediate (prelexical) representations between the speech signal and the lexicon. Various models, such as LAFS (Klatt, 1977, 1989) and Cohort (Marslen-Wilson, 1987), propose such a solution.

The second solution is that some kind of representation is computed between the acoustic signal and the lexicon. As just mentioned, this prelexical representation has commonly been considered to be the phoneme (Cutler & Norris, 1979; Foss & Blank, 1980; McClelland & Elman, 1986; Pitt & Samuel, 1990a). However, other researchers have proposed and considered larger units (Savin and Bever, 1979). In a seminal paper, Mehler, Dommergues, Frauenfelder, and Seguí (1981) provided clear experimental data in support of larger units in speech perception. In their experiments, subjects had to monitor for either consonant-vowel (CV) or CVC sequences in bisyllabic words that started with CV or CVC syllables. Experimental items were pairs of words starting with the same CVC sequence (e.g., for instance *PALace* and *PALmier*), but one of the members of each pair had an initial CV syllable (such as *PALace*), whereas the other had a CVC syllable (such as *PALmier*). If the syllable was a prelexical unit, it would be expected that when subjects had to detect fragments at the beginning of words matching their syllabic structure, they would be faster than when there was no such match. In contrast, if the phoneme was the speech segmentation unit no syllabic effect would be expected, but there would be an overall advantage of CV fragment detection times over CVC fragment detection times. Results showed that when subjects had to detect *pa* in *palace,* they reacted faster than when they had to detect *pa* in *palmier,* and the reverse occurred when subjects had to detect *pal.* From these results, Mehler et al. concluded that subjects had segmented the speech stream into syllable-sized units before accessing the lexicon.

Cutler, Mehler, Norris and Seguí (1983, 1986) tried to replicate in english the experiments of Mehler et al., which had been performed in French, but they could not obtain the original pattern observed in French: an interaction between the structure of the initial syllable of the word and that of the target fragment. English subjects showed a pattern that presented an overall advantage in detecting CV and CVC sequences in CV words over CV[C] words. In fact, it has been impossible, up to now, to show any syllabic effect in English in spite of the variety of experimental procedures used. Therefore, it seems safe to surmise that English speakers do not segment the speech stream into syllable-sized units before contacting the lexicon. What kind of strategy do English speakers use to segment the speech signal? Using a wide variety of experimental procedures and data, Cutler and her coworkers (Cutler, 1990; Cutler & Norris, 1988) have been able to establish that English speakers seem to segment the speech signal at the onset of every strong syllable. This strategy is considered in detail in the following sections.

The consequences of these studies have been very important: They have proved the existence of language-specific mechanisms in speech segmentation. More recent research has found language-specific segmentation strategies in other languages, such as Japanese (Otake, Hatano, Cutler, & Mehler, 1993), Dutch (Zwitserlood, Schriefers, Lahiri, & Donselaar, 1993; Vroomen and de Gelder, in press), Portuguese (Morais, Kolinsky, Cluytens, & Pasdeloup, 1993), Spanish, and Catalan. In the following sections, I review the work carried out in these two last languages.

STUDIES ON THE STATUS OF THE SYLLABLE IN CATALAN AND SPANISH

In explaining the differences between the patterns of results obtained in French and English, Cutler et al. (1983, 1986) argued that they reflected differential ways the phonological properties of the languages are treated by native speakers. In short, French, being a Romance language, has clear syllabic boundaries, whereas English, a Germanic language, has widespread ambisyllabicity.[2] The lack of clear syllabic boundaries prevents English speakers from using syllables as suitable segmentation units. However, the phonological structure of English can be properly described in terms of metrical rhythmic structures, such as *feet*. Feet are suprasyllabic structures that characterize the rhythm of a language. English rhythm is characterized by groups of syllables all starting with a strong (not a reduced) vowel.

Cutler et al. predicted that the pattern of results obtained in French would be replicated in other syllabic languages. Nevertheless, the differences between the French and English experiments of Mehler et al. and Cutler et al. did not concern the existence, or nonexistence, of clear syllabic boundaries. First, French is a language with fixed stress: All words are stressed on the last syllable; English is a language with variable stress. Furthermore, the types of stimuli employed in the two experiments also differed in terms of stress value: Whereas the French words were stressed on the second (i.e., last syllable), the English words were stressed on the first. Second, French does not have vowel reduction,

---

[2]In English, a word like *lemon* can be syllabified as *le·mon, lem·on* or even *le[m]on* (the *m* belonging to both syllables at the same time). This phenomenon is known as *ambisyllabicity,* because the same phoneme can belong to two different syllables at the same time.

whereas English does. Given these differences between the two languages, it was worthwhile to run an experiment in other languages that could confirm or disprove the explanation proposed by Cutler et al. for the discrepancies between the French and English results in terms of the lack of syllabic boundaries. The differences observed between the two languages may simply have been due to a difference in the material, and may have had nothing to do with the phonological properties of the languages.[3]

Sebastián, Dupoux, Seguí and Mehler (1992) performed a replication of the French and English studies, controlling for these differences. Catalan and Spanish were the perfect choices: Both languages have clear syllabic boundaries; therefore, if the explanation in terms of the existence or non-existence of syllabic boundaries is valid, both languages would show the same pattern as French. However, both also have variable stress position. If this was the determining factor, they would show patterns of results close to the English case. Finally, Catalan has vowel reduction, whereas Spanish does not. If the existence of vowel reduction prevented subjects from showing a syllabic effect, Spanish would show a pattern close to the French, whereas Catalan subjects should perform the task without showing syllabic effects (as the English subjects did). The stimuli for the Catalan and Spanish studies included first- and second-syllable stressed words. The pattern of results are shown in Tables 1.1 and 1.2.

The Catalan pattern of results, that is, a lack of syllabic effect on reaction time (RT) in stressed syllables and a significant syllabic effect in unstressed syllables, supported the hypothesis that the differences between the French and English data were due to differences in the materials. However, the pattern of results in Spanish counter this explanation. No syllabic effects were found in Spanish for any type of material. This was surprising. First, all hypotheses predicted some syllabic effects in Spanish (if they had also been found in Catalan). Second, other research (Bradley, Sánchez-Casas and García-Albea, 1993; Sánchez-Casas, 1988) had found significant syllabic effects (although with different materials, and slightly different experimental procedures[4]) in Spanish.

---

[3]In fact, such an explanation was partially contested by the fact that the French subjects, when presented with the English stimuli, still showed a syllabic effect. When the English-speaking subjects were presented with the French stimuli, they did not show any syllabic effects in performing the task. Recent research, however, has shown that French subjects have difficulty perceiving stress in other languages (Dupoux, Pallier, Sebastián & Mehler, 1995), and it may also be the case that the way stress is encoded in French makes it very difficult for English speakers to perceive it correctly.

[4]In these experiments, trisyllabic items were employed, all second-syllable stressed. Moreover, catch trials were included in the filler lists; in these trials, the target shared either the first consonant or the first vowel of the critical word. This type of trial did not exist in any of the other reported

TABLE 1.1

Mean RTs (in ms) in the Fragment Detection Task in Catalan

	First syllable stressed		Second syllable stressed	
	CV word	CVC word	CV word	CVC word
Target CV	329	350	338	343
Target CVC	342	359	353	332

TABLE 1.2

Mean RTs (in ms) in the Fragment Detection Task in Spanish

	First syllable stressed		Second syllable stressed	
	CV word	CVC word	CV word	CVC word
Target CV	355	373	373	385
Target CVC	372	379	382	394

Sebastián et al. (1992) offered an explanation of this lack of effect in terms of the *acoustic transparency* of Spanish. Spanish is a language with few vowels (five) and a relatively reduced syllabic inventory. Given the characteristics of the task, it could be that, under certain circumstances (e.g., involving fast responses), subjects perform the task using low-level information of an acoustic type. This may account for the lack of effects in Spanish (for stressed and unstressed syllables) and partially in Catalan (stressed syllables). In fact, RTs in the Sánchez-Casas experiments were much longer than those obtained by Sebastián et al. (575 ms *vs.* 373 ms respectively).

To test this explanation, two more experiments were performed in which subjects' responses were slowed down by their having to perform a concurrent task (subjects were asked to pay attention to the semantic relations that could arise between words in the list). Results are shown in Tables 1.3 and 1.4.

As expected, clear syllabic effects (interaction between target structure and word structure) were found in both stressed and unstressed syllables in both languages. Therefore, the data obtained in Catalan and Spanish confirmed the original explanation of the differences between French- and English-speaking

experiments (not even the French and English ones).

subjects in terms of a contrast in the way the speech signal is analyzed by speakers of the two languages. Speakers of languages with clear syllabic boundaries (e.g. French, Spanish, and Catalan) seem to syllabify the speech signal, whereas speakers of languages with widespread ambisyllabicity do not.

TABLE 1.3
Mean RTs (in ms) in the Fragment Detection Task in Catalan With Slow Responses

	First syllable stressed		Second syllable stressed	
	CV word	CVC word	CV word	CVC word
Target CV	456	502	493	515
Target CVC	501	490	515	515

TABLE 1.4
Mean RTs (in ms) in the Fragment Detection Task in Spanish With Slow Responses

	First syllable stressed		Second syllable stressed	
	CV word	CVC word	CV word	CVC word
Target CV	589	643	586	640
Target CVC	614	625	612	616

These studies show that the picture is far more complex than was previously thought. Although syllabic effects were obtained in both Catalan and Spanish, subjects seemed to be able to respond without taking into account the full syllabic structure of the words. Syllabic effects may come and go, depending on the subjects' speed of response. Therefore, further research was needed to support the conclusion that Spanish speakers syllabify the speech signal. Pallier, Sebastián, Felguera, Christophe, and Mehler (1993; see also Sebastián & Felguera, 1992), used a totally different technique to assess this assertion.

In their experiments, they asked subjects to detect phonemes inside words or pseudowords. Experimental stimuli appeared in the third phonemic position, but they could be either the onset of a syllable (e.g., p in capricho) or the coda (e.g., p in captura).[5] These stimuli were embedded in two different lists; in one,

---

[5]In fact, there were other experimental conditions, but these two are enough for our purposes.

target fillers were almost always in the onset position, in the other, target fillers were almost always in the coda position (although, as with the experimental stimuli, the targets were in the third phonemic position). Half of the subjects were tested with the *onset list* (target fillers in the onset position), and the other half with the *coda list* (target fillers in the coda position). If subjects did not build the syllabic structure while listening to the speech stimuli, the two groups of subjects should display the same RTs for the two types of experimental stimuli, because all of them almost always detected stimuli in the third phonemic position. But if the syllabic structure of the words had been computed, then the two groups should be induced to expect the targets in a precise syllabic position: Subjects detecting most of the fillers in the onset position should be slowed down when experimental targets appeared in the coda (unexpected) position, but not when they appeared in the onset (expected) position, and the reverse pattern should be obtained for subjects detecting most of the fillers in the coda position.

Pallier et al. (1993) obtained a pattern of results consistent with the hypothesis that subjects computed the syllabic structure of the stimuli. This result was obtained with both French and Spanish subjects and materials. Interestingly, Pallier (1994), using the same technique and experimental setting, did not find this pattern with American English-speaking subjects.

THE IMPORTANCE OF METRICS: THE ROLE OF STRESS

The research just described clearly shows that in languages with clear syllabic boundaries (such as Romance languages), listeners segment the speech stream into syllable-sized units before accessing the mental lexicon. It also shows that listeners of languages like English compute stress while segmenting the speech signal. However, although French does not have contrastive lexical stress and English does not have clear syllabic boundaries, Spanish and Catalan have both clear syllabic boundaries and lexical stress. The research described in the previous section made it possible to test the segmentation of the speech signal into syllable-sized units by speakers of Catalan and Spanish. However, it did not test whether speakers of these two languages also use information concerning the stress value of the syllables in accessing the lexicon.

Before going into a description of my research, it is useful to describe how stress is encoded in different languages. Stress is a property that may vary in (mainly) three dimensions: intensity, duration, and pitch. Which dimensions are more important than others when stress is encoded differ from language to language. For instance, in Spanish, the most important difference between a stressed vowel and an unstressed vowel is in intensity; the difference in duration is of secondary importance, and the difference in pitch is minimal. Contrary to this, in English, the main difference between stressed and unstressed segments is a difference in pitch and duration; differences in terms of intensity are not very important. It is fundamental to keep these discrepancies in mind when doing crosslinguistic research. Studies about stress have apparently led to contradictory results, but this may be because in some cases, the true subject under study has not been the same, although the name (*stress*) may have been.

Although the literature on the role of different structural units in speech perception is quite extensive, there is little on the role of stress. As stated earlier, Cutler and her colleagues have shown that English speakers segment the speech signal at the onset of every stressed syllable or, more exactly, at the onset of every strong syllable.[6]

Cutler and Norris (1988) proposed a strategy, based on a metrical structure, Metrical Segmentation Strategy (MSS), that listeners of languages like English appear to use to segment the speech signal. In a series of experiments, these authors found that listeners were slower to detect the embedded real word in *mintaif* (where the second syllable has a full/strong vowel), than in *mintef* (where the second vowel is reduced/weak). This is because English listeners, when perceiving continuous speech, are said to hypothesize a word beginning at the onset of every strong syllable. Predictions derived from MSS have been tested in a large variety of experimental situations (see Cutler, 1990, for a review) and computer simulations. Recently, Vroomen and de Gelder (in press) have found converging evidence in Dutch, a language metrically similar to English.

But the role of stress in speech perception has also been studied in other contexts. Using a phoneme monitoring task, Cutler and Foss (1977) found that RTs were faster when the target phoneme was in a stressed syllable than in an unstressed one. Cole and Jakimik (1980) and Bond and Garnes (1980) found that subjects were twice as fast in detecting mispronunciations in a stressed than in an unstressed syllable. Nonetheless, Pitt and Samuel (1990b) argued that some of these results may have been due to acoustic differences between stressed and unstressed syllables (intensity, duration, and pitch). However, they also proposed that the acoustic clarity of stressed syllables could make those syllables perceptually outstanding anchors. These anchors could, in turn, be used by the perceptual system to parse the speech signal. Cutler (1976) found that the perceptual system is sensitive to the presence of stress in sentence processing: In a phoneme detection task, subjects responded faster when the targets appeared

---

[6]Strong syllables (again according to Cutler) are defined in terms of vowel quality: syllables with full vowels are said to be strong, while syllables with reduced vowels are said to weak.

in places where (emphatic) stress was expected, even though, all acoustic correlates had been deleted by cross-splicing the materials. Moreover, Wanner and Gleitman (1982) proposed that, in the very first stages of language acquisition, the newborn may use stressed syllables as perceptual islands where speech segmentation is triggered.

However, some experimental data point in a different direction. Cutler (1986) and Cutler and Clifton (1984) maintained that stress plays no role in the process of attaining lexical access. The strongest experimental evidence comes from a series of experiments where the crossmodal priming technique was used. Cutler (1986) found that minimal pairs of words differing only in accent (like *trustee/trusty* and *foregoing/forgoing*) behaved as true homophones. Cutler's proposal was that stress appears to play a role in speech segmentation (it helps us in identifying where a word is most likely to start) and gives us anchors from which to start processing, but does not play a role in the specific processes of word recognition.

However, as I noted, stress is differentially encoded in different languages. Although differences in stress (as in *foregoing/forgoing*) can be of little importance for English listeners, they may be of paramount importance for speakers of Spanish. Spanish, unlike English, does not have the distinction between strong and weak vowels: the same vowels are found in stressed and unstressed positions. Therefore, the only difference between a stressed vowel and an unstressed vowel (e.g., in a bisyllabic word) is that the stressed vowel is where the primary stress falls. Although pairs of words differing only in the position of the primary stress are not very frequent in English, they are very common in Spanish. Given these differences between English and Spanish[7], let us explore the role of stress in speech perception in Spanish.

THE ROLE OF STRESS IN SPEECH PERCEPTION IN SPANISH

Several authors (Bradley et al., 1993; Pallier et al., 1993; Sebastián et al., 1992) have shown that Spanish speakers are sensitive to syllables in segmenting the speech signal. What about stress? This question has been addressed in two series

---

[7]A totally different case is Catalan, a language with full and reduced vowels (like English); however, given the fact that most of the research on stress perception has been carried out with Spanish, we will center our exposition on the latter language.

of experiments. Previous research has tended to divide languages according to whether speakers use syllables or stress in segmenting the speech signal. Although this distinction can be applied to French and English, other languages may use both types of information in speech perception. Indeed, French speakers could not use stress in speech perception, because French does not have contrastive stress; it therefore plays no role in differentiating lexical entries. English speakers would not parse the speech signal into syllable-sized units, because such units do not seem to be naturally used in their language. (From a phonological point of view, it is not possible to assume that French does not have metrical units, or that English does not have syllables. The point is that these theoretical phonological units seem not be used in the same way by speakers of the two languages). It may be, however, that speakers of Spanish make use of both types of information.

In a series of experiments, Sebastián (1995) has tested the hypothesis that Spanish speakers are also sensitive to metrical information when perceiving speech. In these experiments, subjects were asked to perform a generalized syllable detection task. They were presented with trisyllabic pairs of pseudowords. These pseudowords (all becoming pseudowords at the third phoneme) had a CVCVCV structure and differed in the position of stress. Subjects were presented with pairs, such as *pebádi–pebadí*, in which they had to detect the first syllable (*pe*), and pairs like *míbepa–mibépa*, where the syllable to be detected was the last one (*pa*); there were other types of pairs, too, but they are not critical to the hypothesis being discussed here. If subjects were not sensitive to the metrical structure, there would be no difference between the RTs of each two member of the pair; it should take the same amount of time to detect *pe* in *pebádi* as in *pebadí*, and to detect *pa* in *míbepa* and in *mibépa*. However, if subjects computed the metrical structure of the stimuli while listening, there could be statistically significant differences in the detection of the target syllables between the two members of each pair.

Spanish (like English) is a language with a trochaic metrical structure; that is, stress groups (feet) have the stressed syllable at the onset of the group. For instance, a stimulus like *pebádi* has a metrical structure of *<pe>(bádi)*, whereas *pebadí* has a metrical structure of *(peba)(dí)*. In a similar way, *míbepa* has a metrical structure of *(míbe)<pa>*, and *mibépa* of *<mi>(bépa)*. If subjects compute this metrical structure while listening to speech, it should be easier to detect *pe* in *pebádi* than in *pebadí*, because in the first case there are both syllable and foot boundaries between the first and the second syllables, whereas in *pebadí* there is only a syllable boundary. The same reasoning can be applied to the *míbepa–mibépa* pair, so, it should be easier to detect *pa* in *míbepa* than in *mibépa*. Results showed a statistically significant advantage of 16 ms ($p < .02$), for detecting syllables when both syllable and foot boundaries existed, over stimuli with only a syllabic boundary.

These results demonstrate that Spanish speakers compute not only the syllabic structure of stimuli when listening to speech, but the metrical structure, as well. However, the data tell us nothing about the question of the effective use of this information in lexical access. It could be that subjects compute the stress value of syllables before accessing the lexicon, but that this information is not relevant for lexical access. To assess this, another series of experiments was performed.

It has been found that RTs for detecting phonemes at the onset of stimuli are faster for words than for pseudowords, if the stimuli are monosyllabic (Cutler, Mehler, Norris, & Seguí, 1987; Rubin, Turvey, & van Gelder, 1976). However, if they are polysyllabic, RTs do not differ (Foss & Blank, 1980; Seguí, Frauenfelder, & Mehler, 1981). Several explanations for this have been proposed. One of the most popular is the race model (Cutler et al., 1987; Newman & Dell, 1978). To perform the task, subjects can use two different procedures. One of the procedures, the lexical route, involves parsing the speech signal into syllable-sized units and using these units to access the lexicon. Once a lexical candidate has been selected, information concerning its phonemes is available. The other procedure, the nonlexical one, is an *adhoc* strategy: Subjects determine which is the initial phoneme in a given stimulus. It is obvious that both procedures are available when stimuli are words, but only the latter can be used for pseudowords. Subjects are believed to base their responses on the first available information.

How does this model explain the word advantage only for monosyllabic stimuli? Let us assume that the individual parses the speech signal into syllable-sized units prior to accessing the lexicon and that these units are used to start the lexical search. In the case of monosyllabic units, this first package of information is the whole word, and therefore word recognition is fast. This implies that information concerning the initial phoneme is recovered through this route, and that it is faster than the nonlexical one. This explains why initial phonemes are detected faster in words than in pseudowords. For polysyllabic stimuli, however, this initial package of information (initial syllable) may not be large enough to allow word recognition. The lexical route needs more information (and hence more time) to identify longer words. This extra time makes the advantage of words over pseudowords disappear. It may be that the nonlexical route has completed the process of phoneme identification in a comparable time. Therefore, this model predicts that with longer words, the word advantage will disappear.

The present description of this model does not include any reference to the possible role of stress in accessing the lexicon. This possibility has been tested

(Sebastián, 1994; Sebastián & Dupoux, 1995) in a series of experiments comparing the performances of French-, Spanish-, Catalan- and English-speaking subjects. In these experiments, different types of monosyllabic (CVC-*pan*-CCVC-*tren*) and bisyllabic (CVCV-*bala*-CVCV(C)-*canal*) stimuli were presented. Wherever possible (i.e., in all languages but French), two types of bisyllabic stimuli were presented: first- and second-syllable stressed. If stress does not play a role in accessing the lexicon, no statistically significant differences would be esxpected between words and pseudowords. The pattern of results showed however, that subjects were faster at detecting the initial phoneme of a word than its matched nonword when the initial syllable of these stimuli was unstressed (e.g., subjects were faster at detecting *p* in *peral* than *p* in *peril*). This word advantage was not observed for first-syllable stressed stimuli (i.e., there were no significant differences in detecting the initial phoneme in pairs of stimuli like *capa* and *capi*). This pattern of results was obtained in all the languages with variable stress (Spanish, Catalan, and English), but not in French, a language with fixed stress. A possible explanation for this pattern of results is that lexical search starts with stressed syllables. Let us look at the mechanism proposed in slightly more detail. Both stress value and structure parsing are computed for each syllable. If the syllable is a stressed one, the lexical search is triggered; if the syllable is not stressed, the process waits until a stressed one is found. Thus, first-syllable stressed bisyllabic stimuli involve two information processing packages, whereas second-syllable stressed bisyllabic stimuli involve only one. The race model assumes that when two-package processes are involved in recognizing a word, words lose their advantage over pseudowords. As already stated, several authors have already proposed that in language acquisition (Wanner & Gleitman, 1982) and in adult speech processing (Pitt & Samuel, 1990b) stressed syllables may function as anchors of information from which speech processing could proceed. The present explanation is along the same lines.

But what happens with French subjects? French subjects did not show any word advantage for bisyllabic items stressed on the second syllable. Stress has no contrastive value in this language; so it is possible that French subjects do not compute stress values when listening to speech. Current research (Dupoux, Pallier, Sebastián, & Mehler, 1995) seems to point in this direction.

In fact, a detailed analysis of the patterns of data obtained in Spanish, Catalan, and English seems to indicate that the parameters of stress (accent) studied in these experiments could play slightly different roles in the three languages. In fact, the effect was stronger in Spanish than in the other two languages, whereas in English it was only significant in the subjects analysis (and marginally significant in the item analysis). This is not surprising. Spanish, unlike Catalan and English, does not have vowel reduction; therefore, the only way stress is encoded is through the accent. English and Catalan also encode stress through the difference between full and reduced vowels. Although no data are available about the importance of this distinction for Catalan listeners, Cutler and her coworkers have provided extensive proof of its enormous importance for English speakers.

CONCLUDING REMARKS

Slightly over a decade has elapsed since Cutler et al. (1983) tried to replicate the pattern of data obtained by Mehler et al. (1981) with French subjects. The original explanation of the differences between the data obtained with French and English subjects, though still partially valid, cannot explain the whole picture. Research conducted in Spanish and Catalan (as well as in other languages) has shown that when listening to the speech stream, we parse it at different levels: structural and metrical. More important, the precise nature of this parsing depends on the phonological properties of each language. French speakers seem to pay little (if any) attention to the stress value of the segments, probably because French has no stress-based differences at the lexical level. English speakers seem to rely primarily on stress, and more specifically, on the differences between strong (full) and weak (reduced) vowels when segmenting the speech stream; and Spanish subjects seem to make use of both types of information.

In the introduction of this chapter, I asserted that there were both theoretical and practical reasons for conducting crosslinguistic research. From a theoretical point of view, the current knowledge of how speech is perceived has advanced greatly. Nevertheless, there are many questions still to be answered. The developmental question of how babies acquire a language must take into consideration what is now known about adult speech perception. The process of developing a system to compute speech is not a convergent one, but a divergent one. Adult speech segmentation seems to contrast in a multidimensional grid in which different dimensions have different weights. The way these different weights are established in the process of language acquisition is currently an important focus of research.

Another key theoretical question is the relationship between speech perception and production. Most of the data available for speech production have come from studies of speech errors. Detailed analysis of these corpora has shown some divergences in the phonological encoding of information (Igoa, this volume, chap. 11). The development of experimental techniques, such as the *picture-*

naming interference task[8] will probably help us in understanding how phonological information is encoded. Indeed, Costa (1994) has found on-line evidence for syllabic representation in speech production in Spanish. Using the picture-naming interference task, he observed lesser interference when the auditory and visual stimuli shared segmental and structural information, and both types of variables were significant and additive. Future research should try to extend this line of research to other variables, languages, and different techniques. Fuller knowledge of the nature of the phonological representations in speech production will help us to understand how perception and production are related.

A final theoretical question concerns the relationship between the different variables that play a role in speech perception (and, probably, production). If, as the data seem to suggest, Spanish speakers use both structural (syllabic) and metrical (stress) information when parsing the speech stream, the relationship between the two should be determined. Are both computed at the same time? Is there a preferential way to order them?

A final group of interests in studying crosslinguistic differences in speech processing is applied. In 1977, two Boeing 747s crashed in what was the worst civil aviation accident on record: 583 people were killed. Many causes have been put forward to explain why the KLM plane was trying to take off, in spite of the fact that it had not received clearance to do so, or why the Pan American aircraft was on the runway, when it should not have been there. One of the reasons was that "there was considerable misunderstanding between the pilots and the air traffic controllers" (Norman, 1988, p. 130). The pilots and the air traffic controllers were either native speakers or highly skilled second-language speakers of English (only English is spoken in air traffic communications), but even so, "misunderstanding" took place (in an already quite chaotic situation or, maybe, because of it). Listening to a foreign language in a bad acoustic environment or under extreme pressure is not an easy task. Determining the language-specific properties of speech perception will be of considerable help in preventing accidents of this type.

---

[8]In this technique, subjects are asked to name a picture aloud while they are hearing auditory stimuli. Depending on the stimulus onset asynchrony (SOA) between the visual and the auditory stimuli, either semantic or phonological interferences may be observed.

ACKNOWLEDGMENTS

Preparation of this manuscript and the research described here was made possible by the following research grants: HFSP project, *Processing Consequences of Contrasting Language Phonologies;* Spanish Ministerio de Educación y Ciencia contract CE90-008; Human Capital project, *Language as a Cognitive Activity;* and special funding from the Catalan Government (Generalitat de Catalunya). I would like to thank the members of the LSCP laboratory of the CNRS (in Paris) for their continuous support throughout the research, especially Jacques Mehler and Emmanuel Dupoux. Finally, I acknowledge the help of Sergi Pérez, Joaquim Llauger, Teodora Felguera, Ana Parreño, Jordi Pons, Perfecto Herrera, Ventura Fábregas, and especially Laura Bosch and Albert Costa, for their valuable help all these years.

REFERENCES

Bond, Z.S., & Garnes, S. (1980). Misperceptions of fluent speech. In R.A. Cole (Ed.), *Perception and production of fluent speech* (pp. 115–132) Hillsdale, NJ: Lawrence Erlbaum Associates.

Bradley, D.C., Sánchez-Casas, R., & García-Albea, J.E. (1993). The status of the syllable in the perception of Spanish and English. *Language and Cognitive Processes, 8,* 197–233.

Cole, R.A., & Jakimik, J.A. (1980). A model of speech perception. In R.A. Cole (Ed.), *Perception and production of fluent speech* (pp. 133–163). Hillsdale, NJ: Lawrence Erlbaum Associates.

Costa, A. (1994). *El papel de la sílaba en la producción del lenguaje.* [The role of the syllable in speech production]. Unpublished master thesis, University of Barcelona, Spain.

Cutler, A. (1976). Phoneme-monitoring reaction time as a function of preceding intonation contour. *Perception & Psychophysics, 20,* 201–220.

Cutler, A. (1986). Forbear is a homophone: Lexical prosody does not constrain lexical access. *Language and Speech, 29,* 201–220.

Cutler, A. (1990). Exploiting prosodic probabilities in speech segmentation. In G.T.M. Altmann (Ed.). *Cognitive models of speech processing: Psycholinguistic and computational perspectives* (pp. 105–121). Cambridge, MA: MIT Press.

Cutler, A., & Clifton, C. (1984). The use of prosodic information in word recognition. In H. Bouma & D.G. Bouwhuis (Eds.), *Attention and performance X: Control of language processes* (pp. 183–196). Hillsdale, NJ: Lawrence Erlbaum Associates.

Cutler, A., & Foss, D.J. (1977). On the role of sentence stress in sentence processing. *Language and Speech, 20,* 1–10.

Cutler, A., Mehler, J., Norris, D., & Seguí, J. (1983). A language-specific comprehension strategy. *Nature, 304,* 159–160.

Cutler, A., Mehler, J., Norris, D., & Seguí, J. (1986). The syllable's differing role in the segmentation of French and English. *Journal of Memory and Language, 25,* 385–400.

Cutler, A., Mehler, J., Norris, D., & Seguí, J. (1987). Phoneme identification and the lexicon. *Cognitive Psychology, 19,* 141–177.

Cutler, A., & Norris, D.G. (1979). Monitoring sentence comprehension. In W.E. Cooper & E.C. Walker (Eds.), *Sentence processing: Psycholinguistic studies presented to Merrill Garrett* (pp. 113–134). Hillsdale, NJ: Lawrence Erlbaum Associates.

Cutler, A., & Norris, D.G. (1988). The role of strong syllables in segmentation for lexical access. *Journal of Experimental Psychology: Human Perception and Psychophysics, 14,* 113–121.

Dupoux, E., Pallier, C., Sebastián, N., & Mehler, J. (1995). *A distressing deafness in French?* Manuscript submitted for publication.

Foss, D.J., & Blank, M. (1980). Identifying the speech codes. *Cognitive Psychology, 12,* 1–31.

Igoa, J.M. (1995). The relationship between conceptualization and formulation processes in sentece production: Some evidence from Spanish. In M. Carreiras, J.E. García-Albea, & N. Sebastián (*Eds.) Language Processing in Spanish.* Hillsdale, NJ: Lawrence Erlbaum Associates.

Klatt, D. (Ed.). (1977). Review of the ARPA speech understanding project. [Special Issue]. *Journal of the Acoustic Society of America, 62(6).*

Klatt, D. (1989). Review of selected models in speech perception. In W.D. Marslen-Wilson (Ed.) *Lexical representation and process.*   Cambridge, MA: MIT Press.

Marslen-Wilson, W.D. (1987). Functional parallelism in spoken word recognition. *Cognition, 71,* 71–102.

McClelland, J.L., & Elman, J.L. (1986). The TRACE model of speech perception. *Cognitive Psychology, 18,* 1–86.

Mehler, J., Dommergues, J.Y., Frauenfelder, U., & Seguí, J. (1981) The syllable's role in speech segmentation. *Journal of Verbal Learning and Verbal Behavior, 20,* 298–305.

Morais, J., Kolinsky, R., Cluytens, M. & Pasdeloup, V. (1993). Unidades no reconhecimento da fala em Portugues [Speech recognition units in Portuguese]. *Actas do Primero encontro de processamento da lingua portuguesa.* Lisbon, Portugal: Fundaçao Calouste Gulbenkian.

Newman, J.E., & Dell, G.S. (1978). The phonological nature of phoneme monitoring: A critique of some ambiguity studies. *Journal of Verbal Learning and Verbal Behavior, 17,* 359–374.

Norman, D.A. (1988). *The psychology of everyday things.* New York: Basic Books.

Otake, T., Hatano, G., Cutler, A., & Mehler, J. (1993). Mora or syllable? Speech segmentation in Japanese. *Journal of Memory and Language, 32,* 258–278.

Pallier, C. (1994). *Rôle de la syllabe dans la perception de la parole: Études attentionnelles* [The role of the syllable in speech perception: Attentional studies]. Unpublished doctoral dissertation, École des Hautes Études en Sciences Sociales, Paris, France.

Pallier, C., Sebastián, N., Felguera, T., Christophe, A., & Mehler, J. (1993). Attentional allocation within the syllabic structure of spoken words. *Journal of Memory and Language, 32,* 373–389.

Pitt, M.A., & Samuel, A.G. (1990a). Attentional allocation during speech perception: How fine is the focus? *Journal of Memory and Language, 29,* 611–632.

Pitt, M.A., & Samuel, A.G. (1990b). The use of rhythm in attending to speech. *Journal of Experimental Psychology: Human Perception and Performance, 16,* 564–573.

Rubin, P., Turvey, M.T., & van Gelder, P. (1976). Initial segments are detected faster in spoken words than in non-words. *Perception & Psychophysics, 19,* 394–398.

Sánchez-Casas, R. (1988). *Access representation in visual word recognition.* Unpublished doctoral dissertation, Monash University, Melbourne, Australia.

Savin, H., & Bever, T. (1979). The non-perceptual reality of the phoneme. *Journal of Verbal Learning and Verbal Behavior, 9,* 295–302.

Sebastián, N. (1994). The role of accent in speech perception. *Dokkyo International Review, 7,* 231–248.

Sebastián, N. (1995). *Feet and rhythmic structure perception in Spanish.* Unpublished Manuscript.

Sebastián, N., & Dupoux, E. (1995). *Stress effects in phoneme monitoring: An investigation in Spanish, Catalan, English, and French.* Manuscript submitted for publication.

Sebastián, N., Dupoux, E., & Mehler, J. (1995). *Lexical superiority effects in phoneme monitoring. An investigation in French, Catalan, Spanish, and English.* Manuscript submitted for publication.

Sebastián, N., Dupoux, E., Seguí, J., & Mehler, J. (1992). Contrasting syllabic effects in Catalan and Spanish. *Journal of Memory and Language, 31,* 18–32.

Sebastián, N., & Felguera, T. (1992). Detección de fonemas en ataques y codas silábicos [Phoneme monitoring of syllable's onset and coda]. *Cognitiva, 4,* 173–191.

Seguí, J., Frauenfelder, U., & Mehler, J. (1981). Phoneme monitoring, syllable monitoring and lexical access. *British Journal of Psychology, 72,* 471–477.

Vroomen, J., & de Gelder, B. (in press). Competition in spoken word recognition. Response competition or lateral inhibition? *Journal of Experimental Psychology: Human Perception and Performance.*

Wanner, E., & Gleitman, L. (Eds.). (1982). *Language acquisition: The state of the art.* Cambridge, MA: Cambridge University Press.

Werker, J.F., Gilbert, J.H.V., Humphreys, G.W., & Tees, R.C. (1981). Developmental aspects of cross-language speech perception. *Child Development, 52,* 349–355.

Werker, J.F., & Tees, R.C. (1983). Developmental changes across childhood in the perception of nonnative speech sounds. *Canadian Journal of Psychology, 37,* 278–286.

Werker, J.F., & Tees, R.C. (1984). Cross-language speech perception: Evidence for perceptual reorganization during the first year of life. *Infant Behavior and Development, 7,* 49–63.

Zwitserlood, P., Schriefers, H., Lahiri, A., & van Donselaar, W. (1993). The role of syllables in the perception of spoken Dutch. *Journal of Experimental Psychology: Learning, Memory and Cognition, 19,* 260–271.

2

Lexical Access in Visual Word Recognition: The Contribution of Word Form

Rosa M. Sánchez-Casas
Universitat Rovira i Virgili
Tarragona, Spain

INITIAL INPUT REPRESENTATIONS IN VISUAL WORD RECOGNITION

An essential part in the process of comprehending a written sentence is the task of accessing the meaning of the words the sentence is composed of. The reader must associate a portion of the sensory input with a stored lexical representation. This chapter evaluates various proposals about what might constitute the input representation, here termed the *access representation*, that is used to mediate the sensory-to-lexical association process. The main focus is on those proposals that claim that partial information about the written word can serve as the initial input representation for access purposes.

Since the 1970s, a variety of studies using different experimental paradigms and visual materials has provided evidence suggesting that the lexical system may routinely attempt access without having identified all the letters of a word. Evidence from eye movement studies, for instance, has shown that the initial letters of a word, identified parafoveally, may be used in accessing the word when it is subsequently foveated (Inhoff, 1987; Lima & Inhoff, 1985; Rayner, 1978; Rayner, McConkie & Ehrlich, 1978; Rayner, McConkie, & Zola, 1980; Rayner, Well, Pollatsek, & Bertera, 1982). Another type of evidence supporting the salience of word beginnings in the process of lexical access comes from studies in isolated word recognition (Broerse & Zwaan, 1966; Bruner & O'Dowd, 1958; Lima & Pollatsek, 1983; Sánchez-Casas, García-Albea, & Bradley, 1991; Taft, 1979, 1987; Taft & Forster, 1976). These studies seem to indicate that the initial part of a word can provide the basis for contacting the lexicon. Despite this evidence, however, the data available do not allow us to draw definitive conclusions about how that initial part is defined, how far the access process can proceed with the information provided by that part of the word, or by mechanism an initial input representation provides the basis for access. Thus, the aim of this chapter is to discuss some of the evidence that addresses these questions in an attempt to provide some more definitive answers.

The main body of evidence comes from experiments carried out in Spanish. The motivation for these experiments was to explore the issue of universality as it applies to lexical processing systems and, in particular, access representation proposals. Although it seems reasonable to assume that all languages share some basic underlying principles, languages do differ in the details of their structural properties', how much these differences influence language processing is an open question. Crosslanguage research is, therefore, the only way to determine which of the language processes that are claimed to be basic are universal and which are language-specific (see Frauenfelder, 1985). The access proposals that are examined in this chapter were originally tested in English, but English differs from Spanish in important phonological aspects (Bradley, Sánchez-Casas, & García-Albea, 1993; Harris, 1983; Sebastián-Gallés, Dupoux, Seguí, & Mehler, 1992). Those differences might be relevant in determining the sort of representation that speakers use to access the lexicon during word recognition. Exploring the universality of language processing is not the only contribution that crosslanguage research can make to psycholinguistics, however. As Cutler (1985) pointed out, sometimes this research is the only way to answer a given question (e.g., Slobin, 1982) or offers the appropriate control conditions when the characteristics of a particular languages may not suffice (e.g., Cutler, Mehler, Norris, & Seguí, 1987). The use of Spanish for the experiments presented here provides excellent conditions in which to test the proposals about access representation under examination.

Lexical Access Models: A General Overview

Before we consider how an initial input representation is to be characterized, it is important to examine the different models put forward to account for how a word is accessed. What is relevant here is what these models are constrained to say about the ways a written word can be parsed for access purposes; no detailed description or evaluation of particular models is undertaken.

Many lexical access models have been proposed since the 1970s (see Forster, 1985; and Norris, 1986; for a discussion). For one family of models, access is directly achieved from the physical features of the input. Detectors individually compare them with the input, determining their activation levels without the intervention of a central processor. The association between the sensory input and the appropriate mental representation is achieved via a detector reaching a threshold level of activation (e.g., Morton, 1969, 1970, 1979), via competition among detectors (e.g., McClelland & Rumelhart, 1981; Rumelhart & McClelland, 1982), or via the re-creation of the input pattern across a set of activation units in a parallel distributed network (e.g., Seidenberg, 1989, 1990).

Another family of models suggests that access is not direct (e.g., Becker, 1976, 1979; Forster, 1976, 1979, 1989; Rubinstein, Garfield, & Millikan, 1970). These models do not view the lexical system as a detector-based system, but as analogous to a computer-implemented information-retrieval system. Here, words are represented discretely as database entries, with no necessary provision for interaction between them. Some of these models assume that candidates are generated via an activation mechanism, incorporating a checking phase where the best candidate is selected from the generated set (e.g., Norris, 1986; Taft, 1991; Taft & Hambly, 1986). In other models, access is gained via a search process, where a central processor executes serial comparisons between input representations and the array of stored data or lexical entries until the appropriate lexical entry to match the input is located (Forster, 1976, 1979, 1989).

The distinctive characteristics of these types of models impose different constraints on the sort of initial input description through which lexical contact can be achieved during the process of visual word recognition. For instance, the activation model proposed by Morton (1969, 1970, 1979) does not allow for internal parsing within a word: A single threshold device, a *logogen,* is postulated for each word, and no independent threshold values are set for any letter or cluster of letters within the word. Thus, in this type of activation model, in the absence of contextual information, the entire input needs to be available for the appropriate logogen to reach the threshold. However, as mentioned earlier, there is evidence that supports the role of sublexical units in lexical access, and indeed indicates that the access system routinely attempts access without having identified all letters (e.g., see Sánchez-Casas, 1988; Taft, 1991, for reviews).

More sophisticated versions of an activation model, such as the parallel distributed processing (PDP) model proposed by McClelland and Rumelhart (1981), do allow for internal parsing within words, and could therefore evolve to account for effects suggesting partial inputs being used for access. In these models, any part of the word can cause activation within the network of detectors, and bias within the connections between detectors can favor particular properties or parts of the input, so that the presentation of those parts induces more activation that others in the appropriate detectors (McClelland & Rumelhart, 1981; Mozer, 1987). McClelland and Rumelhart's PDP model incorporates detectors below those for the whole word, such as letter features, letters, and letter clusters, each of which computes its own level of activation. In more recent PDP models, internal parsing is allowed by having distributed, instead of local, representations. That is, in these models there are no detectors at the word level, but one detector is used to represent more than one word (e.g., McClelland & Rumelhart, 1981; Seidenberg, 1989, 1990). Whether using local or distributed representations, PDP models provide a very flexible system, in that there are no principled limitations on the descriptions that can initiate the recognition process.

Nondirect access models restrict the flexibility with which the lexical access system can operate more than do the PDP ones. Nevertheless, they also allow for internal parsing of the word to take place in order to gain access, by proposing the construction of an initial description of the input (e.g., Forster, 1976, 1979, 1989; Taft & Hambly, 1986). Here, as in PDP models, more than one input description could be used, and the initial description might well reflect less than the entire word. For instance, models within the search framework (Forster, 1976, 1979), could easily incorporate a bias for a particular part of the word to be used as an access unit, because these models require neither that the initial input description used in the search process be constructed over the entire input nor that the representation be the same as the one used later, when the set of possible candidates is examined in more detail. In contrast to PDP-type models, however, the notion of an initial input representation for access purposes would have to be incorporated as a structural feature of the model, because lexical access is not achieved from the physical features of the input directly, but in stages. This implies that what constitutes the word's access representation has to be specified somehow in the entry, either as a subheading or marked in the entry itself. Any of these possibilities could be incorporated into the model, but with restrictions. This would be possible if one stipulates that the part of the word to be used as an access representation be the same for all words (e.g., the beginning); or that one parses by the application of some sort of principle (Taft, 1979; Taft & Forster, 1976). However, a nondirect access model will face problems if it is shown that there can be multiple access representation units, with more than one part of the word being equally effective in initiating access. For example, it would not be easy for a search model to explain the finding that a word can be accessed through the beginning part and the end part with equal efficiency.

Both activation and search models seem to be able to incorporate the notion of an access representation based on partial information about the word. PDP models provide a more flexible lexical access system than search models, because they allow a greater variation in the sort of input descriptions that can be used to determine the appropriate word's mental representation. In those models, there are many free parameters that can be adjusted, and thus, they could evolve to account for variations in the way words are recognized in a more parsimonious way than the search models can. However, because PDP models in word recognition are based on simulation studies, there seem to be no principled restrictions on the sort of predictions that can be made and, as Estes (1988) pointed out, they are "too powerful to be susceptible of direct empirical test" (p. 207). In contrast, by restricting the flexibility in the operation of the lexical access system, search models allow one to make very specific, falsifiable predictions. What is relevant here, is that what can constitute the word's access representation suggested in the framework of the search model (Taft, 1979; Taft & Forster, 1976) is "commendably vulnerable by virtue of its explicitness" (Henderson, Wallis, & Knight, 1984, p. 219).

Word Access Parsing Procedures

Within the context of these models, two sorts of proposals about how words can be parsed for access purposes can be suggested. One asserts that parsing procedures are guided by the linguistic characteristics of the word, where some principle or rule is applied to all words, to give rise to the input description that is used to initiate lexical access. A proposal along these lines was suggested by Spoehr and Smith (1973, 1975), who claimed that the written word is parsed into syllable-like units, known as *vocalic center groups* (VCGs), that are then translated into a phonological code in order to drive access to the lexical representation. Spoehr and Smith's proposal contrasts with that suggested by Taft and Forster (1976) and Taft (1979). Within the context of Forster's (1976) search model, these authors also proposed a parsing procedure based on linguistic principles, but argued that access relies only on the initial syllable of the word, defined not by phonotactic rules, but on the basis of morphological and orthographic considerations. An alternative method of parsing the initial access representation is one that is not determined by any a priori rule or principle, but operates idiosyncratically for each word. That is, what is relevant is not the syllabic or morphemic status of a given part of the word, but the extent to which the information presented in that part allows that word to be discriminated from the other words in the language (as in the cohort model of Marslen-Wilson & Tyler 1980; Marslen-Wilson & Welsh 1978). Thus, in this sort of proposal, what determines the part of the word that constitutes its access representation are the statistical properties of the lexicon, which reflect those of the language (e.g., Sánchez-Casas et al, 1991; Seidenberg, 1987, 1989, 1990).

Empirical evidence from Spanish concerning the validity of these two proposals is presented in the following sections. As I show further on, findings about initial input representations have implications for the sorts of mechanism that can be proposed to carry out the sensory-to-lexical association process. Thus, issues concerning this process are also considered. I report three experiments. The first attempted to determine whether the initial syllable can be claimed to be the word's access representation in Spanish, evaluating definitions of this syllable in phonological terms and on the basis of orthographic and morphological considerations. The aim of the second experiment was to determine how far the access process can proceed with the information provided in the initial part of the word, manipulating both word frequency and the length of the initial string. Finally, the third experiment was designed to explore the alternative parsing procedure, in which the access representation is determined for each word idiosyncratically, according to the statistical properties of the language.

THE INITIAL SYLLABLE OF THE WORD: HOW IS IT TO BE DEFINED?

Perhaps the most immediate problem that one confronts in proposing that the initial syllable is used in accessing lexical information is in defining what counts as a syllable in the written domain, especially in a language like English, where this proposal originated. English syllabification is frequently unclear or ambiguous, and it is often difficult to determine where the boundaries between syllables are located. Phonologists have put forward various views on how English syllabic structure is to be represented, but there is no single accepted theory of how words are syllabified (Anderson & Jones, 1974; Kahn, 1976; Selkirk, 1982; Treiman & Danis, 1988; Treiman & Zukowski, 1988). One possibility is to adopt a definition of the written syllable in phonological terms as Spoehr and Smith (1973, 1975) suggested. There are specific problems with Spoehr and Smith's parsing procedure as a method of arriving at a phonological code with which to address the lexicon, however (e.g., Coltheart, 1978; Massaro,

1974). For instance, Coltheart (1978) has shown that VCG parsing gives syllabifications that are inappropriate as inputs to the grapheme-to-phoneme translation process. Moreover, there is evidence that suggests that, at least in English, syllables defined in phonological terms are not involved in the treatment of written forms, regardless of the rules one uses. For instance, Prinzmetal, Treiman and Rho (1986) used reports of letter color and letter identity to examine the nature of the units used in parsing written words. They asked subjects to report the color of a given letter target in a word briefly presented. They found that subjects were more likely to report the target's color as matching that of other letters within the same syllable, rather than adjacent letters belonging to a different syllable. The pattern of errors was not determined purely by phonological factors, but by specifically orthotactic constraints on the co-occurrence of consonant letters within a syllable and by considerations of morphological structure (see also Prinzmetal, 1990).

For any English syllabification proposal based on phonotactic rules, one must consider a general problem that is relevant in evaluating the role of the phonological syllable being accessed: In many cases, surface syllabification does not preserve morphological relationships among words (Taft, 1979; Taft & Forster, 1976). There is evidence, however, that morphologically related words are represented under the same lexical entry (see Taft, 1985, 1991, for reviews of the extensive literature). Thus, if one is to propose that only the word's initial syllable is used to initiate the access process, it seems important to take into account the morphological relations between words at that stage in the process, so that they reflect the assumed commonalities of their full lexical representations.

As an alternative solution, Taft (1979) suggested that the syllable that provides the basis for access in the recognition of written inputs should not be defined in phonological terms. Instead, he proposed a first syllable that is orthographically and morphologically defined, according to what he termed the *basic orthographic syllabic structure* (BOSS) principle. The BOSS principle states that the first syllable through which lexical access is achieved includes "as many consonants following the first vowel of the word as orthotactic factors will allow without disrupting the morphological structure of that word". (Taft, 1979, p. 24). In particular, Taft proposed that the BOSS syllable is not a parsing unit, but corresponds to the representation under which the lexical entry is listed: it is the word's access representation. A reiterative left-to-right parsing isolates an input's BOSS syllable. In this procedure, a lexical search is carried out for all the letter combinations beginning at the initial letter of the word, until the resulting letter string corresponds to the BOSS. Only when the BOSS syllable is obtained can access to the appropriate lexical entry be achieved (see Taft, 1979).

Taft's definition of a word's initial syllable in orthographic and morphological terms seems to overcome some of the problems encountered by definitions stated in purely phonological terms. However, the grounds for claiming that the BOSS syllable is the only representation under which a word is accessed are not very strong. Although some studies have provided data compatible with such a claim (e.g., Sánchez-Casas, 1988; Taft, 1979, 1986), others have failed to do so (e.g., Lima & Pollatsek, 1983; Sánchez-Casas, 1988; Sánchez-Casas et al., 1991; Taft, 1987). For instance, in Taft's original experiments, input divisions were imposed by placing the word's physical division either at a point that corresponded to a phonologically defined syllable boundary (i.e., Spoehr & Smith's VCG unit; e.g., *lan tern, fi ber*), or at the BOSS break (e.g., *lant ern, fib er*). Taft (1979) demonstrated that BOSS divisions gave faster reaction times (RTs) than divisions based on phonological syllabification, but Lima and Pollatsek (1983) using the same sort of input divisions, found no reliable difference between BOSS and phonological divisions (see Lima & Pollatsek, 1983; Sánchez-Casas, 1988; Taft, 1987, for more conflicting data regarding the validity of the BOSS).

There seems to be no clear explanation for the discrepancies found in these studies. They cannot be attributed entirely to differences in the experimental paradigm or in the sorts of words the authors used, because some of these studies employed exactly the same experimental technique using similar materials, and still showed different patterns of results (e.g., Lima & Pollatsek, 1983; Taft, 1979). It might be possible, however, that something other than the BOSS is at work and that what determines how lexical access is achieved is an input description defined in other terms (e.g., Forster & Taft, 1994; Sánchez-Casas, 1988; Sánchez-Casas et al., 1991; Taft, 1992). In the next section, I review some data from experiments using Spanish as the test language that seem to shed light on this possibility.

Testing Phonological and BOSS Syllabification Proposals in Spanish

In English, as is common in stress-timed languages, there is a tendency for syllable boundaries to be modified by stress; in particular, consonants tend to associate with adjacent stressed syllables. This tendency makes assessment of syllabification difficult in English, regardless of whether it is characterized as consonantal ambisyllabicity (Kahn, 1976) or as phonological expansion due to a resyllabification phenomenon (see Selkirk, 1982, for more details). The reason for this is that a preference for segmentations that take in additional consonants (e.g., *sal ary* being preferred over *sa lary*) can indicate one of two things: either that there is something like the BOSS at work, or that visual recognition may simply be sensitive to phonetic detail (Sánchez-Casas, 1988). Spanish may provide a way around this problem. In contrast to English, Spanish has syllables with clearly defined boundaries that are resistant under stress movement (see Harris, 1983), so that BOSS syllabification can be guaranteed to differ from phonological syllabification.

In addition, even if Taft's BOSS proposal can be shown to be appropriate for English, it may not be for other languages with different characteristics. For instance, it might be that in a language like Spanish, with closer grapheme-to-phoneme correspondence, more regular syllabic structure, and clearly defined boundaries, a phonologically based access representation can be used in the recognition of written forms, just as has been argued for Serbo-Croatian (Feldman, Kostic, Lukatela & Turvey, 1983).

In order to examine these possibilities, BOSS and phonological syllabification proposals were tested in a series of Spanish experiments using the same temporal separation technique as that employed by Sánchez-Casas (1988) in English. In the version used in these experiments, the items were presented in two stages: The initial part of the word was displayed for 200 ms, and then the item was completed, so that the whole word remained on the center of the screen for 500 ms. RT was measured from the onset of the completed item. Such a temporal separation has been shown to be effective as a method of imposing the desired input segmentation. That is, subjects appear to take the isolated string of the input as a unit, without submitting it to any further analysis (see Sánchez-Casas et al., 1991, for details of how the action of the technique was tested). In the first experiment, and following Taft's initial experiments, Sánchez-Casas (1988) used monomorphemic words with consonant-vowel (CV) pairs in their initial syllables (e.g., *moneda, física*) as targets for a lexical decision.[1] For each item, two initial letter sequences were selected to be presented prior to the complete word. The long sequence corresponded to the BOSS syllable (e.g., *mon* for *moneda, fís* for *física*), defined according to Spanish orthotactic rules,

---

[1]It should be noted that more than half the syllables in Spanish have a simple CV structure, and that a syllable nucleus (vowel or diphtong) cannot be closed by more than two consonants word-medially, or one consonant word-finally. The reason I used only words with CV-initial syllables was that they are the most frequent ones, and, more importantly, they allow us to distinguish between BOSS and phonological input divisions. In words with CVC- or VCC-initial syllables (e.g., *montura, abstemio*), BOSS and phonological syllabification coincide. The only CVC words in which the two syllabification types could be contrasted are words like *consejo,* where the cluster *ns* is possible as the coda of the first syllable (e.g., *cons* in *construcción*). Because words of this sort are not very common, it is difficult to control for the variables of length, number of syllables, grammatical category, and morphemic structure.

whereas the short sequence included one less consonant, corresponding to the phonological syllable (e.g., *mo* for *moneda*, *fí* for *física*). In the nonword items, both the short and the long sequences were possible word beginnings (e.g., *ge* and *ger* for *gerusa*).

As can be seen from the data in Table 2.1, I did not find clear support for the BOSS syllable in Spanish. Although there is a trend in the direction predicted by the BOSS, the overall effect of type of initial string was not reliable, with $F_1(1, 22) = 5.16$, p < 0.05 and $F_2(1, 44) = 3.39$, $p > .05$. No significant effects of initial string were found in the error analysis, F_1 and $F_2 < 1$. These findings also suggest that the close grapheme–phoneme correspondence, characteristic of the Spanish language, does not favor a phonologically based access representation, at least when that representation is defined as an initial syllable.

TABLE 2.1
Mean RTs (in ms) and Percentages of Errors as a Function of String Types in Spanish Words

Item Type	Example	RT	% Errors
Short string	*mo*	599	9.2
Second stress	*moneda*		
Long string	*mon*	580	9.5
Second stress	*moneda*		

This pattern of results was replicated in Sánchez-Casas (1988), when both phonological and BOSS syllabifications of the same type of words were tested on subjects who were Spanish-dominant Spanish-English bilinguals; that is, these speakers showed no reliable differences between the two syllabification types. It seems therefore that Spanish-speaking subjects use neither BOSS nor phonological strategies to segment the visual input for access purposes. What, then, might be the word access procedure they use? Sánchez-Casas et al. (1991) carried out an experiment that suggests a possible answer to this question. In that paper, two important issues were addressed before exploring further the sort of partial information that can provide the basis for access: The first, was providing an account of how the RT advantage observed with this technique occurs and how this advantage is to be interpreted in terms of access. Although studies testing access representation proposals have commonly assumed that the RT advantage produced by a word's initial syllable is evidence that access has occurred, these studies have neither formulated a detailed account of what access via the initial part means nor provided evidence that this access does, in fact, takes place. The second, was determining to what extent the facilitation effects obtained in the temporal separation technique could be due to the number of letters contained in the initial string. In the Spanish experiments that have been reported, the advantage of the BOSS syllable is not reliable, but in the materials used, the initial string corresponding to the BOSS syllable generally contains one letter more than those strings that coincided with the phonological syllable. Thus, it was important to investigate systematically if what determines the advantage in the information presented as the initial string is the number of letters that such a string contains, not its syllabic status.

How Far Can the Access Process Advance With the Initial Letters of the Word?

In order to examine which lexical processing stage is achieved with the temporally isolated initial string, my colleagues and I manipulated a variable that has been shown to be a good predictor of lexical access and that is incorporated in most word recognition models (e.g., Forster, 1976; McClelland & Rumelhart, 1981: Paap, Newsome, McDonald, & Schvaneveldt, 1982). This variable is the frequency of occurrence of a written word in the language. We proposed that the presence or absence of frequency effects can act as a sensitive label of partial input information. In particular, if this information restricts the number of lexical candidates sufficiently, no frequency effects should be obtained. I consider in some detail the line of arguments that establishes this point.

We adopted the interpretation of frequency effects proposed in Forster's search model (Forster, 1976, 1989). This model places the locus of these effects in the process of accessing the entry. High-frequency words are recognized faster than low-frequency words because they are encountered earlier in the search path (see Bradley & Forster, 1987, for a discussion). This prelexical interpretation of the frequency effect allows an examination of how far access processing can advance with partial inputs, under the following argument. Let us suppose that access is obtained from partial inputs; that is, the system begins the access process at the stage where the initial string is presented. Only the entire string contains sufficient information to select among the words sharing an access representation, however. Then, to the extent that there is a delay between the frequency sensitivity subprocess and the arrival of the information necessary for completion, frequency effects will be diminished in the overall measure of performance.

With the temporal separation technique used in these experiments, the initial string is presented for 200 ms. If, during this time, the initial string allows access to an appropriate entry, then what the system could do is to wait until the entire word is available and use the full specification within the selected entry to carry out a check on the completed stimulus. If a second search is not carried out, then one would not expect to find frequency effects, because by the time the system makes its final response when the full stimulus is available, any advantage from gaining access to high-frequency words (rather than to low-frequency words) would have dissipated. For this to be a sensible strategy, however, the system must be really certain that the entry that has been selected on the basis of the initial string is likely to be the appropriate one. This certainty could be achieved in those cases where there is only one candidate, or perhaps very few candidates, that match the initial string.

If the information provided in the initial string is not enough to restrict the number of these candidates to very few, the system would have to initiate a second search when the entire stimulus is available, and frequency effects would emerge. Sánchez-Casas et al.'s argument exposes two different approaches. The first is the view already detailed, where restriction of the number of lexical candidates is essential, or the advantage of having access to full specification is lost. For Taft, however, access and restriction of the set of lexical candidates need not be related. For example, access from partial inputs can occur with a large number of potential candidates, that share the same BOSS (e.g., *mina, mineral, miniatura, minimizar, ministro, minuto, minoría*, and so on, sharing the BOSS *min*). Taft's view would require some extra assumptions in accounting for the facilitatory effects of the BOSS inputs. One possibility would be to adopt a priming account of the facilitation effects. According to his account, if an initial string can contact the lexical entry, then that entry is primed. That is, the initial contact of the entry will leave that entry in an altered state, so that the recognition of the subsequently presented entire word is facilitated (see Davis, 1990; Forster & Davis, 1984). When the full stimulus is available (and gets primed), a second search is carried out, and with this search, a frequency effect would be generated.

In sum, by using both high- and low-frequency words, Sánchez-Casas et al. were able to examine what the facilitation effects produced by an initial string mean in terms of lexical processing. If facilitation reflects savings due to the omission of a second search when the full stimulus occurs, then one should not find evidence of frequency effects at that point where facilitation reaches its peak. However, if the initial portion allows for access, and this access itself produces the facilitation, then the occurrence of a frequency effect is still possible. To test these possibilities, words of high and low frequency were selected. All the words were nouns with bisyllabic stems, had stress on the second syllable, and varied in length from 6 to 8 letters. Each had one of two syllabic structures: single consonant after the first vowel or a double consonant after the first vowel (e.g., *manera* and *manzana*, respectively). The frequency data were taken from *El Recuento del Vocabulario Español* (Rodríguez Bou,

1952).[2] For the single-consonant words, the high-frequency range was from 102 to 707 occurrences per million (geometric mean= 287.1), and the low-frequency range was from 13 to 32 occurrences per million (geometric mean= 22.8). For the double-consonant words, high frequencies ranged from 109 to 1,059 occurrences per million (geometric mean= 279.4), and low frequencies ranged from 2 to 35 per million (geometric mean= 19.4). The mean length for the single-consonant words was 6.3 letters, and for the double consonant words, 7.3 letters ($SDs = 0.5$).

In addition, to manipulate the frequency of the words, we manipulated the length of the initial string to determine whether facilitation effects were due to the number of letters contained in the initial string. Thus, three different types of initial string were used: They contained the first two (CV), three (CVC), or four (CVCV in words like *manera*, and CVCC in words like *manzana*) letters. In these latter two word types, the BOSS syllable corresponds to the three-letter string (i.e., *man*) and the four-letter string is BOSS + 1. However, although the two-letter string constituted the phonological syllable of the single-consonant words, the three-letter string is the double consonant word's phonological syllable. Therefore, in just those words, BOSS and phonological syllabification coincide.

According to the BOSS principle, in both word types, the three-letter strings (i.e., the BOSS) should produce faster RTs than the two-letter strings; and the RTs to those strings may or may not be different from those produced by the four-letter strings (BOSS + 1). According to phonological syllabification, the expected pattern of results in these two types of words will differ. In double-consonant words, the three-letter string should also produce faster RTs than the two-letter ones, because it corresponds to the phonological syllable. In the case of single-consonant words, one would expect the two-letter string to produce faster RTs than either of the other two strings. However, it might be possible that the three string types here do not differ from each other, because all of them contain the word's phonological syllable as a subpart. Findings from the previous experiments, in fact, have shown that BOSSs and phonological syllables do not differ. If what is important is not the syllabic status of the initial string, but the number of letters, one should expect the longer strings to produce the fastest RTs uniformly.

The nonwords were constructed along the same lines as the words: Half of them had a single medial consonant (e.g., *conira*), and the other half had two

---

[2]This book is less well-known than the *Frequency Dictionary of Spanish Words* of Juilland and Chang Rodríguez (1964), but is based on a larger sample of words, so that frequency data for all the words used in the experiment could be found.

consonants (e.g., *corpeto*). As in the words, the nonword length varied from 6 to 8 letters. The three types of strings for the nonwords were chosen in the same way as in the words (e.g., *co, con,* and *coni* for *conira;* and *co, cor,* and *corp* for *corpeto,* single- and double-consonant nonwords, respectively), and all were possible word beginnings (e.g., *co, con,* and *coni* from *cónico;* and *co, cor,* and *corp* from *corpiño*).

TABLE 2.2

Mean RTs (ms) and Percentages of Errors as a Function of String Type for Single- and Double-Consonant Words

Item Type	Example	RT	% Errors
Single-consonant words			
Two-letter string	*ma*	522	5.3
	manera		
Three-letter string	*man*	523	7.5
	manera		
Four-letter string	*mane*	477	3.9
	manera		
Double-consonant words			
Two-letter string	*ma*	528	6.6
	manzana		
Three-letter string	*man*	493	3.0
	manzana		
Four-letter string	*manz*	472	3.0
	manzana		

Once again, the temporal separation technique from previous experiments was used to present the items in stages. Table 2.2 presents the mean RTs and percentages of errors as a function of initial string length for single- and double-consonant words.

It is clear that the pattern of facilitation effects is not compatible with an access representation based on the BOSS syllable. The single-consonant words showed no advantage for the BOSS strings over the string corresponding to the phonological syllable (two-letter string), with the four-letter string (BOSS + 1) producing the fastest reaction times. These strings showed an advantage of 45 msec over the two-letter string, $\underline{\min}F'(1, 46) = 12.97, p < .01$, and were responded to 46 ms faster than when preceded by the BOSS string itself, $\underline{\min}F'(1, 59) = 14.32, p < .01$. The latter comparison also reached significance in the error analyses, with BOSS strings producing higher error rates than BOSS

+ 1 strings, $F_1(1, 27) = 5.66$, $p < .05$, and $F_2(1, 33) = 4.35$, $p < .05$.

Similarly, in the double-consonant words, the four-letter strings produced response times 21 ms faster than the three-letter strings, $\underline{\min}F'(1, 58) = 5.41$, $p < .05$, and 56 ms faster than the two-letter strings, $\underline{\min}F'(1, 59) = 32.82$, $p < .01$. However, here, there was also an advantage (35 ms) for the three-letter strings (both the BOSS and the phonological syllable) over the shorter strings, $\underline{\min}F'(1, 55) = 12.57$, $p < .01$. Two-letter strings were found to produce higher error rates than three-letter strings, although the difference between them was only significant by subjects $F_1(1, 27) = 5.34$, $p < .05$ and $F_2(1, 33) = 2.71$, $p > .05$.

If these findings with respect to facilitation are incompatible with the claim that the BOSS contributes to lexical access, then they work also against any claim based on the phonological syllable. In the complex data pattern, there is one particularly striking fact: Four-letter strings produced faster RTs than any strings corresponding to the initial phonological syllable. In the single-consonant words, a four-letter string gives the first two syllables of the word; in the double-consonant words, it contains one letter more than the string corresponding to the phonological syllable and is an illegal phonological shape. Thus, with the exception of the results obtained with the two- and the three-letter strings in the single-consonant cases, this experiment suggests that the longer the string, the greater the facilitation effect, regardless of its syllabic status.

Data for both single- and double-consonant words as a function of word frequency are presented in Table 2.3.

When the single-consonant words were preceded by the two-letter string, the results showed a 21 ms difference between high- and low-frequency words. This difference was only significant in the subject analysis, $F_1(1, 27) = 5.08$, $p < .05$, with $F_2(1, 33) = 1.39$, $p > .05$. Similar results were obtained with the three-letter string corresponding to the BOSS syllable. Here, the difference between high- and low-frequency single-consonant words was 25 ms, and was also significant by subject, $F_1(1, 27) = 6.45$, $p < .05$, but not by items, $F_2(1, 15) = 2.07$, $p > .05$. Finally, with the four-letter string, the difference between the two types of words was reversed, failing to reach significance in either analysis, $F_1(1, 27) = 1.32$, $p > .05$ and $F_2 < 1$. No significant effects were obtained in the analyses of the error data.

The double-consonant words show a similar pattern of results. In this case, the RT difference between high- and low-frequency words was 22 ms when they were preceded by the two-letter string. This difference reached significance by subjects, $F_1(1, 27) = 4.34$, $p < .05$, but not by items, $F_2(1, 15) = 2.98$, $p > .05$. When words were preceded by either the three-letter (BOSS) or the four-letter (BOSS + 1) string, there was no evidence of frequency effects, F_1 and $F_2 < 1$. None of these effects reached significance in the analyses of the error data on words preceded by three- or four-letter strings. When the two-letter strings were used, low-frequency words tended to produce more errors than high-frequency words. Such a tendency was significant by subjects, $F_1(1, 27) = 6.00$, p < .05, but not by items, $F_2(1, 15) = 2.98$, $p > .05$.

TABLE 2.3

Mean RTs (in ms) and Percentages of Errors, as a Function of Word Frequency for Single- and Double-Consonant Words With Different Initial Strings.

Item Type		Word Frequency	RT	% Errors
Single-consonant words				
	Two-letter string	High	511	5.0
		Low	532	5.5
		Low-High	21	
	Three-letter string	High	511	6.7
		Low	536	8.3
		Low-High	25	
	Four-letter string	High	484	2.8
		Low	471	5.0
		Low-High	-13	
Double-consonant words				
	Two-letter string	High	518	3.3
		Low	540	10.0
		Low-High	22	
	Three-letter string	High	488	2.8
		Low	499	3.3
		Low-High	11	
	Four-letter string	High	467	1.1
		Low	476	5.0
		Low-High	9	

Although the pattern of frequency effects in the data was not reliable, it provides some suggestion of what the observed facilitation effects may mean: An increase in facilitation effects, as shown by the four-letter string relative to the three-letter string, was accompanied by a marked diminution of frequency sensitivity, with facilitation effects being maximal for the four-letter string, where no evidence of frequency effect was found. According to Sánchez-Casas et al.'s argument, it seems clear that it is only in the case of the four-letter string that one can claim that a limited set of lexical candidates was found and, therefore, that access via the information in this string was achieved initially. With the four-letter strings, the results showed a nonsignificant frequency effect. Although the frequency effects were not reliable with the two- and three-letter strings, they were larger for each of those strings.

As an exploratory analysis, Sánchez-Casas et al. tried to determine the extent to which the initial strings used in the experiment actually restricted the number of candidates. In order to perform such an analysis, a theory-neutral count of the number of word completions was carried out with each of the initial string types. This count used a dictionary containing the 10,000 most frequent words of the Spanish language (Rodríguez Bou, 1952), where derivations, but not inflections, were listed as separate entries. This count constitutes an estimate, not an absolute measure, of the number of possible word completions. Given an initial string (e.g., *ma*), all the words beginning with that string, except proper nouns, were included in the count as possible word completions. The results are shown in Table 2.4.

This preliminary word count clearly shows that the four-letter strings restricted the number of possible word completions to a smaller number compared with those estimated when two- or three-letter string were considered. As Sánchez-Casas et al. pointed out, the fact that the two- and three-letter strings already reduced the number of candidates to some extent might explain why, in those cases, frequency effects failed to reach significance in the item analysis: The restriction was sufficient to allow access. In any case, it seems reasonable to conclude that the data are at least consistent with the claim that restrictiveness may be an important factor in determining the word recognition system's use of partial inputs.

TABLE 2.4

Geometric Means of the Number of Word Completions as a Function of Word and Initial String Length for Single- and Double-consonant Words

	Word Type	
Initial String Length	*Single-consonant*	*Double consonant*
Two-letter	122	116
Three-letter	15	19
Four-letter	4	4

THE RESTRICTIVENESS HYPOTHESIS: AN ALTERNATIVE ACCOUNT

The Spanish data I have reported so far can be interpreted as evidence that the syllabic status of the initial string, by itself, is not able to account for patterns of facilitation. Taken together, they suggest that what determines these effects tends to vary inversely with frequency sensitivity. Facilitation effects were not controlled simply by whether the BOSS or the phonological syllable had been presented, weakening the claim that these corresponded to the word's access representation. Rather, a fair predictor of the size of the facilitation effect was whether a frequency effect had been obtained. Within the framework of this technique, the more an input string limits a set of candidates, the less need there is for a second search and its concomitant frequency effects. Although the estimates of restriction are inexact, and what the maximum size of the lexical set may be before a second search is required remains unknown, there is at least some suggestion of a causal link between these variables. It should be emphasized, however, that the notion of restrictiveness does not necessarily reduce to the notion of increased length (cf. initial strings, in Taft, 1987).

The notion of restrictiveness, as defined by Sánchez-Casas et al. (1991), though different from previous access proposals, still belongs within the access representation tradition, because it assumes a left-to-right parsing of the visual input (e.g., Taft, 1979). Such a notion also overlaps the idea of the *uniqueness point* proposed in the cohort model of spoken word recognition (Marslen-Wilson & Tyler, 1980, Marslen-Wilson & Welsh, 1978). The uniqueness point is defined for each word as the moment at which its initial sequence of phonemes differentiates it from all other words, and this has been found to be a good predictor of the moment at which a spoken word is recognized (e.g., Marcus & Frauenfelder, 1985; Marslen-Wilson, 1984). In this extension of the idea of the uniqueness point, the degree of restrictiveness can be defined for each word for a given initial sequence, but in terms of grapheme, rather than phoneme, sequences (see Johnson & Pugh, 1994, for a recent proposal of a cohort model of visual word recognition).

Testing the Restrictiveness Hypothesis in Spanish

A word parsing procedure in which access can be achieved via an initial string only when it restricts the number of possible candidates to very few would imply that what constitutes the word's access representation is determined for each word according to the statistical properties of the language. The results obtained by Sánchez-Casas et al. (1991) suggest that a parsing procedure defined in those terms might be used by Spanish speakers when they access the lexicon from partial inputs. In order to provide more definitive evidence to support this possibility, it is necessary to examine the notion of restrictiveness more directly, and to control gramatically the degree to which the letters presented as the initial string restrict the number of lexical candidates. This is precisely what the next experiment carried out by Sánchez-Casas (1993), attempted to do, using the masked priming technique developed by Forster and Davis (1984). This technique has some advantages over the temporal separation technique used previously, allowing more appropriate testing conditions to determine whether the restrictiveness hypothesis can offer an alternative account of what constitutes a word access representation. For instance, it ensures that strategic factors do not affect subjects' performance, reducing greatly the possibility that subjects guess at responses. In addition, with the masked priming technique, one does not confront the problem that subjects can find it unusual or unnatural to be presented with fragments of words.

In addition, the masked priming technique has been shown to be sensitive to effects taking place at the level of processing that is of interest here: the lexical level (e.g., Davis, 1990; Forster, 1987; Forster, Davis, Schoknecht, & Carter, 1987; Mildred, 1986; Sánchez-Casas, Davis, & García-Albea, 1992). It is not possible to analyze all the evidence here in detail. What should be emphasized at this point is the finding that priming can be obtained with nonidentical primes, or *form-priming* (e.g., Forster et al., 1987), and that these effects can be interpreted as taking place at the lexical level. Three important findings support a lexical intepretation of the form-priming effects: (a) the sensitivity of those effects to a property of lexical organization (i.e., *neighborhood density,* defined in terms of letter and/or subsyllabic unit similarities; e.g., Forster et al., 1987; Forster & Taft, 1994; Grainger, 1990; Grainger, O'Regan, Jacobs & Seguí, 1989, 1992); (b) the evidence of full-sized priming effects with morphologically related pairs (Forster et al., 1987); and (c) the existence of cross-language priming effects with cognate prime–target pairs (Mildred, 1986; Sánchez-Casas et al., 1992). Having shown that nonidentical primes can produce reliable priming effects, one can manipulate the information that is presented in the prime in different ways and discover what information is sufficient for an initial contact with the lexicon.

In asking whether partial information about a word can, by itself, provide the basis for access, the experiment designed by Sánchez-Casas (1993) differs critically from those discussed in the previous section. First, it uses the masked priming effects as a tool to manipulate the information presented in the prime and to discover what information is sufficient for an initial contact with the lexicon. Second, the part that is claimed to be the word's access representation is defined in this experiment in terms of neither the BOSS nor as the phonological syllable, but in terms of how much it restricts the number of possible word completions. Third, the degree of restrictiveness of either the initial or the final fourletters of the words is now manipulated, to provide a more complete test of the restrictiveness hypothesis and to compare directly the priming effects obtained with initial and final word fragments. It was argued that if restrictiveness is all that is relevant in determining whether a subpart of the word is sufficient for lexical contact, and if the initial part of the word has no special accessrepresentation properties, then one should find comparably sized priming effects with restrictive endings. Fourth, the words used in this experiment were selected from the dictionary computer database of 10,000 entries. In contrast to Sánchez-Casas et al.'s (1991) experiment, the dictionary was now addressed to list all words that contained a specified sequence in any position. Thus, instead of having the dictionary list words beginning *comp-*, or ending *-tura*, the words listed contained the sequence in any position. For instance, the words *completo* and *incompetente* would both be listed if the sequence *-comp-* were given, and the words *pintura* and *obturador* would be given for *-tura-*. This change in the estimation procedure was introduced because, if the access mechanism opportunistically uses the word fragment presented in the prime, one cannot assume that the mechanism will have information about the position in a word from which such a fragment comes. The criteria used in counting the possible word completions were: (a) Inflections and derivations were not counted as separate lexical entries, (b) compound words were included in the count as separate entries from their components and (c) very low-frequency words and proper nouns were not included in the count. The *restrictiveness* of a given four-letter sequence was defined as the degree to which it reduced the total number of words to those that contained that sequence. If the letter sequence was unique or was shared by just a few words (3 or less), it was considered to be *restrictive* (e.g., *-miem-*, *-yeta-*), but if many words contained the sequence (15 or more), it was called *unrestrictive* (e.g., *-comp-*, *-ente-*).

Sánchez-Casas (1993) selected four types of words to manipulate the degree to which their initial or final four letters restricted the number of word completions: (a) words that contained four-letter restrictive beginnings (e.g., *miembro*); (b) words containing four-letter unrestrictive beginnings (e.g., *completo*); (c) words containing four-letter restrictive endings (e.g., *pupitre*); and (d) words with unrestrictive four-letter endings (e.g., *decente*). The words varied in length from 6 to 8 letters. It should be emphasized that in the first two types of words (restrictive- and unrestrictive- beginning words), the four-letter sequence presented as the prime did not correspond with either the BOSS or the phonological syllable: 93% of these sequences corresponded to the BOSS + 1, and 95% of them contained more than one syllable, with 35% containing two complete syllables (e.g., *gusa, gobi, lagu*); the remaining ones corresponded to one syllable plus one letter more (e.g., *cast, comp, miem*). Nonwords were also constructed without manipulating the restrictiveness of either their beginnings or their endings. Half of the nonwords were made by adding a different ending to a four-letter word beginning (e.g., *sortera*), and the other half were made by adding a different beginning to a four-letter word ending (e.g., *estamia*).

The masked priming technique in the version employed by Forster et al. (1987) was used to present both words and nonwords as targets in a lexical decision task. A target item could be preceded by two types of primes: the four initial or the four final letters of the target, depending on whether it was a beginning-type target (e.g., *miem/miembro; comp/completo*) or an ending-type target (e.g., *itre/pupitre; ente/decente*); and a control prime containing four letters different from the target. None of the four letter of the control prime (whether it was a beginning or an   ending one) ever concided with any of the letters in the same position in the target (whether it was a word or nonword; e.g., *pent/miembro; sent/completo, tuga/pupitre, tera/decente*). Both primes and targets were displayed centered on the screen, so that the letters of the prime were never spatially aligned with those of the targets.

The mean RTs and percentages of errors are shown in Table 2.5 and 2.6 for the words and nonwords, respectively.

If restrictiveness is the relevant variable in determining priming, facilitatory effects are obtained only in the restrictive cases, and not in the unrestrictive ones, whether the prime was a beginning or an ending sequence. Four-letter primes gave an advantage of 33 ms over control primes for the restrictive cases, $minF'(1, 44) = 4.34$, $p < .05$, whereas for the unrestrictive cases, the 8 ms difference was reversed and did not reach significance in either analysis, F_1 and $F_2 < 1$. Critically, no interaction was found between type of prime and part of the word in either restrictive, $F_1(1, 18) = 1.51$, $p > .05$ and $F_2(1, 28) = 0.21$, $p > .05$, or unrestrictive, F_1 and $F_2 < 1$, cases.

In the error data, there was no significant effect of prime type in either the restrictive cases, $F_1(1, 18) = 1.69$, $p > .05$ and $F_2(1, 28) = 1.76$, $p > .05$, or the unrestrictive cases, $F_1(1, 18) = 1.84$, $p > .05$ and $F_2(1, 28) = 2.63$, $p > .05$. As in the RT data, no interaction was found between the prime and the part of the word, in either the restrictive or in the unrestrictive cases, F_1 and $F_2 < 1$.

The results also showed that RTs tended to be faster for target words preceded by a beginning prime than for those with an ending prime. However, the difference only reached significance for the restrictive cases, $F_1(1, 18) = 8.59$, $p < .05$ and $F_2(1, 28) = 5.87$, $p < .05$, and not for the unrestrictive cases, F_1 and

$F_2 < 1$. The same pattern of effects was found in the error analysis. Here, ending primes produced higher error rates than beginning primes, $\underline{\min}F'(1, 45) = 5.44$, $p < .05$, but only in the restrictive cases. A difference in frequency of occurrence between the target words of the different sets might be responsible for these effects. Finally, it should be mentioned that the nonword data did not show any significant effects of the manipulations.

TABLE 2.5
Mean RTs (in ms) and Percentages of Errors as a Function of Word and Prime Type

Item Type	Example	RT	% Errors
Restrictive-beginning words			
Four-letter fragment prime	*miem* *miembro*	619	1.9
Control fragment prime	*pent* *miembro*	660	4.3
Restrictive ending words			
Four-letter fragment prime	*itre* *pupitre*	672	10.0
Control fragment prime	*tuga* *pupitre*	697	12.0
Unrestrictive beginning words			
Four-letter fragment prime	*comp* *completo*	684	7.5
Control fragment prime	*sent* *completo*	662	10.6
Unrestrictive ending words			
Four-letter fragment prime	*ente* *decente*	676	5.0
Control fragment prime	*tera* *decente*	682	8.1

The pattern of results reported in this experiment clearly demonstrate that fragment primes, whether beginnings or endings, produce reliable and equivalent priming effects, but only in the restrictive word set. According to this finding, no specific part of the word appears to have a special status in lexical access, independent of the degree to which it restricts the number of possible lexical candidates. Any of the two fragmets of the word, either its beginning or its ending, seems to be able to drive lexical access, as long as it provides enough positive evidence to allow the lexical processor to output the corresponding lexical entry as one of, at most, very few candidates.

TABLE 2.6
Mean RTs (in ms) and Percentages of Errors for the Nonwords as a Function of Prime Type

Item Type	Example	RT	% Errors
Beginning			
Four-letter fragment prime	*sort* *sortera*	786	7.5
Control fragment prime	*aven* *sortera*	785	9.0
Ending			
Four-letter fragment prime	*amia* *estamia*	787	10.0
Control fragment prime	*ucto* *estamia*	792	8.4

The results obtained by Sánchez-Casas (1993) constitute further evidence of the lexical nature of the masked priming effects by showing that the presence or absence of those effects is determined by the degree of restrictiveness of either the initial or the final part of the word. Like the notion of neighborhood density, the notion of restrictiveness refers to a property of lexical organization, because it concerns the number of lexical entries that match a given input. Only if priming effects are taken as evidence that the corresponding lexical entry has been located or activated can one explain why only restrictive beginnings and endings have been found to produce reliable priming effects.

Neither a low-level interpretation of the masked priming effects as the result of lack of interference at the visual level, nor an interpretation in terms of competition at the orthographic level can be sustained on the basis of some of the findings reported here. Visual interference could not account for facilitatory effects with fragment primes, because the letters of the fragment primes were never presented aligned with those of the targets (when primes and targets were presented centered on the screen, their component letters did not coincide). Orthographic competition (see Evett & Humphreys, 1981; Humphreys, Evett, Quinlan, & Besner, 1987) does not suffice either, because it predicts priming effects for both restrictive and unrestrictive fragments, and for nonwords, as well. Finally, if priming effects reflect visual interference or orthographic competition, they should also have been observed for nonword targets, but nonwords failed to show reliable priming effects (see Table 2.6). It seems, therefore, that to account for the role of restrictiveness in determining priming effects, one has to claim that these effects reflect lexical contact, regardless of how this contact is held to take place.

The sort of priming effects obtained in these experiments provide clear evidence against proposals that claim that the initial part of the word constitutes the only input description through which a word's lexical representation can be accessed. The strongest evidence against these proposals is the finding that the end of a word also produces priming effects when the information it includes restricts the number of lexical matches sufficiently. Although one might be able to propose an access mechanism that operates on the basis of the initial part of the word and is flexible enough to account for the existence of priming only with restrictive beginnings, it is not at all obvious how such a mechanism could handle the evidence of facilitatory effects when the end of the word is used as a prime. In addition, it has been shown that neither the BOSS nor the phonological status of the letter sequence presented as the prime determines whether lexical contact is achieved.

Recent evidence reported by Carreiras, Alvarez, and de Vega (1993), however, suggests that the syllable does play a role in the process of lexical access in Spanish. In a series of experiments, Carreiras and his colleagues showed that the *positional frequency* of syllables (defined as the number of times a syllable appears in a particular position in words) has an effect on subjects' RTs in a lexical decision task. In particular, they found that words with high-frequency syllables were responded to slower than words with low-frequency syllables. Carreiras et al.'s experiment differs in important respects from mine (e.g., Carreiras et al. did not use masked priming and did not examine the role of partial information), but it is still interesting to see whether syllabic frequency might have had an effect in my study. Although my materials were not selected according to syllabic frequency, some preliminary analyses suggest that this variable is not relevant in determining priming effects. First, the four-letter sequences presented as primes did not always constitute a possible syllable (e.g., *cast, mbio*). This was true when these sequences corresponded to the beginning or to the end of both restrictive and unrestrictive words. Second, in those cases where the four-letter sequences corresponded to complete syllables (35% of the cases), syllabic frequency did not seem to differ between the restrictive and unrestrictive cases. Although no definitive conclusions can be drawn from this preliminary analysis, it seems that syllabic frequency, by itself, cannot account for the pattern of priming effects, at least when partial information is used. However, more experiments need to be done to examine this issue under more stringent conditions.

In sum, on the basis of the results from the set of experiments reported in this chapter, it can be concluded that, in Spanish, the notion of restrictiveness has a crucial role in determining when lexical contact is achieved from partial inputs, suggesting that there may be alternative ways of gaining access (see Chambers, 1979; Forster & Taft, 1994, for a similar conclusion regarding the existence of multiple paths to the lexicon).

The Universality of an Access Representation Based on the Notion of Restrictiveness

Exploring the issue of universality concerning different word access procedures was one of my goals carrying out the Spanish experiments I have discussed. Thus, it is important to address now the question of whether a word parsing procedure of the sort characterized here for the Spanish language might also be used by speakers of other languages. Although not many findings of this sort have been reported in the literature, some available data suggest that the notion of restrictiveness plays a role in determining what drives access in English (Sánchez-Casas, 1988; Sánchez-Casas et al., 1991). The most relevant data are those provided by Sánchez-Casas (1988) in a lexical decision experiment using a masked priming paradigm and words that could contain restrictive and unrestrictive beginnings and endings. The design and experimental procedure of this experiment were the same as those in Sánchez-Casas (1993). The same pattern of results was found in English as in Spanish. That is, restrictive four-letter sequences, from the beginning (e.g., *thun* from *thunder*) or the end (e.g., *dred* from *hundred*) of the word, produced reliable priming effects, $\underline{\min}F'(1, 61)$ = 6.84, $p < .05$, 18 and 2 ms, respectively). However, for the unrestrictive cases, the 7 ms between the two prime types did not reach significance either by subjects, $F_1(1, 22) = 1.76$, $p > .05$, or by items, $F_2(1, 40) = 0.53$, $p > .05$. Moreover, no interaction was found between type of prime and part of the word in either restrictive or unrestrictive cases, F_1 and $F_2 < 1$ for both. Similarly, no significant effects were obtained in the nonword data. As in the Spanish experiment, the fragments presented as the primes did not correspond systematically to the BOSS or to the phonological syllable. Thus, the syllabic status of the word fragment does not seem to determine whether lexical access can be achieved when English is used[3].

Sánchez-Casas' (1988, 1993) findings in Spanish and English are not the only evidence that lexical access can make use of word-ending constraints as effectively as word-beginning constraints. A different sort of evidence has been reported by O'Regan and Holmes (1987, cited by O'Regan & Levy-Schoen, 1987), in an eye-movement experiment with French materials and French subjects. This experiment showed that the "most convenient" viewing position (i.e., the first fixation position within the word where recognition is most rapid) changes with the informational structure of the word. That is, for words that are uniquely determined by their first six letters (e.g., *hirondelle*), the convenient viewing position is near the fourth letter. Although the convenient viewing position is less well defined in words with unique endings (e.g., *architecte*), it is clearly shifted rightward, somewhere near the middle of the words (see Lima & Inhoff, 1985, for findings regarding fixation duration, gaze duration, and restriction manipulations in English). In another study, Slowiaczek, Nusbaum, and Pisoni (1987) have provided evidence in the auditory domain that listeners use both word-initial and word-final information in the recognition process. In particular, the probability of correctly identifying target words embedded in noise increases when the targets are preceded by primes that share the three phonemes at the beginning or the end, relative to a condition where the targets are presented preceded by a prime sharing zero, one, or two phonemes, or by no prime at all. These results clearly suggest that ending information can also be relevant in the domain of auditory word recognition.

Although these different types of evidence are consistent with the claim that word access procedures may be universal, more research is needed to test further

---

[3]Recently Forster and Taft (1994) have provided some evidence in English that the printed word can be coded into subsyllabic units, in particular, word bodies and antibodies. A *word body* is the orthographic equivalent of the rhyme in a syllable (e.g., *erd* is the body of *herd*). A *word antibody* corresponds to the onset and the nucleus of the syllable (e.g., *pru* is the antibody of *prune*). In a series of experiments using the masked priming paradigm, Forster and Taft showed that form-priming effects are determined jointly by the neighborhood density, defined in terms of letters and in terms of bodies and antibodies (see Forster & Taft, 1994, for details of the interaction of these two variables). It might be that bodies and antibodies also play a role in determining priming effects in the masked priming experiment reported here. Further experiments need to be done to test this possibility. It should be noted that Forster and Taft only used monosyllabic words (*perd/herd, prute/prune;* though see Taft, 1992, for an examination of the role of the body in the initial syllables of polysyllabic words). Sánchez-Casas (1988, 1993), however, used polysyllabic words, employing either the beginning or the end of the word. Thus, in order to determine whether the notion of restrictiveness has an effect independent of that of the subsyllabic units defined by Forster and Taft, it would be interesting to examine the role of these units in polysyllabic words, considering both initial and second syllables, and under conditions where only part of the word is used.

the notion of restrictiveness, as well as to determine whether these results can be replicated in other languages besides Spanish and English.

Lexical Access Models and the Notion of Restrictiveness

As mentioned at the beginning of the chapter, findings concerning access representations do not only give information about the input description that is constructed from the sensory input, but also have implications for the sort of mechanisms that can be proposed to carry out the sensory-to-lexical matching process. It is, therefore, important to consider how search and activation models of lexical access can account for the findings reported here and what constraints these findings impose on any proposal for an access mechanism.

Both search and activation models are able to incorporate the notion of an access representation based on partial information about a word. However, neither of them seems to be able to explain the reported findings, without some modifications. In evaluating the two types of models, I only consider the priming data, because they are the most conclusive regarding the role that the notion of restrictiveness can play in lexical access.

Search Models

In search models like that proposed by Forster (1976, 1987), access is achieved via a search mechanism, where some abstract representation of the stimulus is first used to select a set of compatible lexical candidates. Those candidates are then said to be examined in parallel for their congruency with a fuller specification of the stimulus (*post-access check*); once an appropriate match is found, the contents of the lexical entry are said to be accessed, and can be made available to other processors. Within this approach to lexical access, the finding of both identity and form-priming effects (Forster, 1987; Forster et al., 1987; Forster & Davis, 1984) has been interpreted as evidence that lexical contact has taken place. That is, these effects are said to occur as a result of the prime accessing a lexical entry, which then remains in an altered state, so that when the target is subsequently presented and contacts that same entry, the information it contains can be retrieved more rapidly. Priming generated in such a fashion should give rise to an all-or-nothing effect. That is, there will be an effect if the target contacts the same entry as the prime, but there will be no effect if it contacts a different entry.

The circumstances in which form-priming occurs seem quite specific, although identical priming is quite general. The picture that is emerging is that for secure priming of the former type, targets should not resemble too many other words (thus ruling out effects for unrestrictive words and effects of neighborhood density, defined in terms of letters or subsyllabic units similarity). The very fact of nonidentical priming forces a modification of the search model, because the action of the prime is not limited to a single lexical entry. Findings reported here (as well as in Forster, 1987; Forster & Taft, 1994; Sánchez-Casas, 1988) suggest that when the prime is presented, both the lexical entry of the ultimate target, and others that match the input closely are contacted. It should be noted that there are, at the moment, no independent reasons why close matches, as well as perfect matches, should be accessed by the prime. This property is consistent with a nonterminating search that has a rather lax match criterion. It can be speculated that this version of search-based lexical access could support rapid error recovery, given a context, for possible errors in the input or in the system itself (see Forster, 1989; Forster & Taft, 1994, for a discussion).

The masked priming experiments reported in this chapter show that lexical contact from partial inputs is possible, but also provide evidence that what determines whether this occurs is the degree to which the input restricts the number of possible lexical matches: Only primes that restrict that number to just one, or very few, produce reliable facilitation effects. The finding that those effects are not produced by unrestrictive primes means that the extent of the form match between an input and a lexical representation does not, by itself, control access. The question, then, is whether a search model can account for the role of restrictiveness in controlling the occurrence of priming effects.

One way of dealing with this would be to suggest that restrictiveness operates at the stage where a set of lexical candidates is selected in the initial pass through the lexicon. That is, when the prime is presented, an initial pass will mark all the candidates that match the input (with a definition of what might count as a match still to be specified, see further on); if the resulting candidate set is too large, however, any further consideration simply lapses. Only when the letter sequence presented as a prime is shared by very few other words will the system list those words as possible candidates for further evaluation. The assumption of a limit on the number of lexical entries that can be accessed by the prime covers the fact that only restrictive primes produce reliable priming effects, but has no independent motivation. An apparently similar assumption might be invoked to account for the finding that priming effects are only obtained with target words that have very few neighbors (Forster, 1989). It should be noted that, although all the target words used in the masked priming experiments reported here had very few neighbors (being long), here restrictiveness is a property applying to primes and not to targets. Thus, neighborhood density and restrictiveness may reflect different aspects of lexical processing or lexical organization.

For an account of restrictiveness as a variable operating at the initial stage of access, the model needs to determine which entries match the input, but establishing what counts as a match presents further difficulties for a model of lexical access within the search framework. In Forster's model, what is claimed to be the word's access representation need not correspond to the entire input, although it has to be implemented as a structural feature of the model. That is, the part of the input that provides the basis for access could be said (a) to correspond to the heading under which the word is lexically represented (e.g., Taft, 1979), or (b) to be marked somehow in the lexical entry (e.g., *MIEMbro*, *pupITRE*, where the uppercase letters represent the highly restrictive portions, and hence, information that is highly weighted). Only when the initial input representation matches that specification in the lexical entry does that entry become included in the set of possible candidates. As mentioned in the first section of this chapter, either of these possibilities could be implemented in a search model, but with certain limitations. Those limitations stem from a constraint in the model: Before access, the contents of any entry are not available to other entries in the lexicon. (This could be seen as a highly local version of *encapsulation,* in the sense that Fodor, 1983, used the term.) Thus, the matching criteria for each entry to be accessed must be predetermined. If the beginning of the word can serve as the word's access representation, it must be marked in the entry, and so, too, for the end of the word. Problems of parsimony arise, however, if more than one part of the word can be used as its access representation.

The problem is a real one, because Sánchez-Casas' (1993) experiment has provided evidence that both beginnings and endings can produce priming effects, as long as they sufficiently restrict the number of possible lexical matches. Assuming that these effects reflect lexical contact, this means, for instance, that the entry corresponding to word like *miembro* can be contacted via its four initial letters, *miem*, and that of a word like *pupitre* can be contacted via its four final letters, *itre*. However, if it is the degree of restrictiveness that determines whether lexical contact takes place from a partial input, there may well be more than one part of a word that allows for such a restriction on the number of candidates. For example, in the word *bayeta*, both *baye* and *yeta*, are restrictive; in the word *pueblo*, this is true for *pueb* and *eblo*. Although only restrictive and unrestrictive beginnings and endings have been used as primes in the experiments reported here, there is no reason to expect different outcomes if middle parts of words were to be used (except, perhaps, that Nooteboom, 1981, has noted that middles are generally less informative than beginnings and endings). It is not clear how multiple partial inputs could be implemented as access representations in a search model.

One possible solution is that for each lexical entry there is a critical number of letter matches that has to be achieved for that entry to be accessed. That is, the model might incorporate a criterion bias device of the sort implemented in some activation models (e.g., Morton, 1969). This matching criterion would have to be calculated separately for each word, and might be characterized in terms of the proportion of letters of the word that must be present in the input. For the majority of words, more than one matching criterion will be needed, so the essence of the problem that restrictiveness presents is that specific combinations of letter matches are sufficient, but not necessary, for access.

A model that incorporates multiple matching criteria begins to resemble models within the activation approach (e.g., Morton, 1979), although it may not entirely lose its search character. However, a multiple criterion device would damage the model's explanatory power, reducing its role with respect to the phenomenon entailed here to a largely descriptive one. It is exactly on these grounds that criticism has been leveled against the activation models. In sum, it does not seem easy for a search model to account for the sort of masked priming findings reported here without making extra assumptions, the implementation of which will weaken the explanatory nature of the model considerably. The main problem for the model is that of incorporating the notion of restrictiveness, because it depends on statistical properties of the lexicon as a whole. If there is no clear way for all of a word's possible access representations to be listed in an individual lexical entry, then a search model does not have a natural way to determine what counts as a match and what does not in any given instance. The next question, then, is whether activation models themselves can account more readily for the notion of restrictiveness and for an access representation based on the notion of restrictiveness.

Activation Models

The notion of restrictiveness fits more naturally with the activation framework of the PDP approach (e.g., McClelland & Rumelhart, 1981). Although different models within this approach make different assumptions about a system's precise architecture and the details of how it may operate (see McClelland, 1987, 1988), most of them share the notion of competing interaction as the basic mechanism through which recognition is achieved. It is the commitment to interaction that allows these activation models the potential to account parsimoniously for variable restrictiveness as a determinant of access from partial inputs.

In contrast to the search model, where lexical representations are seen as encapsulated database entries, detectors within the activation system interact with each other via their inhibitory and excitatory connections. This means that at any given time, the level of activation reached by any detector is calculated not only on the basis of the detector's direct activation response to the incoming input (according to the degree to which it matches), but also takes into account the responses of competing detectors within the network. Another feature that distinguishes search models from acivation models is that processing within activation models does not take place in stages, but in a continuously graded fashion. The notion of *cascading activation* is basic to the way these models operate; that is, when any part of the input is presented, activation is generated in the feature and letter detectors at the bottom of the network. Without having to reach any threshold, activation from those detectors spreads throughout the entire network. The word detectors that are compatible with parts of the input (to whatever degree) become activated and compete with each other via their inhibitory connections. The word that finally emerges as the best candidate to match the input is the one whose pattern of activation stabilizes at the highest level, as a result of such competition.

A model that operates like this apparently has a natural way of accounting for the fact that the number of lexical candidates is a factor in whether a word will be accessed when only partial information is available. Competition among elements in the lexical pool allows the level of activation reached by a given detector to reflect how many other detectors match the given input, and thus, the restrictiveness notion can be handled; cascading activation allows for any part of the word to generate activation in the network, and thus to activate lexical-level representations, even when the full specification of the stimulus is not available. What needs to be done now is to tie these considerations to how the model accounts for priming effects.

There seem to be different ways priming effects can be explained within these sorts of models. One possibility is to see priming as the result of *persisting activation* (cf., Evett & Humphreys, 1981). That is, when the prime is presented, it induces activation in the appropriate word detector, as well as in other word detectors that resemble the stimulus to any degree. The induced activation is then assumed to persist after stimulus offset, so that when the target is subsequently presented, the corresponding word detector is ready. Under this assumption, the amount of priming is proportional to the orthographic overlap between prime and target, with the strongest effects being produced by identical primes.

Another possibility, available only to the PDP models such as the network model of McClelland and Rumelhart (1981,) is that that priming effects are the result of a temporary increase in the strength of the connections among appropriate network nodes (e.g., McClelland & Rumelhart, 1985; Rueckel, 1990). That is, when the prime stimulus is presented, the weights of connections among the feature, letter, cluster, and word nodes involved are raised, and remain so, at least temporarily, after stimulus offset. So, when the target is presented, the state of the connections that lead to the appropriate word node facilitates that node's activation. In effect, the system is showing learning, just as it did in its original training.

To account for the role of restrictiveness in determining priming effects, the activation produced by the prime has to be maintained for restrictive words and suppressed for unrestrictive words. Given the learning interpretation I have offered, it seems that connections would be strengthened in both the restrictive and unrestrictive words; thus, it is not clear how this system would explain their differential priming effects. Interpreting priming effects as stemming from partial activation, however, I can attempt an explanation of that differential pattern.

With such an interpretation, it may be possible to explain why unrestrictive primes do not produce reliable facilitation effects. These sequences are shared by many words in the language and, so, will produce activation in many word detectors within the system. The large number of competing detectors can be assumed to inhibit each other, effectively suppressing whatever activation has been produced. Thus, in these cases no residual activation remains for a subsequent target to build on, and consequently, there is no priming. It is less easy, however, to explain how restrictive letter sequences produce priming effects, because those sequences need not restrict the number of candidates to just one, but only to a few. Let us take, first, the straightforward cases: when the letter sequence fully matches a particular word (an identity prime) or the fragment has only one lexical candidate. For these, one word node will receive maximum activation from the corresponding letter and cluster detectors. The maintenance of this activation for later sampling of the target does not seem problematic. Competition drives down the activation that has been produced in any less appropriate word detectors. Thus, a unique match maintains its own activation when the system stabilizes. But what happens in restricted, but nonunique, candidate cases, where the input does not definitively favor one over the few others? If competition is the mechanism blocking facilitation from unrestrictive primes, the question must be why activation persists over any set whose size is greater than one. It seems that for restrictive primes to produce an effect, the model has to assume, rather arbitrarily, that two or three competing candidates will not annihilate each other, although any greater number will. Further, the model has to find a way to maintain the pattern of activations that each of these candidates produces. Such an assumption is necessary not only to explain priming effects in restrictive cases, but also to explain, for instance, how words that differ by one letter can prime each other (see Forster, 1987; and also McClelland's, 1986, blackboard model, for a possible way patterns of activation can be maintained).

Even without the force of the current results, a system that allows a limited set of competitors to annihilate each other will not be a very efficient one, because there may be cases where the information available is ambiguous in form; that is, it is not sufficiently specified for the system to decide on the particular lexical candidate that best matches the input. Imagine, for instance, what happens when one reads long. It is likely that, for long words, more than one fixation is necessary. If only part of the input is processed during the first fixation, and that part is matched by two or three candidates, then it will be important for the system to maintain the activation of those candidates so that, when further information becomes available from further fixations, the appropriate representation to match the input is selected.

Similar problems will be faced by other PDP models such as that suggested by Seidenberg (1989, 1990), which use distributed, instead of local, representations. Seidenberg's model does not incorporate an activation–inhibition mechanism to achieve word identification, but postulates the re-creation of the input pattern as spreading activation across a set of units. Thus, this model will overcome the problem of competitors annihilating each other. It is not clear, however, how this type of model could evolve to maintain a pattern of activation over time to account for form-priming effects and for the differential priming effects for unrestrictive and restrictive words.

In sum, to account for the masked priming effects reported in this chapter, activation models, like search models, are forced to make new and arbitrary assumptions, particularly in the handling of priming effects in terms of partial activation. In addition, the partial activation interpretation confronts further problems in explaining some of the findings that have already been reported in the literature on masked priming (Forster, 1989; Forster et al., 1987; Mildred, 1986; Sánchez-Casas et al., 1991). As mentioned earlier, evidence of full priming effects has been found when the prime was morphologically related to the targets. The persisting activation account predicts an effect graded by the number of similar letters; the more letters shared by the prime and the target, the greater the priming effects should be. Because morphologically related primes do not share all their letters with the target, they should produce smaller priming effects than identical ones.

CONCLUDING REMARKS

I have tried here to examine how a written input is parsed to gain access to the word's lexical representation. The Spanish data suggest that although the structure of the language characterized according to linguistic notions does not play a role in determining what the access representation is, the general shape of the language, in terms of what parts are more restrictive, does. Moreover, this is also true when English is used, supporting the claim that access proposals may be universal.

Regarding the success of the two types of models in handling the findings reported here, I have argued that they both face some problems that need to be addressed: Search models are stable structural models that incorporate frequency-ordered table look-up as the mechanism of association between the sensory input and the word's stored representation. Activation models, by contrast, are dynamic models that owe their ancestry more to learning theory, and have a flexibility based on their response characteristics being defined relative to a background of the entire network. In attempting to account for the data, the virtues of the search model are the pitfalls of the activation model, and vice versa. That is, because the data entries in a search model are isolated from one another, it faces problems in explaining restrictiveness as a variable determining access from partial inputs. However, because such a model allows representations to be stored individually and permanently, a natural explanation is provided of how priming of a lexical entry can persist over short time spans to facilitate subsequent access to its contents. Further, it allows for a set of candidates to be initially selected for further evaluation, and thus for a rapid resolution of possible ambiguities in the input. The opposite picture holds in the case of activation models. These models can account more readily for the role of restrictiveness in lexical access, because their structure demands that processing should occur in an interactive fashion throughout the lexicon. However, the very flexibility of their structure makes it difficult for them to hold specific information over time. Thus, they have problems in explaining how candidate matches to a given input can be maintained to direct benefits in a limited way. More generally, these models have many free parameters that can be adjusted to account for different sets of findings. The lack of constraints makes them too powerful and, thus, difficult to test empirically.

One might conclude that the findings I have reported in Spanish not only point out what the problems of the two classes of models are, but also force both the search and the activation models to consider each other's positive features. Although this is an important step in the modeling of processes in visual word recognition, the simple solution of combining the two models must be avoided. It makes little sense, for instance, to propose a search model that incorporates an initial activation phase, or an activation model which incorporates additional permanent individualized representations. Such a solution might be able to account for the data, but will do so at the cost of weakened explanatory power. For research to be fruitful, it has to to be carried out within a framework that imposes strong constraints, and, at this moment, it is search models, not activation models, that fulfill such a requirement. The further requirement, that a constrained model should nonetheless be able to account for new experimental findings, has not yet been satisfied within the search approach. Whether an account in these terms remains elusive will depend largely on the refinement that future research gives to the critical notion of restrictiveness.

REFERENCES

Anderson, J., & Jones, C. (1974). Three theses concerning phonological representations. *Journal of Linguistics, 10,* 1–26.

Becker, C.A. (1976). Allocation of attention during visual word recognition. *Journal of Experimental Psychology: Human Perception and Performance, 2,* 556–566.

Becker, C.A. (1979). Semantic context and word frequency effects in visual word recognition. *Journal of Experimental Psychology: Human Perception and Performance, 5,* 252–259.

Bradley, D.C., & Forster, K.I. (1987). A reader's view of listening. *Cognition, 25,* 103–134.

Bradley, D.C., Sánchez-Casas, R.M., & García-Albea, J.E. (1993). The status of the syllable in the perception of Spanish and English. *Language and Cognitive Processes, 8,* 197–233.

Broerse, A.C., & Zwaan, E.J. (1966). The information value of initial letters in the identification of words. *Journal of Verbal Learning and Verbal Behavior, 5,* 441–446.

Bruner, J.S. & O'Dowd, D. (1958). A note on the informativeness of parts of words. *Language and Speech, 1,* 98–101.

Carreiras, M., Alvarez, C. J., & de Vega, M. (1993). Syllable frequency and visual word recognition in Spanish. *Journal of Memory and Language, 32,* 766–780.

Chambers, S.M. (1979). Letter and order information in lexical access. *Journal of Verbal Learning and Verbal Behavior, 18,* 225–241.

Coltheart, M. (1978). Lexical access in simple reading tasks. In G. Underwood (Ed.), *Strategies of information processing* (pp. 151–216). London: Academic Press.

Cutler, A. (1985). Cross-language psycholinguistics. *Journal of Linguistics, 23,* 659–667.

Cutler, A., Mehler, J., Norris, D., & Seguí, J. (1987). Phoneme identification and the lexicon. *Cognitive Psychology, 19,* 141–177.

Davis, C. (1990). *Masked repetition priming.* Unpublished doctoral thesis, Monash University, Clayton, Victoria, Australia.

Estes, W.K. (1988). Toward a framework for combining connectionist and symbol-processing models. *Journal of Memory and Language, 27,* 196–212.

Evett, L.J., & Humphreys, G.W. (1981). The use of abstract graphemic information in lexical access. *Quarterly Journal of Experimental Psychology, 33A,* 325–350.

Feldman, L.B., Kostic, A., Lukatela, G. & Turvey, M.T. (1983). An evaluation of the "Basic Orthographic Syllabic Structure" in a phonologically shallow orthography. *Psychological Research, 45,* 55–72.

Fodor, J.A. (1983). *The modularity of mind.* Cambridge, MA: MIT Press.

Forster, K.I. (1976). Accessing the mental lexicon. In R.J. Wales & E. Walker (Eds.), *New approaches to language mechanisms* (pp. 257–287). Amsterdam: North-Holland.

Forster, K.I (1979). Levels of processing and the structure of the language processor. In W.E. Cooper

& E. Walker (Eds.). *Sentence processing: Psycholinguistic studies presented to Merrill Garrett* (pp. 27–85). Hillsdale, NJ: Lawrence Erlbaum Associates.

Forster, K.I. (1987). Form-priming with masked primes: The best match hypothesis. In M. Coltheart (Ed.), *Attention and performance XII: The psychology of reading* (pp.127–146). Hillsdale, NJ: Lawrence Erlbaum Associates.

Forster, K. (1989). Basic issues in lexical processing. In W.D. Marslen-Wilson (Ed.), *Lexical representation and process* (pp. 75–107). Cambridge, MA: MIT Press.

Forster, K.I., & Davis, C. (1984). Repetition priming and frequency attenuation in lexical access. *Journal of Experimental Psychology: Learning, Memory, and Cognition, 10,* 680–698.

Forster, K.I., Davis, C., Schoknecht C., & Carter, R. (1987). Masked priming with graphemically related forms: Repetition or partial activation? *Quarterly Journal of Experimental Psychology, 39A,* 211–251.

Forster, K.I., & Taft, M. (1994). Bodies, antibodies, and neighborhood-density effects in masked form priming. *Journal of Experimental Psychology: Learning, Memory, and Cognition, 20,* 844–863.

Frauenfelder, U.H. (1985). Cross-linguistic approaches to lexical segmentation. *Journal of Linguistics, 23,* 669–687.

Grainger, J. (1990). Word frequency and neighborhood frequency effects in lexical decision and naming. *Journal of Memory and Language, 29,* 228–244.

Grainger, J., O'Regan, J.K., Jacobs, A.H., & Seguí, J. (1989). On the role of competing word units in visual word recognition. *Perception and Psychophysics, 45,* 189–195.

Grainger, J., O'Regan, J.K., Jacobs, A.H., & Seguí, J. (1992). Neighborhood frequency effects and letter visibility in visual word recognition. *Perception and Psychophysics, 51,* 49–56.

Harris, W.J. (1983). Syllable structure and stress in Spanish: A nonlinear analysis. *Linguistic Inquiry Monographs.* Cambridge, MA: MIT Press.

Henderson, L., Wallis, J., & Knight, D. (1984). Morphemic structure and lexical Access. In H. Bouma & D.G. Bouwhuis (Eds.), *Attention and performance X: Control of language processes* (pp. 403–418). Hillsdale, NJ: Lawrence Erlbaum Associates.

Humphreys, G.W., Evett, L.J., Quinlan, P.T., & Besner, D. (1987). Orthographic priming: Qualitative differences between priming from identified and unidentified primes. In M. Coltheart (Ed.), *Attention and performance XII: The psychology of reading* (pp. 105–125). Hillsdale, NJ: Lawrence Erlbaum Associates.

Inhoff, A.W. (1987). Parafoveal word recognition during eye fixations in reading: Effects of visual salience and word structure. In M. Coltheart (Ed.), *Attention and performance XII: The psychology of reading* (pp. 403–418). Hillsdale, NJ: Lawrence Erlbaum Associates.

Johnson, N.F., & Pugh, K.R. (1994). A cohort model of visual word recognition. *Cognitive Psychology, 26,* 240–346.

Juilland, A., & Chang-Rodríguez, E. (1964). *Frequency dictionary of Spanish words.* The Hague: Mouton.

Kahn, D. (1976). *Syllable-based generalizations in English phonology.* Unpublished doctoral dissertation, Massachusetts Institute of Technology, Cambridge.

Lima, S.D., & Inhoff, A.W. (1985). Lexical access during eye fixations in reading: Effects of word-initial letter sequence. *Journal of Experimental Psychology: Human Perception and Performance, 11,* 272–285.

Lima, S.D., & Pollatsek, A. (1983). Lexical access via an orthographic code? The basic orthographic syllable structure (BOSS) reconsidered. *Journal of Verbal Learning and Verbal Behavior, 22,* 310–332.

Marcus, S.M., & Frauenfelder, U.H. (1985). Word recognition: Uniqueness or deviation? A theoretical note. *Language and Cognitive Processes, 1,* 163–169.

Marslen-Wilson, W.D. (1984). Function and process in spoken word recognition: A tutorial review.

In H. Bouma & D. G. Bouwhnis (Eds.), *Attention and Performance X: Control of language processes* (pp. 125–150). Hillsdale, NJ: Lawrence Erlbaum Associates.

Marslen-Wilson, W.D., & Tyler, L.K. (1980). The temporal structure of spoken language understanding. *Cognition, 8,* 1–71.

Marslen-Wilson, W.D., & Welsh, A. (1978). Processing interactions and lexical access during word recognition in continuous speech. *Cognitive Psychology, 10,* 29–63.

Massaro, D.W. (1974). Perceptual units in speech recognition. *Journal of Experimental Psychology, 102,* 199–208.

McClelland, J.L. (1986). The programmable blackboard model of reading. In J.L. McClelland, D.E. Rumelhart, & the PDP Research Group (Eds.), *Parallel distributed processing: Explorations in the microstructure of cognition* (Vol. 2, pp. 122–169). Cambridge, MA: Bradford Books.

McClelland, J.L. (1987). The case for interactionism in language processing. In M. Coltheart (Ed.),*Attention and performance XII: The psychology of reading* (pp. 3–36). Hillsdale, NJ: Lawrence Erlbaum Associates.

McClelland, J.L. (1988). Connectionist models and psychological evidence. *Journal of Memory and Language, 27,* 107–123.

McClelland, J.L., & Rumelhart, D.E. (1981). An interactive activation model of context effects in letter perception: Part 1. An account of basic findings. *Psychological Review, 88,* 375–407.

McClelland, J.L., & Rumelhart, D.E. (1985). Distributed memory and the representation of general and specific knowledge. *Journal of Experimental Psychology: General, 114,* 159–188.

McClelland, J.L., Rumelhart, D.E., and the PDP research group (1986). *Parallel distributed processing: Explorations in the microstructures of cognition: Vol. 2: Psychological and biological models.* Cambridge, MA: Bradford Books.

Mildred, H.V. (1986). *Masked priming effects between and within languages.* Unpublished honours thesis, Monash University, Clayton, Victoria, Australia.

Morton, J. (1969). Interaction of information in word recognition. *Psychological Review, 76,* 165–178.

Morton, J. (1970). A functional model of human memory. In D.A. Norman (Ed.), *Models of human memory.* New York: Academic Press.

Morton, J. (1979). Facilitation in word recognition: Experiments causing change in the logogen model. In P.A. Kolers, M.E. Wrolstad, & M. Bouma (Eds.). *Processing of visible language* (Vol. 1, pp. 259–268). New York: Plenum.

Mozer, M. (1987). Early parallel processing in reading: A connectionist approach. In M. Coltheart (Ed.), *Attention and performance XII: The psychology of reading* (pp. 83–104). Hillsdale, NJ: Lawrence Earlbaum Associates.

Nooteboom, S.G. (1981). Lexical retrieval from fragments of spoken words: Beginnings versus endings. *Journal of Phonetics, 9,* 407–424.

Norris, D. (1986). Word recognition: Context effects without priming. *Cognition, 22,* 93–136.

O'Regan J.K., & Lévy-Schoen, A. (1987). Eye-movement strategy and tactics in word recognition and reading. In M. Coltheart (Ed.), *Attention and Performance XII: The psychology of reading* (pp. 363–383). Hillsdale, NJ: Lawrence Erlbaum Associates.

Paap, K.R., Newsome, S.L., McDonald, J.E., & Schvaneveldt, R.W. (1982). An activation-verification model for letter and word recognition: The word superiority effect. *Psychological Review, 89,* 573–594.

Prinzmetal, W. (1990). Neon colors illuminate reading units. *Journal of Experimental Psychology: Human Perception and Performance, 16,* 584–597.

Prinzmetal, W., Treiman, R., & Rho, S.H. (1986). How to see a reading unit. *Journal of Memory and Language, 25,* 461–475.

Rayner, K. (1978). Foveal and parafoveal cues in reading. In J. Requin (Ed.), *Attention and performance VII*. Hillsdale, NJ: Lawrence Erlbaum Associates.

Rayner, K., McConkie, G.W., & Ehrlich, S. (1978). Eye movements and integrating information over fixations. *Journal of Experimental Psychology: Human Perception and Performance, 4,* 529–544.

Rayner, K., McConkie, G.W., & Zola, D. (1980). Integrating information across eye movements. *Cognitive Psychology, 12,* 206–226.

Rayner, K., Well, A.D., Pollatsek, A., & Bertera, J.H. (1982). The availability of useful information to the right of fixation in reading. *Perception and Psychophysics, 31,* 537-550.

Rodríguez-Bou, I. (1952). *Recuento del vocabulario Español* [Frequency of Spanish vocabulary]. San Juan, Puerto Rico: Oea & Unesco.

Rubinstein, H., Garfield, L., & Millikan, J.A. (1970). Homographic entries in the internal lexicon. *Journal of Verbal Memory and Verbal Behavior, 9,* 487–494.

Rueckel, J.G. (1990). Similarity effects in word and pseudoword repetition priming. *Journal of Experimental Psychology: Learning, Memory, and Cognition, 16,* 374–391.

Rumelhart, D.E., & McClelland, J.L. (1981). An interactive model of context effects in letter perception: Part 2. *Psychological Review, 89,* 60–94.

Sánchez-Casas, R.M. (1988). *Access representation in visual word recognition.* Unpublished doctoral dissertation, Monash University, Melbourne, Victoria, Australia.

Sánchez-Casas, R.M. (1993). *El papel de la restrictividad en el acceso al léxico* [The role of restrictiveness in lexical access]. Paper presented at the Primer Symposium de Psicolingüística, Tenerife, Canary Islands, Spain.

Sánchez-Casas, R.M., Davis, C.W., & García-Albea, J.E. (1992). Bilingual lexical processing: Exploring the cognate/noncognate distinction. *European Journal of Cognitive Psychology, 4,* 293–310.

Sánchez-Casas, R.M., García-Albea, J.E., & Bradley, D.C. (1991). On access representation in visual word recognition: The temporal separation technique. *Psychological Research, 53,* 53–61.

Sebastián-Gallés, N., Dupoux, E., Seguí, J. & Mehler, J. (1992). Contrasting syllabic effects in Catalan and Spanish. *Journal of Memory and Language, 31,* 18–32.

Seidenberg, M.S. (1987). Sublexical structures in visual word recognition: Access units or orthographic redundancy? In M. Coltheart (Ed.), *Attention and performance XII: The psychology of reading* (pp. 245–263). Hillsdale, NJ: Lawrence Erlbaum Associates.

Seidenberg, M.S. (1989). Visual word recognition and pronunciation: A computational model and its implications. In W.D. Marslen-Wilson (Ed.), *Lexical representation and process* (pp. 25–74). Cambridge, MA: MIT Press.

Seidenberg, M.S. (1990). Lexical access: Another theoretical soupstone? In D.A. Balota, G.B. Flores d'Arcais, & K. Rayner (Eds), *Comprehension process in reading* (pp. 33–71). Hillsdale, NJ: Lawrence Erlbaum Associates.

Selkirk, E.O. (1982). The syllable. In H. van der Hulst & N. Smith (Eds.), *The structure of phonological representation* (pp. 337–383). Dordrecht: Foris.

Slobin, D.I. (1982). Universal and particular in the acquisition of language. In E. Wanner & C.R. Gleitman (Eds.), *Language acquisition: The state of the art.* Cambridge, England: Cambridge University Press.

Slowiaczek, L.M., Nusbaum, H.C., & Pisoni, D.B. (1987). Phonological priming in auditory word recognition. *Journal of Experimental Psychology: Learning, Memory, and Cognition, 13,* 64–75.

Spoehr, K.T., & Smith, E.E. (1973). The role of syllables in perceptual processing. *Cognitive Psychology, 5,* 71–89.

Spoehr, K.T., & Smith, E.E. (1975). The role of orthographic and phonotactic rules in perceiving letter patterns. *Journal of Experimental Psychology: Human Perception and Performance, 104,* 21–34.

Taft, M. (1979). Lexical access via an orthographic code: The Basic Orthographic Syllable Structure (BOSS). *Journal of Verbal Learning and Verbal Behavior, 18,* 21–39.

Taft, M. (1985). The decoding of words in lexical access: A review of the morphographic approach. In D. Besner, T.G. Waller, & G.E. MacKinnon (Eds.), *Reading research: Advances in theory and practice* (Vol. 5, pp. 83–123). Orlando, FL: Academic Press.

Taft, M. (1986). Lexical access codes in visual and auditory word recognition. *Language and Cognitive Processes, 1,* 49–60.

Taft, M. (1987). Morphographic Processing: The BOSS re-emerges. *Attention and performance XII: The psychology of reading* (pp. 265–279). Hillsdale, NJ: Lawrence Erlbaum Associates.

Taft, M. (1991). *Reading and the mental lexicon.* Hillsdale, NJ: Lawrence Erlbaum Associates.

Taft, M. (1992). The body of the BOSS: Subsyllabic units in the lexical processing of polysyllabic words. *Journal of Experimental Psychology: Human Perception and Performance, 18,* 1004–1014.

Taft, M., & Forster, K.I. (1976). Lexical storage and retrieval of polymorphemic and polysyllabic words. *Journal of Verbal Learning and Verbal Behaviour, 15,* 607-620.

Taft, M., & Hambly, G. (1986). Exploring the cohort model of spoken word recognition. *Cognition, 22,* 259–282.

Treiman, R., & Danis, C. (1988). Syllabification of intervocalic consonants. *Journal of Memory and Language, 27,* 87–104.

Treiman, R., & Zukowski, A. (1988). Units in reading and spelling. *Journal of Memory and Language, 27,* 466–477.

3
Automatic and Strategic Processes in Lexical Access

José J. Cañas and María Teresa Bajo
Universidad de Granada
Granada, Spain

MODELS OF PRIMING AND LEXICAL ACCESS

The processing of a word during language comprehension involves accessing stored information about its meaning. Since the early experiments reported by Meyer and Schvaneveldt (1971), there has been little doubt that the context in which a word is presented can influence the way its meaning is accessed. In their experiment, subjects had to decide if two simultaneously presented visual letter strings were English words. They found that displays containing two related words (e.g., *doctor-nurse*) produced faster and more accurate responses than displays containing two unrelated words (e.g., *bread-nurse*). These results have been replicated many times with different priming procedures (e.g., Balota & Chumbley, 1984; Neely, 1977, Tweedy, Lapinski, & Schvaneveldt, 1977). Many of these procedures involve the presentation of a single word (the *prime*) to which no overt response is required, followed by the presentation of a second word or letter string (the *target*) to which subjects are required to make a word/nonword decision. In this procedure, a related prime provides a semantic context and facilitates response.

These priming effects have been the focus of considerable attention in most word recognition models (Becker, 1980, 1985, Collins & Loftus, 1975; Norris, 1986), and several processes have been suggested as causes. For example, *automatic spreading activation* has been proposed as a process that produces priming in the lexical decision task (Anderson, 1983, Collins & Loftus, 1975). This model explains priming as the result of automatic processes. Memory is held to consist of a network of concepts (*nodes*) organized in such a way that the activation of a concept activates the related nodes; that is, the presentation of a word activates its network representation, and this activation spreads out automatically via the links connecting the representation in the mental lexicon to neighboring nodes (those representing concepts related to the one presented). Therefore, if a target word is preceded by a related prime, the concept node for the target word is already activated to some degree when the target appears, so it is recognized relatively faster than targets that are preceded by unrelated primes. This automatic activation is supposed to decay over time and distance. More activation reaches concepts that are closely related to the prime than those that are weakly related to it. This activation from the prime reaches the target node only if there is an 80-400 ms interval between the appearance of prime and the appearence of the target (Stimulus onset asynchrony, SOA).

A second model concerned with priming effects postulates two processing modes that may be responsible for facilitation (Neely, 1977; Posner & Snyder, 1975). An automatic processing mode initiates an automatic spread of activation, which facilitates the processing of related nodes. This process is similar to the automatic spreading activation proposed by Collins and Loftus (1975). This processing mode is fast-acting and strategy-free, and occurs in parallel with other mental activities. The second processing mode, in contrast, is the result of an attentional mechanism and is capacity-limited and slow-acting. According to this model, priming effects can be the result of both modes of processing. As in the spreading activation model, when a word is presented, it automatically activates its node, and this activation spreads to related nodes. In addition, subjects can intentionally focus attention on the word presented and its related nodes. This attentional process facilitates the processing of related concepts, but at the cost of inhibiting the processing of unrelated ones. This inhibitory process is a consequence of the attentional shift that occurs when the target is unrelated to the prime. Because the automatic and attentional processing modes differ in their temporal parameters, the model predicts that priming and inhibition should vary as a function of the interval between the prime and the target. Because automatic activation is fast acting, automatic priming should be evident at short prime–target intervals (e.g., 0 to 250 ms). In contrast, attentional priming and inhibition effects should only be apparent at longer prime–target intervals, because the attentional processing mode is slow-acting.

A third type of model proposes that priming effects are based entirely on subjects' strategies (Becker, 1980, 1985, Norris, 1986). In these accounts, the processes invoked are assumed to be strategic because they are flexible; their presence is held to depend on the experimental conditions. Therefore, they are not a necessary result of stimulus presentation, and they need time to act. Subjects do not need to be aware of their use, however. Two types of strategic processes have been suggested: a prelexical *expectancy generation* strategy, and a postlexical *checking* strategy. When the prelexical expectancy strategy is invoked, subjects are assumed to use the prime to predict the target. When the prime is presented, the subject presumably forms a set of related words that is likely to include the target. Once this expectancy set is formed, the subject randomly selects candidate words and matches them with the input coming from the target. Related targets are facilitated because they are probably among the words included in the predicted set. The composition of the expectancy set may vary, depending on the stimulus conditions. When the prime–target relationship is narrowly defined (e.g., antonyms or very strongly related primes), the expectancy set would only include the small set of items that meets those conditions. When the prime–target relationship is broadly defined, however (e.g., all types of associative relations or wide ranges of associative strength), the expectancy set would include a large and varied set of items. Therefore, the type of prime–target relation that can produce facilitation would depend on the composition of the set and on the stimulus conditions (Becker, 1980, 1985; Cañas, 1990; Cañas & Bajo, 1994). This expectancy process is said to be *prelexical* because it affects the speed of lexical access.

The post-lexical checking strategy, in contrast is assumed to have its effects later (de Groot, 1985; Neely, 1991; Neely, Keefe, & Ross, 1989; Norris 1986). For example, in the checking model proposed by Norris (1986), as perceptual analyses proceed, sets of perceptually consistent words are identified and checked for their relationship with the context. If one of these words is related to the context (the prime), the word would be considered plausible in that context, and its recognition criterion would be lowered. If the word is unrelated to the prime, however, it would not be consistent with the context, and its recognition criterion would be raised. In lexical decision, subjects have to decide whether the target is a word or a nonword. The finding of an associative relation between the target and the prime is evidence that the target is a word, because a nonword cannot be related to the prime. However, if no relation is found between the prime and the target, then the target could be either an unrelated target or a nonword. Subjects would be slower on these trials than on related trials, because word–nonword discrimination would be more difficult. This strategy is said to be *postlexical* because it affects decision processes occurring after some lexical information has been accessed.

Empirical Evidence

Although each of these theoretical explanations of priming has focused on a single process, there have been recent suggestions that a complete account of priming phenomena must include the independent contributions of at least three processes: automatic activation, expectancy processes, and postlexical checking (Cañas & Bajo, 1994; Neely, 1991). This suggestion is based on data showing that it is possible to pull apart each process by manipulating critical variables. In addition, it is possible to set up conditions in which one or another priming mechanism is likely to be at work.

For example, evidence of automatic activation processes has been provided by experiments in which priming stimuli are presented for durations too brief to allow conscious awareness of the items' identification (e.g., Balota, 1983; Carr, McCauley, Sperber, & Parmelee, 1982; Dagenbach, Carr, & Wilhelmsen, 1989); by experiments showing facilitation on a single critical trial, when subjects had not experienced any other pairs of associates before this critical trial (Fischler, 1977); and by experiments introducing conditions in which conscious attention was directed toward different semantic categories (Neely, 1977). Thus, in Neely (1977), subjects were informed that word targets following certain category-name primes (e.g., *body*) were very probably exemplars of a different prespecified category (e.g., were likely to be exemplars of the category, *part of a building* such as *door*). Thus, when *body* was the prime, subjects' attention was directed toward the category *part of a building*. In a small proportion of trials, the targets were exemplars of a nonattended category, and were either related (e.g., *arm*) or unrelated (e.g., *sparrow*) to the prime (*body*). Results showed that at short SOAs, facilitation occurred for related targets (e.g., *arm*) independent of whether subjects' attention was directed to a different category (e.g., *part of a building*). However, at these short SOAs, facilitation and inhibition effects were not present for unrelated targets. The facilitation effect for related targets was interpreted as evidence of an automatic fast-acting spread of activation from the category name (*body*) to related exemplars (e.g., *arm*).

On the other hand, the pattern of facilitation and inhibition at long SOAs has provided evidence of the use of attentional strategies. For example, in Neely's experiment, when the SOA was long, facilitation occurred for attended targets (e.g., *door*, following the category-prime *body*) and inhibition occurred for unattended ones, regardless of whether they were related to the prime (e.g., *arm* following *body*) or unrelated to it (e.g., *sparrow* following *body*). This facilitation and inhibition were interpreted as evidence of an attentional mechanism that produces conscious activation of attended targets and conscious inhibition of unattended ones. The type of attentional mechanism suggested by Neely's data was prelexical in nature, because it appeared to work before lexical access had occurred. In addition, data showing that the composition of the stimulus list influences which targets are facilitated have also been interpreted as being the result of subjects' expectations. For example, in his Experiment 2, Becker (1980) used high- and low-typicality category name/category exemplar pairs, whereas in Experiment 5, he used antonyms, strong associates, and high- and low-typicality category name/category exemplar pairs. Results showed that facilitation for low-typicality exemplars was present in Experiment 2 and absent in Experiment 5. This absence of facilitation for low-typicality exemplars was interpreted as being due to the expectancies generated by the large proportion of strong prime–target relations present in Experiment 5. In such conditions, less strong (low-typicality) targets would not be expected and, therefore, would not be facilitated. Similarly, results showing that the relative proportion of related and unrelated primes produces variations in the magnitude of facilitation (Tweedy, et al., 1977; Henik, Friedrich, Tzegold, & Tramer, 1994) have been attributed to the workings of the expectancy mechanism.

Finally, the effects of backward priming (Koriat, 1981; Seidenberg, Waters, Sanders, & Langer, 1984) and the nonword ratio (Neely, et al., 1989) have been attributed to the use of postlexical checking strategies (Balota & Lorch 1986; Seidenberg et al., 1984). In backward priming (e.g., *hop*:prime and *bell*:target), the association between the prime and the target can only become apparent after the target has been presented and lexical access for it has already occurred. Therefore, backward priming exerts its influence in the decision process, rather than in the speed of lexical access. Consistent with this interpretation, backward priming does not occur in naming, in which decision processes are not involved. Similarly, the effect of the nonword ratio has been explained by postlexical checking processes. The *nonword ratio* refers to the probability of a target being a nonword given that it is unrelated to the prime that precedes it. Results show that larger nonword ratios are associated with larger priming effects. Obviously, the larger the probability of the target being a nonword given that it is preceded by an unrelated prime, the more useful and efficient the postlexical checking strategy will be, producing in this way, larger priming effects.

Despite the evidence showing the possible effects of these three priming mechanisms, many theoretical accounts have tried to ascribe all strategic effects in the lexical decision task to postlexical mechanisms (Norris, 1986; Seidenberg et al., 1984). The purpose of the studies described here was to explore further the relative role of these mechanisms in producing strength effects in lexical decision. In this chapter, we consider priming in word recognition as a flexible process that can be accomplished via different mechanisms. These mechanisms will vary depending on the stimulus conditions, the type of task, or even the language involved. The experiments that follow try to show the involvement of two of these mechanisms—automatic spreading activation and prelexical expectancy processes—in producing associative priming in lexical decision.

ASSOCIATIVE STRENGTH EFFECTS

Automatic and Strategic Contributions

A related finding within the lexical decision task is that the size of the priming effect varies as a function of the strength of the relation between the prime and the target. Primes that are more strongly related to the target word produce larger facilitation effects than primes that are more weakly related (Cañas, 1990; de Groot, Thomassen, & Hudson, 1982). This strength effect is held to result from the action of the same mechanism that produces priming. Thus, in a spreading of activation framework, this effect is considered to be the result of an automatic fast-acting process. Activation is believed to spread to related nodes, with less activation reaching less related nodes. Because weaker relations are represented in the network by longer links, and activation decays over time and distance (Collins & Loftus, 1975), the amount of activation reaching a node would depend on the prime–target strength. Thus, facilitation would be smaller for weaker prime–target related pairs. Similarly, from the position of a prelexical attentional theory, strength effects would be a consequence of the smaller probability of weakly related targets being included in the expectancy set (Becker, 1980, 1985). Finally, in a postlexical framework, the effect would be due to the slower and weaker evidence for wordness provided by weaker targets when they are checked against the prime (de Groot, 1985; Norris, 1986).

Thus, as with priming, it might be possible to pull apart the contributions of these mechanisms by manipulating critical variables and experimental conditions. Our first series of experiments (Exps. 1 to 4) attempted to study the relative role of automatic and strategic processes in producing the strength effect. The second series (Exps. 5 and 6) explored the relative merit of proposing prelexical and postlexical mechanisms in lexical decision. Our working hypothesis was that automatic processes, as well as prelexical and postlexical strategies, are needed to explain the full range of results concerning priming in lexical decision. Because backward priming and nonword ratio effects are difficult to explain by prelexical mechanisms (Neely, 1991), and the need for proposing prelexical mechanisms has been questioned (Norris, 1986), in the second part of the chapter we tried to establish conditions in which prelexical accounts make clear predictions.

AUTOMATIC AND STRATEGIC PROCESSES

Experiment 1

To investigate whether strategic factors were responsible for the appearance of strength effects in lexical decision, the prime–target associative strength and the relative proportion of related and unrelated pairs were manipulated at various SOA durations (Cañas, 1990). Relative proportion was introduced as a strategic variable in an attempt to manipulate the efficacy of strategy use. Thus, when the proportion of related to unrelated pairs was high, the strategic-attentional use of the prime–target relation would be enhanced in comparison with conditions in which this proportion was low. In addition, SOA was manipulated to introduce some conditions where automatic processes were more likely to occur (short SOAs) and other conditions where strategic processes were more likely to appear (long SOAs). Therefore, our expectations were that with short SOAs, as the result of automatic processing, strength effects would be present independent of the relative proportion of related–unrelated pairs. However, with long SOAs, we expected that the strength effect would be present only when the experimental conditions made clear the efficacy of strategies leading to priming and strength effects. In this experiment, we did not make predictions regarding the use of prelexical or postlexical strategies, because the proportion manipulation would enhance the use of both; that is, when the proportion of related targets was high, subjects would be encouraged to use the prime to predict the target or to take the prime–target relation as evidence of wordness.

    Three groups of subjects were assigned to three conditions of proportion of related-unrelated pairs. All three groups had the same set of items divided into eight blocks each containing 12 word–word pairs and 12 word–nonword pairs. In the first proportion condition (more-related), each block contained 10 related pairs (5 strongly related and 5 weakly related) and 2 unrelated pairs. In the second proportion condition (equal-number), each block contained 6 related pairs

(3 strong and 3 weak) and 6 unrelated pairs. In the third proportion condition (more unrelated), each block contained 2 related pairs (1 strongly related and 1 weakly related) and 10 unrelated pairs. Each of these groups of subjects was divided into three subgroups with different SOA conditions (200 ms, 500 ms and 1000 ms).

Although the instructions did not mention the proportion of related words or the SOA used, subjects could infer the value of these two variables before the actual experiment: To familiarize subjects with the experimental procedure, practice lists were introduced with the same SOAs and proportions as in the experiment.

Each trial consisted of the presentation on a computer screen of two fixation crosses for 500 ms; followed by the presentation of a prime word lasting 200 ms; and the presentation of the target stimulus (word or nonword) after a blank interval of 0, 300, or 800 ms following the prime. Therefore, SOAs of 200 ms, 500 ms, and 1000 ms were obtained by varying the blank interval between the offset of the prime and the onset of the target. Subjects responded to the target by pressing one of two keys (*yes* or *no*) on the computer keyboard.

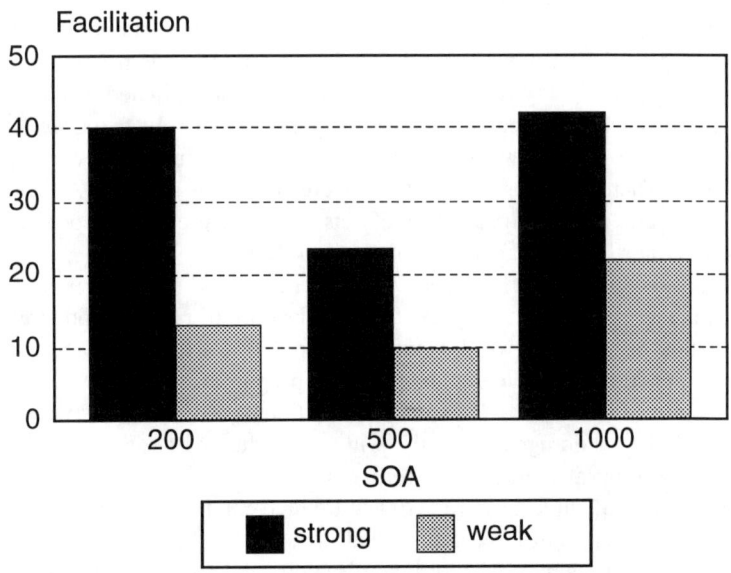

FIG. 3.1a. Facilitation as a function of the strength of the prime–target association and the proportion of related and unrelated pairs (Exp. 1). Adapted from Cañas (1990).

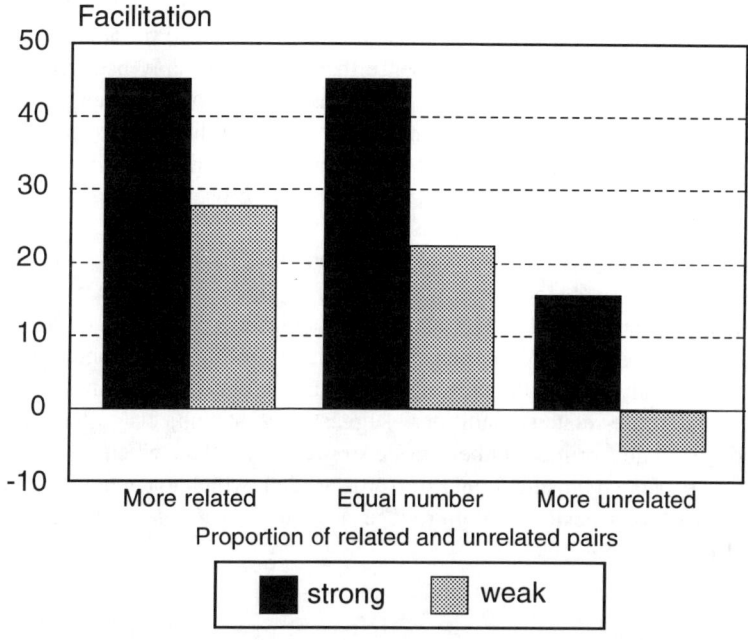

FIG. 3.1b. Facilitation as a function of SOA (Exp. 1). Adapted from Cañas (1990).

The English words forming the experimental list were selected from controlled association norms (Nelson & McEvoy, 1979), and variables of frequency and word length were controlled. The subjects were 108 students at the University of South Florida, all native speakers of English, with 12 serving in each of the 9 between-subjects conditions.

Contrary to our predictions, strength effects appeared independently of SOA and proportion. An analysis of variance (ANOVA) on the reaction time (RT) data showed a significant interaction of relatedness (related vs. unrelated) and strength (strong vs. weak), $F(1, 99) = 5.21$, $p < .01$, indicating that there was more priming (difference between related and unrelated prime–target pairs) for strong targets than for weak targets. Strength did not interact with any of the other variables. Figures 3.1a and 3.1b show the magnitude of priming (related minus unrelated) for weak and strong targets in each of the SOA and proportion conditions.

These results suggested that, contrary to our expectations, strength effects might be due to the automatic spreading of activation processes and might not be affected by attentional factors and strategic manipulations. However, this interpretation is not consistent with most priming theories or with previous data. Therefore, we thought that perhaps the conditions introduced to induce strategic processing were not specific, in the sense that they might only be affecting the general use of related pairs, without any consideration of the strength of that relation. For example, the proportion of related to unrelated pairs might have promoted a very general strategy that produced differential processing of related relative to unrelated targets, but did not affect the processing of strongly and weakly related targets.

This possibility received some support from the data, because the interaction of proportion and relatedness was significant, $F(2, 99) = 3.32$, $p < .05$. Thus, the difference between related and unrelated pairs (priming) was larger in the equal-number and more-related conditions than in the more-unrelated condition. This effect was mainly due to the slower RTs to the unrelated targets in the equal-number and more-related conditions, suggesting that subjects' attention was focused on related primes (either strong or weak), so that, when an unrelated target was presented, an attentional shift was needed, which made the RT slower. Experiment 2 was designed to introduce a strategic variable that specifically affected the strength effect.

Experiment 2

To find out whether the persistence of the strength effect in Experiment 1 was due to the automaticity of the process producing it or to the lack of specificity of the strategic variables used, Experiment 2 introduced a variable that would directly affect strength if this effect was sensitive to attentional manipulations. Three groups of subjects were tested in a lexical decision task. All subjects had the same proportion of word–nonword pairs (13 word and 13 nonword) and the same proportion of related and unrelated pairs (10 related and 3 unrelated) in each block of trials; this proportion was selected to encourage attentional processing. Similarly, an SOA of 500 ms was selected to ensure that there was enough time for attention to act. However, the three groups differed in the proportion of strongly and weakly related pairs in their lists. One group (the more-strong group) had 80% strongly related pairs and 20% weakly related pairs. A second group (the equal-number group) had 50% strongly related pairs and 50% weakly related pairs. The third group (the more-weak group) had 20% strongly related pairs and 80% weakly related pairs. We expected that the presence of the strength effect in this experiment would depend on the proportion condition. In the more-strong condition, subjects would be encouraged to make more use of strong relations than of weak ones. For example, if they were using the prime to predict the target (prelexical expectancy strategy), the presence of many strongly related prime–target pairs would induce them to include only strong candidates in their expectancy sets, so only strongly related targets would be facilitated. If the postlexical strategy was selected, subjects would probably use only strong relations as evidence of wordness. Therefore, in the more-strong condition, strategic processing would cause the appearance of strength effects.

At the other extreme, the more-weak condition would induce subjects to use weak and strong relations as part of their attentional strategy. Thus, prelexical expectancy sets would   include weak and strong candidates, and postlexical checks would take weak and strong relations as evidence of wordness. Therefore, in this condition we expected equal facilitation for weak and strong targets.

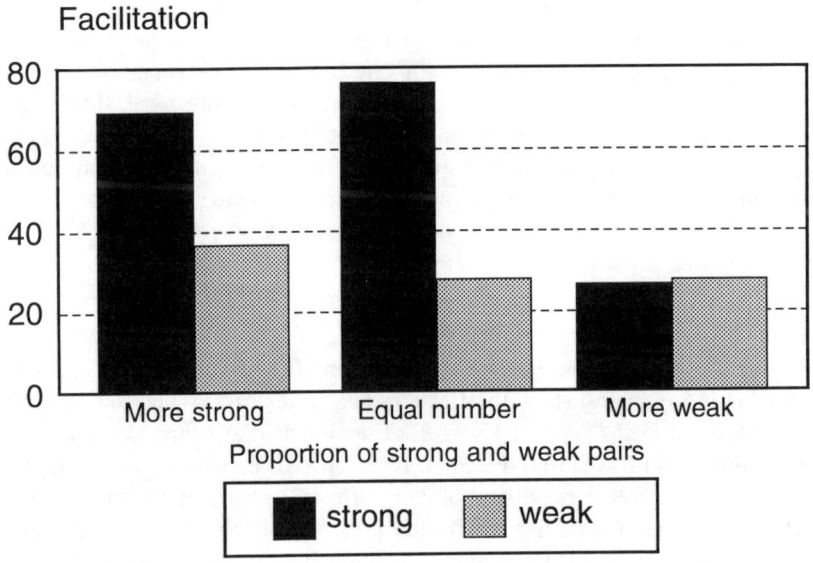

FIG. 3.2. Facilitation as a function of the strength of the prime–target association and the proportion of strongly and weakly related pairs. SOA = 500 ms (Exp. 2). Adapted from Cañas (1990).

The sequence of events within each trial was the same as that in the 500 ms SOA condition of Experiment 1. A new set of stimuli was selected, however, because this experiment, and the subsequent ones, were conducted with Spanish-speaking subjects. The new set of words that formed the experimental list was selected from Spanish association norms (Algarabel, Sanmartin, García, & Spert, 1985). The selection procedure was similar to the one used in Experiment 1, except that an independent set of unrelated prime–target pairs was selected for all subjects. Therefore, strength and relatedness were considered a single variable with three levels: strong, weak, and unrelated. Subjects were 60 university students at the University of Granada, with 20 serving in each of the three between-subjects conditions.

As expected, the main effect of type of relation (strong, weak, unrelated) was significant, $F(2, 114) = 27.92$, $p < .001$. Targets preceded by strongly related primes were recognized faster than targets preceded by weakly related primes, and both were recognized faster than targets preceded by unrelated primes. More importantly, this variable interacted with the relative proportion of strong and weak pairs, $F(4, 114) = 2.27$, $p = .05$. This interaction is shown in Fig. 3.2. As can be seen, in both the more-strong condition and the equal-number condition, the difference in RT between the strong and weak targets was significant (31 ms and 47 ms, respectively). However, in the more-weak condition, this difference was not significant (1 ms).

The disappearance of the strength effect in the more-weak condition is consistent with the use of attentional strategies. When more weak than strong primes are present in the experimental list, both types of primes are equally effective in predicting the target (prelexical locus) or in providing useful information for the checking mechanism (postlexical locus).

Experiment 3

The purpose of Experiment 3 was to explore further the role of strategic processing in producing strength effects in lexical decision. Therefore, an even longer SOA interval (1000 ms) was used, and a neutral prime condition (the word *blanco,* white) was introduced. The presence of a neutral prime condition was intended to explore possible inhibitory effects, because attentional strategic processing is usually associated with the presence of inhibition. According to Posner and Snyder's (1975) original formulation, attentional processing involves intentional focusing on a particular lexical representation. This focusing facilitates the processing of words related to the prime at the cost of inhibiting the processing of words unrelated to it. Thus, inhibition would be caused by the shift of attention that must occur when the target is unrelated.

Extending this framework to our previous manipulations, inhibition should be present not only for unrelated words, but also for weakly related words when they are not included in the expectancy set or are not taken as evidence of wordness. Hence, the relative proportion of strongly and weakly related pairs (more-strong vs. more-weak) was manipulated, with the prediction that weakly related targets would be more inhibited than neutral targets in the more-strong condition.

Forty new students from the University of Granada participated in this experiment, with 20 assigned to each proportion condition. The procedure and materials of the two proportion conditions were similar to those used in the more-strong and more-weak conditions of Experiment 2, but a new set of 15 words was selected to be used as targets in the neutral prime condition. Within a block, three trials consisted of a neutral prime (the word *blanco*) preceding word targets, and three trials consisted of a neutral prime preceding nonword targets. Thus, as in Experiments 1 and 2, the type of prime (strong, weak, unrelated, or neutral) was manipulated within subjects.

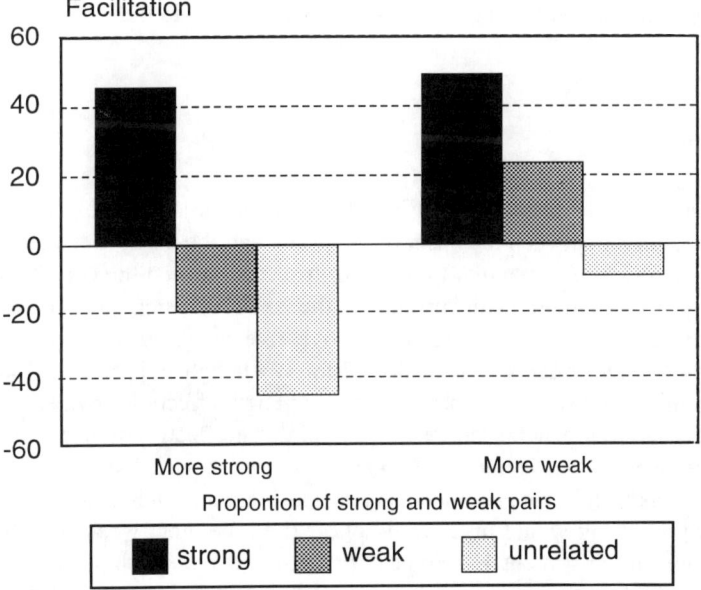

FIG. 3.3. Facilitation and inhibition as a function of the strength of the prime–target association and the proportion of strongly and weakly related pairs. SOA = 1000 ms (Exp. 3). Adapted from Cañas (1990).

Figure 3.3 shows the pattern of facilitation and inhibition for strongly related, weakly related, and unrelated primes in each proportion condition. Facilitation and inhibition were calculated by subtracting from the neutral condition.

As the figure shows, targets preceded by strongly primes were facilitated in both the more-strong and the more-weak conditions. However, targets preceded by weakly related primes were facilitated in the more-weak condition and inhibited in the more-strong condition. Finally, unrelated targets were inhibited in both proportion conditions, although the magnitude of the inhibition effect was larger in the more strong condition. An ANOVA on the raw RT data showed that the interaction of type of prime and proportion was significant, $F(3, 114) = 2.84$, $p < .05$.

Again, this pattern of results is consistent with the use of attentional strategies at long SOAs. Thus, targets within the attentional focus are facilitated (strong targets in both conditions and weak targets in the more-weak condition), whereas targets outside this focus are inhibited (weak targets in the more-strong condition and unrelated targets). In addition, the presence of strength effects in the more-strong condition and the absence of this effect in the more-weak condition replicate the findings of Experiment 2 and extend them to longer SOA intervals.

Experiment 4

Experiments 2 and 3 showed the effect of a strategic variable in lexical decision when the interval between the onset of the prime and the onset of the target was large enough to allow attention to act, and therefore showed the contribution of strategic processes in producing priming in the lexical decision task. The purpose of Experiment 4 was to explore the relative role of automatic processing in producing strength effects in lexical decision. Although Experiment 1 showed evidence indicating some automaticity of the strength effect, this evidence might have been due to a general failure to manipulate an effective strategic variable. Therefore, we thought it important to show that at short SOAs, the difference between weakly and strongly related targets was present even in conditions where strategic processing would make it disappear (i.e., the more-weak condition).

Hence, in Experiment 4, the type of prime–target relationship (strong, weak, and unrelated) was the only variable manipulated; and the stimuli, materials, and procedure were similar to those of the more-weak condition of Experiment 2. The only difference was that the prime word was presented for only 75 ms and the blank interval following the prime was 25 ms. The SOA interval, therefore, was 100 ms. A new group of 20 students from the University of Granada participated in this experiment.

As expected, at the short SOA interval used in this experiment, there was a difference between targets preceded by strongly and weakly related primes. Thus, the effect of type of prime was significant, $F(2, 38) = 11.43$, $p < .001$. Targets preceded by strongly related primes were recognized faster (845 ms) than targets preceded by weakly related primes (888 ms), and both were recognized faster than targets preceded by unrelated primes (929 ms). Thus, at short SOAs, strength effects seem to be independent of subjects' attentional strategies.

Summary

The results of Experiments 1 to 4 are consistent with theoretical frameworks proposing the existence of automatic and attentional processes in the lexical decision task. At short SOA intervals (250 ms and 100 ms), targets that were strongly related to the prime were recognized faster than targets that were weakly related to the prime. This strength effect was not sensitive to attentional variables such as the relative proportion of related and unrelated pairs (Exp. 1) or the relative proportion of strong and weak pairs (Exp. 4), intended to change subjects' strategies. Therefore, at short SOAs, this effect appears to be the result of automatic activation of the prime representations spreading to related concepts, with more related concepts receiving more activation than concepts located further away. On the other hand, at long SOAs (500 ms and 1000 ms), the strength effect depended on the subjects' strategy. If subjects used both strongly and weakly related primes to predict the prime (prelexical strategy) or if they used both strong and weak relations as evidence of wordness (postlexical strategy), both types of targets were facilitated and the strength effect disappeared. Thus, this effect was not present in the more-weak condition of Experiments 2 and 3. However, if the composition of the stimulus list encouraged subjects to use strong relations as the only source on which to base their strategies (the more-strong condition of Expes. 2 and 3 and the equal number condition of Exp. 2), the strongly related targets were facilitated, whereas the weakly related targets were inhibited (the more-strong condition of Exp. 1). Hence, the strength effect at long SOAs seems to be dependent on the composition of the stimulus list and on other possible variables affecting attentional processing.

PRELEXICAL AND POSTLEXICAL CONTRIBUTIONS

Experiments 5 and 6 were designed to explore the relative contributions of pre-lexical expectancy strategies and postlexical checking in the lexical decision task. Postlexical accounts of priming often neglect the role of expectancy processes in lexical decision (Norris, 1986; Stanovich & West, 1983). The presence of postlexical processes in lexical decision is clearly supported by the presence of backward priming (Koriat, 1981) and nonword ratio effects (Neely et al., 1989) in lexical decision, and their absence in naming. Therefore, our primary aim was to seek support for the existence of prelexical processes in lexical decision. Pre-lexical theories assign an important role to the composition of the stimulus list for producing priming and strength effects. Expectancy sets are formed to resemble the stimulus lists. Therefore, the size and composition of a set would directly depend on the experimental list. If these conditions encourage the generation of large expectancy sets, lexical decision responses would slow down as longer searches through the set need to be conducted (Becker, 1980, Cañas, 1990). If, in contrast, the generation of small sets is encouraged, search processes would be narrowed, and lexical decision responses would be speeded up.

Experiments 1 to 4 showed that the composition of the stimulus list plays an important role in lexical decision. However, postlexical accounts of priming could easily accommodate those findings, because the efficacy of the checking strategy would depend on the number and strength of the related pairs. Thus, larger numbers of related pairs would make the checking strategy more useful, and stronger relationships would produce faster checking processes. From many postlexical theories (e.g., Norris 1986), but it is not clear why strength and proportion should interact, it would be possible to assume that the composition of the stimulus list also affects the efficacy of the checking process. For example, it is possible that when many strong targets are introduced in the list, only strong relations are taken as evidence of wordness, whereas when many related pairs are included, both weak and strong relations would be taken as evidence of wordness.[1]

In Experiments 5 and 6, we introduced a variable whose possible effects could only be explained by the action of a prelexical strategy. As already

---

[1]This account is problematic if one assumes that strong prime-target relations are checked much faster than weak ones, so that they provide faster and stronger evidence for wordness. Postlexical checking would be a useful strategy provided that the semantic checking of the prime and target finish before the lexical decision has been made; hence, only fast checking processes (e.g., checking for strong relations) would produce priming. This assumption leads to the prediction of strength effects, regardless of whether the stimulus list contains a large number of weakly related pairs.

discussed, expectancy accounts of priming predict that decision times depend not only on the composition of the set (whether strong or weak candidates are included), but also on its size. Once the set is formed, subjects have to search through the set and recover the candidate word that matches the target. The larger the set, the longer the search process will be. Therefore, if a prelexical expectancy strategy is used, the size of the set of related words defined by the prime is a variable that should show its effects at long SOAs. Nelson, Lalomia, and Cañas (1991) reported data showing that the size of the set of related words defined by a prime affects decision times, depending on search-related variables. The size of the set of related words defined by the prime refers to the number of different related words produced by a large group of subjects to a given word (the prime). The size of the set can be estimated from normative data (Algarabel et al., 1985; Nelson & McEvoy, 1979); because those norms usually contain words producing both large and small numbers of related words, it is possible to select primes that define large and small sets.

Expectancy theories of priming predict that the effect of this variable will also depend on the composition of the stimulus list. When the composition of the list encourages subjects to generate expectancy sets that include strongly and weakly related words (i.e., to include all the words related to the prime), the size of the expectancy set would vary with the size of the set of related words defined by the prime. Primes defining large associative sets would produce large expectancy sets, and primes defining small associative sets would produce small expectancy sets. Panel A of Fig. 3.4 illustrates these conditions. In contrast, when the composition of the stimulus list encourages subjects to generate expectancy sets that include only strongly related words, the size of this set would always be relatively small, regardless of the number of words associated to the prime. However, when the prime has a large number of associates, many of those (the weak ones) would be left out of the expectancy set and would not be facilitated. This would produce strength effects. When the prime defines a small number of associates, all of them (weak and strong) would probably be entered into the expectancy set, because this small number of associates is the only basis on which to generate the expectancy set. This would reduce or eliminate the strength effect. Panel B of Fig. 3.4 illustrates conditions in which small expectancy sets are generated.

It is obvious from the figure that there are large differences between different conditions in the number of words that subjects have to search through. According to expectancy theories, these differences should show their effects on priming. Clearly, the size of the set of related words defined by the prime should not play any role in the checking process. Therefore, in a postlexical framework, the size of the set of associates to the prime should not affect the magnitude of priming. The result of preliminary perceptual analyses of the target is supposed to be checked against the context provided by the prime. Because the prime and the possible targets are already available to the subject for the checking mechanism to work, it is evident that a variable that mainly depends on search processes could not influence it.

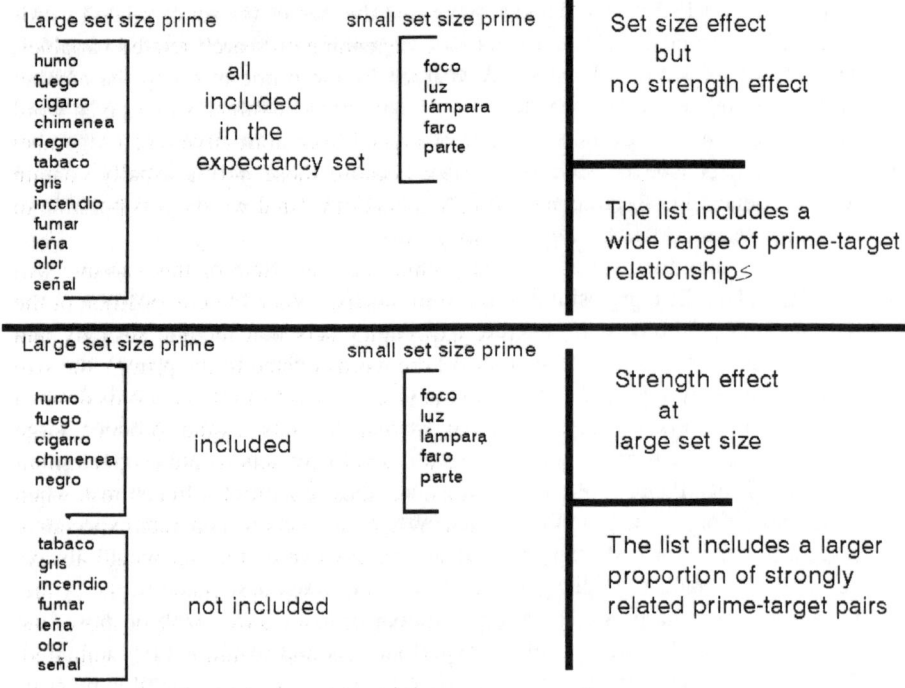

FIG. 3.4. Theoretical expectancy sets and predicted effects as a function of the stimulus list's composition. Adapted from Cañas and Bajo (1994).

Experiment 5

Experiment 5 attempted to create conditions (illustrated by Panel A of Fig. 3.4) in which the composition of the stimulus list encouraged the generation of expectancy sets that included all types of related words. Thus, a large variety of prime–target relationships were included in the experimental list. The strength of the relationships varied from very weak (.01–.10) to very strong (.31–.40) with two medium levels (.11–.20, and .21–.30). One third of the target words were preceded by related primes, one third were preceded by unrelated primes, and one third were preceded by a string of asterisks (neutral condition). Half of the prime words defined large sets of associated words, and the other half defined small sets of associated words. From an expectancy point of view, the presence of different types of relations would encourage subjects to generate expectancy sets that included all possible associates to the prime. Hence, all types of related targets would be facilitated. In these conditions, the size of the set of words associated to the prime would be an important variable. Because all of the associates to the prime would be included in the expectancy set, the larger the associative set, the larger the expectancy setn and the longer the decision times. Therefore, we expected that the size of the set would have an effect, whereas the strength of the prime–target relationship would not (equal facilitation for all type of relations).

For this experiment, 96 words were selected from Algarabel et al.'s (1985) associative norms. Forty-eight of the selected pairs had primes that defined associative sets of 19 or more words ($M = 23.5$), and 48 had primes that defined sets of fewer than 18 words ($M = 15.06$). Within each set of 48 pairs that defined the set size variable, 4 subsets of pairs were formed, each with a strength of association as indicated earlier. Variables that have usually been found to affect lexical decision, such as frequency and word length, were controlled. As indicated, the proportion of word to nonword targets and the proportion of related to unrelated words was 50%. Similarly, within the related-word condition, the proportion of pairs for each strength condition was 25%. The experimental procedure was similar to that of Experiment 3. Thus, the SOA was 1000 ms (200 ms stimulus presentation and 800 ms blank interval). The neutral prime for this experiment was a string of asterisks. Thirty new subjects from the University of Granada participated in this experiment.

The main effects of type of prime (related, unrelated, neutral) and set size (large vs. small) were significant, $F(2, 58) = 21.08, p < .001$ and $F(1, 29) = 5.81$, $p < .03$. On the other hand, the main effect of strength (.01–.10, .11–.20, .21–.30 and .31–.40) was not. As expected, related targets were recognized faster (672 ms) than unrelated targets (710 ms) and than targets preceded by neutral primes (748 ms). Surprisingly, unrelated targets were recognized faster than targets preceded by neutral primes. Hence, in contrast to Experiment 3, neutral primes produced slower responses than unrelated primes, and it was not possible to assess inhibitory effects. This finding is not without precedent. Some previous studies have also shown slower responses to targets preceded by strings of asterisks (e.g., de Groot et al., 1982), and, although there is no clear explanation, it has been suggested that different types of neutral primes may play different roles in modulating facilitation effects (Borowsky & Besner, 1991).

More important for our predictions were the set size by type of prime and strength by type of prime interactions. As predicted, the Set size × Type of prime was significant $F(2, 58) = 4.83$, $p < .03$, whereas the strength by type of prime and the strength by type of prime by set size interactions were not ($Fs < 1$). Further analyses of the set size by type of prime were performed on the data. To make sure that our facilitation effects were not affected by the type of baseline (unrelated or asterisks), two separate analyses were performed on the data, one taking unrelated primes as the baseline and the other taking asterisks as the base for comparisons. Similar results were obtained in the two analyses.

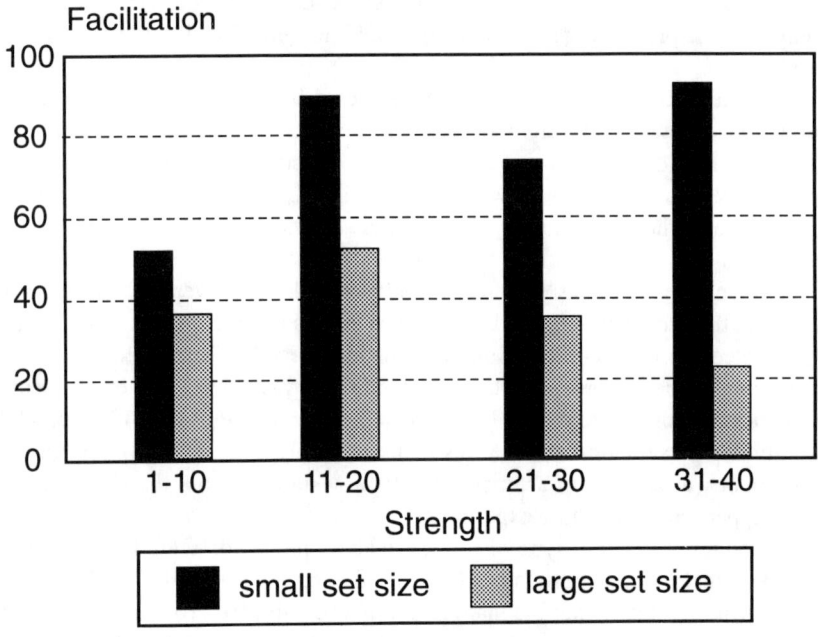

FIG. 3.5. Facilitation effects as a function of the size of the associative set defined by the prime and the strength of the prime–target association (Exp. 5). Adapted from Cañas and Bajo (1994).

Figure 3.5 shows the magnitude of facilitation for each of the strength and set size conditions. The facilitation depicted in this figure was calculated by subtracting mean RTs to related targets (.01–.10 large, .01–.10 small, .11–.20 large, .11–.20 small, .21–.30 large, .21–.30 small, .31–.40 large or .31–.40 small) from the mean RTs for the equivalent unrelated and asterisk conditions. Therefore, the baseline for facilitation was the mean of the neutral and unrelated conditions.

As can be seen, the set size by strength interaction was due to the larger facilitation shown by targets preceded by small set size primes compared to targets preceded by large set size primes. This larger facilitation appeared in all strength conditions. There were some additional variations in the magnitude of priming for different strength conditions, but these variations were not enough to produce reliable differences. Therefore, weak, medium, and strong primes produced equivalent amounts of facilitation.

These results are consistent with an expectancy account of priming and with the data from Experiments 2 and 3 showing that, when subjects are encouraged to include weak and strong targets in the expectancy set, the strength effect disappears. In addition, as predicted by these theories, when all types of candidate words were included in the expectancy set, the size of the associative set of the prime was an important variable: The larger the associative set of the prime, the larger the expectancy set and the longer the search process through the related candidate words.

These results fit nicely with a prelexical expectancy account, but they are very inconsistent with theories attributing priming effects at long SOAs to the unique role of postlexical strategies. Priming effects should not be influenced by the set size of the prime, because the checking mechanism is not affected by search-related variables. As stated, postlexical processes check for the consistency between the target and its context (prime) after lexical information about the prime and possible targets is already available to the subject. Variables such as proportion of related pairs or strength influence these postlexical processes by encouraging them to provide stronger evidence of wordness. However, it is far from evident how a search-related variable, such as the size of the set of associates to the prime, could affect the presence or efficacy of the checking process.

Experiment 6

Another prediction that follows from a prelexical framework is the reduction of the set size effect in some conditions in which strong associates are the only candidate words entered into the expectancy set. If only strong targets are included in the expectancy set, the size of this set would be small, with only a few strong candidate words included. Hence, the overall effect of the set size of the prime should be small. However, the presence of strength effects would be dependent on this variable. This is illustrated by Panel B of Fig. 3.4. When primes that define large set sizes are used as the basis on which to generate expectancy sets of only strongly related candidates, weak associates to the primes will be left out of the expectancy sets. In these conditions, weakly related targets will not be facilitated. In contrast, when the sources for generating expectancy set are primes with small set of associated words, weak and strong associates would be included in the sets, because there are few candidate words to be selected into them.[2] Therefore, we expected that primes defining large associative sets would produce strength effects, whereas primes defining small associative sets would produce small or null strength effects. Experiment 6 was designed to create conditions encouraging subjects to generate small expectancy sets that mainly included strongly associated words.

In this experiment, only two levels of strength (strong and weak) were included, and 75% of the related pairs were strong primes. A new set of 96 related pairs was selected from Algarabel et al.'s (1985) associative norms. Forty-eight of them defined small associative sets ($M = 16.10$), and 48 defined large associative sets ($M = 24.7$). Within each of these sets, 36 had strong prime–target relations ($M = 0.26$), and 12 had weak ones ($M = 0.02$). As in Experiment 5, one third of the target words were preceded by related primes, one third were preceded by unrelated primes, and one third were preceded by a string of asterisks (neutral condition). In contrast to Experiment 5, however, within the related-word condition, 75% of the pairs were strongly related and 25% were weakly related. In all other respects, the procedure was the same as the one used in Experiment 5. Forty-eight new subjects from the University of Granada participated in this experiment.

Figure 3.6 shows the magnitude of priming as a function of strength and set size. Facilitation was again calculated by subtracting RTs to related targets (strong large, strong weak, weak large, or weak small) from the mean RTs for the equivalent unrelated and asterisk conditions. As can be seen, the magnitude of priming varied with both strength and set size. Most important, these two variables interacted. Thus, for the Set size × Strength × Type of Prime interaction, $F(2, 94) = 4.35$, $p < .02$.

As predicted, primes defining large sets of associated words produce strength effects, with weak primes failing to facilitate responding to the target.

---

[2]This prediction is made on the assumption that expectancy sets that include at least three or four candidates are always generated. If that initial assumption were wrong, strength effects similar to the ones obtained in the previous condition would be found. Therefore, possible differences between conditions regarding strength effects would also provide some insight into possible constraints on generating the sets.

An ANOVA on type of prime (related, unrelated, neutral) and strength on the large set size condition showed a significant Strength × Type of Prime interaction, $F(1, 94) = 5.65, p < .03$. When primes defined large sets, the strength effect was mainly due to the lack of facilitation of weak primes. This is consistent with predictions based on the use of expectancy strategies. In these conditions, weakly associated words would be left out of the expectancy set and would not be facilitated.

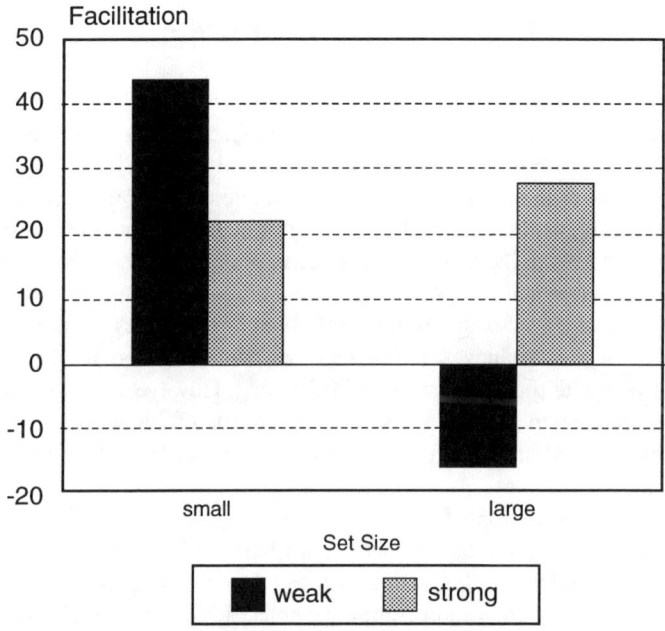

FIG. 3.6. Facilitation effects as a function of the size of the associative set defined by the prime and the strength of the prime–target association (Exp. 6). Adapted from Cañas and Bajo (1994).

In contrast, targets defining small associative sets did not produce strength effects. An ANOVA on type of prime and strength in the small set size condition indicated that the interaction of these two variables was not significant. Thus, targets preceded by related primes were responded to faster than targets preceded by either unrelated or neutral primes, and this was true for both weakly and strongly related primes. Again, this is consistent with prelexical accounts of priming. Primes defining small associative sets had very few strongly related words to be included in the expectancy set, so weakly related words were also needed to generate this set. Hence, both strongly and weakly related words were included in the set, and both were facilitated.

This pattern of results is again inconsistent with proposals attributing priming effects to the use of postlexical checking mechanisms. The effect of the set size variable and the dependence of strength effects on this variable are not easy to fit into postlexical frameworks.

CONCLUDING REMARKS

In this chapter, priming effects in lexical decision were studied. These priming effects have been considered evidence of lexical access. The presentation of a related prime activates its lexical representation, and this activation is supposed to facilitate access to the target's lexical representation. Both automatic spreading activation processes and prelexical expectancy strategies attribute priming effects to the speeded access to the target's lexical representation when it is preceded by a related prime. Thus, automatic spreading activation from the prime is believed to activate the target's lexical representation before its presentation, and the generation of an expectancy set that includes words related to the prime is supposed to facilitate the target's lexical processing. However, recent postlexical accounts of priming in lexical decision attribute this effect to a facilitation of decision processes occurring after the prime and target lexical representations have been accessed.

The main contribution of this chapter is to show that priming effects in lexical decision are not due to the single contribution of any of these processes. Thus, the priming effects in Experiments 1 and 4 were interpreted as due to the automatic spreading of activation from the primes' lexical representations to the representations of related targets, and Experiments 2, 3, 5, and 6 seem to demonstrate the role of expectancy attentional strategies in producing priming effects. In addition, the latter experiments indicated that it is possible to predict when and how these processes will show their effects. Spreading activation appears to exert its role at short SOAs, and produces more facilitation for strong than weak primes, independent of the stimulus conditions (Exps. 1 and 4). In contrast, attentional expectancy strategies seem to exert an influence at long SOAs, and the type of targets being facilitated would depend on the stimulus conditions: Targets whose representation enters the expectancy set would be facilitated, whereas targets whose representation is left out of the set would not. Weakly related targets are especially susceptible to expectancy strategies. Thus, when stimulus conditions encourage subjects to generate small expectancy sets mainly composed of strong associates, weak targets are not facilitated (weak targets in the more strong condition of Exps. 2 and 3), unless the number of associates to the prime is so small that they are needed to form the set (weak target in the small prime set size condition). However, when the stimulus conditions encourage subjects to include strongly and weakly related candidate words in the expectancy sets (more-weak conditions of Exps. 2 and 3, and Exp. 5), weakly related targets are also facilitated. Hence, the joint work of prelexical automatic spreading activation and expectancy strategies easily explain the pattern of results of the experiments reported in this chapter.

Other data, however (Koriat, 1981; de Groot, 1985; Stanovich & West, 1983; Seidenberg et al., 1984; Neely et al., 1989), also show the contribution of postlexical strategies in producing priming effects in lexical decision. Other effects, such as backward priming and nonword ratio, are better explained as due to the effects of postlexical checking in the decision process. Taken together, results showing priming effects in lexical decision suggest that a complete account of priming phenomena must include the independent operations of at least these three processes. Therefore, an important research goal is to identify conditions in which each of them may work.

ACKNOWLEDGMENTS

Preparation of this chapter was supported by a DGICYT grant (PB92-0938) from the Spanish government to María Teresa Bajo.

REFERENCES

Algarabel, S., Sanmartin, J., García, J., & Spert, R. (1985). Normas de asociacion libre para investigación experimental [Associative norms for experimental research]. *Informes del laboratorio de aprendizaje y memoria: Informe N° 1.* Department of Experimental Psychology, University of Valencia, Spain.

Anderson, J.R. (1983). *The architecture of cognition.* Cambridge, MA: Harvard University Press.

Balota, D.A. (1983). Automatic semantic activation and episodic memory encoding. *Journal of Verbal Learning and Verbal Behavior, 22,* 88–104.

Balota, D.A., & Chumbley, J.I. (1984). Are lexical decisions a good measure of lexical access: The role of word frequency in the neglected decision stage. *Journal of Experimental Psychology: Human Perception and Performance, 10,* 340–357.

Balota, D.A., & Lorch, R. (1986). Depth of automatic spreading activation: Mediated priming effects in pronunciation but not in lexical decision. *Journal of Experimental Psychology: learning, Memory and Cognition, 12,* 336–345.

Becker, C.A. (1980). Semantic context effects in visual word recognition: An analysis of semantic strategies. *Memory and Cognition, 8,* 493–512.

Becker, C.A. (1985). What do we really know about semantic context effects during reading? In D. Besner, T.G. Waller, & E.M. MacKinnon (Eds). *Reading research: Advances in theory and practice* (Vol.5, pp. 125–166). New York: Academic Press.

Borowsky, R., & Besner, D. (1991). Visual word recognition across orthographies: On the interaction between context and degradation. *Journal of Experimental Psychology: Learning, Memory, and Cognition, 17,* 272–276.

Cañas, J.J. (1990). Associative strength effects in the lexical decision task. *Quarterly Journal of Experimental Psychology, 42A,* 121–145.

Cañas, J.J., & Bajo, M.T. (1994). Strategic associative priming in the lexical decision task. *Quarterly Journal of Experimental Psychology, 47A,* 383–405.

Carr, T.H., McCauley, C., Sperber, R.D., & Parmalee, C.M. (1982). Words, pictures and priming: On semantic activation, conscious identification and the automaticity of information processing. *Journal of Experimental Psychology: Human Perception and Performance, 8,* 757–777.

Collins, A.H., & Loftus, E.F. (1975). A spreading activation theory of semantic processing. *Psychological Review, 82,* 407–428.

Dagenbach, D., Carr, T.H., & Wilhelmsen, A. (1989). Task-induced strategies and near threshold priming: Conscious effects on unconscious perception. *Journal of Memory and Language, 28,* 412–443

de Groot, A.M.B. (1985). Word-context effects in word naming and lexical decision. *Quarterly Journal of Experimental Psychology, 37A,* 281–297.

de Groot, A.M.B., Thomassen, A., & Hudson, P. (1982). Primed lexical decision: The effects of varying the stimulus onset asynchrony of prime and target. *Acta Psychologica, 61,* 17–36.

Fischler, I. (1977). Associative facilitation without expectancy in a lexical decision task. *Journal of Experimental Psychology: Human Perception and Performance, 3,* 18–26.

Henik, A., Friedrich, F.J., Tzegold, J., & Tramer, S. (1994). Capacity demands of automatic processes in semantic priming. *Memory and Cognition, 22,* 157–168.

Koriat, A. (1981). Semantic facilitation in lexical decision as a function of prime–target association. *Memory and Cognition, 9,* 587–598.

Meyer, D.E., & Schvaneveldt, R.W. (1971). Facilitation in recognizing pairs of words: Evidence of a dependence between retrieval operations. *Journal of Experimental Psychology, 90,* 227–234.

Neely, J.H. (1977). Semantic priming and retrieval from lexical memory: Roles of inhibitionless spreading activation and limited-capacity attention. *Journal of Experimental Psychology: General, 106,* 226–254.

Neely, J.H. (1991). Semantic priming effects in visual word recognition: A selective review of current findings and theories. In D. Besner & G. Humphreys (Eds.) *Basic processes in reading: Visual word recognition* (pp. 264–336). Hillsdale, NJ: Lawrence Erlbaum Associates.

Neely, J.H., Keefe, D.E., & Ross, K. (1989). Semantic priming in the lexical decision task: Roles of prospective prime-generated expectancies and retrospective semantic matching. *Journal of Experimental Psychology: Learning, Memory, and Cognition, 15,* 1003–1019.

Nelson, D.L., Lalomia, M.J., & Cañas, J.J. (1991). Dissociative effects in different priming domains. *Memory and Cognition, 19,* 44–62.

Nelson, D.L., & McEvoy, C.L. (1979). Encoding context and set size. *Journal of Experimental Psychology: Human Learning and Memory, 5,* 292–314.

Norris, D. (1986). Word recognition: Context effects without priming. *Cognition, 22,* 93–136.

Posner, M.I., & Snyder, C.R.R. (1975). Attention and cognitive control. In R.L. Solso

(Ed.),*Information processing and cognition: The Loyola Symposium*. Hillsdale, NJ: Lawrence Erlbaum Associates.

Seidenberg, M.S., Waters, C., Sanders, M., & Langer, P. (1984). Pre- and post-lexical loci of contextual effects on word recognition. *Memory and Cognition, 12,* 315–328.

Stanovich, K.E., & West, R. (1983). On priming by a sentence context. *Journal of Experimental Psychology: General, 7,* 77–85.

Tweedy, J.R., Lapinski, R.H., & Schvaneveldt, R.W. (1977). Semantic context on word recognition: Influence of varying the proportion of items presented in an appropriate context. *Memory and Cognition, 5,* 84–89.

4

Dual-Route Models in Spanish: Developmental and Neuropsychological Data

Francisco Valle-Arroyo
Universidad de Oviedo
Oviedo, Spain

Since the 1970s, reading has received a great deal of attention. English-speaking authors, basing themselves on lexical decision and naming data from normal subjects and on the errors of acquired dyslexics, have defended *dual-route models of reading,* because there seem to be two different ways of reading, each with its own set of processes. The Spanish writing system, however, presents striking contrasts with English; therefore, what seems unquestionable in English may not even be true in Spanish.

In this chapter, I present reading data from normal children of different ages and some neuropsychological results from acquired dyslexics that, as a whole, match almost point by point the predictions made from dual-route models of reading. This seems to show that Spanish and English readers use fundamentally the same reading procedures, despite the great differences between their respective writing systems.

PSYCHOLINGUISTIC CONSIDERATIONS REGARDING WRITING SYSTEMS

Writing systems can be divided into two main categories: alphabetic and logographic. The former follow *alphabetical* principle: Orthographic symbols (letters or clusters of letters) are associated with sounds (phonemes). This means that the written word always indicates how the visual form is to be read or pronounced, because every word is composed of letters that are usually pronounced in a given way. Alphabetic writing systems are phonographic (Sampson, 1985) and, in a way, can be considered as the first recording devices. In logographic systems, such as Chinese, on the other hand, the whole written word (logogram) stands for a meaning to which a certain pronunciation corresponds, but it is impossible to say that a particular part of the string of phonemes corresponds to a particular part of the logogram. In a nontrivial manner, a logogram is similar to a picture or drawing that can be named, but the whole pronunciation corresponds to the entire picture. If one is shown a picture of a tomato, and is asked to give its name—i.e., to "read it"—one can surely do it, but no one would ever say, for example, that the first syllable /tə/corresponds to the left third of the picture, the second /mei/ to the middle third and so on. The string of phonemes /təmeitəu/, as a whole, is the phonological form of the whole picture. Logographic systems are more meaning oriented; this is why written texts can be understood by educated people from different regions of China, even though they speak different languages (Sampson, 1985).

Given these facts, it is reasonable to assume that the process of reading cannot be the same in logographic and alphabetic writing systems.[1] Learning to read in a logographic system implies the acquisition of the specific phonological form and the specific meaning associated with each logogram so that even expert readers are limited in the number of logograms they can read: just those logograms that they have seen in the past. Sasanuma (1980), referring to *kanji,* the logographic system in Japanese, wrote, "It is not unusual, for instance, for even a highly educated person to sometimes be unable to pronounce some low-frequency kanji words although the same person could usually recognize or figure out the meaning of these words" (p. 54). Thus, the determining factor in reading in these languages is *familiarity,* of which frequency is, in statistical

---

[1]This may not be completely true. Paradis (1989) stated that 25 % of the Chinese logograms provide sufficient information through the phonic radical about their correct and unique pronunciation. In this respect, logographic systems could be considered as the most opaque writing systems, but may not be radically different from English. Regarding Japanese kanji, see Paradis, Hagiwara, and Hildebrandt (1985).

terms, a good approximation. In general, high-frequency logograms should be familiar, whereas the less frequent a logogram is the less likely it is to be known by the subject.

Learning to read in an alphabetic system may consist of acquiring orthography–sound mappings that are not specific to particular words, but generic (i.e. applicable to all words). Therefore, once the orthography–sound equivalences are sufficiently learned, any word can be read. This last assertion only holds for alphabetic writing systems that have consistent orthography–sound mappings (with no exceptions) or, even better, univocal grapheme-to-phoneme conversion rules, such as Spanish and Italian, but alphabetic orthographies differ in their consistency. At one extreme are the so-called *transparent* writing systems (e.g., Italian, Finnish, and Spanish); at the other, *opaque* languages (e.g., English and maybe French). Opaque languages also vary in their degree of opacity, some being more opaque than others. The transparency–opacity dimension, therefore, is a continuum, and alphabetic writing systems occupy different locations along it: Some are closer to the transparent pole, others to the opaque one. In completely transparent orthographies (e.g., Spanish),[2] the same letters or groups of letters (graphemes) always produce the same sounds. In less transparent writing systems, such as English, there are some graphemes that consistently produce a single sound, others have multiple phonological realizations not entirely determined by context, and others have idiosyncratic pronunciations. (For a more detailed exposition of English, see Patterson & Morton, 1985.)

From what has been said up to this point, reading Chinese (or any other logographic writing system) aloud should be different from reading Spanish (or any other transparent alphabetic orthography). The Spanish reader has to identify the sequence of letters making up the word and then convert these orthographic symbols into the sounds specified by the phoneme–grapheme conversion rules, thus obtaining the correct pronunciation. This form of reading is called *nonlexical reading* in dual-route models. In Chinese, because the logogram is not decomposable into sublexical units, this nonlexical way of reading is impossible; the reader has to recognize and comprehend the logogram to be able to assign to it the correct pronunciation: *lexical* reading in dual-route models.

In opaque writing systems, nonwords should be read nonlexically, but irregular words would be correctly pronounced only by chance if this nonlexical route is employed. Therefore, the lexical route is also needed to guarantee accurate reading.

In brief, (a) logographic systems should be read, at least in a high number

---

[2]Writing in Spanish, however, is partially opaque, because there are several phonemes that can be written in two or three different ways.

of cases, lexically; (b) in completely transparent orthographies known or unknown words, real or invented, can all be read nonlexically; and (c) opaque systems need both ways of reading: the lexical route is required for reading irregular words and the nonlexical one is necessary for unknown regular words and nonwords.

Nonetheless, it is not theoretically impossible for known words in transparent writing systems to be read lexically. The English reader of words of idiosyncratic pronunciation (e.g., *yacht*) has to learn that the string of letters <y>, <a>, <c>, <h>, <t> represents the meaning, "a light sailing-vessel used for pleasure," to which the pronunciation /jot/ corresponds. Every word in Spanish is also a unique string of letters that sounds a certain way and means something; therefore, Spanish speaking readers could, in principle, read known words lexically. For this reason, although the nonlexical routine would be sufficient to read all types of linguistic stimuli (words and nonwords) in a transparent ortography, lexical reading *might be used* with familiar words. As a matter of fact, we all know that preschool children can "read" some words that they have frequently seen, and the same is true for illiterate adults (e.g. the *stop* on a stop sign). Therefore, it is not unlikely that expert readers who have seen lots and lots of words—some of them thousands of times—may read in this way, that is, without applying grapheme–phoneme conversion rules.

DUAL-ROUTE MODELS OF READING

Simple linguistic considerations about the nature of writing systems—specifically about how logographic, transparent and opaque languages encode phonology in the written stimulus—suggest there are two different ways of reading: lexically and nonlexically. But to what extent are these theoretical considerations supported by empirical data? Many studies on visual word recognition and naming in English (Baron & Strawson, 1976; Berndt & Mitchum, 1994; Coltheart, 1978, 1987; Humphreys & Evett, 1985) have validated these assumptions and have led to the development of dual-route models, which, roughly speaking, propose a dictionary look-up procedure (lexical reading) and a letter-to-sound procedure (nonlexical reading).

How are these two routes of reading supposed to work? Adult readers know a considerable number of words in their orthographic and phonological forms and also their meanings. This knowledge is symbolized in Fig. 4.1 by the Orthographic Input Lexicon, the Phonological Output Lexicon, and the Semantic System, respectively.

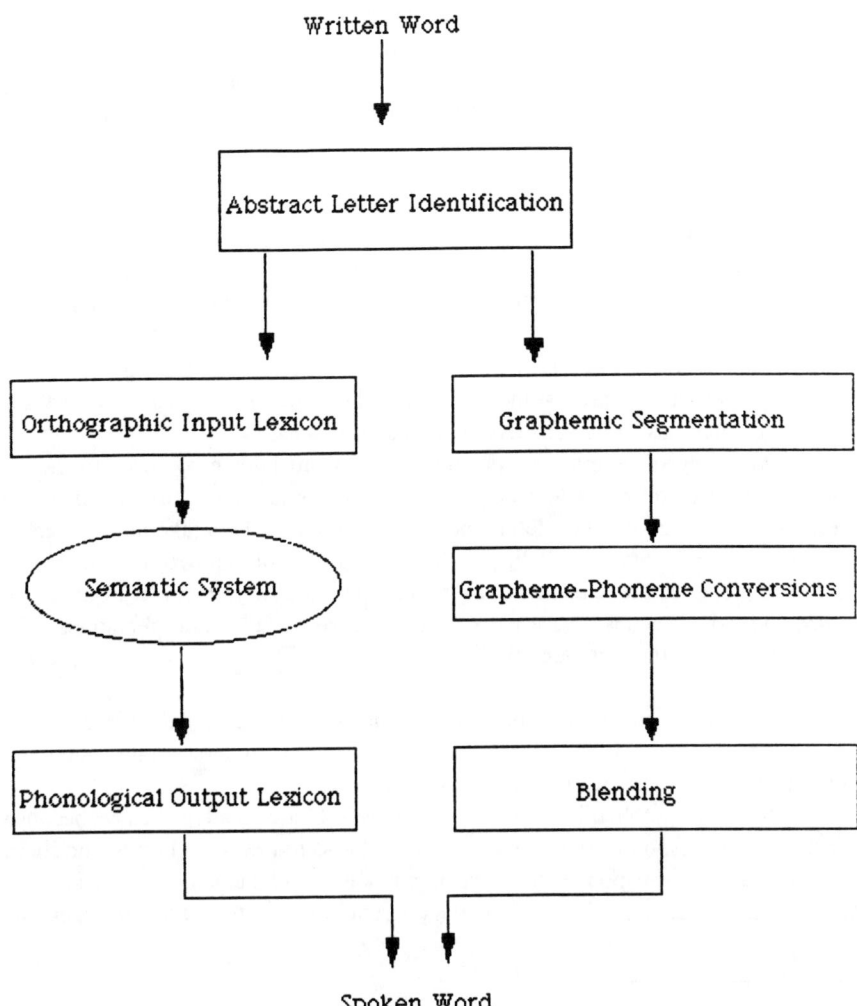

FIG. 4.1. A dual-route model of reading. Adapted from Coltheart (1985).

At the same time, they also know what graphemes make up a phoneme, and how such graphemes are converted into sounds. That is, they are able to do *graphemic segmentation* and *grapheme-to-phoneme conversion* (GPC; Morton,

1979; Morton & Patterson, 1980; Patterson & Shewell, 1987).[3]

To read a written linguistic stimulus, we must first identify the string of letters making up the stimulus. The sequence of letters identified may be known or unknown. If the letter string corresponds to a known word, the subject may access its meaning, and give its phonological form in way similar to speaking, where a concept or idea is translated into a sound. These processes are the main constituents of lexical reading. In other words, the orthographic form activates the meaning, and the meaning activates the phonological form corresponding to that meaning. If any one of these operations fails or is defective, then the final output will not be correct. Clearly, this reading routine is mediated by meaning in such a way that, if the subject does not understand the meaning, he or she will not be able to give the sound. It is likely that synonym substitutions (reading *dad* as *father*) may occur since by definition both words /dæd/ and /'fa:θər/ approximately represent the same meaning. Finally, semantic variables (e.g. imageability) might have some effect on this way of reading, because the semantic stage has to be sensitive to semantic factors.

If the string of letters does not match any word known by the subject, the other way of reading has to be used.[4] Here, the subject must first segment the letter string into graphemes, letters or clusters of letters that make up a phoneme (graphemic segmentation). If the reader tries to read the nonword *chattarshap,* for example, once the letters have been identified, the subject has to group <ch>, <tt>, and <sh>, because these pairs of letters give rise to single phonemes. The final product of this segmentation would be <ch>, <a>, <tt>, <a>, <r>, <sh>, <a>, <p>.

Only then can the conversion of graphemes into phonemes take place to give the correct pronunciation. If one or more of these processes fails, then the pronunciation given will not be the expected one.

In Spanish, graphemic segmentation and GPC are relatively easy, because each letter corresponds to a phoneme, except for <ch>, <ll>, and <rr>, and there is a one-to-one correspondence between graphemes and phonemes. The last stage in nonlexical reading is *blending,* which requires that the obtained string of

---

[3]In this figure, I do not include the so-called *direct* route of reading for two reasons. First, for me, reading implies going from a visual to a phonological form and comprehending its meaning; in this case, comprehension does not occur. Second, the main reason for postulating this route was the existence of some cases of visual non-semantic dyslexia in which there is a co-occurring deficit in speech comprehension.

[4]Because subjects do not know in advance whether the stimulus is going to be a word or nonword until they have recognized it, it is usually assumed that both routes begin to work in parallel and the first to reach the output wins over the other (Henderson, 1982).

phonemes be retained and assembled in order to give the pronunciation as a whole, the result of a unique articulatory program that prevents reading syllable by syllable. In this way of reading, comprehension occurs after blending has taken place and is based on phonology, rather than orthography, as is the case in speech comprehension. This is clearly seen in surface dyslexics, who define the word according to pronunciation and not orthography (Coltheart, Masterson, Byng, Prior, & Riddoch, 1983).

If lexical reading is semantically mediated, nonlexical reading aloud is phonologically mediated. Therefore, subjects who read by this means should have problems with homophone comprehension, because nobody can distinguish, by sound alone, two homophones.

PREDICTIONS BASED ON PSYCHOLINGUISTIC CONSIDERATIONS

If the processes specified in Fig. 4.1 are real, then, following Sternberg's (1969) steps, it should be possible to find variables that affect each of these processes; if there is some independence among them, the positive or negative effects should be additive in nature, producing a consistent increment or decrement in the reaction times (RTs) or in numbers of errors. Some of the linguistic variables that would have an effect on reading accuracy and RT are lexicality, frequency, regularity, and length.

If someone read *lexically and only lexically,* the only variable that should have an effect on reading would be familiarity. Only if he or she knew the sequence of letters of the stimulus to be read could the meaning and sound be associated with it; otherwise, reading would be impossible. Lexical reading guarantees a perfect reading of known words and the impossibility of reading unknown words and nonwords. Going back to the linguistic variables outlined earlier, lexicality should be an extremely good predictor of reading accuracy, because only words can be known by the reader, not nonwords. For the same reason, frequency should differentially influence reading: High-frequency words would be expected to be read accurately, because they are probably known by the reader, but low-frequency words (or at least some of them) may not have been encountered before and, in consequence, will not be read appropriately. In general, then, one could expect a good reading of high-frequency words, but a poorer reading of low-frequency words. Neither regularity nor length, if they are controlled for frequency, could influence reading. As stated before, the only relevant factor would be familiarity. If the reader knows the sequence of letters composing the word and its sound, he or she should be able to read it, independent of whether the word is regular or irregular, short or long.

If, on the other hand, one only reads *nonlexically,* the two factors that can influence reading accuracy and RT are regularity and length. Regularity is the most important factor, because the reader has to convert graphemes into phonemes, and irregular words, by definition, are those words that do not follow GPC rules. The prediction would be good reading of regular words (known and unknown) and nonwords, but regularized—and, as such, incorrect—reading of irregular words. Length should also show some effect, unless the GPC rules are completely mastered. If they are insufficiently learned, more errors are likely to occur in long than in short stimuli, because, in general, there will be more GPC rules in longer words and nonwords than in shorter ones. The distinction between words and nonwords (lexicality) is not relevant in this context, because orthography–sound mappings are equally valid in both types of stimuli. Lexical frequency cannot have any reliable effect in this way of reading: GPC rules are the same in frequent as in infrequent words. The only frequency that might have an effect on nonlexical reading is that of the syllable (or other sublexical unit), because the more frequent a syllable is, the more likely it is that the conversions implied have been used in the past and the better consolidated they will be.

Given that Spanish is a completely transparent writing system with no irregular words, the regularity cannot be controlled in experiments. The predictions based on psycholinguistic considerations for Spanish will be those in Table 4.1.

TABLE 4.1
Variables That Should and Should Not Influence Both Ways of Reading in Spanish

	Lexicality	Frequency	Length
Lexical Reading	Yes	Yes	No
Nonlexical Reading	No	No	Yes

In the following two sections, I present data from normal subjects (children with different reading levels) and from patients with acquired dyslexia in order to show the extent to which these data match the predictions just formulated. In anticipation, these data seem to show, in general, that, even in Spanish, both ways of reading are used, and that the lexical procedure becomes more and more important as the degree of expertise increases. However, this position is not universally defended. As in English, some authors think that the nonlexical route is the only one employed by Spanish-speaking readers. In each section, besides my own data some other relevant studies holding the contrary view are also briefly commented on. In this manner, readers contrast the data and form their own opinions.

DEVELOPMENTAL DATA

In the previous section, I explained which linguistic variables should influence lexical reading and which should influence nonlexical reading. The predictions were made for extreme cases, that is, for those readers who read only by the lexical route or only by the nonlexical route. How should these predictions be modified when applied to children of different reading levels? To answer this question, I describe briefly the school system and teaching methods of reading used in Spain. Compulsory kindergarten begins at the age of 4 and lasts 2 years. Primary school begins at 6. In kindergarten, children are not usually taught how to read, but some teachers introduce the most elementary rules in the second half of the second year in kindergarten, as was the case in the study reported here. Teaching methods are based on phonics, and the GPC rules are explicitly taught with words. This means that when younger children learn how to convert a grapheme into a phoneme, they are acquiring visual experience with real words at the same time. Therefore, both ways of reading may develop hand-in-hand. Older children would be expected to have a much bigger orthographic input lexicon and to know GPC rules much better than younger children. Yet, given the unequivocal nature of Spanish orthography–sound mappings, even the youngest children should have a good knowledge of GPC rules, despite their very limited orthographic lexicon.

In summary, given the complete transparency of the Spanish writing system and the use of GPC rules in teaching, the younger children should mainly show the characteristics associated with nonlexical reading, whereas the older children might show effects of the variables that influence lexical reading to a greater extent, despite the fact that their knowledge of orthography–phonology mappings is surely deeper and better.

The data I present here, from a doctoral thesis done under my direction and supervision (Lozano, 1992), confirms and extends my own results (Valle-Arroyo, 1989a, 1989b) and those of Domínguez and Cuetos (1992).

Two hundred forty children participated in the experiment: 80 first graders (6 years old, with about 7 months of reading practice), 80 third graders (8 years old, with 2½ years of reading experience) and 80 sixth graders (11 years old, with 5½ years of reading experience). They had all been taught by a phonics method.

The children were given 144 stimuli to read aloud in a randomized mixed presentation. Half were words and half were nonwords obtained from real words by changing one letter in the initial, medial, or final position. Words were controlled for frequency and length; nonwords were conrolled for length.

Number and type of errors were the dependent variables. Words and nonwords were the units of analysis; that is, if the pronunciation given for the whole stimulus was incorrect, one error was counted, even though more than one phoneme might have been in error. The maximum possible number of errors per group and condition was 5760 (80 subjects × 72 words/nonwords).

Results

Data were analyzed using analysis of variance (ANOVA) procedures.

Numbers of Errors

In the quantitative analysis (number of errors), the most relevant findings were as follows:

Lexicality. Table 4.2 shows the mean number of errors in each experimental condition. Overall, lexicality exerted a significant effect. At each grade level, the number of errors was much higher for nonwords than for words, but the effect of lexicality increased with grade. Although first graders made 1.5 errors in nonwords for each error in words, in third grade the relation was 3 to 1 and in sixth grade it was 6 to 1. These results suggest several things. First, words and nonwords are not read in the same way, and this is true even for first graders. If they were, that is, if all verbal stimuli were read by the application of GPC rules, then the same number of errors would occur in both categories. Second, because the relative proportion of errors in nonwords increased with the number of schooling years, this effect shows the progressive dominance of lexical reading with age. Older children seemed to rely on a lexical method much more than younger children. This effect cannot be due to a better knowledge of GPC rules, because then the proportion of errors in nonwords would remain constant, or even decrease, with age.

TABLE 4.2
Mean Number of Errors per Subject on Words and Nonwords

	Words	Nonwords
First graders	11.26	17.15
Third graders	4.13	12.10
Sixth graders	1.98	12.14

Length. Pooling words and nonwords, length had a significant effect in all grades (see Table 4.3). The number of errors decreased significantly from long to short stimuli. This general data pattern can be clarified by considering length by frequency and length by lexicality interactions. For first and third graders, the interaction Length × Frequency (in words) was significant, because no length effect appeared for high-frequency words, but it was highly reliable with words of medium and low frequency. For sixth graders, the overall length by frequency interaction was not significant, but when only nonwords were included in the analysis, length produced a significant effect. Therefore, sixth-grade reading was affected by length, but only when the stimuli were nonwords.

TABLE 4.3
Mean Numbers of Errors per Subject on Words and Nonwords of Different Lengths

	Words			Nonwords		
	Long	Medium	Short	Long	Medium	Short
First graders	4.48	3.56	3.23	6.85	5.98	4.32
Third graders	1.80	0.80	1.53	4.71	4.58	2.81
Sixth graders	0.89	0.45	0.64	4.96	4.69	2.49

From these data, one may conclude that nonword reading (which must be done following the nonlexical procedure) is sensitive to length, as predicted; words, on the other hand (which can be read lexically, as well as nonlexically), seem to be read lexically by sixth graders, as though they were all part of the childrens' orthographic lexicons. First and third graders also might have read high-frequency words by the lexical route, because there was no effect of length in this subgroup of words. This result is consistent with predictions: High-frequency words are most likely to be known by younger children because of their frequent use, and are therefore the best candidates for a lexical method of reading.

Frequency. The ANOVA showed a significant effect of frequency in first and third graders, but no reliable effects in sixth graders (see Table 4.4). The younger children made considerably fewer errors on high-frequency words than on low-frequency words, but the oldest ones made a statistically equivalent number of errors across frequency groups.

TABLE 4.4
Mean Number of Errors as a Function of Word Frequency

	Words				Nonwords
	Frequency				
	High	Medium	Low	Overall	
First graders	3.16	4.34	3.76	11.26	17.15
Third graders	0.89	1.49	1.75	4.13	12.10
Sixth graders	0.49	0.61	0.88	1.98	12.14

Overall, this result seems to be contrary to expectations: Older children, supposedly lexical readers, should make fewer errors as word frequency becomes higher, whereas younger children—who might predominantly use the nonlexical pathway—should not show frequency effects or, if they do, should do so to a lesser degree. Are these data really contrary to predictions? I do not think so; they are in complete agreement with what we have already seen in the lexicality and length analyses. It seems that the sixth graders knew all the words included in the list, or at least such a high number of them that the effects of frequency did not reach reliable levels. Remember that, in order to read lexically, one has to know the words via previous exposure to them. In consequence, only if a relevant number of words is unknown should the frequency effect appear. The sixth graders performed as though they knew all the words included in the experiment. This interpretation is not unreasonable, because Juilland and Chang-Rodríguez's (1964) dictionary of frequency contains the 5.000 words most frequently used in Spanish, those that appear at least 5 times per half-million. This explanation is consistent with the fact that frequency effects did show up in first and third graders. For them, there are some familiar words (probably most of the high-frequency group) and some that are unfamiliar (mostly in the low-frequency group): The former can be read lexically, but the latter should be read through GPC rules. I am implicitly assuming that lexical reading is more efficient and faster (Coltheart, 1978), and is less likely to produce errors than nonlexical reading. This last assumption is also based on data. In Valle-Arroyo (1989a, 1989b), as well as in Lozano (1992), the number of errors on consonant-vowel (CV) and CVC syllables where the first consonant's pronunciation is context-dependent (*c* and *g* in Spanish) is almost 3 times higher in nonwords than in words.

Types of Errors

Naturally, the total number of errors was significantly lower in sixth graders than in third graders, and in third graders than in first graders. However, the decrease was not evenly distributed across types. Some types of errors were more common in the sixth graders than in the first graders.

Of the various types of errors recorded, I report on only two: lexicalizations (nonwords that are read as visually similar real words) and their opposite, conversions of words into nonwords. These two types are probably the most directly related to the question at hand: deciding whether Spanish children use one and/or the other reading route. Table 4.5 presents the percentages of errors of each type in the three groups of subjects.

TABLE 4.5
Percentages of Lexicalizations and Word–Nonword Conversions by Grade

	1st Graders	3rd Graders	6th Graders
Lexicalizations	25%	32%	43%
Word–nonword conversions	75%	18%	7%

Sixth graders made 43% of the total number of lexicalizations, a percentage nearly double that of first graders. In contrast, 75% of word–nonword conversions were made by first graders. Lexicalizations are usually considered to reflect lexical influence and are, therefore, more numerous in older children, who have shown a predominance of the lexical routine over the nonlexical one, but it is important to note that even in first graders, this type of error is not negligible. Word–nonword conversions, whatever their nature, cannot be interpreted as due to lexical influence, because, especially in first graders, producing a nonword in place of a word probably reflects an incompete mastery of GPC rules.

Discussion

The effects of psycholinguistic variables that, in principle, should influence one or the other type of reading, are not completely dissociated in the data. However, a complete dissociation would be possible if and only if nonlexical readers only read by letter–sound conversions and lexical readers only used a dictionary look-up procedure. First graders, even when they are taught GPC rules, apply and practice these rules on real words. Therefore, they gradually acquire an orthographic lexicon that includes repeatedly encountered words. These words can be read either lexically or nonlexically. Sixth graders have acquired a larger sight vocabulary and have developed a better knowledge of GPC rules. Consequently, what can reasonably be accomplished as reading experience accrues is a gradual predominance of lexical variables (frequency and lexicality) and a gradual decrease of the factors that influence nonlexical reading.

This is, in fact, what we found. Sixth graders made six times more errors on nonwords than on words, showed no length effect on words (which could be read lexically), but made a significantly higher number of errors on long than on short nonwords (which should be read nonlexically); furthermore, most of their errors consisted of lexicalizations. All of these findings support the predominance of a lexical route for reading in older children. The only finding that did not fit the predictions was the lack of frequency effects on word reading, but, as already stated, this may be due to the relatively high frequency of low-frequency words. Had we used words not included in the Spanish dictionary of frequencies, perhaps the effect would have appeared. Moreover, it should be noted that error counting is a coarser measure than RT. Using RTs, the lexical frequency effect occurs, even with university students (Carreiras, Alvarez, & de Vega, 1993, Exp. 2; García-Albea, 1982).

First graders, according to predictions, showed a significant length effect for nonwords and medium- and low-words (probably those unfamiliar to them), and most of their errors consisted of word–nonword conversions. Contrary to expectations, however, they made more errors on nonwords than on words and did show a frequency effect. Neither of these phenomena should appear if they could read *only* nonlexically, but it is quite evident that the high-frequency words, at least on this list, must be in their orthographic lexicon; consequently, there was no reason why the frequency effect should not have occurred, or why the number of errors on words would not be lower than on nonwords, because some words are known by these young children.

Overall, then, the developmental data agree with the predictions made from a dual-route model of reading, and the minor discrepancies can be accounted for in the terms outlined. It is important to note that the data reported cannot be explained by assuming that older children simply have a better knowledge of GPC rules. According to this explanation, the following data patterns should have been obtained:

1. The effects—the relative proportion of errors in younger and older children—should have been constant and independent of linguistic variables, but they varied considerably in words and nonwords. Even though there were significant differences between first and sixth graders in the number of errors on both words and nonwords, the Grade × Lexicality interaction was highly significant. On nonwords, older and younger children produced similar numbers of errors (22% fewer errors in sixth than in first grade); on words, in contrast, the number of errors made by the older children was 82% lower than in younger children.

2. The numbers of all types of errors should have been higher in the youngest children than in the oldest children, but lexicalizations were almost double in the oldest age group.

3. The longer stimuli should have produced a higher number of errors than the shorter ones, but in the sixth graders, although for words as well as nonwords this was factually true, the effect was only reliable in nonwords; in first graders, for both words and nonwords, the length effect was reliable, except for high-frequency words.

Only by assuming a developmental shift from nonlexical to lexical reading as age increases, which is tantamount to acknowledging a dual-route model of reading in Spanish, can these data be explained.

Now, if there is a developmental shift in reading (Backman, Bruck, Hebert, & Seidenberg, 1984; Barron, 1981, 1986; Perfetti & Hogaboam, 1975) from a mainly nonlexical approach to a mostly lexical one as one goes from first to sixth grade, it would be natural to assume that adult readers would use the lexical form of reading with all words, except maybe for the very unusual ones, yet evidence from adult readers is controversial. Some studies (Bajo, A. Burton, E. Burton, & Cañas, 1994; García-Albea, 1982; Sebastián, 1991) seem to support the point I have upheld, but other authors (de Vega, Carreiras, Gutiérrez, & Alonso, 1990) defend the use of the nonlexical route as the more prominent in Spanish. This situation echoes a similar debate that took place in English (Coltheart, Curtis, Atkins, & Haller, 1993; Patterson, Seidenberg, & McClelland, 1989; van Orden, Johnston, & Hale, 1988).

In a recent study, Carreiras et al. (1993) carried out five experiments with university students: Two of these experiments used lexical decision and the other three, naming (reading) tasks. Only the naming experiments are commented on here. In these three experiments (Exp. 2 with words, Exp. 4 with words and nonwords in blocked presentation, and Exp. 5 with words and nonwords in mixed presentation), subjects had to read high- and low-frequency words, as well as nonwords, and their RTs were measured. Half of both types of words (and nonwords) were made up of high-frequency syllables, and the other half were made up of low-frequency syllables.

The results were not consistent across experiments. Lexical frequency reached statistical significance in experiment 2 (high-frequency words had shorter RTs than low-frequency words), but not in Experiments 4 and 5. Syllable frequency had two contrasting effects. In words (Exps. 2 and 4), syllable frequency increased RTs: The more frequent syllables produced reliably longer latencies and the less frequent syllables showed faster RTs. In nonwords (Exps. 4 and 5), syllable frequency produced the "classical" frequency effect: Increased frequency gave speeded RTs. From these data, the authors conclude that "these results are consistent with the idea of a mandatory phonological (nonlexical) route for Spanish readers" (Carreiras et al., 1993, p. 770) and that "phonological activation could be a routine and essentially an automatic part of word identification in Spanish, as it could be in other shallow (transparent) languages" (p. 778), and they cited Serbo-Croatian (Lukatela & Turvey, 1990).

These conclusions clearly conflict with the arguments presented in this chapter. How firmly grounded are Carreiras et al.'s conclusions? In my opinion, the paper is interesting, and the syllable frequency effect poses some problems for the dual-route models in Spanish, because a sublexical unit has beeb shown to affect on reading times, which may indicate that the word is not treated as a whole but as something decomposable into smaller entities. Nonetheless, I do not think that these problems are as serious as the authors say.

Let us look at their results from the perspective of the predictions made earlier. If words and nonwords were read in the same way, that is, by orthography–sound conversion rules as the authors seem to assume, then no significant differences between words and nonwords should be obtained. Furthermore, if Spanish-speaking readers follow the nonlexical route in reading, the only variable that might have some positive effect on reading times would be syllable frequency, because high-frequency syllables, by definition, would have been seen more often while reading than low-frequency syllables, and, therefore, the GPC rules implied would be more consolidated. None of these predictions was fulfilled. Words had significantly shorter RTs than nonwords (although this was not reported in the paper), consistent with the existence of a double method of reading and with the assumption that the lexical route is faster than the nonlexical one (Coltheart, 1978). In fact, in Experiments 4 and 5 the mean RTs for words were 632 ms and 748 ms, respectively, whereas those for nonwords were 667ms and 832 ms, respectively. This means that in Experiment 4 the difference between words and nonwords was 35 ms and in Experiment 5, 84ms. These differences must be statistically significant, because much smaller differences (of 18 or 20 ms) were reported as significant. The second prediction was fulfilled, but only for nonwords. For words, syllable frequency did not speed reading times, but, contrary to expectations, slowed them. Syllable frequency, then, had opposing effects on words and nonwords. That is why I think that the conclusion that their data are consistent with the idea of a mandatory phonological route for Spanish readers is unwarranted; their data are basically consistent with dual-route models of reading Spanish.

Therefore, Carreiras et al.'s (1993) results, as well as my developmental data, support dual-route models of reading in Spanish. As a matter of fact, de Vega et al. (1990) concluded, on the basis of more consistent data, that the lack of interaction between graphemic and lexical frequencies "suggests that Spanish readers used the lexical route, at least in a third of words" (p. 178).

NEUROPSYCHOLOGICAL DATA

If, as developmental data seem to show in transparent writing systems, lexical and nonlexical routes of reading are functional, then cerebral lesions in Spanish-speaking adults might selectively impair one of them, leaving the other intact or relatively well preserved. Such double dissociations have been extensively reported and commented on English- and French-speaking patients (Coltheart, Patterson, & Marshall, 1980; Malatesha & Whitaker, 1984; Patterson, Marshall, & Coltheart, 1985). Phonological and deep acquired dyslexics, on the one hand, and surface dyslexics, on the other, present contrasting patterns in the way they read. Phonological and deep dyslexics read a significantly higher number of words—both regular and irregular—than nonwords although there are other differences between these groups. The most immediate explanation for this dissociation (and, at the same time, one of the strongest sources of support for dual-route models) is that these patients have lost the nonlexical reading routine, or it is substantially impaired, whereas the other way of reading remains intact or in a relatively good state. In opaque writing systems, surface dyslexics show a higher number of errors on words than on nonwords, this effect being due to regularizations of irregular words. The fact that they make more mistakes in irregular than in regular words and that these errors consist of regularizations, seems to imply that these patients use the nonlexical reading routine, probably because of destruction to, or deterioration of, the lexical route.

Some cases of acquired dyslexia have been documented in transparent languages, too, for example, in Italian (Bisiacchi, Cipolotti, & Denes, 1989; de Bastiani, Barry & Carreras, 1988; Sartori, Barry, & Job, 1984). In Spanish, however, as far as I know, until very recently not a single case of acquired dyslexia had been reported. Indeed, some outstanding figures have openly manifested doubts about the possibility of ever finding a true deep or phonological dyslexic in Spanish.

Ardila, Rosselli, and Pinzón (1989) and Ardila (1991) conducted an investigation with 62 Spanish-speaking aphasics divided into eight classical groups (Brocas, Wernickes, anomics, and so on). These patients were given letters, nonsense syllables, nonwords, and words to read aloud. Because of the absence of semantic paralexias in their samples, the authors drew the same conclusion in both studies, namely, that semantic errors do not occur because of the phonological nature of the Spanish writing system, asserting "reading in Spanish is always mediated through phonology" (Ardila, 1991, p. 444) and, consequently, semantic errors can never occur in reading isolated Spanish words. It is true that no semantic errors should occur if Spanish-speaking readers always followed the nonlexical route (see Fig. 4.1), yet the implication does not hold in the other direction: Given that no semantic paralexias are produced by Spanish aphasics, they (and Spanish readers in general) should use a phonologically mediated (nonlexical) way of reading. To do so is to commit what logicians call the fallacy of the consequent: Nonlexical reading is not the only possible reason for the lack of semantic errors in reading; another possible reason could be simply that the search has not been exhaustive. In this respect, the very limited number of items (10 or 12) included in each of the reading tasks is quite disturbing. Had the lists of words and nonwords been long enough, one would have expected some semantic errors to appear. Even with these brief lists of items, however, there is some indication that words and nonwords were read in different ways. For example, the mean percentage of errors was considerably lower for words (24.75) than for nonwords (34.38), and lexicalizations—a type of error produced under lexical influence—came fifth among the 13 types of errors studied. That is why it is not surprising that, with in-depth case studies, the classical double dissociation between phonological and surface dyslexia has emerged in Spanish, as well.

In this section, I review the cases of acquired dyslexia already published, and those that are in press or have been presented at recent conferences. These include three deep dyslexics, ON, MG, and JMK (Ferreres & Miravalles, 1995; Ruíz, Ansaldo, & Lecours, 1994); three phonological dyslexics, AA, YM, and AD (Cuetos, Valle-Arroyo, & Suárez, in press; Ferreres, 1994), and one surface dyslexic, DC (Ruíz, Cid, Mantiñán, Recalde, & Tetelboim, 1994). All of them, as far as I know, had no prior problems in reading, but began to experience difficulties in reading as a consequence of a cerebral lesion.

In neuropsychological studies, although there are a few cases of complete dissociation (Funnell, 1983; McCarthy & Warrington, 1986), most subjects show a relatively well preserved performance in one area (e.g., reading words) and a very poor performance, though not total incapacity, in another (e.g., in nonword reading). This is probably because the lesion has not been selective enough to impair only one reading procedure and has therefore damaged both of them, although to varying degrees. The situation is similar to the one found in the developmental study, where we saw a gradual strengthening of lexical variables with age and a gradual decline of nonlexical ones, but never a complete dissociation.

Phonological and Deep Dyslexias: Lexical Reading

The received interpretation of the dissociated reading performance of phonological and deep dyslexia is, as has already been stated, that patients suffering these types of reading disorder use only the lexical routine, because the nonlexical one has been destroyed or impaired. Therefore, they should show not only the lexicality effect, but the other characteristics associated with this form of reading as well: the frequency effect in word reading, and no effects of length or regularity (Patterson, 1981).

A number of difficulties attend attempts to see the effects of linguistic variables on the patients' reading accuracy. Not all authors present their data from the point of view I have followed in the description of developmental data, but rather from the standpoint that has been traditional since Marshall and Newcombe published their (1973) paper: They report the numbers or percentages of morphological, visual, and semantic errors (see Table 4.6), but do not give sufficient information about frequency and the other linguistic variables. As much as possible, I use the same criteria here I used in reporting the developmental data.

How do these variables affect our sample? Table 4.6 presents the overall percentages of words and nonwords correctly read by each of the six patients. It also shows how frequency, length, imageability, and grammatical class influence word reading. (Imageability and grammatical class are included, because deep dyslexics read highly imageable (and content) words better than less imageable (and function) words.)

Overall, the patients read 57% of the lexical stimuli and only 9% of the nonlexical letter strings. For all of them, the number of errors on words was significantly lower than on nonwords, despite the fact that some of the patients read as much as 89% of the words and others read only 8%; a similar disparity was found for nonwords (from 35% to 0%). Everyone made more errors on low-frequency than on high-frequency words; these differences were statistically significant in some patiens, but not in others. There may be a number of reasons for discrepancy. First, the lists of words varied in length. (In general, the longer the list, the greater the likelihood of including more low-frequency items and the higher the probability of obtaining the frequency effect.) Second, the criteria for inclusion in one or the other frequency list varied from author to author (some included words in the low-frequency list that others consider as high-frequency). And finally—and this is the most important point—patients might have differed in their degree of dependence on lexical and nonlexical routes.

TABLE 4.6
Effects of Linguistic Variables on Reading Accuracy: Percentages of Correct Answers

Patient Author(s)	Stimuli								
	W	NW	HF	LF	SW	LW	HI	LI	GC
ON[1]	75	2	100	75	?	?	94	79	Y
MG[1]	65	8	87	80	?	?	85	77	Y
JMK[2]	8	0	19	14	14	10	26	2	Y
AA[3]	37	0	77	49	53	41	74	42	Y
YM[3]	69	9	97	83	73	72	90	84	Y
AD[4]	89	35	93	82	90	88	90	85	Y
Overall	57	9	79	64	57	53	77	61	Y

[1]Ruíz, Ansaldo, et al., (1994); [2]Ferreres, & Miravalles (1995); [3]Ferreres, (1994); [4]Cuetos, et al. (in press).
Abbreviations: W = words, NW = nonwords, HF = high frequency, LF = low frequency, SW = short words, LW = long words, HI = high imageability, LI = low imageability, GC = grammatical class effect, Y = yes.

Therefore, lexicality and frequency, the two variables that would influence reading accuracy if a person reads mainly by a lexical strategy did, in fact, produce the expected effects, although in some cases the differences in performance did not reach the required level of reliability.

This dissociation between word and nonword reading is hard to understand unless one bears in mind that the processes involved in word reading are different from those used in nonword reading. If they were exactly the same, the dissociation would be impossible. ON, for example, read 75% of words, reaching 100% correct on high-frequency nouns, but read only 2% of nonwords. If words were really read in Spanish as Ardila et al. (1989) assumed, there is no reason why ON would be unable to read nonwords: In general, the same letters and the same GPC rules were involved, with the nonwords differing from words by just one letter.

TABLE 4.7
Percentages of Types of Paralexias, Omissions Included

				Type of Paralexia			
Patient	S	V	M	V/S	FWS	OM	OT
ON	23	27	36	14	0	0	0
MG	15	33	40	12	0	0	0
JMK	22	5	6	4	2	47	14
AA	5*	27	30	2	6	28	2
YM	0	35	49	0	4	12	0
AD	0	80	3	6	0	0	11

Abbreviations: S= semantic, V= visual, M= morphological, V/S= visual and/or semantic, and visual then semantic, FWS= function word substitutions, OM= omissions, OT= others.
*AA is included in the group of phonological dyslexics, although he made some semantic errors, because, as Ellis and Marshall (1978) have shown, if pairs of words are randomly selected, about 10% of the pairs will be semantically related; and, therefore "real" deep dyslexics should show a higher percentage of semantic paralexias.

Let us imagine that ON can read *casa* (house) and *dama* (lady), both high-frequency nouns, and that he is unable to read the nonword *dasa*. Let us further assume that he reads by following these operations: (a) identification of the string of letters making up the stimulus (e.g., <c>, <a>, <s>, <a>), and (b) application of these GPC rules: *c* -> /k/, *a* -> /a/, *s* -> /s/, and so on. If these two assumptions were true, then he would be able to read *dasa,* because exactly the same letters and orthography–sound mappings are involved. Only by positing that words are read in a different way, namely, by assigning to the global sequence of letters the global pronunciation associated with it, can this dissociation be explained. This conclusion would receive convergent empirical support if one could show that one or several of the operations of the nonlexical routine were totally or substantially impaired and, as such, responsible for the nonword reading impairment. (This is pursued further on.)

What about length? As mentioned earlier, its effect on reading accuracy should be marginal, at most, but four of the six patients summarized in Table 4.6 for whom information is available read short words better than long ones; only in AA, however, was this difference statistically reliable.

Why is the nonlexical reading process deficient in these patients? Logically, abstract letter identification should be functioned in all members of the sample, because they all could read words, and in order to accomplish this task, letters had to be identified. The failure should be found in the three operations of the nonlexical routine. In Spanish, graphemic segmentation is rather trivial (each letter is a grapheme, and even *ll, rr* and *ch* are called letters and, until recently, had independent entries in the dictionary), so the plausible loci of impairment should be either GPC rules or blending. In other languages, patients have been found to be deficient in each one alone or in both (Beauvois & Derouesné, 1979; Derouesné & Beauvois, 1985; Funnel & Humphreys, 1991). Patients RG (Beauvois & Derousné, 1979) and Clive (Funnel & Humphreys, 1991) were unable to give the sounds corresponding to the single letters of the alphabet (an inability to convert graphemes into phonemes) or to give the first phoneme of a word they had already read correctly (/'windəu/ -> /w/). Patient LB (Derouesné & Beauvois, 1985), on the other hand, had no problems in converting letters into sounds, but was unable to blend them into a whole. None of the published reports, except for Cuetos et al.'s (in press), has examined these processes systematically and in detail. Therefore, it is risky to decide where they failed, but I would guess that ON, JMK, and AA, the subjects with the lowest percentages in nonword reading, failed on GPC rules not only because of their low percentage in nonword reading, but also because they did not even try to read them. AD had no problems with GPC; he was able to give the sound associated with a letter in 95% of the cases and even read single CV nonsense syllables with relatively good accuracy (84%), but he had real problems with blending (21% correct answers); also, he could not distinguish between a word and a nonword when the experimenter provided him with the sequence of phonemes making up the example.

It is quite remarkable and, for the layperson, counterintuitive that word–nonword dissociation can happen in reading Spanish, because it is implicitly assumed that words and nonwords are read in the same manner. But if words and nonwords are read using different processes, and phonological and deep dyslexics are supposed to have lost the nonlexical route of reading, then the question is, why do most phonological, and, to a lesser extent, deep dyslexics still read some nonwords? The reason may lie in the residual functioning of this nonlexical route. Those whose lexical route is completely destroyed will be unable to read any nonword. In contrast, if there is still some residual functioning of the nonlexical route, short nonwords are most likely to be read correctly. (This length effect in nonword reading is present in AD). The residual nonlexical reading ability could also explain the types of errors made by phonological dyslexics in nonwords: Some patients mostly make lexicalizations (Derouesné & Beauvois, 1985; Patterson, 1982), but others give another nonword visually and phonologically similar to the nonword stimulus (Bisiacchi et al., 1989). This last type of error is likely to occur when the patient has some residual capacity to read nonlexically.

In summary, the neuropsychological data lead to the same conclusion drawn from the developmental data: Spanish speakers read in substantially the same manner as English speakers.

The remaining variables of Table 4.6 (imageability and grammatical class) have been included, because, in all deep dyslexic patients, reading efficiency depends on both: Highly imageable words are read better than those low in imageability, and nouns are read better than verbs and function words. In all the deep dyslexics in this sample, there was a highly significant imageability effect and in all (phonological dyslexics included) there was a part-of-speech effect. Surprisingly, in Spanish, the part of speech that consistently presents the more serious problems are verbs; in English, in contrast, function words get the lowest scores, but it is hard to tell why this might be so.

Surface Dyslexia: Nonlexical Reading

Before discussing the data from surface dyslexics, something should be said about the tests that can be used in a transparent writing system to detect the existence of this disorder; to do so, it is important to remember the characteristics of surface dyslexia. Surface dyslexics are believed to read by using GPC rules that produce regularization errors in irregular words; lexical and semantic access is gained through sound, not orthography. This last property will result in homophone confusions when such subjects are required to give the meaning of one member of a homophonic pair e.g., *gauge* read as /goːdʒ/ and defined as *canyon* or *gorge;* in Spanish, *baca* /'baka/ [luggage rack] defined as *cow* because it sounds like *vaca* /'baka/, which means *cow*.) The usual way to test the regularity effect, is to present a list of regular and irregular words and compare performance on the two halves (regular and irregular). In Spanish, there are no irregular words, because pronunciation can always be derived and obtained by the strict application of rules. Therefore, alternative means must be used. One possible substitute for the regular–irregular list is a combination of Spanish words and foreign words that are used in Spanish, such as *pizza, boutique,* or *hall,* and that, if read according to Spanish orthography–sound mappings, would produce regularization errors: /'piθθa/, /bou'tike/, and /al/, respectively. Another is the use of homophones. One may present one word of the homophonic pair and ask the patient to define it, or present both words and one picture and ask the patient to point to the word that corresponds to the picture. If recognition is also achieved through sound, another possibility is a lexical decision task with pseudohomophones (see Valle-Arroyo & Cuetos, 1989, in press). These ideas and methods can be used in evaluating surface dyslexia.

Although information about Ruíz, Cid, et al.'s (1994) patient (DC) is limited, the available data are enough to assert that he suffers from surface dyslexia. The investigators showed him a list of words, nonwords and foreign words frequently used in the River Plate region of Argentina. In fact, these are the words Argentinians employ instead of the equivalent Spanish ones, such as the French *bijouterie* /bidʒu'tri/ for the Spanish *bisutería* (costume jewelry). The percentage of the Spanish words and nonwords correctly read was high and approximately the same (73% and 81%, respectively). Most of the foreign words were regularized, that is, read following Spanish GPC rules (*bijouterie* -> /bidʒoute'rie/) and, consequently, incorrectly, despite the fact that these foreign words are the words Argentinians use instead of the equivalent Spanish ones. Of 35 such words, DC read only 1 correctly. Of the 34 mistakes, 24 were perfect regularization errors, and the other 10 consisted of phonological approximations to the stimulus, as though it were a Spanish word.

To test homophone confusions, Ruíz, Cid, et al. paired two homophonic words with one picture, because their patient's speech was nonfluent. His score was 65% correct, not statistically different from chance.

The authors recorded reading times for both words and nonwords and found that DC read the two types of stimuli at the same speed, in contrast to control subjects, and his RTs were significantly higher than those of control subjects, mainly for words; it was on this basis that the authors maintained that RTs can be used as another way of detecting surface dyslexia in Spanish, following Coltheart's (1978) assertion that lexical reading is faster and more efficient than nonlexical reading.

Although the information available is still rather limited, and this study has not yet been completed, these data are precisely what one would expect from a nonlexical reader: There was no lexicality effect (words and nonwords were read in approximately the same proportion); and, although frequency was not reported, one would guess that it could not have been an important determinant of reading accuracy, because the same proportion of errors was made in nonwords as in words, and legal nonwords can be considered as "words" of the lowest possible frequency. Length, which could have had some influence on reading, was not reported. Therefore, this patient seems to read by the application of GPC rules, because his reading exhibits all the characteristics associated with it.

Taken together, phonological and surface dyslexics constitute a double dissociation of the nonlexical and lexical routines of reading and show that adult Spanish readers use both ways of reading. The rationale underlying this conclusion is the following: Because the reading characteristics of these patients began to appear immediately after brain damage, they cannot be the result of new learning, but rather reflect previous reading skills.

CONCLUDING REMARKS

Based on linguistic considerations alone, I have acknowledged that Spanish verbal material (words and nonwords) can be read by applying orthography–sound conversion rules; therefore, the nonlexical way of reading should be enough. At the same time, I maintain that there is no theoretical impossibility for Spanish words to be read lexically, that is, by identifying the string of letters making up a word and assigning the corresponding pronunciation to that letter string. This possibility is made clear by understanding what an English-speaking person has to do to read an irregular word, such as *yacht*. The only necessary and sufficient condition is to know that the sound /jot/ corresponds to the letter sequence, <y>, <a>, <c>, <h>, <t>. This is possible with any Spanish word.

The data reported in this chapter have shown that this possibility is real: Spanish-speaking people have available and utilize both ways of reading, just as opaque language users do. This fact could be interpreted as suggesting that the functional architecture of the reading system is not as dependent on linguistic characteristics as one might think, but is relatively independent of them and, therefore, as universal as it can be. (Logogram readers can never have, as far as I know, a strictly GPC system, because their orthography does not allow it.)

Developmental data support the idea that lexical reading begins to develop early and is well developed by sixth grade. Although the data produced by first graders are overwhelmingly explicable by nonlexical variables, some results show, already at this early age, certain lexical effects such as a higher number of errors on nonwords and a lower number of errors on high-frequency words. That may mean that a few visual encounters are sufficient for the words to be incorporated into the orthographic lexicon. It is even possible, as Stuart and Coltheart (1988) have argued, that learning of the GPC rules might speed up the process of building up the orthographic lexicon. In many cases, except for those in which some dubious phoneme (/b/, /θ/, /x/)[5] intervenes, GPC rules predict with total reliability how a word has to be written. This developmental shift seems to be approaching its end by sixth grade, because sixth graders' data match what would be expected if familiarity were really the most determining factor in reading accuracy.

Yet, although this lexical way of reading overtakes the nonlexical one, it does not eliminate it. The two continue to coexist. Older children are better not

---

[5]Any of these phonemes can be written in two different ways: /b/ as *b* and *v*, /θ/ as *z* and *c* (before *e* and *i*), and /x/ as *j* or *g* (before *e* and *i*).

only at word reading, but at naming nonlexical stimuli, as well. One might wonder, then, whether this better knowledge of GPC rules is the real cause of their superior reading scores. The answer is surely "no," because on nonwords, which must be read by the application of GPC rules, sixth graders are no better than third graders, and even the youngest children do not make a dramatically higher number of errors than the other two age groups. Where the difference is huge is in word reading. Why? Probably because sixth graders know the majority of the words used in the experiment and, consequently, can read them by direct assignment of meaning and sound to the identified visual forms. If a better knowledge of GPC rules were responsible for the much better performance of older children than younger ones, similar patterns of results would have been obtained in words and nonwords.

In brief, it seems that knowledge of GPC rules develops quite rapidly and that the processes involved in lexical reading are acquired more slowly. First graders, after about 7 months of reading practice, seem to be relatively good at making grapheme–phoneme correspondences, and by third grade these correspondences are almost completely mastered. That is why there were no differences in nonword reading between third and sixth graders. Lexical reading, on the other hand, takes longer, and only in sixth grade do its effects begin to show in a significant way.

This conclusion may have consequences for neuropsychological studies. Acquired dyslexics are individuals who have lost some reading ability in which they were competent before their accident. Nnobody can lose or preserve what he or she has not acquired, so phonological and deep dyslexia can only appear in people who have had a certain degree of schooling and/or have maintained some reading activity over the years to enable them to develop a lexical way of reading. Although it is very unlikely that in the absence of deep dyslexics Ardila et al.'s study (1989) can be accounted for in these terms, because the average level of schooling was 8.32 years, this may explain why other investigators have had difficulty finding phonological and deep Spanish dyslexics. By way of confirmation, of the three deep dyslexics reported in this chapter, two (Ruíz, Ansaldo, et al., 1994) had university degrees, and the third had at least 12 years of schooling.

Nonetheless, the cases reported here provide convergent support for the existence of a double pathway of reading. Only because adult readers use these two forms of reading can a lesion selectively destroy one of them, leaving the other intact; because they exist and are used, they can remain intact or be altered. If all verbal stimuli were named by converting sublexical orthographic units into phonemes, any lesion affecting the reading system should show exactly the same pattern of errors, so that only their overall percentages would be higher or lower, depending on the severity of the impairment. What neuropsychological data make clear is that phonological and deep dyslexics, on the one hand, and surface dyslexics, on the other, exhibit complementary patterns. The former are able to read known stimuli well and even perfectly, if they are high-frequency words, but do rather poorly on unknown nonwords. For the latter stimulus familiarity makes no difference, but regularity does. As soon as the pronunciation of a word (e.g., bijouterie) cannot be derived from orthography–sound mapping rules, they mispronounce and regularize it, because they read it as though it followed the Spanish GPC rules. Taken together, developmental and neuropsychological data provide very strong support for dual-route models of reading in Spanish.

There are many questions that have been left aside, but there is one final point I would like to address. The neat dissociations between lexical and nonlexical reading found in some neuropsychological patients have been used not only to assert the *existence* of these two forms of reading, but also their *independence* (Coltheart, 1985, among others). I think that what the dissociations tell us is that one route can function independently of the other in extreme cases, but they do not confirm whether the routes cooperate in normal subjects, because, if there is an interaction in normal circumstances, when dyslexics lose one of them, they also lose the possible interaction. For this reason, I think that other methods of study should be used to disentangle this issue.

REFERENCES

Ardila, A. (1991). Errors resembling semantic paralexias in Spanish speaking aphasics. *Brain and Language, 41,* 437–445.

Ardila, A., Rosselli, M., & Pinzón, O. (1989). Alexia and agraphia in Spanish speakers: CAT correlations and interlinguistic analysis. In A. Ardila & F. Ostrosky-Solís (Eds.), *Brain organization of language and cognitive processes* (pp. 147–175). New York: Plenum.

Backman, J., Bruck, M., Herbert, M., & Seidenberg, M.S. (1984). Acquisition and use of spelling and sound correspondences in reading. *Journal of Experimental Child Psychology, 38,* 114–133.

Bajo, M.T., Burton, A., Burton, E., & Cañas, J.J. (1994). Word recognition across orthographies: Another look at the interaction between context and degradation. *European Journal of Cognitive Psychology, 6,* 171-193.

Baron, J., & Strawson, C. (1976). Use of orthographic and word-specific knowledge in reading words aloud. *Journal of Experimental Psychology: Human Perception and Performance, 2,* 386–393.

Barron, R.W. (1981). The development of visual word recognition: A review. In G. E. MacKinnon & T.G. Waller (Eds.), *Reading research: Advances in theory and practice* (Vol. 3). New York: Academic Press.

Barron, R.W. (1986). Word recognition in early reading: a review of the direct and indirect access hypothesis. *Cognition, 24,* 93–119.

Beauvois, M.F., & Derouesné, J. (1979). Phonological alexia: Three dissociations. *Journal of Neurology, Neurosurgery and Psychiatry, 42,* 1115–1124.

Berndt, R.S., & Mitchum, C.C. (1994). Approaches to the rehabilitation of "phonological assembly": Elaborating the model of nonlexical reading. In M. J. Riddoch & G. W. Humphreys (Eds.), *Cognitive neuropsychology and cognitive rehabilitation* (pp. 503–526). Hove, UK: Lawrence Erlbaum Associates

Bisiacchi, P., Cipolotti, L., & Denes, G. (1989). Impairment in processing meaningless verbal material in several modalities: the relationship between short-term memory and phonological skills. *Quarterly Journal of Experimental Psychology, 41A,* 293–319.

Carreiras, M., Alvarez, C.J., & de Vega, M. (1993). Syllable frequency and visual word recognition in Spanish. *Journal of Memory and Language, 32,* 766–780.

Coltheart, M. (1978). Lexical access in simple reading tasks. In G. Underwood (Ed.), *Strategies of information processing* (pp. 151–216). London: Academic Press.

Coltheart, M. (1985). Cognitive neuropsychology and the study of reading. In M. I. Posner & O. S. M. Marin (Eds.), *Attention and performance XI: Mechanisms of attention* (pp. 3–37). Hillsdale, NJ: Lawrence Erlbaum Associates.

Coltheart, M. (Ed.). (1987). *Attention and performance XII: The psychology of reading.* Hillsdale, NJ: Lawrence Erlbaum Associates.

Coltheart, M., Curtis, B., Atkins, P., & Haller, M. (1993). Models of reading aloud: Dual-route models and parallel-distributed-processing. *Psychological Review, 10,* 589–608.

Coltheart, M., Masterson, J., Byng, S., Prior, M., & Riddoch, J. (1983). Surface dyslexia. *Quarterly Journal of Experimental Psychology, 35A,* 469–495.

Coltheart, M., Patterson, K., & Marshall, J.C. (1980). *Deep dyslexia.* London: Routledge & Kegan Paul.

Cuetos, F., Valle-Arroyo, F., & Suárez, M.P. (in press). A case of phonological dyslexia in Spanish. *Cognitive Neuropsychology.*

de Bastiani, P., Barry, C., & Carreras, M. (1988). Mechanisms for reading nonwords: Evidence from a case of phonological dyslexia in an Italian reader. In G. Denes, C. Semenza, & P. Bisiacchi (Eds.), *Perspectives on cognitive neuropsychology* (pp. 253–267). Hove, UK: Lawrence Erlbaum Associates.

de Vega, M., Carreiras, M., Gutiérrez, M., & Alonso, M. (1990). *Lectura y comprensión: Una perspectiva cognitiva* [Reading and Comprehension: A cognitive perspective]. Madrid: Alianza.

Derouesné, J., & Beauvois, M.F. (1985). The "phonemic" stage in the nonlexical reading process: evidence from a case of phonological alexia. In K. Patterson, J. C. Marshall, & M. Coltheart (Eds.), *Surface dyslexia* (pp. 399–457). Hove, UK: Lawrence Erlbaum Associates.

Domínguez, A., & Cuetos, F. (1992). Desarrollo de las habilidades de reconocimiento de palabras en niños con distinta competencia lectora [Development of word recognition abilities in children of different reading levels]. *Cognitiva, 4,* 193–208.

Ellis, A.W., & Marshall, J.C. (1978). Semantic errors or statistical flukes? A note on Allport's "On knowing the meaning of words we are unable to report". *Quarterly Journal of Experimental Psychology, 30,* 569–575.

Ferreres, A.R. (1994, October). *Phonological alexia in Spanish.* Paper presented at the 33rd Congreso Argentino de Neurología, Mar del Plata, Argentina.

Ferreres, A.R., & Miravalles, G. (1995). The production of semantic paralexias in a Spanish-speaking aphasic. *Brain and Language, 49,* 153–172.

Funnell, E. (1983). Phonological processes in reading: New evidence from acquired dyslexia. *British Journal of Psychology, 74,* 159–180.

Funnell, E., & Humphreys, G. (1991). *Teaching programmes in cognitive neuropsychology: Video 2. Words and sentences: A case study of phonological dyslexia.* Hove, UK: Lawrence Erlbaum Associates.

García-Albea, J.E. (1982). Algunos aspectos en el estudio del procesamiento del lenguaje [Some aspects of the study of language processing]. In I. Delclaux & J. Seoane (Eds.), *Psicología cognitiva y procesamiento de la información.* Madrid: Pirámide.

Henderson, L. (1982). *Orthography and word recognition in reading.* London: Academic Press.

Humphreys, G.W., & Evett, L. (1985). Are there independent lexical and nonlexical routes in word processing? An evaluation of the dual route theory of reading. *Behavioral and Brain Sciences, 8*, 689–739.

Juilland, R., & Chang-Rodríguez, E. (1964). *Frequency dictionary of Spanish words.* The Hague: Mouton.

Lozano, L. (1992). *Análisis de las diferentes estrategias lectoras en los alumnos de EGB: el modelo evolutivo de doble ruta ante el diagnóstico de las dislexias* [An analysis of the different reading strategies in primary school children: The developmental dual-route and the diagnosis of dyslexias]. Unpublished doctoral dissertation, Universidad de Oviedo, Oviedo, Spain.

Lukatela, G., & Turvey, M.T. (1990). Phonemic priming with words and pseudowords. *European Journal of Cognitive Psychology, 2*, 325–343.

Malatesha, R.N., & Whitaker, H. (1984). *Dyslexia: A global issue.* Dordrecht: Martinus Nijhoff.

Marshall, J.C., & Newcombe, F. (1973). Patterns of paralexia: A psycholinguistic approach. *Journal of Psycholinguistic Research, 2*, 175–199.

McCarthy, R., & Warrington, E.K. (1986). Phonological reading: phenomena and paradoxes. *Cortex, 22*, 359–380.

Morton, J. (1979). Word recognition. In J. Morton & J. C. Marshall (Eds.), *Pycholinguistic series: Vol. 2. Structures and processes* (pp. 107–156). London: Elek.

Morton, J., & Patterson, K.E. (1980). A new attempt at an interpretation, or, an attempt at a new interpretation. In M. Coltheart, K. Patterson, & J. C. Marshall (Eds.), *Deep dyslexia* (pp. 91–118). London: Routledge & Kegan Paul.

Paradis, M. (1989). Linguistic parameters in the diagnosis of dyslexia in Japanese and Chinese. In P. G. Aaron & R. M. Joshi (Eds.), *Reading and writing disorders in different orthographic systems* (pp. 231–266). Dordrecht: Kluwer.

Paradis, M., Hagiwara, H., & Hildebrandt, N. (1985). *Neurolinguistic aspects of the Japanese writing system.* New York: Academic Press.

Patterson, K.E. (1981). Neuropsychological approaches to the study of reading. *British Journal of Psychology, 72*, 151–174.

Patterson, K.E. (1982). The relation between reading and phonological coding: Further neuropsychological observations. In A. W. Ellis (Ed.), *Normality and pathology in cognitive functions* (pp. 77–111). London: Academic Press.

Patterson, K., Marshall, J.C., & Coltheart, M. (Eds.). (1985). *Surface dyslexia.* Hove, UK: Lawrence Erlbaum Associates.

Patterson, K.E., & Morton, J. (1985). From orthography to phonology: An attempt at an old interpretation. In K. E. Patterson, J. C. Marshall, & M. Coltheart (Eds.), *Surface dyslexia* (pp. 335–359). Hove, UK: Lawrence Erlbaum Associates.

Patterson, K.E., Seidenberg, M., & McClelland, J.L. (1989). Connections and disconnections: acquired dyslexias in a computational model of reading processes. In R. G. Morris (Ed.), *Parallel distributed processing: Implications for psychology and neuropsychology* (pp. 131–181). Oxford, England: Clarendon.

Patterson, K.E., & Shewell, C. (1987). Speak and spell: Dissociations and word-class effects. In M. Coltheart, G. Sartori, & R. Job (Eds.), *The cognitive neuropsychology of language* (pp. 273–294). Hove, UK: Lawrence Erlbaum Associates.

Perfetti, C.A., & Hogaboam, T.W. (1975). The relationship between single word decoding and reading comprehension skill. *Journal of Educational Psychology, 67*, 461–469.

Ruíz, A., Ansaldo, A.I., & Lecours, A.R. (1994). Two cases of deep dyslexia in unilingual hispanophone aphasics. *Brain and Language, 46,* 245–256.

Ruíz, A., Cid, C., Mantiñán, N., Recalde, S., & Tetelboim, L. (1994, October). *¿Alcanza una sola vía para la lectura y la escritura en español?* [Is one route sufficient for reading and spelling in Spanish?]. Paper presented to the 33rd Congreso Argentino de Neurología, Mar del Plata, Argentina.

Sampson, G. (1985). *Writing systems.* London: Hutchinson.

Sartori, G., Barry, C., & Job, R. (1984). Phonological dyslexia: A review. In R. N. Malatesha & H. A. Whitaker (Eds.), *Dyslexia: A global issue* (pp. 339–356). The Hague: Martinus Nijhoff.

Sasanuma, S. (1980). Acquired dyslexia in Japanese: Clinical features and underlying mechanisms. In M. Coltheart, K. Patterson, & J.C. Marshall (Eds.), *Deep dyslexia* (pp. 48–90). London: Routledge & Kegan Paul.

Sebastián, N. (1991). Reading by analogy in a shallow orthography. *Journal of Experimental Psychology: Human Perception and Performance, 2,* 471–477.

Sternberg, S. (1969). Memory scanning: Mental processes revealed by reaction time experiments. *American Scientist, 57,* 421–457.

Stuart, M., & Coltheart, M. (1988). Does reading develop in a sequence of stages? *Cognition, 30,* 139–181.

Valle-Arroyo, F. (1989a). Errores en lectura y escritura: Un modelo dual [Errors in reading and spelling: A dual-route model]. *Cognitiva, 2,* 35–63.

Valle-Arroyo, F. (1989b). Reading errors in Spanish. In P. G. Aaron, & R. M. Joshi (Eds.), *Reading and writing disorders in different orthographic systems* (pp. 163–175). Dordrecht: Kluwer.

Valle-Arroyo, F., & Cuetos, F. (1989). Las dislexias desde el enfoque neurocognitivo [Dyslexias from the neurocognitive standpoint]. *Sant Pau, 10,* 9–19.

Valle-Arroyo, F., & Cuetos, F. (in press). *EPLA: Evaluación del Procesamiento Lingüístico en la Afasia* [PALPA: Psycholinguistic Assesments of Language Processing in Aphasia]. Hove: UK: Lawrence Erlbaum Associates [Translation, revision, and adaptation of J. Kay, R. Lesser, & M. Coltheart, *PALPA*]

van Orden, G., Johnston, J.C., & Hale, B. (1988). Word identification in reading processes proceeds from spelling to sound to meaning. *Journal of Experimental Psychology: Learning, Memory and Cognition, 14,* 371–386.

5

On the Origin of Phonological Representations in Deaf People

Jesús Alegría
Université Libre de Bruxelles
Brussels, Belgium

PHONOLOGICAL REPRESENTATIONS IN COGNITION IN THE DEAF

Reading, writing, and spelling, as well as numerous other mental activities, are supported in normally hearing people by phonological codes. One of the best documented domains in which the presence of these codes has been established is short-term memory (STM). Conrad (1962, 1964) has shown that some of the errors in STM experiments are similar to those made when hearing noise. These results have been extended by demonstrations that the memory span depends on phonological similarity between items: the *rhyme effect*. In the same vein, it has been shown that short words are easier to retain than longer words: the *length effect*. One of the models of STM proposed to account for these data is a rehearsal device that reactivates the phonological representations of the items to be retained (Baddeley, 1981; Baddeley & Hitch, 1974; Baddeley & Lewis, 1981).

STM experiments have revealed another phonologically related phenomenon. Typically, the items presented last are better retained than those in the middle part of the list: the *recency effect.* Interestingly enough, this happens with heard, but not with read, materials: the *modality effect.* This fact appears to be related to speech processing. The precategorical acoustic storage (PAS) proposed by Crowder and Morton (1969) supposed that a raw copy of the acoustical message is briefly stored prior to phonological categorization for subsequent lexical processing (Baddeley & Hitch, 1974). More recently, it has been shown that lip-read materials behave like heard, not seen, information (Campbell & Dodd, 1980; Spoehr & Corin, 1978). The recency effect is indeed almost as pronounced in lip-reading as it is in hearing (Campbell, 1987a; Crowder, 1986). An interpretation of the modality effect in terms of sensory input–visual versus auditory–must be excluded. A more abstract code common to both hearing and lip-reading, but not implied in reading nor in identifying objects or pictures, seems necessary to explain all of the data. This code is probably involved in on line speech processing. A model capable of dealing with the whole puzzle must include at least two kinds of phonological coding: the first one supporting rehearsal, independent of the input modality, related to speech production activities, and responsible for the presence of phonological errors in STM and for the rhyme and length effects (Baddeley, 1981; Conrad, 1964); and the second one related to speech processing, auditory as well as lip-read, and responsible for the differences in the recency effect as a function of input modality (Campbell, 1987b; Crowder, 1986).

The properties of the STM system probably determine basic aspects of speech perception. The fact that two kinds of phonological codes, each with its own time constraints, are at work during hearing and reading, greatly influences the size of the processing units. If those phonological codes were deficient or simply absent, as could be imagined in the case of deaf people, the consequences for speech processing would probably be considerable. It seems that STM has been tailored by speech perception at its size. STM processes not supported by phonological codes are, however, conceivable. An important case in the present context concerns deaf persons whose mother tongue is sign language. It has been shown in STM tasks that the rehearsal processes for some of them involve the activation of internal representations of the lexical units of sign language (Bellugi, Klima, & Siple, 1975).

The STM paradigm was one of the first used to explore the question of phonological coding in the deaf within the present theoretical context (Conrad, 1970, 1972, 1979). In the 1979 study, Conrad submitted a large group of deaf youngsters, the whole population of deaf schoolers between 15 and 16-and-a-half years old of age in England and Wales in 1975–1976, to an STM task with two types of words: phonologically similar but orthographically different (*do, few, true, through*, etc.), and phonologically different but presenting visually similar whole words shape (*bare, have, farm,* etc.). A subject was assumed to use phonological codes if he made more errors in the first than in the second condition. In the opposite case, he was assumed to use visuo-orthographic cues. The results revealed the existence of both kinds of codes. Moreover, a strong correlation appeared between the use of phonological coding and speech intelligibility on the one hand, and between phonological coding and reading ability on the other. These correlations remained substantial and significant even when the effects of hearing loss were controlled.

Convergent evidence has been found using the Stroop color–word interference task (Leybaert & Alegría, 1993; Leybaert, Alegría & Fonck, 1983). A number of experiments with hearing people have demonstrated that Stroop interference is considerably greater when the subject has to name the color (the *naming* condition) than when he has to push a key as a function of the color according to a preestablished code, the *manual response* condition (Pritchatt, 1968). It has been hypothesized that in the naming version of the task, the word and the color inputs are automatically identified, and consequently their corresponding phonological codes are evoked. The greatest part of the observed interference comes from the competition between these two phonological output codes. In the manual response condition, however, the interference is weaker, because the phonological code evoked by the identification of the word does not interfere (or inteferes less) with the response code imposed by the instructions (Lupker & Katz, 1981). Leybaert et al. (1983) examined the interference in a manual and a naming Stroop task in two groups of orally trained deaf subjects, one with good speech intelligibility and the other with poor intelligibility, and in a group of hearing controls. The interference in the manual task evaluated by the difference between the interfering condition (e.g., *blue* written in red) and the control one (e.g., a series of consonants written in red) was significant and identical in all groups (23 ms, 19 ms, and 19 ms, respectively). A significant and rather substantial increase in interference was observed in the naming task only in the hearing group and in the good intelligibility deaf group (the interference in the naming task reached 110 ms and 145 ms respectively). The increase in interference in the poor intelligibility group was smaller and not-reliable (44 ms). All subjects in the experiment were profoundly deaf. So, as in Conrad's STM study, intelligibility differences cannot be explained in terms of hearing loss. These results indicate that word, as well as color, identification may not automatically evoke the corresponding phonological output code in deaf individuals who have not developed intelligible speech, although it does in those who have developed it. An obvious relationship exists between this interpretation and the one proposed by Conrad to explain the correlation between speech intelligibility and phonological coding in STM tasks.

A third source of evidence concerns spelling. In an experiment aimed at exploring the use of phonological representations in spelling by deaf school children (Leybaert & Alegría, in press), a comparison was made between their performance with words whose spelling was directly derivable from the surface phonology (e.g., in French, *bleu, cartable*) and their performance with words that were ortographically opaque (e.g., in French: *pull, attention*). The results showed an important effect of derivability at all ages: In the younger group (mean age 10;9–10 years, nine months), the percentage of errors was 40% and 57% in the derivable and opaque conditions, respectively. The corresponding results for the older group (mean age 13;10) were 15% and 26%, respectively. This effect, although highly reliable, was considerably weaker than the one obtained with groups of hearing children matched with the deaf groups for their performance in the opaque condition: The group matched with the younger deaf (mean age 7;5) produced 12% errors in the phonologically derivable condition; the one matched with the older group of deaf (mean age 9;1) produced only 6% of errors. This demonstrates that deaf children possess and use the phonological representations of the words they know in order to write them down. If their spelling mechanisms were based exclusively on orthographic representations of words, no advantage for the phonological over the opaque condition would be observed. It also suggests that the accuracy of those representations and/or the accuracy of their translation into orthography improves with age, although it remains far below the level demonstrated by hearing controls (see Hanson, Shankweiler, & Fischer, 1983, for converging evidence from deaf adults).

Error analysis confirms this interpretation. In the group of normally hearing children, more than 90% of the errors were an acceptable transcription of the surface phonology of the target word. This proportion was considerably lower in the deaf. It depended on age, and in accordance with previously reported data, on the subjects' speech intelligibility. To examine this aspect of the results, each age group was split into two identical subgroups as a function of the quality of the subjects' speech. In the younger group, the percentage of phonologically acceptable errors was 32% and 22% for the more and less intelligible subgroups, respectively. The corresponding values in the older group were 53% and 21%, respectively. The increase in phonologically acceptable substitution errors was only present in the more intelligible group of deaf subjects.

The three situations examined so far—STM, Stroop color–word interference, and the analysis of spelling performance—show an interesting convergence. In each case, individual differences depended on the intelligibility of the speech production of the subjects. In the first two cases the activation of phonological codes had detrimental effects on performance (this was particularly strong in the Stroop case, where the subjects were totally aware of the negative effects of their tendency to pronounce the word's name). The presence of those codes suggests that their activation is automatic in the deaf, as it is in normally hearing subjects.

It is important to add that the phonological codes revealed in these experiments are all postlexical. This does not prove the existence of phonological codes that determine access to the lexicon in the deaf. In the case of the normally hearing subject, phonological access to the lexicon is guaranteed by the existence of an auditory processor, but this is obviously not the case in the profoundly prelingual deaf. It could be useful to examine some evidence concerning the possibility of its existence.

Models of written word identification in normally hearing people involve the activity of a mechanism that translates orthographic strings into phonological ones: the *phonological assembler* (Patterson & Morton, 1985). The relevance of this device comes from the existence of phonological access to the lexicon. Its presence in deaf subjects would strongly suggest the existence of functional phonological access to their lexicon. The evidence concerning the activity of the phonological assembler comes from experiments combining factors such as the frequency and/or lexicality of the items to identify, on the one hand, with factors such as length and spelling-to-sound regularity, on the other. The basic assumption is that factors determining the contribution of the phonological assembler to word identification would interact with factors such as word frequency, that are supposed to reveal direct access. The notion of identification does not apply to pseudowords, for obvious reasons. In that case, the assembling of a phonological code necessarily depends on the activity of the phonological assembler.

With this theoretical background, a group of 19 deaf adolescents aged 14 to 20 years was tested on a series of tasks involving reading isolated items aloud (see Leybaert, 1993, for a more extended report of these data). The items were presented one by one on the screen of a computer, and the latency of the response was measured from the stimulus presentation to the beginning of the subject's response. The oral response was also recorded and its accuracy subsequently analyzed. Adequate precautions were taken to separate genuine reading errors from articulatory ones.

Numerous aspects of the results demonstrate that the reading of the deaf involves phonological assembling. The most obvious evidence was their basically correct pronunciation of pseudowords, which testifies to their ability to segment written material into strings and attribute to them the corresponding phonology. The performance for pseudowords derived from words by changing one letter (e.g., *tur* from *dur,* hard) was poorer than the performance for the corresponding words. This was also the case in the control group of hearing subjects. It is important to emphasize that this effect of lexicality was not because it is easier to articulate familiar words (*dur*) than never pronounced pseudo-words (e.g. *tur*). This potential explanation of the data was dismissed by including a condition with two kinds of pseudowords: pseudohomophones and the corresponding control pseudowords. The pseudohomophones were pronounced like real words (e.g., *maizon* and *wazau*, which are pronounced like the French words *maison*, house and *oiseau*, bird), so a lexical facilitation at the response level could be detected. The results show that the effect of lexicality was still present with the pseudohomophones, but it was significantly lower than that obtained with the control pseudowords. These data reveal the activity of the phonological assembler in pronouncing pseudowords.

To explore the activity of the phonological assembler in word identification, a comparison was made between frequent and infrequent words of four, six or eight letters (e.g., *seul*, alone; *soleil*, sun; and *souvenir*, often; vs. *scie*, saw; *surnom*, nickname, and *salsifis*, salsify). The effect of frequency was present in the latency and accuracy of the responses in both the deaf and the normally hearing groups of subjects. As expected, the effects of length were weaker for the frequent than for the infrequent words in both groups of subjects. This indicates that both the deaf and the hearing subjects have developed an assembling procedure that contributes substantially to the identification of infrequent words.

This conclusion depends heavily on the data collected on the pronunciation of pseudowords and infrequent words, some of which were probably unknown to the deaf children. To ascertain that the assembling procedure really participates in word identification, the reading of irregular words was analyzed. The application of an assembling procedure in this case produces regularizations (e.g., reading /fem/ instead of /fam/ for *femme*, woman), which can interfere with the postlexical correct pronunciation directly found in the word's address. Special precautions were taken, because sometimes deaf children produced the regularized response not only when presented with the written version of some words, but also when spontaneously pronouncing them. This is because part of the internal phonology associated with words could be derived from the alphabetic orthography itself for certain words (see data on rhyme decision task, further on). To eliminate this artifact, the subjects were asked to name a drawing of each of the irregular words used in the experiment. Only words correctly pronounced in this case were considered. This control guarantees that the words were known by the subjects, and, more important, that they possessed the correct phonology. The results show a small but reliable effect of regularity with frequent words (with 17% and 25% errors for regular and irregular words, respectively) and a stronger one with infrequent words (17% and 43% errors, respectively).

The evidence just reviewed leads to the conclusion that written word identification in deaf children is not limited to visuo-orthographic recognition: they possess and use a device that elaborates phonological codes aimed at identifying words (see Leybaert, 1993, for a more detailed discussion on this point). The mere existence of this device can be taken as positive evidence of the accessibility to the internal lexicon through phonology. Combining this with the results of experiments on STM, Stroop interference in a color naming task, and the analysis of spelling production, it seems likely that a substantial proportion of the deaf population possesses language representations that are accessible via a phonological path: The access to one particular item in the lexicon automatically evokes the corresponding phonological code.

These results and interpretations raise a number of questions. An important one, which cannot be discussed here, concerns the origin of individual differences: Why do children with similar auditory handicaps and similar family and school histories sometimes differ so strongly at the level of the phonological representation of language? The answer is not readily available, but efforts to reach it should help us understand speech processing in both deaf and hearing individuals. The following section examines a problem that is related to that of individual differences: the origin of the phonological representations in the deaf observed so far.

THE ROLE OF LIP-READING IN SPEECH PERCEPTION

Lip-reading improves speech understanding in both deaf and hearing subjects, but the role assigned to lip-reading until the mid-1970s was rather modest. One obvious reason was that the visual dimension of the speech signal is not necessary for understanding speech. Indeed, hearing subjects understand radio programs and phone calls, and children born blind develop normal speech comprehension.

The role attributed to lip-reading used to be confined, almost exclusively, to poor listening conditions (Binnie, Montgomery, & Jackson, 1974; Erber, 1969, 1974; Sumby & Pollack, 1954). More recently, the benefits of lip-reading have been extended to cases where the auditory signal was easy to hear, but the message was difficult to understand: for example, listening to an unfamiliar language or a difficult text (Reisberg, McLean, & Goldfield, 1987). In all of these cases, the results can be interpreted without attributing any role to lip-reading at the level of phonological processing. Its role can be limited, for example, to facilitating auditory speech perception, by drawing the listener's attention to the moments when important acoustic events could happen. This notion is incompatible with data reported by Summerfield (1991), who showed that fluorescent lips in the dark improve speech comprehension, but a circle whose diameter is modulated by the gap between the lips does not. This last stimulus preserves the temporal pattern given by the lips, but apparently this is not the relevant input. Some constraints on ecological validity seem necessary for the visual input to be admitted into the phonological processing device.

In all of these cases, it is more or less explicitly supposed that the lip-reading information is optional. Data collected since the early 1980s using normally hearing subjects have shown that when the speaker's face is seen, the visual information accompanying speech production is inevitably integrated into an audiovisual compound that might differ from both the visual and the auditory speech signals. McGurk and MacDonald (1976) showed that seeing a face pronouncing the syllable /gah/ together with a simultaneous auditory /bah/ produces an intermediate percept /dah/. The subject reports hearing a clear /dah/ instead of any sort of /bah/-/gah/ compound. Similarly, a visual /kah/ combined with an auditory /pah/ produces a heard /tah/. If auditory and visual stimuli are inverted; that is, when the visual stimulus presents a bilabial feature, /bah/ or /pah/, this feature is inevitably included in the subjects' impression, which sounds /bgah/ or /bdah/ (or /pkah/-/ptah/). The main point of these data is that they convincingly demonstrate that lip-reading intervenes at the speech processing level. An interpretation of the results in terms of, say, improving attention, seems too weak to explain audiovisual speech perception. These results have been confirmed, and their consequences for speech processing theories developed, by Massaro (1987, 1989).

It is worth noting that numerous results collected in the "ventriloquism" paradigm show that the mere existence of a temporal correlation between auditory and visual events located at different places can bring about a spatial recalibration of both systems, even in rather abstract combinations, such as voice intensity modulating the light intensity of a screen (Radeau & Bertelson, 1977, 1978). Realistic constraints do not seem to act in the spatial recalibration studies. There is an interesting suggestion that the audiovisual integration observed in speech processing is a speech-specific phenomenon, as long as it doesn't follow the more general rule derived from audiovisual spatial location (ventriloquism) studies. The results of Summerfield (1991) suggest that the simple spatiotemporal coordination is not sufficient to obtain integration in the speech area. In the same vein, Bertelson, Vroomen, Wiegeraad, and de Gelder (1994) have recently shown a dissociation within the McGurk effect that is independent of the spatial separation of the auditory and visual stimuli; the McGurke effect was strongly reduced if the face pronouncing the visual syllable was presented upside-down, whereas the ventriloquism effect showed the opposite pattern (see Radeau, 1994a, 1994b, for a thorough examination of these matters).

One obvious reason why the speech processing apparatus incorporates the lip-reading information is that human beings are, from the very beginning, presented with a highly correlated audiovisual speech signal. Studies of the McGurk effect in children have shown that it is present in 4- to 6 year-olds (Massaro, 1987; McGurk & MacDonald, 1976). At those ages, the connection between yhe two events has had plenty of time to establish itself. More impressive are the results obtained with infants using the paradigm of preference. Dodd (1979) showed that 10- to 16-week-old infants devote more attention to speech when sound and lip movements were synchronized than when they were out-of-synchrony by 400 ms. In a similar vein, Kuhl and Meltzoff (1982) and MacKain, Studdert-Kennedy, Spieker, and Stern (1983) demonstrated that 4- to 6-month-old infants presented with two faces prefer to look at the face executing the articulatory gesture corresponding to the stimulus simultaneously presented through audition. These results cannot be interpreted in terms of a simple sensitivity to audiovisual synchronization, because both visually presented syllables were temporally synchronized with the auditory stimulus. These results indicate that the visual lip-read information is processed in a linguistically relevant manner. Impressive though they are, these data do not definitively prove that lip-reading is integrated into a genuine hard-wired speech module. Indeed, the connection between heard and seen speech could become established during the first weeks of life. Two empirical facts are compatible with this hypothesis: first, the capacity to imitate facial gestures, most of them involving the mouth, soon after birth (Field, Woodson, Greenberg, & Cohen, 1982; Meltzoff & Moore, 1977); second, the delicate sensitivity to phonologically relevant auditory contrasts that can be observed at the age of 3 or 4 weeks (Bertoncini, Bijeljac-Babic, Jusczyk, Kennedy, & Mehler, 1988; Eimas, Siqueland, Jusczyk, & Vigorito, 1971).

Knowing the role played by audiovisual correlations in the development of an integrated speech processing device is important in a discussion concerning the deaf because such correlations cannot exist in the absence of audition. If, in contrast, the exposure to massive highly correlated audiovisual speech is not necessary because the speech module is prewired, it is conceivable that the exposure to lip-reading alone activates the module.

To summarize, the notion that lip-reading must be integrated into the speech perception device forces one to admit the existence of rather abstract representations, common to the auditory and the visual speech signals (see Massaro, 1987; Vroomen, 1992, and specially Summerfield for a thorough discussion of the shape that this common metric must possess, and Liberman & Mattingly's 1985 revision of the motor theory of speech perception). So, the phonological codes that are involved in a number of mental activities also have a visual lip-reading dimension, at least in normally hearing individuals. From the perspective of the deaf, this evolution can be considered as good news, because it draws their phonological representations closer to those of the normally hearing subjects. The main problem for deaf individuals is that lip-reading alone is insufficient to deliver much useful speech because of its intrinsic ambiguity. To take an example from the earliest referential items, French words like *papa* /papa/ (father) and *maman* /mamã/ (mother) are identical in lip-reading. The next section examines the possible effects of a substantial reduction of this ambiguity.

MANUAL AIDS TO LIP-READING: CUED SPEECH

Audition without vision allows speech to develop, as demonstrated by the blind, whereas vision without audition does not. This is derived from the fact that visual information is far more ambiguous than auditory information. Lexical development requires relatively systematic relationships between referents and their corresponding phonological sequences, and lip-reading cannot reliably supply them. Lip-reading accounts for most of the phonological development in deaf children (Dodd, 1976). At the same time, the deaf rarely develop useful speech from lip-reading alone. This situation has frequently brought speech therapists and teachers of the deaf to add systematic signals, usually visual, but sometimes tactile, to lip-reading, in order to reduce its ambiguity. A strong illustration of this idea taken from the literature on normally hearing subjects is the demonstration that the understanding of lip-reading improves dramatically if an auditory buzzer modulated by the vocal fold activity is added. Although the buzzer sequence without lip-reading is uninterpretable, the vocal fold activity gives essential information about voicing, a basic phonological feature that is totally invisible (Rosen, Fourcin, & Moore, 1981).

This section deals with a system of manual aid, Cued Speech (CS), developed to help deaf children to understand speech by eliminating the ambiguity of lip-reading (Cornett, 1967; see also Périer, 1987, for a comparison of CS with some other similarly motivated concurrent systems). The speaker holds one hand near his or her mouth while speaking, so the listener can see both the lips and the hand at the same time. In the French version of CS, the hand can adopt eight shapes and five different positions around the mouth. Hand shapes are for disambiguating consonants; hand positions disambiguate vowels. Consonants and vowels are independently grouped into sets of two or three items, and each set has its specific shape or place. The system is designed to complement lip-reading in a natural way by adding discriminating information selectively. Shapes and places are assigned to groups of consonants and vowels in such a way that items sharing the same hand shape or hand place are easy to discriminate by lip-reading, whereas items that are difficult to discriminate belong to different groups. Thus, a particular hand shape is shared by /p,d,ʒ/ , a different one by /b, n, w/, a third one by /f, t, m/ and so on. For the vowels one place is shared by /i,ɔ̃,ã/ , a second one by /a,o,ə/, and so on. As a result of this organization, each time the speaker produces a cue (a particular hand shape at one specific place) while pronouncing a consonant-vowel (CV) syllable, he is giving unambiguous phonological information about this syllable. Syllables presenting different structures, such as VC, CCV, and CVC, include additional cues that reveal the supplementary phones (this question is not considered here; for a thorough examination of it see Alegría, Charlier, & Mattys, 1995). The whole system appears, at first sight, somewhat complex and artificial. In fact, it is relatively easy to learn, and, with some practice, normally hearing adults manage to use it while speaking, with only a slight reduction in speed.

It is worth contrasting CS with other systems sharing similar aims. A well-known one is fingerspelling. This system differs from CS in that it consists of an alphabetic representation of speech using hand shapes for letters, whereas CS represents speech at a strictly phonetic level. In a number of other systems, the hands (or other devices accompanying speech, such as tactile cues) give phonemic information in a direct way, often at a subphonemic level. A typical case is that in which particular signs are used to indicate that an item is voiced, or nasal, or contains some other phonetic feature. This is radically different from CS, in which the hands alone give no direct phonetic information: There is no hand shape or hand position that can be interpreted in terms of a phonetic feature without taking the lips into consideration (except one hand shape for /g/ in the French version).

As mentioned at the beginning of this section, the ambiguity of lip-reading information about speech is an obstacle to referential clarity and, hence, to speech understanding and speech development. CS is a system that, in principle, eliminates all of these ambiguities. Let us suppose that this is the only obstacle. In that case, nothing essential would distinguish deaf children raised in a family using CS to communicate from their normally hearing peers. Whatever the uncertainties involved in that statement, an interesting situation has been created by the fact that some schools around the world, one of them in Brussels, have adopted CS. Furthermore, some parents have adopted it to communicate with their deaf children from the very beginning. This situation, in the context of the evolution of ideas about lip-reading discussed earlier, constitutes a real challenge for research in cognitive psycholinguistics. Can words made of a sequence of lip postures accompanied by a systematic sequence of hand shapes and positions be processed, interpreted, stored, retrieved, and used in cognitive activities in a way equivalent to audiovisual speech? The a priori answer of Cornett (1967) was "yes". There is now one piece of empirical evidence that allows us to go further.

The Role of CS in Speech Processing

The first systematic research on speech understanding with CS to be published was conducted in Australia (Nicholls, 1979; Nicholls & Ling, 1982). A group of 18 deaf youngsters, aged 9 to 16, attending a school where CS had been introduced about 10 years before and exposed to it for at least 4 years, were presented with sentences for lip-reading alone or accompanied by CS. Their task was to identify the last word in the sentence. The percentage of correct responses increased from 40% in the lip-reading to 95% in the CS condition.

In a similar vein, we examined a group of 55 deaf subjects, aged 5;11 (five years, eleven months) to 16;1 ($M = 10;7$) (Charlier, Hage, Alegría, & Périer, 1990; a preliminary report with a group of 24 subjects was published in Périer, Charlier, Hage, & Alegría, 1988). Fourteen used CS at home (the home group), the others exclusively at school (the school group). They were presented with sentences to lip-read with and without CS. Their task was to choose the drawing out of a set of four that corresponded to the seen sentence. The results showed that CS brought significant improvements in the critical condition in both groups. The improvement was weaker in the school group (the percentage of correct responses in the most difficult condition in the experiment rose from 37% correct to 53% without and with CS, respectively), than in the home group (their results reached 39% and 72% respectively), however, suggesting that the age at which the child began to use CS was significantly and negatively correlated with the gain it allowed: The sooner children were exposed to CS the greater the observed improvements. This variable was confounded, however, with the total duration of the exposure to CS and with the home–school factor. The data were reanalyzed in an attempt to explore this question. Subgroups of home and school children paired for the duration of their exposure to CS were considered. The former subgroup was obviously younger than the latter: 8;6 and 12;1 years, respectively. The improvement observed when CS was introduced into the task was still greater in the home than in the school group (10.71% and 4.79% respectively), despite the age factor that plays against the younger children belonging in the home group.

A third experiment examined the extent to which CS improves lip-reading in deaf schoolchildren (Alegría, et al., 1995). One of the main aims of this experiment was to study the effects of the age at which children were exposed to CS. Two groups were considered: early and late. Early subjects had started using CS with their parents at home before the age of 2 years, as their ordinary way to communicate. The late group had begun later in their lives (usually at age 6) and, with two exceptions, used it exclusively at school (the two exceptions corresponded to cases where the parents had adopted CS after the age of 2 and used it in a rather unsystematic way). The task consisted of identifying frequent words and phonologically paired pseudowords in lip-reading with and without CS. All of the items had four phonemes grouped into two syllables. Pseudoword material was included to obtain clearer data concerning how CS participates in the perception of phonological strings without any lexical help. For this reason, separate blocks were run for words and pseudowords.

The percentages of correct responses per group and condition, together with same basic data about the age of the subjects and the duration of their exposure to CS, appear in Table 5.1.

TABLE 5.1

Mean Percentages of Correct Responses in the Phonological Strings Identification Task per Condition and Group.[*]

	Early	Late		
		Whole group	Age matched[1]	Exposure matched
n	7	24	6	12
Mean age	10;9	14;10	12;2	14;7
Age Range	8;6-12;0	11;8-19;10	11;8-18;9	
CS Exposure	9;6	7;10	9;5	
Words				
Lip-reading	41.5	47.3	27.6	47.1
CS	73.7	67.3	40.1	66.2
PS words				
Lip-reading	17.9	9.4	2.1	10.4
CS	54.9	32.8	12.0	32.0

[*] Adapted from Alegría et al. (1995).

The performance of early and late groups, without taking conditions into account, was similar: 47% and 39% of correct responses, respectively. It is important to notice that the late group was considerably older than the early group: 14;10 and 10;9, respectively. The difference between early and late groups

---

[1] *Exposure matched* and *Age matched* sub-groups of the *Late* group were selected to match the subjects of the *Early* group in age and duration of exposure to CS respectively.

became significant when the age effect was eliminated, as shown by the data produced by a subgroup of six children out of the late group matched by age with the early group (see Table 5.1). The gain induced by CS was significantly greater in the early than in the late group, even though age was not controlled. It is important to add that the group by lexicality interaction was significant, indicating that, although the groups did not differ from each other in word identification, a reliable difference favoring the early group appeared in pseudoword processing. The differences observed between the early and late groups of children cannot be immediately attributed to the precociousness of the exposure to CS, because this factor was confounded with the duration of exposure to CS. To disentangle these factors, the late group was split into two subgroups, depending on the duration of exposure to CS. Table 5.1 presents the results obtained by a subgroup of late subjects matched with the early group by the duration of exposure to CS. The analysis replicated that just reported. The overall difference between groups failed to reach a significant level, but the group by cuing and group by lexicality interactions were both significant. This indicates that CS processing, as well as pure, non lexical, phonological processing depended more strongly on the timing of exposure to CS than on the duration of the exposure to it.

The results presented so far show that in deaf children exposed to CS at an early age and, to a lesser extent, in those exposed to it later on and/or exclusively at school, CS strongly reduces the ambiguity of lip-reading. This suggests that it could be a basic element of speech development. Two projects aimed at exploring some aspects of this question were undertaken. The first concerns the development of morphological and syntactic items that are poorly represented in the lip-read; CS could be especially efficient at this level. The second concerns the role played by CS in the lexical representations of deaf people.

To begin with the first problem, the capacity of deaf children who had learned CS to deal with French grammatical gender was explored. This problem was chosen for several reasons. First, derivational and grammatical morphology is quite poor in deaf children (see Swisher, 1976, for an examination of their performance on on Brown, 1973, classical first 14 English morphemes; see also a study in Italian by Taeschner, Devescovi, & Volterra, 1988, showing delays, and in some cases deviations, in gender morphology), although normally hearing French-speaking children have productive control of gender morphology by age 3 (Karmiloff-Smith, 1979). Second, gender is phonologically marked at noun endings in a way that is not totally systematic: nouns that end with /ɛtə/ are almost certainly feminine and those that end in /o/ are masculine, whereas /wa/ endings are unmarked, so that there are as many words ending with /wa/ that are feminine as masculine. To develop productive competence in gender morphophonology, the subject has to relate noun endings with other gender-marked morphemes: articles, pronouns, adjectives, and so on. The task is difficult for the deaf, because these classes of words are often short and are usually unstressed, like noun endings. The experiment consisted of asking subjects to classify drawings of common and unfamiliar objects into feminine and masculine categories (Hage, 1994; Hage, Alegría, & Périer, 1991). In the 1991 experiment, nine subjects who had had intensive CS practice (three at school only for at least 8 years and the other six at school and at home since before the age of 2) were studied. Their mean age was 10;11 (range: 4;6 to 21;0). The experimenter showed each drawing to the subject while pronouncing its name using CS. The subject had to repeat the name orally, preceded by the corresponding article. The results for common names were quiet good for marked, as well as unmarked, items (90% and 94% correct respectively). For the unfamiliar unmarked nouns, exactly 50% of the responses were correct (chance level), showing that the subjects did not know them. The score reached 75% correct for the unfamiliar marked items, significantly better than chance. These results indicate that subjects intensively exposed to CS were able to derive the grammatical gender of an unknown word based solely on its phonological properties to an exceptionally high degree compared with the normal standards for the deaf.

This issue was further explored with another group of deaf subjects with different family and school histories (Hage, 1994). Two groups of children were considered, one that had had CS at home, and another intensively trained by oral methods that did not include CS. The children in the groups were matched for vocabulary knowledge and lip-reading ability. The CS group contained 32 children, mean age 11;3 (range: 6;11 to 17;8). The classic oral group contained 21 children, mean age 13;8 (range: 6;11 to 17;8). The oral training of this group had begun at home between 3 and 30 months. It was expected that at equivalent levels of lexical ability, CS children would do much better than children in the purely oral group in dealing with grammatical gender. That is because grammatical gender understanding involves the ability to manipulate short and inconspicuous phonological strings, such as word endings and articles.

Both groups performed almost perfectly for the common words (between 82% and 99% correct). The groups differed, however, with unfamiliar words: 66% and 48% for the CS and oral groups, respectively, with unmarked words, and 76% and 61% with marked ones. The difference observed between groups in attributing grammatical gender to unmarked unfamiliar words indicates that the CS group knew more about these items than the oral group; therefore, the difference between groups in improvement observed from unmarked to marked words could not be unambiguously interpreted.

To deal with this question, subgroups of subjects from both groups, matched on the basis of the results with unfamiliar unmarked words, were considered. The results obtained by these groups appear in Table 5.2. The effect of marking on unfamiliar words was now reliably greater in the CS group than in the oral group. So, when tested on subtle morphophonological information, children selected because they had had intense and precocious oral training and had attained exceptional success at lexical comprehension assessed by vocabulary knowledge, nevertheless performed worse than those who had had CS. The advantage of the CS group probably results from its efficiency in revealing aspects of the morphophonology usually hidden in lip-reading.

TABLE 5.2
Mean Percentages of Correct Responses in the Grammatical
Gender Attribution Task per Condition and Group[*]

	CS^2	Oral
n	14	10
Mean age	10;8	14;10
Age Range	6;11-14;11	10;11-11;79
Common words		
Unmarked	99	82
Marked	97	94
Unfamiliar words		
Unmarked	57	56
Marked	80	67

[*] Adapted from Hage (1994).

The next question to consider concerns the possible role of CS in the development of phonological representations attached to lexical items in the internal lexicon. Two experimental tasks—one STM and one rhyme decision—were used to examine this question (Charlier, 1994). As previously mentioned, the results of numerous experiments with the STM paradigm demonstrate a considerable variety of internal codes in the deaf: phonological, visuo-orthographic, dactylic, sign-language based, and so on, partially depending on their linguistic and school background. Deaf subjects were divided into two groups: the early group, composed of children whose parents had adopted and used CS at home before the child was 3; and the late group, children attending

---

[2] *CS:* deaf children who have been exposed to CS. *Oral:* deaf children who have had oral training exclusively.

schools that had adopted a variety of methods of communication, including Signed French, dactylology, and CS. A control group of hearing children was also included. Three series of eight drawings each were used. In the control condition, the names of the drawings were monosyllabic (*chat,* cat; *feu,* fire; *banc,* bench; etc.). In the rhyming condition, the names of the drawings rhymed (*dé,* dice; *nez,* nose; *thé,* tea; etc.). In the length condition the words were of three or four syllables (*crocodile; télévision; portemanteau,* coat rack; etc.). The experimenter showed a number of cards, one at a time, for about 2 seconds while pronouncing the name of the object; then she put them in a row, face down. As soon as the last card had been presented, the experimenter put a strip of cardboard on the table on which the eight cards from that condition appeared. The child was asked to push each of the face down cards in front of the corresponding ones on the strip. The number of cards was individually determined in the control condition so that performance was slightly higher than 50% correct.

TABLE 5.3*

Mean Percentage of Correct Responses in the Short Term Memory Task per Condition and Group.

	Early[3]	Late	Hearing
n	12	14	30
Mean age	8;8	10;9	9;4
Age Range	5;8-11;0	8;0-13;0	8;5-11;0
CS Exposure	7;3	6;11	
Control	63.8	54.5	63.6
Rhyme	48.9	57.1	47.4
Length	49.7	57.6	57.6
Mean span	5.2	4.9	5.2
Range	4-6	4-5	4-7

* Adapted from Charlier (1994).

Table 5.3 summarizes the results. The children from the early group and the normally hearing controls presented a very similar pattern of results, whereas the

[3] Early: deaf children exposed to CS at home before the age of three years. Late: deaf children whose training includes CS only at school. CS Exposure: mean duration of children's Exposure to CS.

late group showed no differences in recall between conditions. Both early CS and hearing controls showed marked sensitivity to rhyme and to spoken wordlength in their recall. If anything, the effects of lengthening the words and of rhymes impaired early CS children more than they impair hearing children. Indeed, length failed to reach significance in the hearing group. There may be several reasons for this. The most likely is that hearing children rehearsed using shortened version of the words (*croco* for *crocodile*, *tévé* for *télévision*, etc.).

A further task (Charlier, 1994) tested the role of CS in deciding whether two items rhymed or not. The items were presented in pairs of drawings. Half of the pairs rhymed. In this case, there were two conditions: rhyming, orthographically identical (*pain–train*, bread–train) and rhyming, orthographically different (*tasse–glace,* cup–ice). The nonrhyming items were also divided into two conditions: nonrhyming, but identical on lip-reading (*train* /tRɛ/–*pied* /piɛ/: the items' endings, /ɛ/ and /ɛ/, are identical for lip-reading), and nonrhyming, differing in lip-reading (*robe* /Rɔb/–bale /bal/). The subjects belonged to three groups according to the same criteria as the previous (STM) experiment. The results appear in Table 5.4.

TABLE 5.4[*]

Mean Percentages of Correct Responses in the Rhyme Decision Task per condition and Group.

	Early	Late	Hearing
n	16	18	12
Mean age	10;1	12;7	8;7
Age Range	6;10-15;10	7;4-16;8	7;0-12;0
CS Exposure	7;4	7;11	
Rhyme			
Orthographically similar[4]	97;4	84;4	96;8
Orthographically different	94.4	73.9	97.0
NonRhyme			
Lip-read, ending similar	93.4	68.3	97.7
Lip-read, ending different	100.0	95.6	92.2

[*] Adapted from Charlier (1994).

---

[4] Orthographically similar and ortographically different: rhyming pairs with identical and different ortographic endings, respectively. Lip-read, ending similar and Lip-read, ending different: non-rhyming pairs with identical and different lip-reading endings, respectively. Groups: see Table 5.3.

All groups approached ceiling performance for orthographically similar rhymes and for lip-reading different nonrhymes. In the rhyming but orthographically different condition, however, the late group fell to 74% correct "yes" responses, whereas the other two groups remained at levels higher than 90% correct. So, when items rhyme but do not have similar orthographical endings, subjects trained exclusively at school with CS were induced into false negative responses. It must be borne in mind that the items were presented as drawings, so the experiment itself did not induce orthographically based responses. One possible interpretation of these errors is that some subjects trained in the classic oral tradition derived the phonology of words from their orthographic representation. It is important to notice, however, that the score reached by this group clearly demonstrated that their rhyme judgments were not based exclusively on orthographic information (see Campbell & Wright, 1988; Hanson & Fowler, 1987; Hanson & McGarr, 1987, for partially contrasting results). The fact that early CS and hearing subjects were not influenced by orthography suggests that their phonological representations are sufficiently accurate and complete to support their rhyme judgments.

The results in the nonrhyming but similar lip-reading condition revealed important differences between groups. Here, the late group's performance fell to 68% correct, while the other two groups remained above 90% correct. This confirms the data and speculations proposed by Dodd and Hermelin (1977) and Dodd (1987) suggesting that lip-reading constitutes the main input for phonological development in the deaf. The present results reveal that some deaf children tend to consider as homophones items that are identical on lip-reading. The results of the early CS group, by contrast, indicate that the precocious use of CS allows the development of an awareness of phonological contrasts in words having subtle distinctions that are not visible on the lips.

SUMMARY AND CONCLUDING REMARKS

The starting point of this chapter was the notion that a large portion of cognitive activity is supported by phonological representations whose development is closely related to the integrity of the auditory apparatus. The question, then, concerned how some deaf children apparently develop and use this phonological system. The results obtained by deaf youngsters in different experimental tasks—STM, Stroop color–word interference, spelling, and so on—show that some of them possess those representations, and that those representations work in these deaf individuals the same way they work in normally hearing people.

The evidence of phonologically related mental activity was strongly correlated with the subjects' speech intelligibility. This points toward a potentially unique determinant of these effects, that is, the ease with which the phonological codes of words can be retrieved.

These data, however, concern exclusively postlexical phonology. In the case of the deaf, there is no compelling reason to posit the existence of prelexical phonological codes as an interface between the auditory signal and the lexical word representation. The analysis of the mechanisms involved in written word identification was motivated by the search for evidence concerning the existence of a phonological route to the lexicon. Numerous aspects of the results produced by deaf children educated in a classical oral tradition show that they carry out phonological assembling as hearing readers do. The conclusion is that the deaf do possess phonological access to their lexical knowledge.

There is no doubt concerning the reality of phonological processing and representation in deaf children, but we can ask about its origin. One obvious source of phonology is lip-reading. Dodd (1976) argued convincingly that the development of a phonological system in the deaf child can be easily understood by positing lip-reading as its main source. Some aspects of our data on spelling (Leybaert & Alegría, 1995), as well as on the rhyme decision task (Charlier, 1994), reveal that lip-reading visibility has substantial effects on the phonological representations of words.

CS, which aims to eliminate lip-reading ambiguity, was examined in this context. Experiments comparing the perception of speech materials with and without CS conclusively demonstrated improvements when CS was added to lip-reading, especially in children exposed to CS from an early age. These children also showed a greater ability to manipulate word endings related to French grammatical gender.

The STM and the rhyme decision tasks revealed notable differences between children precociously exposed to CS at home and children who had a classic oral training including CS at school. In the latter group, the representations of words were mainly based on lip-reading, and may have been improved by orthographic knowledge. The subjects of the former group, however, had phonological representations of words indistinguishable from those of hearing children. It seems reasonable to submit that CS fostered the establishment of phonemic contrasts in the subjects' lexicon which are invisible in lip-reading.

The data discussed so far demonstrate that CS participates both in speech processing and in speech representation in memory. The question for future studies would be to determine how lip-reading and CS articulate with each other to elaborate a unique speech percept. Two extreme models seem possible. One supposes that the CS–lip-reading compound is perceived phonemically. The phoneme is the minimal speech unit allowing meaning distinctions. It is an abstract unit, so there is no logical obstacle to considering that CS, together with visual lip-read information, elaborates phonemic contrasts. The second supposes that both lip and hand cues are hierarchically organized processes, the former providing the core phonological information and the latter intervening afterward to resolve the remaining ambiguities.

In the hierarchical view, the participation of CS in the speech perception processes is somewhat superficial. It works as an additional index in a problem-solving situation. In the phonemic view, by contrast, CS is conceived as one of the inputs of the automatic speech processing device. An obvious objection to the phonemic view could be that the speech processing device cannot handle artificial inputs, like the hand shapes and positions of CS. Some aspects of the results reported by Rosen et al. (1981) are worth noting in this context. These authors demonstrated that the addition of an auditory nonspeech signal (a buzzer modulated by the pitch contour of the speaker's voice) to lip-reading substantially improves speech perception. This suggests that an artificial nonspeech stimulus can be integrated with natural lip-reading in speech processing. R. Campbell (personal communication, 1992) mentioned that, after some training, the subjects in the task experienced the introduction of the buzzer as if "the sound was added to the TV images." In a similar vein, Fowler and Dekle (1991) have shown that acoustic syllables are integrated with synchronously presented haptic information (the subject places his or her fingers on the lips of the model pronouncing a syllable), producing a McGurk-like effect.

These examples suggest that the speech processing system can accept extraneous signals as if they possessed a phonemic value. The case of CS cannot be directly assimilated to the case of the buzzer or to that of haptic perception. One important reason is that the subjects in those experiments were normally hearing adults who possessed representations of the cues given by the buzzer or felt by the lips. It is certainly not obvious that a 5- or 6-year-old deaf child who has no phonological representations of some phonemic contrasts (e.g., voicing) can use CS to distinguish /p/ from /b/, and /ʒ/ from /ʃ/. The question is different when CS is used as a way to communicate between infants and parents. The question then is not whether CS could participate in the perception of phonemic contrasts, but rather whether it participates in the *development* of these contrasts. This probably depends on the early use of CS. Indeed, the results showing that the early and/or home, but not the late and/or school, groups of deaf children possess speech representations indistinguishable from those of the normally hearing subjects support this hypothesis. So, the way in which lip-reading and CS are integrated in speech processing can differ in the two groups. Subjects exposed to CS early could process it phonemically, because they have developed normal phonemic representations of speech. Subjects exposed to CS later may be limited to using it as an artificial signal in a problem-solving way. It is hard to go further in this discussion without empirical evidence to constrain speculation; however, the question is important because it involves basic properties of the speech processing module, particularly its permeability to more or less exotic inputs. If it could be demonstrated that CS is indeed incorporated into this module in at least some deaf children, as is clearly the case for lip-reading in the normally hearing, the notion of hearing lips and hands would be upheld.

ACKNOWLEDGMENTS

This work was supported by the Belgian F.R.S.M. (Fonds de la Recherche Scientifique Medicale) convention No. 3.4571.94. I wish to thank my "old" colleagues, Olivier Périer and Jacqueline Leybaert, and even more, my "new" ones, Brigitte Charlier and Catherine Hage, whose recent doctoral dissertations form the core of this chapter.

REFERENCES

Alegría, J., Charlier, B.L. & Mattys, S. (1995). *The role of lip-reading and Cued Speech in the processing of phonological information in deaf children.* Manuscript submitted for publication.

Baddeley, A.D. (1981). The concept of working memory: A view of the current state and probable future development. *Cognition, 10,* 17–23.

Baddeley, A., & Hitch, G.S. (1974). Working memory. In G. H. Bower (Ed.), *The psychology of learning and motivation* (Vol. 8, pp. 47–90). New York: Academic Press.

Baddeley, A., & Lewis, V.J. (1981). Inner active processes in reading: The inner voice, the inner ear, and the inner eye. In A. M. Lesgold & C. A. Perfetti (Eds.), *Interactive processes in reading* (pp. 107–129). Hove, UK: Lawrence Erlbaum Associates.

Bellugi, U., Klima, E.S., & Siple, P. (1975). Remembering in signs. *Cognition, 3,* 93–125.

Bertelson, P., Vroomen, J., Wiegeraad, G., & de Gelder, B. (1994). Exploring the relation between McGurk interference and ventriloquism. *Proceedings of the 1994 international conference on spoken language processing* (Vol. 2, pp. 559–562).

Bertoncini, J., Bijeljac-Babic, R., Jusczyk, P.W., Kennedy, L., & Mehler, J. (1988). An investigation of young infants' perceptual representations of speech sounds. *Journal of Experimental Psychology: General, 117,* 21–33.

Binnie, C.A., Montgomery, A.A., & Jackson, P.L. (1974). Auditory and visual contributions to the perception of consonants. *Journal of Speech and Hearing Research, 17,* 619–630.

Brown, R. (1973). *A first language: The early stages.* Cambridge, MA: Harvard University Press.

Campbell, R. (1987a). The cerebral lateralization of lip-reading. In B. Dodd & R. Campbell (Eds.), *Hearing by eye: The psychology of lip-reading* (pp. 215–226). Hove, UK: Lawrence Erlbaum Associates.

Campbell, R. (1987b). Lip-reading and immediate memory processes or on thinking impure thoughts. In B. Dodd & R. Campbell (Eds.), *Hearing by eye: The psychology of lip-reading.* Hove, UK:

Lawrence Erlbaum Associates.

Campbell, R., & Dodd, B. (1980). Hearing by eye. *Quarterly Journal of Experimental Psychology*, *32*, 85–99.

Campbell, R., & Wright, H. (1988). Deafness, spelling and rhyme: how spelling supports written word and picture rhyming skills in deaf subjects. *Quarterly Journal of Experimental Psychology*, *40A*, 771–788.

Charlier, B. L. (1994). *Le développement des représentations phonologiques chez l'enfant sourd: étude comparative du Langage Parlé Complété avec d'autres outils de communication* [The development of phonological representations in deaf children: a comparison between Cued Speech and other communication tools]. Unpublished doctoral dissertation, University of Brussels, Brussels, Belgium.

Charlier, B.L., Hage, C., Alegría, J., & Périer, O. (1990). Evaluation d'une pratique prolongée du LPC sur la compréhension de la parole par l'enfant atteint de déficience auditive [Evaluation of the effects of prolonged Cued Speech practice upon speech understanding in deaf children]. *Glossa*, *22*, 28–39.

Conrad, R. (1962). An association between memory errors and errors due to acoustic masking of speech. *Nature*, *193*, 1314–1315.

Conrad, R. (1964). Acoustic confusions in immediate memory. *British Journal of Psychology*, *55*,, 75–84.

Conrad, R. (1970). Short-term memory processes in the deaf. *British Journal of Psychology*, *81*, 179–195.

Conrad, R. (1972). Speech and reading. In J.F. Kavanagh & I.G. Mattingly (Eds.), *Language by ear and by eye* (pp. 205–240). Cambridge, MA: MIT Press.

Conrad, R. (1979). *The deaf school child*. London: Harper & Row.

Cornett, O. (1967). Cued speech. *American Annals of the Deaf*, *112*, 3–13.

Crowder, R.G. (1986). Auditory and temporal factors in the modality effect. *Journal of Experimental Psychology: Learning, Memory, and Cognition*, *12*, 269–279.

Crowder, R.G., & Morton, J. (1969). Precategorical acoustic storage (PAS). *Perception & Psychophysics*, *5*, 365–373.

Dodd, B. (1976). The phonological system of deaf children. *Journal of Speech and Hearing Disorders*, *41*, 185–198.

Dodd, B., (1979). Lip-reading in infants: Attention to speech presented in- and out-of-synchrony. *Cognitive Psychology*, *11*, 478–484.

Dodd, B. (1987). Lip-reading, phonological coding and deafness. In B. Dodd & R. Campbell (Eds.), *Hearing by eye: The psychology of lip-reading* (pp. 177–189). Hove, UK: Lawrence Erlbaum Associates.

Dodd, B., & Hermelin, B. (1977). Phonological coding by the prelinguistically deaf. *Perception & Psychophysics*, *21*, 413–417.

Eimas, P.D., Siqueland, E.R., Jusczyk, P.W., & Vigorito, J. (1971). Speech perception in infants. *Science*, *171*, 303–306.

Erber, N.P. (1969). Interaction of audition and vision in the recognition of oral speech stimuli. *Journal of Speech and Hearing Research*, *12*,, 423–424.

Erber, N.P. (1974). Visual perception of speech by deaf children: Recent developments and continuing needs. *Journal of Speech and Hearing Research*, *39*, 178–185.

Field, T.M., Woodson, R., Greenberg, D., & Cohen, D. (1982). Discrimination and imitation of facial expressions by neonates. *Science*, *218*, 179–181.

Fowler, C.A., & Dekle, D.J. (1991). Listening with eye and hand: Cross-modal contributions to speech perception. *Journal of Experimental Psychology: Human Perception and Performance*, *17*, 816–828.

Hage, C. (1994). Développement de certains aspects de la morpho-syntaxe chez l'enfant à surdité profonde: Rôle du Langage Parlé Complété [Some aspects of morpho-syntactic development in profoundly deaf children: role of Cued Speech]. Unpublished doctoral dissertation, University of Brussels, Brussels, Belgium.

Hage, C., Alegría, J. & Périer, O. (1991). Cued speech and language acquisition: The case of grammatical gender morpho-phonology. In D. S. Martin (Ed.), *Advances in cognition, education, and deafness* (pp. 395–399). Washington, DC: Gallaudet University Press.

Hanson, V.L., & Fowler, C.A. (1987). Phonological coding in word reading: Evidence from hearing and deaf readers. *Memory and Cognition, 15*, 199–207.

Hanson, V.L., & McGarr, N. (1987). Rhyme generation by deaf adults. *Haskins Laboratories Status Report on Speech Research, SR-92*, 137–158.

Hanson, V.L., Shankweiler, D., & Fischer, F.W. (1983). Determinants of spelling ability in deaf and hearing adults: Access to linguistic structure. *Cognition, 14*, 323–344.

Karmiloff-Smith, A. (1979). *A functional approach to child language.* Cambridge, England: Cambridge University Press.

Kuhl, P.K., & Meltzoff, A.N. (1982). The bimodal perception of speech in infancy. *Science, 218*, 1138–1141.

Leybaert, J. (1993). Reading ability in the deaf: The roles of phonological codes. In M. Marschark & M.D. Clark (Eds.), *Psychological perspectives on deafness.* Hillsdale, NJ: Lawrence Erlbaum Associates.

Leybaert, J., & Alegría, J. (1993). Is word processing involuntary in deaf children? *British Journal of Developmental Psychology, 11*, 1–29.

Leybaert, J., & Alegría, J. (1995). Development of the use of linguistic regularities by deaf children in spelling. *Reading and Writing.*

Leybaert, J., Alegría, J., & Fonck, E. (1983). Automaticity in word recognition and word naming by the deaf. *Cahiers de Psychologie Cognitive, 3*, 255–272.

Liberman, A.M., & Mattingly, I.G. (1985). The motor theory of speech perception revised. *Cognition, 21*, 1–36.

Lupker, S.J., & Katz, A.N. (1981). Input, decision and response factors in picture–word interference. *Journal of Experimental Psychology: Human Learning and Memory, 7*, 269–282.

MacKain, K.S., Studdert-Kennedy, M., Spieker, S., & Stern, D. (1983). Infant intermodal speech perception is a left hemisphere function. *Science, 219*, 1347–1349.

Massaro, D.W. (1987). Speech perception by ear and eye. In B. Dodd & R. Campbell (Eds.), *Hearing by eye: The psychology of lip-reading* (pp. 53–83). Hove, UK: Lawrence Erlbaum Associates.

Massaro, D.W. (1989). Speech perception by ear and eye: A paradigm for psychological inquiry [Book review]. *Behavioral and Brain Sciences, 12*, 741–794.

McGurk, H., & MacDonald, J. (1976). Hearing lips and seeing voices. *Nature, 264*, 746–748.

Meltzoff, A.N., & Moore, K.M. (1977). Imitations of facial and manual gestures by human neonates. *Science, 198*, 75–78.

Nicholls, G.H. (1979). *Cued Speech and the reception of spoken language.* Unpublished master's thesis, McGill University, Montreal, Quebec, Canada.

Nicholls, G.H., & Ling, D. (1982). Cued Speech and the reception of spoken language. *Journal of Speech and Hearing Research, 25*, 262–269.

Patterson, K.E., & Morton, J. (1985). From orthography to phonology: An attempt at an old interpretation. In K.E. Patterson, J.C. Marshall, & M. Coltheart (Eds.), *Surface dyslexia: Neuropsychological and cognitive studies of phonological reading* (pp. 335–359). Hillsdale, NJ: Lawrence Erlbaum Associates.

Périer, O. (1987). L'enfant à audition déficiente. Aspects médicaux, éducatifs, sociologiques et psychologiques [The child with an auditory deficit: medical, educational, sociological, and psychological issues]. *Acta Oto-Rhino-Laryngologica Belgica, 41,* 129–420.

Périer, O., Charlier, B.L., Hage, C., & Alegría, J. (1988). Evaluation of the effects of prolonged Cued Speech practice upon the perception of spoken language. In I.G. Taylor (Ed.), *The education of the deaf: Current perspectives. Vol.1: International Congress on Education for the Deaf* (pp. 616–625). Beckenham, Kent, UK: Croom Helm, Ltd.

Pritchatt, D. (1968). An investigation into some of the underlying associative verbal processes of the Stroop color effect. *Quarterly Journal of Experimental Psychology, 20,* 351–359.

Radeau, M. (1994a). Auditory-visual spatial interaction and modularity. *Cahiers de Psychologie Cognitive, 13,* 3–51.

Radeau, M. (1994b). Ventriloquism against audio-visual speech: Or, where Japanese-speaking barn owls might help. *Cahiers de Psychologie Cognitive, 13,* 124–140.

Radeau, M., & Bertelson, P. (1977). Adaptation to auditory-visual discordance and ventriloquism in semirealistic situations. *Perception and Psychophysics, 22,* 137–146.

Radeau, M., & Bertelson, P. (1978). Cognitive factors and adaptation to auditory-visual discordance. *Perception and Psychophysics, 23,* 341–343.

Reisberg, D., McLean, J., & Goldfield, A. (1987). Easy to hear but hard to understand: A lip-reading advantage with intact auditory stimuli. In B. Dodd & R. Campbell (Eds.), *Hearing by eye: The psychology of lip-reading* (pp. 97–113). Hove, UK: Lawrence Erlbaum Associates.

Rosen, S.M., Fourcin, A.J., & Moore, B.C.J. (1981). Voice pitch as an aid to lip-reading. *Nature, 291,* 150–152.

Spoehr, K.T., & Corin, W.S. (1978). The stimulus suffix as a memory code phenomenon. *Memory and Cognition, 6,* 583–589.

Sumby, W., & Pollack, I. (1954). Visual contributions to speech visibility in noise. *Journal of the Acoustic Society of America, 26,* 212–215.

Summerfield, Q. (1987). Some preliminaries to a comprehensive account of audio-visual speech perception. In B. Dodd & R. Campbell (Eds.), *Hearing by eye: The psychology of lip-reading* (pp. 3–51). Hove, UK: Lawrence Erlbaum Associates.

Summerfield, Q. (1991). Visual perception of phonetic gestures. In I. G. Mattingly & M. Studdert-Kennedy (Eds.), *Modularity and the motor theory of speech perception* (pp. 117–137). Hillsdale, NJ: Lawrence Erlbaum Associates.

Swisher, L. (1976). The language performance of the oral deaf. In H. Whitaker & H. A. Whitaker (eds.), *Studies in Neurolinguistics* (Vol. 2, pp. 59–93). New York: Academic Press.

Taeschner, T., Devescovi, A., & Volterra, V. (1988). Affixes and function words in written language of deaf children. *Applied Psycholinguistics, 9,* 385–401.

Vroomen, J.H.M. (1992). *Having voices and seeing lips: Investigations in the psychology of lipreading.* Unpublished doctoral thesis, Katholieke Universiteit Brabant, Tilburg, The Netherlands.

Werker, J.F., & Tees, R.C. (1984). Cross-language speech perception: Evidence for perceptual reorganization during the first year of life. *Infant Behavior and Development, 7,* 49-63.

6

Parsing in Different Languages

Fernando Cuetos
Universidad de Oviedo
Oviedo, Spain

Don C. Mitchell
University of Exeter
Exeter, UK

Martin M.B. Corley
University of Exeter
Exeter, UK

A considerable body of modern science is concerned with the origins of structures and phenomena. Cosmologists engage in intense debate on the origins of the universe, biochemists speculate about the origins of life, and paleontologists and physical anthropologists discuss the origins of hominids and Homo sapiens. Similar debates have played a central part in discussions of numerous phenomena in the study of language (e.g., Bickerton, 1990). Researchers have investigated change, evolution, and innovation in language and have asked whether particular properties or features are innate—perhaps determined by the structure of the human mind—or whether they are acquired as a consequence of the language user's individual experiences. Although it is probably uncontentious that certain aspects of language are acquired (e.g., vocabulary, accents, and specific grammars or dialects), there is a strongly held view among linguists, in particular, that certain structural principles of language are universal and innate (Atkinson, 1992; Chomsky, 1986; Cook, 1988; Pinker, 1994; Radford, 1990). If this is true, it raises the possibility that some of the procedures that people use to process language may also be universal and innate. This question may be addressed at many different levels of language processing, but because of the prominent role of syntax in modern linguistic debate, one of the central battlegrounds in the nature/nurture war zone has been in the field of syntactic analysis or *parsing*. Inevitably, much of the debate revolves around whether a fixed set of parsing strategies is used to process the different languages of the world. The present chapter addresses this question, drawing heavily on empirical studies of sentence processing in Spanish and other Romance languages.

The function of the parser is to compute the syntactic structure of sentences, allowing the reader or listener to determine "who did what and to whom" and, more generally, to infer appropriate relationships between statements and entities expressed by the sentence. Among other things, its raw material consists of the order of occurrence of the individual words in the sentence, together with detailed information about these words (e.g., major category class; subcategorization information; inflections conveying information about number, gender and case; and so on). Other inputs include intonation, prosody, and punctuation.

The parsing process itself is typically completed very rapidly and without conscious awareness. For the most part, its workings are only laid bare when it constructs an erroneous analysis, holding up the operation of the rest of the sentence processing system. In normal circumstances, this occurs most frequently with ambiguous sentences, with the consequence that most of the empirical work on parsing focuses on trying to specify how the mechanism handles materials of this kind. For example, a typical test sentence might be one like (1):

(1)   Vi a Juan cuando iba a la playa
        I saw John going to the beach

Here, there is ambiguity about whether it Juan or the speaker who is going to the beach, and information about the preferred interpretations can provide a window onto the internal machinery of the parser. For comprehensive reviews of the basic empirical findings and their associated theoretical conclusions, the reader is referred to general surveys of the parsing literature (e.g., Frazier, 1987; Frazier & Clifton, 1996, chap.1; Mitchell, 1987b, translated into Spanish in Valle,

Cuetos, Igoa, & del Viso, 1990; Mitchell, 1994).

To address the question of whether these processes operate in essentially the same way from language to language, it is essential to spell out the major theoretical proposals in some detail.

TYPES OF PARSING THEORY

Parsing theories introduced since the 1970s can be classified into three broad categories based on their treatment of crosslinguistic variation (see Mitchell, Cuetos, & Zagar, 1990, for a review). First, there are theories that are essentially universal, in the sense that they assume that the computational machinery and strategies for parsing are effectively identical in all languages (e.g., Bever, 1970; Crocker, 1992; Frazier, 1987; Inoue & Fodor, 1995; Kimball, 1973; Pritchett, 1992). Of course, all such accounts have to make provision for the fact that, at the very least, detailed grammatical rules and items of vocabulary change from language to language. This is typically handled by assuming that language-specific information is made available to the parser in a manner analogous to the use of simple data files by a computer program in the way, for example, a spell-checking routine might uses files consisting of correctly spelled words. This view was apparently the one adopted by Frazier (1987) when she wrote: "we should be able to remove the grammar of English from our theory of sentence processing, plug in the grammar of some other language, and obtain the correct theory of processing of that language" (p.565). The second class of models assumes that the "customization" of parsers goes some way beyond file exchanges which simply replace one grammar with another. In these models, the data file provided by each language includes not only the grammar, but also information about the valence or priority assigned to certain operations in the parser's portfolio of strategies. The eventual choice of strategy can be seen as a consequence of parameter setting during grammar-acquisition, but the assumption is that it is the parsing strategy itself that changes, and not just the rules of the grammar that provide its raw material. These models range from those in which certain syntactic operations take precedence in individual languages (e.g., Gibson, Pearlmutter, Canseco-Gonzales, & Hickok, 1995), through intermediate proposals (e.g., Frazier & Rayner, 1988), to those in which the whole parsing strategy is changed radically (e.g., Mazuka & Lust, 1990). The third, and perhaps most radical class of theories assumes that the data file is subject to much more extreme forms of customization. In fact, they assume that the device starts off with a tabula rasa and goes on to use general learning algorithms during exposure to language to construct analysis procedures that can then be used to handle input (e.g., Bates & MacWhinney, 1987; St. John & McClelland, 1990). With theories of this kind, the parsing decisions are wholly determined by the specific history of training and may be completely specific to the device that has received the input.

In this chapter, we consider the potential of three different types of theory in relation to one fairly specific aspect of syntactic analysis: resolving the ambiguities that typically occur when modifying constructions, such as relative clauses, have to be attached to a word or phrase within a complex noun phrase (NP) in the manner illustrated in (2).

(2)   Someone shot the servant of the actress who was on the balcony.

Sentences of this kind will be referred to as NP-PP-RC sentences (since they included constituent sequences of the form: noun phrase - prepositional phrase - relative clause).

The basic problem is that when a modifier, such as *who was on the balcony,* is preceded by a complex NP in this way, it can typically be attached to more than one of the Ns within the NP–PP complex. Thus, sentence (2) could be interpreted as implying that either the servant or the actress was the person who was on the balcony. More technically, the modifier can be attached to more than one *head* or *host site* within the preceding constituent. To disambiguate the sentence, it is necessary to determine whether the modifier proposition applies to the first potential head or the second. Resolutions of the first kind are referred to as *NP1-attachment* (or *N1-attachment*), *early-attachment* or *high-attachment* (on the grounds that the first site is located at a higher point in the phrase marker for such structures). Correspondingly, links of the second kind are termed *NP2-, N2-, late-* or *low-attachments.*

Because one of the important functions of a parser is to resolve ambiguities of this kind, it is possible to examine fundamental properties of syntactic processing by determining whether such ambiguities are handled in a uniform way or whether the processing strategies vary from language to language. The reason for focusing on this particular structure is that the head-attachment ambiguity, and the associated parsing problems, occur in numerous languages across a range of typological classes. It therefore provides an ideal test case for evaluating the theories we have outlined and investigating the degree to which parsing machinery varies from language to language. In the next section, we consider a number of specific theoretical proposals concerning the resolution of ambiguities of this kind.

Universal Parsers

First, we consider proposals premised on the assumption that parsing procedures are essentially the same for all languages.

Traditional Garden Path Theories

The most widely discussed universal account of parsing is one referred to as the *garden path* theory (Frazier, 1979, 1987; Frazier & Rayner, 1982). This theory is concerned most fundamentally with the question of how the parser operates when it encounters structural ambiguity in the sentences it is required to analyze. The central claim is that, faced with alternative readings, the parsing device very rapidly selects a single interpretation and uses this as the basis for its continuing analysis of the sentence. Where this choice proves to be mistaken, a selection of reanalysis procedures is used to recompute the structural relations within the region of ambiguity (Ferreira and Henderson, 1991; Frazier and Rayner, 1992). A crucial feature of the model is that in the initial analysis, computational effort is devoted exclusively to the interpretation selected by the conflict-resolution device.

Within this framework, a major focus of attention has therefore concerned the way in which this initial analysis is selected. Frazier (1979, 1987) proposed that the decision is based on a small number of structural principles, all of which serve to increase the speed and efficiency with which new material can be incorporated into the ongoing analysis. Of these principles, the most important are Minimal Attachment and Late Closure, which were defined as follows:

(3)   Minimal Attachment: "Do not postulate any potentially unnecessary nodes." (Frazier, 1987, p.562).

(4)   Late Closure: "If grammatically permissible attach new items into the clause or phrase currently being processed (i.e. the phrase or clause postulated most recently)". (Frazier, 1987, p.562).

The principle of minimal attachment ensures that the parser selects for its first analysis a structure that is simple and quick to build, avoiding the additional work involved in assembling more complex structures. The late closure principle ensures that new constituents are immediately integrated with prior material, minimizing the chances of exceeding the memory limits of the sentence processing mechanism. Because these features would presumably produce benefits for all types of readers and listeners, Frazier (1987) argued that they should apply universally across all the languages of the world. Comparable claims for universal parsing strategies have been made by several other investigators (e.g. Bever, 1970; Kimball, 1973; see Mitchell and Cuetos, 1991a; Mitchell, et al., 1990, for reviews).

A comprehensive account of parsing has to say something about how the analysis proceeds once the initial structural choice has been made. In particular, there is pervasive evidence that the syntactic analysis of sentences can be influenced by nonsyntactic factors, such as semantic and discourse information and other contextual sources of influence. According to the garden path theory, these influences are handled, in part, by a device that is completely distinct from the mechanism responsible for making the initial structural choice. This device—originally called the *thematic processor* (Rayner, Carlson, & Frazier, 1983)—introduces information about the thematic relations that the words of the sentence are capable of entering and, in later extensions of the model, was also assigned wider functions in dealing with discourse and other context information (e.g., Clifton & Ferreira, 1989; Frazier, 1990b). Although there are no clear statements about the generality of these operations, in the absence of discussion of the way they may vary across languages, it seems safe to assume that, like the parsing strategies already considered, they are intended to be viewed as universal procedures that apply without exception to the different languages of the world.

In relation to the specific concern of this chapter with modifier attachment, the garden path model predicts that in sentences like (2), the RC should initially be attached to the phrase currently being processed; that is, it predicts low- or N2-attachment to *actress,* rather than high-attachment to *servant.* In another section, we discuss the evidence concerning this prediction.

The Refined Garden Path Theories

Following a series of studies discussed at length in the next section, Frazier (1990a) and de Vincenzi and Job (1993) elaborated considerably on the role of the second phase of processing within the framework of the garden path theory. Following the analysis in earlier versions of the model, Frazier (1990a) argued that once the initial structurally determined choice has been made, the second mechanism kicks in very quickly and sometimes triggers a complete revision of the structural analysis. The refinement consisted largely of a more systematic statement of the discourse-related workings of the second mechanism. In particular, Frazier (1990a) proposed that the device operates in accordance with what she referred to as the *relativized relevance* principle, outlined in (5):

(5)   Other things being equal (e.g., all interpretations are grammatical, informative, and appropriate to discourse), preferentially construe a phrase as being relevant to the main assertion of the current sentence (Frazier, 1990a, p.321).

In certain cases, this can result in a reading that is quite different from the one proposed by the first (structurally guided) mechanism, and the revised analysis is the one that will be most in evidence if the reader's commitments are checked at any point after the second-phase discourse mechanism has come into play.

In further elaborations of this account, de Vincenzi and Job (1993) suggested that there may be certain constraints on the circumstances in which the discourse mechanism can impose its revisions. In particular, they suggested that a phrase or clause can only be reconstrued as being "relevant" to a previously expressed assertion if this earlier assertion is in the same processing region as the constituent to which the clause is initially attached. The processing region they identified as being critical was one they termed the *theta domain:* roughly speaking, a set of words linked either to the last verb or to another word that is capable of assigning semantic roles to NPs (see de Vincenzi & Job, 1993, for details).

As with the original garden path theory, the features and operations of this refined version of the theory are also considered to be universal properties of human language systems.

What predictions does this refined version of the garden path model make in connection with the process of resolving ambiguities of modifier attachment? First, it implies that the RC in sentences like (2) should initially be attached low, to *actress.* At a later point in processing, however, the model predicts that this link should be broken and the modifier should be reattached high to *servant.* This revision should occur because the first phrase *(the servant)* is more likely to be closely connected with the main assertion of the sentence. The discourse interpretation mechanism should therefore follow the relativized relevance principle and shift the attachment from *actress* to *servant.* The end result of this sequence of operations is that high-attachment should prevail after the discourse effects have exerted their influence (cf. Clifton, 1988; de Vincenzi & Job, 1993; Frazier, 1990a).

Construal Theory

In a much more radical refinement of the garden path theory, Frazier, Clifton, and their colleagues (Carreiras & Clifton, 1993; Gilboy, Sopena, Clifton, & Frazier, 1995; Frazier & Clifton, in press) have proposed that the original parsing strategies (such as late closure and minimal attachment) only apply to a certain subset of the structural ambiguities that occur in any given language—namely, those concerned with clauses that are potentially or obligatorily dependent on the main predicate of the sentence, linkages that are termed *primary* relations. For other relations, the theory holds that, rather than being linked at a specific point in the developing phrase marker, the ambiguous material may merely be "construed" as being associated with the constituents within an entire theta domain. Thus, construal theory postulates that with nonprimary relations, such as RC attachment; there is no initial commitment to one structural analysis over another. The standard parsing strategies play no role at all, and all structural biases or preferences are introduced by thematic or discourse processing operations outlined in the garden path precursors to the theory.

This account, then, is explicitly characterized by the proposal that the standard parsing strategies do not apply universally. Instead, the suggestion is that they come into play exclusively for the purpose of analyzing a particular subset of ambiguous structures i.e., primary relations). However, this restriction to specific structures does not extend to its application to different languages. The primary strategies and construal mechanisms are assumed to apply universally across languages.

The prediction for processing sentences like (2) is that the RC should initially be construed or attached to a region incorporating both *servant* and *actress,* with no bias or commitment to one of them. A little later, Gricean and discourse principles would favor low-attachment (to *actress*) in English and high-attachment (to *servant*) in most other languages (cf. Frazier & Clifton, in press; Gilboy et al., 1995). The reason for predicting attachment to *actress* in English is that if the speaker/writer had intended to modify *actress* he or she could have avoided using the postnominal Norman form, selecting instead the unambiguous Saxon genitive, *The actress' servant, who was on the balcony:* Assuming the speaker observes Gricean maxims such as "Be clear," the use of the alternative form might be taken as being deliberate, serving to reduce the tendency to attach the RC to *servant* and shifting the emphasis in favor of low-attachment (to *actress*). In the absence of the alternative form, other languages would reflect a more widespread bias in favor of high-attachment (following principles like relativized relevance).

Parameterized Theories of Parsing

These are theories based, in part, on the fact that there are important qualitative differences between languages—as discussed by Chomsky's (1981, 1986) principles and parameters theory—and in much work on language acquisition (e.g., Atkinson, 1992; Radford, 1990). For example, languages can be classified as being *head-first* or *head-last, pro-drop* or *non-pro-drop,* and so on. The parsing theories considered in this section take into account one or more parameter settings for the language in question and incorporate this parameterized information into the ambiguity-resolving process (see Frazier & Rayner, 1988; Mazuka & Lust, 1990, for related proposals designed to handle ambiguities other than those highlighted here).

Parameterized competition with Special Purpose strategies

Modifier-Straddling Strategy. A simple, parameter-based proposal was put forward by Cuetos and Mitchell (1988; see also, Mitchell & Cuetos, 1991a; Mitchell et al., 1990). The suggestion was that, in certain very specific circumstances, general parsing strategies might not operate alone in determining the initial structural analysis to be pursued. Instead, from time to time they may have to compete with local special-purpose strategies that impose some pressure to select a competing analysis. The effectiveness of these local strategies may vary from language to language, and in particular, Cuetos and Mitchell (1988) suggested that their role might be determined, in part, by parameter-based linguistic properties of the languages under analysis.

The particular illustration used by Cuetos and Mitchell (1988) concerned strategies for handling the attachment ambiguities that are the subject of this chapter. With materials of the kind already discussed, they suggested that a special-purpose strategy may be operative in some languages. The strategy involved "jumping over the modifier" to attach RCs to the first NP in structures of the form NP-modifier-RC. A rationale was given for suggesting that this *modifier straddling* strategy should become an influential competing force in postmodifying languages (where adjectives follow the noun), but not in premodifying languages. The suggestion, then, was that the influence of the modifier-straddling strategy might be switched on in postmodifying languages, perhaps as a result of parameter-setting processes in the course of normal language acquisition.

In a system of this kind, the effects of a general parsing strategy could easily be swamped and reversed by the local effects of the special-purpose strategy. Given the premise that the local effects are parameter-linked, a system of this kind would not be completely universal, in the sense that it would not operate in precisely the same way when implemented in different languages. However, such a routine could be regarded as universal, with a limited amount of parametric variation.

Models of this kind predict that high-attachment preference should prevail in languages where the special-purpose strategy is switched on. Cuetos and Mitchell (1988) suggested that this might occur in languages where adjectives generally follow the nouns they modify (e.g., Spanish, Italian, and French). On this account, the first noun in a complex NP should be selected as the attachment site in languages in this class, whereas the pattern should be reversed in English, Dutch, German, and other premodifying languages.

The Recency/Predicate Proximity model. Recently, Gibson et al., (1995) proposed a somewhat more elaborate model based on parameterized competition between strategies. According to this account, the parser may weigh several different competing factors when making its preliminary structural decisions. For example, in trying to decide between two or more potential attachment sites for a modifier, it might be influenced by a preference to minimize site–modifier separations within the sentence on the one hand (*recency* preference), and a tendency to try to attach the modifier as closely as possible to an *S-node* within the phrase-marker description of the sentence *(predicate proximity)*. In sentences where the different tendencies pull in different directions, the decision about hosting the modifier would depend on the relative strengths of the competing influences. Gibson et al. showed that it is possible to obtain cross-linguistic variation in host preferences by postulating that the relative weight of one of these competing factors has at least two values and varies across languages. Where the effects of recency are weaker than those of predicate proximity, the model predicts a bias in favor of attaching modifiers high (to N1), whereas when the reverse is true the model predicts low, N2-attachment.

As with the model outlined in the previous section, this proposal can be regarded as describing a universal parser, but again with parametric variation.

Tuning Theory

In the previous section, we considered parsers that are subject to limited variation based on the settings of perhaps one or two parameters. It was in the spirit of these proposals that parser variation should be explained by assigning parameter values to entire languages or, arguably, even employing the same settings for entire classes of languages.

We now turn to a much more open-ended proposal, a suggestion that we have called the *tuning hypothesis* (Mitchell, 1994; Mitchell & Cuetos, 1991a; Mitchell, Cuetos, & Corley, 1992). The suggestion is that the initial choice of structural analyses in parsing is determined not by general principles (whether parameterized or not), but by the experience the individual reader or listener may have had on previous encounters with ambiguities of the same kind. Put simply, the proposal is that, faced with an ambiguity, the reader/listener will initially opt for the resolution that has turned out to be appropriate most frequently in the past. Thus, the model proposes that ambiguities are not resolved by any fixed or universal rule, but that their resolution varies according to the individual's exposure to comparable examples in his or her prior experience with the language. Each time a person encounters and resolves a specific form of ambiguity, the syntactic processing mechanism adjusts itself marginally to take account of the new solution. Once the ambiguity has been resolved in a given direction, the mechanism is adjusted in such a way that there will be a slightly greater possibility of choosing that resolution in subsequent encounters with the ambiguous form in question. The more an interpretation has appeared and worked successfully in the past, the higher the chance it will have of being chosen again in the future.

A statistical or experience-based mechanism of this kind would presumably iterate toward a different solution for each ambiguity in its repertoire. If the patterns of resolution in the raw material (i.e., the choices intended by speakers and writers) were themselves governed by some overriding linguistic principles, then an exposure-based parser of this kind would mimic these principles, but in doing so it would not be incorporating the principles themselves. Faced with a totally arbitrary ensemble of resolution patterns, it would home in on the more probable choices just as readily as it would when handling a highly regulated training corpus.

A model of this kind can be regarded as incorporating a fairly extreme form of parameter setting. In any given language, the conflict-resolving mechanism for selecting the initial parse would be informed by the values of perhaps several dozen parameters; varying on continuous scales. Clearly, an account of this kind would be less parsimonious than any model based on a much smaller number of parameters. However, parsimony aside, this type of model could provide a ready explanation of any crosslinguistic variation there may be in the process of ambiguity resolution.

Of course, the tuning hypothesis is based on universal principles of its own. The suggestion is that for all languages the initial reading of an ambiguous constituent will be governed by the statistical properties of that particular ambiguity in the language under consideration. It is just the specific decisions that will be subject to crosslinguistic variation.

Turning to the predictions for RC attachment, the preferred host would be the one that is used most often when comparable ambiguities are resolved in the language under examination. Using a small-scale corpus analysis, Mitchell, et al. (1992) found that in English most of the ambiguities of the form NP1-*of*-NP2-RC were resolved in favor of NP2-attachment. (Indeterminate attachments were excluded from the analysis.) In contrast, a Spanish corpus showed a bias in the opposite direction. The pattern of preferences to be expected on the basis of tuning, then, is one of low-attachment in English and high-attachment in Spanish, with predictions for other languages depending on the details of the corresponding corpus analyses.

Totally Data-Shaped Parsers

The tuning hypothesis is concerned exclusively with the task of determining the initial reading of structurally ambiguous material, and in its current form has nothing at all to say about how the syntactic analysis proceeds beyond this (e.g., how structures are built, how grammatical constraints are monitored, or how reanalysis is handled). However, there is a class of experience-based models that is considerably more ambitious than this. We refer to them here as *totally data-shaped parsers*. According to this type of account, shaping goes beyond determining the initial analysis to be pursued in ambiguous structures: The entire computational machinery for syntactic analysis is assembled on the basis of sustained exposure to language, and the final product is molded by semantic and discourse factors, as well as by strictly syntactic considerations. Tuning processes of this kind play a major role in several language acquisition experiments carried out within the competition model (Bates & MacWhinney, 1987; MacWhinney, 1987). Similarly, in neural network models (McClelland & Rumelhart, 1981; Seidenberg & McClelland, 1989), processing preferences are also determined by exposure to language.

Like the tuning hypothesis, the performance of data-shaped parsers would be expected to reflect the biases represented within the training materials. As before, then, the prediction for relative clause attachment is that the parsing bias should reflect the bias in the corpus statistics. That is, low-attachment should prevail in English and high-attachment in Spanish.

Summary of Models of Modifier Attachment

The proposals summarized until now are concerned with explaining the workings of the rapid-acting parsing system that allocates modifier information to one or another of the potential hosts within a complex NP. The presentation highlights theoretical differences in the extent to which the models view the parsing mechanism as being specially adapted for different languages. As a corollary to this, the various accounts differ markedly in the status they give to late closure or recency. At one extreme, late closure is treated as a central principle for guiding parsing decisions; at the other, it is assigned no real role in the process (although no one rules out the possibility that there is a correlation between Recency and the statistical prevalence of attachment). Between these limits, the principle is seen as a bias that has to compete with others to influence parsing choices. At the heart of the difference between the models is the question of whether these tendencies are hard-wired or are honed by experience.

EVALUATION OF THE THEORIES IN LIGHT OF EMPIRICAL EVIDENCE

We start by outlining a number of general findings concerning the way attachment ambiguity is handled in different languages. In later sections, we go on to consider the implications these results have for the various parsing theories we hav outlined. Within these sections, we also introduce and discuss further, more detailed investigations that have been conducted to evaluate a number of more specific issues within the area.

Basic Observations

Most of the current discussion of the competing parsing theories revolves around their predictions concerning preferred attachments when complex NPs are followed by modifiers (particularly, RCs).

The issue was first examined by Cuetos and Mitchell (1988). In a questionnaire study using NP-PP-RC sentences like (6a-b), we simply followed each item with a question designed to establish how the subjects had resolved the ambiguity.

(6)   a. Someone shot the servant of the actress who was on the balcony.
        b. Alguien disparó contra el criado de la actriz que estaba en el balcón.

The questions were of the form: "Who was on the balcony?" for (6a) and "¿Quién estaba en el balcón?" for (6b), and subjects were required to give a one-word answer in each case. The English readers showed a reliable preference for attaching the RC to the second site (i.e., *actress* was selected on 58% of occasions), whereas the Spanish readers opted predominantly for the first site (*criado* was chosen on 62% of trials).

The Spanish bias in favor of high-attachment was corroborated in a self-paced reading study using materials in which an extra phrase was added to force a low-attachment resolution at the end of the sentence. In the case of (6b), this was achieved by adding the phrase *con su marido* (with her husband). Our assumption was that if our subjects had opted to attach the RC to *criado* (a masculine head-noun) prior to reading this phrase, they would then be faced with the anomaly of a male person being *con su marido*. Assuming that this would trigger reanalysis (disconnecting the RC from criado and reattaching it to *actriz*), we predicted that the reading time would be relatively long. In fact, the results showed that the time taken to read this display was reliably longer than it was in control conditions in which subjects had no need to shift the attachment from one site to another. High-attachment preferences have subsequently been confirmed in numerous questionnaire and reading-time studies using comparable Spanish materials (e.g., Carreiras, 1992; Carreiras & Clifton, 1993; Gilboy et al., 1995; Mitchell & Cuetos, 1991a, 1991b; Mitchell, et al., 1990, and in several unpublished studies we have carried out in Oviedo).

The results show a clear preference for N1- or high-attachment in NP-*de*-NP-RC structures in Spanish. The pattern of findings for English, however, has been less consistent. Mitchell and Cuetos (1991b) reported two further questionnaire studies confirming the earlier evidence for low-attachment preference. However, C. Clifton (personal communication, 1995) obtained the reverse result when the identical questionnaire was used in Massachusetts. Furthermore, using a different questionnaire, Clifton (1988) found additional evidence in favor of high-attachment in American English. To complicate issues further, Clifton and his colleagues have shown clear evidence of low-attachment in at least two different on-line studies using RC with reflexive pronouns (Carreiras & Clifton, 1993; Clifton, 1988; Frazier, 1990a). Several other studies have shown no on-line bias in either direction (e.g., Carreiras & Clifton, 1993, plus several unpublished studies from our lab in Exeter). Overall, the results appear to indicate that the attachment biases in English are reliably different from those in Spanish (however, see Gilboy et al., 1995, who, although documenting further differences, elected to emphasize the overall similarity of the biases shown in a range of different types of structure). Several studies indicate that the shift in preference may be marked enough to reverse the Spanish bias (favoring low- rather than high-attachment). However, for reasons that are not well understood, this particular finding cannot always be replicated reliably.

Following the early investigations, similar on- and off-line studies have been carried out in several other languages. In most cases, the results point to a high-attachment bias similar to that obtained in Spanish. High-attachment preferences have been found in questionnaire studies in French (Mitchell, et al, 1990), Italian (de Vincenzi and Job, 1993), Dutch (Brysbaert & Mitchell, 1993), German (Hemforth, Konieczny, and Scheepers, 1994), and Russian (V. Kempe & R. Radach, personal communication, 1993). On-line results have typically corroborated these conclusions (e.g., Zagar & Pynte, 1992, in French; Brysbaert & Mitchell, 1993, in Dutch). In contrast with this, though, de Vincenzi and Job (1993) claimed to have provided on-line evidence for an immediate low-attachment in Italian. However, as Carreiras and Clifton (1993) have pointed out, this particular result may be subject to segmentation artifacts (discussed further on).

The results considered so far have been concerned with two- site sentences including prepositional phrases with the preposition *of* (or its translation in various languages). For the sake of completeness, it should be mentioned that several studies have shown that the pattern of preferences is altered when different prepositions are used in place of *of* (e.g., Clifton, 1988; Frazier, 1990a; Gilboy et al., 1995; de Vincenzi, & Job, 1993). The experimental evidence on preposition effects is discussed in more detail further on.

So far, we have restricted ourselves to materials in which there are just two potential attachment sites within the complex RC. However, Gibson et al. (1995) have recently gone beyond this to examine the patterns of preferences in three-site materials of the form NP-PP-PP-RC.

They conducted a series of studies in which Spanish–English bilingual subjects were required to indicate whether sentence fragments were grammatically acceptable or not. On a proportion of the trials the verb in the RC agreed (in number) with the first noun, as in (7a). On others, it agreed with the second, as in (7b), or the third (7c).

(7)   a. (...) la lámpara cerca de las pinturas de las casas que fue dañada en la inundación.
        (...) the lamp near the paintings of the houses which was damaged in the flood

        b. (...) las lámparas cerca de la pintura de las casas que fue dañada en la inundación.
        (...) the lamps near the painting of the houses which was damaged in the flood

        c. (...) las lámparas cerca de las pinturas de la casa que fue dañada en la inundación.
        (...) the lamps near the paintings of the house which was damaged in the flood

The results for on-line grammaticality judgment studies for both Spanish and English showed that viewing time for the disambiguating material in the region of the verb dañada was longest for (7b), shortest for (7c), and intermediate for (7a). An off-line study in English revealed a comparable order ((7b) < (7a) < (7c)) for judgments of grammaticality.

In every case considered up to now, the attachment ambiguity has involved linking a RC to a complex made up of a NP followed by one or more prepositional phrases. However, this is not the only kind of structure that can offer competing attachment sites for a subsequent modifying constituent. The same problem may arise with NP-RC-RC sentences like (8).

(8)   Pedro miraba los libros que pertenecían a la chica que...
        Peter was looking at the books that belonged to the girl who/which...

To examine attachment preferences in cases like this, Mitchell and Cuetos (1991a) presented subjects with sentence fragments like (8) and instructed them to complete the sentence in any way they thought plausible. In these circumstances, a continuation with a plural verb would indicate high-attachment to the plural NP *los libros,* whereas a singular verb continuation would suggest low-attachment to *la chica.* The results showed that with these structures subjects had a very strong propensity to attach low (i.e., to the second site).

These findings suggest that attachment preferences depend crucially on the precise internal structure of the complex NP embracing the competing attachment sites. Like all the other findings we have outlined, this is a result that will have to be explained by any viable model of attachment resolution. We now turn to a detailed evaluation of the way in which different models account for these data.

Universal Accounts

Evaluation of the Garden Path theory

Taken at face value, these findings argue against an important aspect of the garden path theory, namely, that the initial attachment of the RC in sentences like (2) should be determined by exactly the same principles in all languages. More specifically, given that principles like minimal attachment do not discriminate between the alternative interpretations of a sentence, the theory specifies that the initial attachment should always be governed by the late closure principle. In other words, the RC should be attached systematically to the second of the two potential attachment sites, rather than the first. The fact that this does not occur raises problems for the garden path theory.

In an early defense of the traditional form of the theory, Clifton (1988) identified several different potential problems in the Cuetos and Mitchell (1988) study. He suggested that the increased reading time for the final display might have occurred not because subjects were forced to reassess a mistaken initial attachment (as we had assumed), but because extra time was required simply to handle a constituent that could potentially be attached to more than one site. On this kind of interpretation, the original findings would not necessarily be taken as evidence against late closure.

In order to evaluate this criticism, Mitchell and Cuetos (1991b) conducted an experiment including conditions that forced early closure, as well as late closure. In this study, there was also a control condition in which neither analysis was rejected in favor of the other. Overall, there were four types of sentences: materials in which late closure was forced (e.g., (9a)), sentences in which early closure was forced (9b), a control condition that could be interpreted by following either early or late closure (9c), and a control nonambiguous condition (9d).

(9)   a. Alguien disparó contra el criado de la actriz / que estaba en el balcón / con su marido.
b. Alguien disparó contra la criada del actor / que estaba en el balcón / con su marido.
c. Alguien disparó contra la criada de la actriz / que estaba en el balcón / con su marido.
d. Alguien disparó contra la actriz / que estaba en el balcón / con su marido.

The results showed that the reading time for the final display, *con su marido* (with her husband), was enhanced only when it forced the reader to adopt the late closure reading (i.e., in (9a)). There were no differences in the three remaining conditions indicating that neither ambiguity per se in (9c) nor forcing early closure (Condition (b)) had the same effect as forcing late closure. Contrary to Clifton's (1988) suggestions, this indicates that there is a genuine bias against late closure in materials of this kind, and that with materials like (9a), readers have to expend effort in overcoming this bias in settling on an appropriate late closure analysis.

Another methodological problem raised by C. Clifton (personal communication, 1988) was that the segmentation employed in the early studies might have biased readers against late closure interpretations. In the Cuetos and Mitchell (1988) study, the sentences were presented in three displays, and the segmentation of the first display always coincided with the end of the NP-PP phrase *el criado de la actriz* (the servant of the actress). Because segmentation is known to influence parsing decisions (e.g., Mitchell, 1987a), it is possible that this altered subjects' biases. However, in later experiments, Mitchell and Cuetos (1991b) and Carreiras (1992) found that the results were essentially unchanged when the segmentation of the materials was altered in such a way that the two first displays of the earlier materials no appeared together (e.g., *Alguien disparó contra el criado de la actriz que estaba en el balcón* or *Somebody shot the servant of the actress who was on the balcony*. Thus there is no evidence to suggest that artificial segmentations of the materials introduced biases that were not already evident from other sources.

Taken together, the findings provide increasing evidence that the late closure strategy is not a procedure that is used to the exclusion of others to settle ambiguities involving modifier attachment. Evidence against low-attachment bias has since been corroborated in several other languages besides Spanish (as noted earlier). At the very least, other factors must be involved in interpreting modifiers in each of these languages.

Evaluation of the Refined Garden Path Theory

Given this clear evidence in favor of high-attachment biases, Clifton (1988) and Frazier 1990a) then focused on another potential weakness of the original study: that the bias was first tested several words after the point near the beginning of the RC where the initial commitment should theoretically have been made. In effect, they acknowledged that there was a high-attachment bias at this relatively late point in the sentence, but attributed this to the effects of a second, discourse-based, phase of processing that reversed the initial bias (still held to be determined by late closure). As spelled out before, this second, lagging, operation has long been accorded an important function in the garden path theory. However, prior to the modifier-attachment studies, its postulated activities had been restricted to those associated with the assignment of thematic roles (e.g., Rayner et al., 1983) and to certain context effects (e.g., Ferreira & Clifton, 1986). In 1990, apparently as a direct response to the Spanish attachment data, Frazier (1990a) elaborated on these proposals, introducing the notion that the second-phase operation also includes specifically discourse-related strategies designed to ensure that modifiers are normally linked up with material that is at or near the "focus" of the text being processed (cf. the relativized relevance principle, Frazier, 1990a, described earlier). Because this involves novel extensions to the original theory, we refer to it as the *refined* version of the model (see also, de Vincenzi & Job, 1993, for further adjustments along these lines).

The refined theory provides a straightforward account of the high-attachment biases that have emerged in the majority of modifier attachment studies. Within a complex NP the first noun is the head of the entire phrase and is arguably the main assertion or *focus* of the constituent. According to the elaborated theory, therefore, this is precisely the site to which the discourse mechanism would be expected to attach the RC. So, Frazier (1990a) accounted for the high-attachment data by maintaining that the demonstrated biases reflect the state of play in the sentence processing mechanism after the discourse operation has exerted its influence.

In support of a discourse element of processing, Frazier (1990a) pointed to evidence that attachment bias is apparently influenced by the informativeness of the RC. In particular, she reported a questionnaire study comparing people's interpretations of clauses carrying very little information (e.g., locatives, such as *who were on the balcony*) with modifiers conveying more informative, attributive information (e.g., the relative clause in *Julie met the friend of the man who reads news on Saturday Night Live*). In line with the refined model, the results showed that the high-attachment preference was more marked in locative sentences (70%) than in the attributive materials (59%).

Although there appears to be some support for the refined version of the garden path model, this account is difficult to reconcile with the data in a number of respects.

The first problem concerns the absence of any clear evidence that reanalysis plays a systematic role in on-line studies of modifier attachment. In the past, wherever there has been persuasive evidence for reanalysis, the effects have been reflected in fairly sizable latency variations (e.g., Frazier, 1987; Frazier, Clifton & Randall, 1983; Frazier & Rayner, 1982; Mitchell, 1987a, 1987b). If comparable operations had played a role in modifier attachment, there should have been similar latency effects in appropriate circumstances. In particular, there should have been clear signs of revision effects (shifts from low- to high-attachment) in all sentences that ultimately showed a high-attachment preference. However, there was no sign of such effects in several different studies (see Mitchell & Cuetos, 1991b, for detailed discussions and analysis). In fact, until now, no study in Spanish—or indeed, in French (Zagar & Pynte, 1992)—has yielded any evidence that there is a phase of processing in which low-attachment bias systematically prevails, and so it is not even clear that the preconditions for these reanalysis effects can be demonstrated.

In contrast with the evidence for Spanish and French, there have been claims that there is a low-attachment (late closure) phase of processing in Dutch and Italian. However, as argued further on, these claims are questionable, and the evidence in support of attachment followed by reattachment remains uncertain.

The evidence for late closure in Dutch was offered by Flores d'Arcais (1990). It was based on ambiguous sentences like (10):

(10)   Jan zag Anneke lopend op het strand.
        John saw Anne running on the beach.

In sentences of this kind, it could be either Jan or Anneke, or both, who were running on the beach. When the sentence was disambiguated with a new sentence indicating that the first person was the one who was running (e.g., *hij was moe,* he was tired), it took subjects longer to read this test sentence than it did when it was disambiguated in favor of the second attachment site (using continuations such as *ze was moe,* she was tired). Although this provides superficial support for the notion that there is a phase of processing in which low-attachment dominates, it falls a long way short of providing definitive endorsement for the view that comparable biases occur in processing NP-PP-RC sentences. For a start, the sentence structure in (10) is totally different, and it is not at all obvious that it is possible to make direct comparisons with the earlier studies. Second, the Flores d'Arcais (1990) experiment involved testing attachment bias after the end of the clause and so, within the framework of the refined theory, it is implausible to argue that the results can be taken as reflecting biases in the initial rather than the later (discourse-based), stage of processing. (Hence, the high-attachment bias is, in fact, completely contrary to expectation, rather than suportive of the theory.) Third, and perhaps most important, the biases in sentences like (10) can be reversed by exchanging one verb for another in the matrix clause (Brysbaert & Mitchell, in press) and cannot therefore be taken as reflecting late closure effects within the Refined garden path theory.

The ostensible support for a recency-governed phase of processing in Italian comes from the de Vincenzi & Job (1993) study we have mentioned several times.

Subjects were presented sentences like (11) in a self-paced reading task, with successive displays marked by the oblique lines (/) in the example.

(11)   L'avvocado diffida / del padre / della ragazza / che si e'tradita-o / al processo.
The lawyer suspects / the father / of the girl / who betrayed herself-himself / at the trial.

Although various aspects of the data appeared to suggest that subjects eventually elected to attach the ambiguous RC high (i.e., to *padre*), the reading latencies for Display 4 turned out to be significantly longer when the (gender-related) contents of the display forced high-attachment (e.g., *che si e'tradito*) than when they forced low-attachment (*che si e'tradita*) de Vincenzi and Job (1993) interpreted this as evidence that the RC is initially attached low (to *ragazza*), but is later decoupled and reconnected to the higher site (*padre*). Going beyond the data, they argued that the parser initially adopts the late closure strategy, and that this preliminary analysis is later overruled by interpretative processes. However, there are problems with this inference, as various investigators (e.g., Carreiras & Clifton, 1993; Frazier & Clifton, in press) have pointed out. Specifically, in contrast to all previous studies of RC attachment, the two potential attachment sites here (*padre* and *ragazza*) were presented in different displays, with the first being removed from view before the second appeared. Because the two sites were not treated in an equivalent fashion, this may have produced an artificial bias in favor of *ragazza*. In support of this possibility, Brysbaert and Mitchell (1993) have shown that parsing biases (in Dutch) can be influenced by altering the way in which the material is segmented. The implication of this is that it is not yet clear whether de Vincenzi and Job's (1993) early low-attachment biases reflect anything other than a segmentation artifact[1].

In short, contrary to the refined theory, there is no clear support for the view that there is a brief phase of analysis during which the RC is temporarily attached low prior to being reattached to the competing site once discourse processes come into play. Nor is there any evidence that time-consuming reanalysis takes place at the points in sentences where these revisions are hypothesized to occur.

This lack of support for the refined theory is also evident in the failure to find evidence that attachment preferences are strongly affected by discourse and semantic considerations. If the putative second phase of processing had been dominated by such effects in the way proposed, then attachment preferences would have been expected to be strongly influenced by semantic and discourse manipulations. However, both Carreiras (1992) and Zagar and Pynte (1992) have failed to obtain such effects. Carreiras (1992) used NP-PP-RC sentences that were semantically biased toward a low-attachment interpretation (e.g., *Alguien disparó contra el criado de la actriz que estaba en el escenario* or *Someone shot the servant of the actress who was on the stage*). Contrary to the hypothesis that attachments are strongly affected by semantic considerations, he found that subjects continued to show a preference for high-attachment in the face of clear semantic biases. Similarly, Zagar and Pynte (1992) failed to induce changes in attachment preferences when they manipulated discourse context to favor low- rather than high-attachment.

In summary, several of the central features of the refined theory have failed to find empirical support in recent studies, and on the present evidence, this modified version of the theory does not seem to be substantially more viable than the garden path theory in its original form.

Construal Theory

The crucial difference between construal theory and the revised garden-path

---

[1]De Vincenzi and Job (in press) have recently repeated the experiment using a different pattern of segmentation. As in the earlier study, reading latency was reliably shorter when the gender marking of the reflexive verb was compatible with low-attachment. In light of these new findings, it is less plausible to write these biases off as segmentation artifacts.

theory is that RCs are treated as nonprimary relations, which are therefore not initially attached to any particular site within the complex NP. Instead, they are *construed* or associated in a general way with an extended sentence region organized around a single verb, in a theta domain. In the absence of differential links within the theta domain, construal differs from refined garden path theory in that it is not undermined by failures to demonstrate successive phases of analysis in which low-attachment is later replaced by high-attachment. Also, in construal theory, the eventual attachment is determined by a wide variety of considerations, including discourse and focus effects, Gricean principles, and semantic information. Given this multiplicity of influences, the theory is not compromised in any way by the failure to show evidence of any particular kind of effect in this stage of processing. Unlike the refined garden path theory, therefore, it is not seriously weakened by the failure to demonstrate that semantic and discourse biases are capable of influencing the final attachment.

Construal theory offers fairly simple accounts of the main findings on parsing preferences in modifier-attachment studies. In structures with complex NPs that include the preposition *of* (or its cognates), the general preference for high-attachment in languages other than English is attributed to the effects of discourse focus operations that take place in the second phase of processing. Principles such as relativized relevance are used to account for the fact that RCs typically end up being linked to the first, and theoretically more focused, attachment site. The fact that there is less propensity for high attachment to occur in English (e.g., Carreiras & Clifton, 1993; Cuetos & Mitchell, 1988) is attributed essentially to the fact that the second phase of processing proceeds on the basis that the writer or speaker always makes an effort to be clear (i.e., that the material to be analyzed conforms to the Gricean maxim of clarity). Frazier (1990a) pointed out that, although there is ambiguity concerning the way modifiers should be attached to postnominal (or Norman) genitives of the form *the servant of the actress,* the same problem does not occur with the prenominal or Saxon genitive form (e.g., *the actress' servant*). In this second case, subsequent modifiers can only be attached to *servant.* Following the Gricean principle that writers and speakers always try to be clear and avoid ambiguity, Frazier (1990a) has argued that they would elect to use the Saxon genitive if they wanted to signal that the modifier is intended to be associated with the head of the complex NP (*servant*). Using the Norman genitive form, therefore, would be a signal that the modifier should be interpreted as being attached to the alternative site (i.e., the nonhead, *actress*). Armed with this information about the alternative interpretations of different expressions, a reader or listener would be biased in the direction of interpreting modifiers following Norman genitives as being attached to the nonhead (i.e., the second site in the complex NP). In contrast with this, languages that do not have the two alternative genitive forms (such as Spanish) would not be subject to the same kind of bias or pressure to choose the nonhead attachment with structures of exactly the same kind (see also, de Vincenzi & Job, 1993; Gilboy et al., 1992).

Although these observations seem to do a good job in explaining the differences between English and the various Romance languages, recent evidence suggests that the Gricean account makes exactly the wrong predictions when it comes to certain other languages that have both Saxon and Norman genitive forms. For example, the proposal wrongly predicts that low-attachment preference should prevail in Dutch and German, which, as already indicated, both seem to show a high-attachment bias (see Brysbaert & Mitchell, in press, for a detailed discussion of this issue). This means that, at least as currently formulated, construal theory lacks a convincing account of crosslinguistic differences in resolution biases in NP-PP-RC sentences.

In contrast, construal theory has a ready explanation for Mitchell and Cuetos' (1991b) observation that Spanish readers seem to show a strong low-attachment preference in identifying modifier heads within complex NPs of the form NP-RC-RC. As indicated earlier, the initial construal process attaches a modifier to an entire theta domain, and then, if there are alternative hosts within this domain, the interpretative processes in the second phase are left to make the final decision. With NP-PP structures, both potential modifier hosts will be within the critical theta domain, and discourse/focus processes will typically cause the first to be selected (as outlined). However, with NP-RC structures, the theta domain will not extend beyond the RC. Because this included just a single potential host in the sentences used by Mitchell and Cuetos (1991b), the theory predicts that this NP will be chosen unambiguously as the attachment site for the final modifier.

This provides a neat explanation of the original observations with *pertenecia* sentences (see our earlier discussion of the finding relating to sentence (8) above). However, the results of a recent study suggest that this proposal may not be entirely adequate as a description of immediate processing in sentences of this kind. In particular, it seems that on-line measures (as opposed to off-line questionnaire measures) fail to show any statistical preference for the second, as opposed to the first, attachment site (Mitchell, Cuetos, & Brysbaert, 1994). According to construal theory a shift to the earlier NP involves detaching the modifier from its preferred theta-domain: a change which should trigger a full-scale reanalysis, causing an increment in processing time which should theoretically be just as large as that associated with any other instance of parsing reanalysis. The fact that this did not occur suggests that the account of ambiguity resolution currently offered by construal theory may be incomplete.

One finding that poses problems for construal theory (and, indeed, for any other universal account of parsing) is that there are stable individual differences in preferences for high- or low-attachment. If it were really true that host selection is determined by interpretative procedures that have universal application, then one would not expect to find systematic differences in biases for different readers. However, questionnaire studies show that people do, in fact, differ significantly in their tendencies to opt for interpretations consistent with high- and low-attachment (Brysbaert & Mitchell, 1993; Mitchell, 1988). In the most detailed examination of this phenomenon to date, Corley (1995) tested 52 subjects on two parallel forms of a questionnaire administered 3 weeks apart. Informants were given incomplete sentences like (12a-b), with noun order and number marking counterbalanced over questionnaire forms.

(12)   a. The court heard about the investigator(s) of the murder(s)...
         b. The court heard about the murder(s) of the investigator(s)...

The task was to provide a completion for the sentence starting with either *who* or *which* followed immediately by either *was* or *were*. In the overwhelming majority of cases, the choice of relative pronoun and verb number was sufficient to indicate whether the subject intended the RC to be attached high or low. The results showed a very high positive correlation ($r = 0.799$, df = 50, $p < .001$) between the proportions of low-attachment choices in the first and second tests. This confirms not only that there are substantial individual differences in attachment preference (figures in this study ranged from 0% to 100% low-attachment), but also that these effects are stable over a substantial period of time and are therefore not likely to be attributable to temporary priming effects and other similar short-lived phenomena.

To account for these findings, the construal theory would, at the very least, have to acknowledge that there must be individual differences in the way different people deploy their parsing and interpretative machinery, a concession that goes against the spirit of any truly universal processing mechanism. If a universal system can be configured in different ways by individual users, then, rather than being completely universal, it must at least be subject to parametric variation. It is to this possibility that we turn in the next section.

Evaluation of Parameterized Accounts

Strategy Competition Models

The original, highly speculative, version of this account was that there is competition between late closure and a special-purpose strategy that deals exclusively with attaching post positioned modifiers to NPs. Specifically, Cuetos and Mitchell (1988) speculated about the role of what we have referred to as the *modifier-straddling* strategy, which is switched on in languages in which adjectives normally precede the noun and switched off in languages with postnominal adjectives. On this account, late closure would be unchallenged in languages like English, whereas in postmodifying languages this strategy would be counterbalanced and potentially overwhelmed, culminating in a high-attachment bias and thus providing a satisfactory account of the early data. However, subsequent research has shown that this particular variant of the model is almost certainly not viable. First, de Vincenzi and Job (1993) observed that in Italian (a postmodifying language in which the straddling strategy should be active), it is easy to find sentences structured like *the servant of the actress who...* examples, but contradict the hypothesis by being interpreted in such a way that they show a low-attachment bias. They pointed out that this can occur even when semantic considerations strongly favor the alternative attachment (e.g., in *Il vino dello zio allungato con l'acqua,* The wine of the uncle diluted with water). Thus, the straddling strategy does not seem to be active in certain sentences in a language where it should be influential. Furthermore, recent data from Dutch show that the putative special-purpose strategy appears to be active in a language in which the straddling strategy should be switched off. Specifically, Brysbaert and Mitchell (1993) found that there were clear high-attachment biases in Dutch, despite the fact that it is a premodifying language. Recent evidence suggests the same may be true of German (R. Radach & V. Kempe, personal communication, 1988). Clearly, if there is a parameter-controlled special-purpose strategy that competes with late closure, the activation of this strategy is not intimately connected with adjective–noun order.

A potentially more plausible candidate for the special-purpose procedure is the one guided by Gibson et al.'s (1995) predicate proximity principle, which introduces a bias in favor of attaching modifiers as closely as possible to the root of a predicate (such as a verb phrase). With structures of the form NP-PP-RC, such a principle would bias the final clause attachment in favor of the first NP, because this node is closer to the predicate incorporating the complex NP as a whole. Gibson et al. (1994) proposed that the cost associated with attaching a modifier to a NP at a fixed distance away from a predicate may be a value that varies parametrically from one language to another. Thus, languages like Spanish and French might be characterized by high parameter values (or costs), with the consequence that nonproximal attachments are strongly discouraged, effectively supporting high-attachment resolutions. Other languages (like English) might have lower values, resulting in weaker biases in favor of high-attachment.

According to the model presented by Gibson et al. (1995), the eventual choice of attachment is governed by the balance of costs imposed by these and other kinds of competing influences. With modifier-attachment sentences of the kind being examined here the main competitor would be recency preference, a bias that favors recent over more distant attachment sites and operates with equal force across languages. To account for the data, Gibson et al. (1995) merely assume that predicate proximity is strong enough to overwhelm the effects of recency preference in some languages (such as Spanish and French), although in other languages (e.g., English), its effects are relatively weak, allowing recency to prevail.

To investigate this hypothesis, Gibson et al. (in press) conducted a series of studies using sentence fragments including three potential attachment sites:

(13)   ... la lámpara cerca de las pinturas de las casas que fue dañada en la inundación.
The lamp near the paintings of the houses which was damaged in the flood

According to the model, the first site (N1) should be favored over N2 and N3 by predicate proximity, whereas recency preference should bias attachments in favor of N3 over N2, and, in turn, of N2 over N1. By making certain simplifying mathematical assumptions, Gibson et al. (1995) predicted that at the outcome of these competing processes, subjects' overall preference would be to attach to N3 more than to N1, with both preferred to N2.

As outlined in the recency/predicate proximity model, Gibson et al. (1995) carried out on- and off-line grammaticality judgment studies to assess the attachment preferences in three-site sentences. As indicated earlier, the results confirmed the predictions. Gibson et al. therefore took the data as support for their proposal that attachment preferences are decided by the balance of two competing principles: predicate proximity and recency. By hypothesis, the same kind of competition would occur in two-site structures of the kind we have discussed at length in this chapter. In particular, the suggestion is that the universal attachment bias (recency Preference) is counterbalanced to different degrees by the varying effects of a language-related special-purpose strategy (predicate proximity preference).

Unfortunately, there are signs that this version of the strategy competition model may fare little better than the earlier modifier-straddling proposal.

The first problem concerns the model's attachment predictions for NP-RC1-RC2 sentences like (8), repeated here as (14), for the reader's convenience.

(14)   Pedro miraba los libros que pertenecían a la chica que...

In this kind of sentence, both potential attachment sites are close to a predicate, and so the predicate proximity principle should not distinguish between the two candidates. According to the model, it follows that the question of modifier attachment should be decided by recency alone. Hence, the prediction is that there should be unequivocal support for low-attachment in this structure. In practice, although this has been confirmed in off-line studies (Mitchell & Cuetos, 1991b; Mitchell, et al., 1994), a recent self-paced reading study has shown that there is no reliable bias of this kind in on-line processing (Mitchell, et al., 1994). Given that numerous studies have shown stable effects when, according to the model, different strategies are in competition with one another, it is difficult to see why the biases should not be at least as emphatic when a single principle (recency) is allowed to act without countereffects. This finding suggests that attachment decisions may be influenced by factors other than those highlighted in the Gibson et al. model.

A second problem is that there is increasing evidence that attachment preferences in NP-PP-RC structures may vary depending on precisely which preposition is incorporated within the PP (Clifton, 1988; de Vincenzi & Job, 1993; Frazier, 1990a; Gilboy et al., 1995). For example, prepositions like *with* (*con*) or *near* (*cerca*) appear to encourage a higher proportion of low-attachments than *of* (*de*) does. Such changes are particularly marked with sentences like *Alguien disparó al criado de aquella actriz que estaba en el balcón* (The servant of that actress who was on the balcony), where there is virtually no doubt that it is *la actriz* (the actress) who was on the balcony. Because lexical changes of this kind would have a very marginal effect, if any, on recency and should have no effect at all on predicate proximity, it seems unlikely that the Gibson et al. model is capable of accounting for these findings as it stands. Of course, Gibson and his colleagues could question these findings on the grounds that these investigators used different experimental tasks and different materials from their own. We therefore carried out a study to examine the lexical effects in further detail.

We administered questionnaires to 112 Spanish speaking subjects: 28 participants in each of four conditions. Two groups were required to make attachment judgments following instructions similar to those used by Cuetos and Mitchell (1988); (see examples further on). The other two groups were required to make grammaticality judgments using instructions modeled on those used by Gibson et al. (1994). In each pair, one of the two groups was presented with sentences similar to those used by Gibson et al. (i.e., *N1 cerca del N2 del N3, N1 near N2 of the N3* - see (15a) and (16a)). In the other group, the word *cerca* (*near*) was removed (i.e., *N1 del N2 del N3, N1 of the N2 of the N3;* see (15b) and (16b)). In the attachment judgment forms of the questionnaire (15a-b), the test material was followed by a question designed to reveal how the subject had resolved the attachment ambiguity. In the grammaticality judgment forms (16a-b), the subject simply had to mark "Si" or "No" to indicate whether the constituent was grammatical or not.

(15)   a. N1 del N2 del N3
        ... el jardín del garaje del edificio que estaba tan deteriorado.
        ... the garden of the garage of the building that was so deteriorated.
        ¿Qué estaba deteriorado?_____
        What was deteriorated?_____

        b. N1 cerca de N2 de N3
        ... el jardín cerca del garaje del edificio que estaba tan deteriorado.
        ... the garden near the garage of the building that was so deteriorated.
        ¿Qué estaba deteriorado?_____

(16)   a. N1 del N2 del N3
        ... el jardín de los garajes de los edificios que estaba tan deteriorado.
        SI   NO

        b. N1 cerca de N2 de N3
        ... el jardín cerca de los garajes de los edificios que estaba tan deteriorado.

The results of the study showed marked preposition effects with both kinds of judgment task. The detailed findings are shown in Tables 6.1 and 6.2.

TABLE 6.1
Percentage of Judgments Favoring N1, N2, and N3 Sites in the Attachment Judgment Task

		Site	
Form of Questionnaire	N1	N2	N3
Cerca	51.19	13.69	34.52
De or Del	34.82	32.74	32.44

The results show that performance was markedly affected by changing the preposition associated with the middle site (N2). In the formal statement of the Gibson et al. model, the parameters for neither recency nor predicate proximity should be affected by this manipulation (see Gibson et al., in press, for precise definitions of the parameter weights). The present findings therefore corroborate earlier evidence that preposition identity influences attachment preference and confirms that certain alterations are needed before the model can account for the data.

TABLE 6.2

Percentage of Items Judged Nongrammatical When the RC was Resolved as Being Attached to Sites N1, N2, or N3 in the Grammaticality Judgment Task

	Site		
Form of Questionnaire	N1	N2	N3
Cerca	28.57	59.82	23.21
De or Del	58.03	70.53	30.36

A notable feature of these findings is that the two tasks (attachment judgment and grammaticality judgment) appeared to show markedly different patterns of attachment preference. To investigate these differences further, we used the grammaticality judgment task to examine attachment biases in two-site materials more similar to those used by Cuetos and Mitchell (1988) and others. There were four versions of the questionnaire, each completed by 20 subjects. In two conditions, the verb within the RC agreed in number with the noun in the first site (high-attachment sentences); in the other two conditions, it agreed with the second site (low-attachment sentences). In two of the versions, the subordinate verb was singular, and in the others it was plural. Examples of the four conditions are given in (17a-d):

(17) a. el criado de las actrices que estaba en el balcón (high-attachment)
       b. el criado de las actrices que estaban en el balcón (low-attachment)
       c. los criados de la actriz que estaba en el balcón (low-attachment)
       d. los criados de la actriz que estaban en el balcón (high-attachment)

The results are shown in Table 6.3. In contrast with other experimental procedures that show a uniform bias in favor of high-attachment, the grammaticality judgment task revealed no reliable differences: 23% and 20% of the high- and low-attached materials, respectively, were judged to be unacceptable. Interestingly, however, there was a substantial effect of verb number. For some reason, people are more likely to say that the sentence is ungrammatical if the verb is singular (27%) than if it is plural (16%).

These results confirm that the grammaticality judgment task generates patterns of data that are markedly different from those obtained in other investigations of modifier attachment. Moreover, anomalous effects, such as the influence of verb number, suggest that performance on this task may be subject to influences other than those associated with modifier attachment. The verb plurality effect is reminiscent of similar nongrammatical effects that have been shown to affect performance in other linguistic tasks. For example, Bock and Miller (1991) demonstrated that subjects show a (plurality-related) tendency to try to make a verb agree with the closest noun, even when this is grammatically incorrect. The current findings suggest that extraneous, nongrammatical biases may also play a role in the grammaticality judgment task. If so, it suggests that it is unsafe to use such tasks to draw direct conclusions about attachment preferences in the way Gibson and his colleagues have sought to do.

TABLE 6.3
Percentages of phrases Judged Ungrammatical, for Singular versus Plural

Characteristics of Complex NP				
First noun	Second noun	Verb	Judged as ungrammatical	
S	P	S	High	30%
S	P	P	Low	15%
P	S	S	Low	25%
P	S	P	High	17%

We are now in a position to evaluate the recency/predicate proximity version of the strategy competition model. The evidence suggests that the model as it stands is not capable of providing a full account of the data. In particular, its predictions for NP-RC-RC structures are disconfirmed; and it fails to explain systematic changes that occur when one preposition within the complex NP is replaced by another. Moreover, the grammaticality judgment task used by Gibson et al. (in press) seems to be subject to various extraneous biases and may not provide a secure basis for evaluating models of attachment preference. However, none of the experimental findings to date specifically rules out any role for either recency preference or predicate proximity, and it is quite possible that these principles will figure in subsequent, fuller accounts of attachment phenomena. A positive feature of the model is that it explicitly predicts a U-shaped function for attachment preferences in three-site materials—a finding that has been corroborated by methods other than grammaticality judgment (as already outlined). A second advantage is that, by postulating crosslinguistic variation in the relative strengths of the two competing principles, it provides a straightforward explanation of differences in attachment preference across languages, and this extends the scope of the model in providing accounts of parsing effects in different languages. At present, there is no clear indication of how these parametric variations might come about. However, Gibson et al. (in press) have outlined various alternatives and this is an issue that could easily be explored further in the future. Overall, then, the recency/predicate proximity model seems likely to provide a useful framework for extending our understanding of attachment phenomena.

Evaluation of the Tuning Hypothesis

The tuning hypothesis allows one to make two different kinds of prediction. The basic proposal is that ambiguities are initially resolved in line with the statistical prevalence of the alternative readings in the language as a whole. So, on the one hand, it is possible to estimate these statistical values (using corpus studies) and hence, predict the patterns of preference to be expected with individual linguistic structures. However, in addition to these static, well-established biases, the model can also be used to predict more local or temporary biases. A central feature of any full account of tuning would be a description of the mechanism used to keep a tally of the occurrence of events in different categories. In order to respond to cumulative frequencies, such a mechanism would have to be subject to incremental change, and, if there were a shift in the input distribution, this would have to be reflected in some way in the device's internal settings. If sufficient weight is given to recent samplings, the tuning hypothesis will predict that preferences will show short-term changes on the basis of exposure patterns over the preceding minutes, days, or weeks. Thus, the model predicts that parsing preferences will change if, during some period prior to testing, the reader or listener has been exposed to an unusual preponderance of one ambiguity resolution, rather than another. In addition to making predictions about long- and short-term biases, the model is easy to reconcile with any evidence that there are individual differences in bias from one person to another. In principle, each ambiguity-resolving device must be tuned on the basis of its own input distributions (i.e., experience). In these circumstances, different devices would be tuned to different subsamples of the language as a whole, and different histories of training could well lead to different parameter settings (particularly if distributions differ, say, in written and spoken language, in broadcast versus immediate social forms, etc.). Thus, the tuning processes could well result in individual differences in preferences that remain stable over time.

Recent corpus studies of long-term effects have provided some encouraging support for the tuning hypothesis. In connection with modifier attachment preferences, Mitchell, et al. (1992) reported a small-scale study of two-site ambiguities in a 450,000-word Spanish corpus: 60% of the resolvable relative clause attachments were linked to the first site, whereas in English use of the million-word LOB corpus revealed that the pattern was reversed (38% high-attachment). If these patterns are confirmed in larger scale studies, this will indicate that the tuning hypothesis makes the correct predictions for on- and off-line attachments in Spanish and English. To our knowledge, no corpus studies of two-site attachments have been carried out in other languages.

Recently, Gibson and Pearlmutter (in press) and Gibson and Loomis (1994) have examined attachment distributions in materials with three potential attachment sites in two different English corpora. The results show that modifiers are attached most frequently to N3, then to N1, with N2 links occurring in only a small proportion of cases. The on- and off- line data reported by Gibson et al. (1994) show that the same pattern of preferences turns up in the results of their grammaticality judgment data. If the same pattern is reproduced in parsing, then this result, too, would be consistent with the tuning hypothesis.

Evidence from other structures is also beginning to accumulate. For example, Tabossi, Spivey-Knowlton, McRae, and Tanenhaus (in press) have compared the corpus statistics and latency data for sentences beginning with a NP followed by a verb with the inflection -ed. In certain circumstances, such verbs are ambiguous, in the sense that they could either be the main verb of the sentence or a subordinate verb within a reduced RC. Tabossi et al. presented evidence that it is the first (i.e., main verb) interpretation that prevails in corpus occurences of these forms, exactly in line with the well-known on-line evidence that this interpretation is given precedence in first-pass parsing (see also, MacDonald, 1994; Trueswell, Tanenhaus, & Garnsey, 1994, for further evidence in relation to this structure; and Trueswell, Tanenhaus, & Kello, 1993, for comparable evidence with a different form of ambiguity).

Another structure in which we have examined the relation between statistical corpus patterns and parsing preferences involves contractions of the English auxiliaries *had* and *would* (Corley, Mitchell, & Cuetos, 1993). In (18), the contracted form *she'd* can either represent *she had* or *she would* and in cases like this, there is no prior syntactic or discourse information to indicate which reading is more appropriate.

(18) The gambler told everyone she'd bet the money to win a fortune.

A corpus analysis revealed that *had* is more frequent than *would,* so presumably the past tense (*she had*) interpretation of *she'd* is more common than the conditional one (*she would*). Given this statistical evidence, the tuning hypothesis predicts that the former interpretation should initially be selected in on-line sentence processing. It follows, therefore, that readers should be garden-pathed more when they read sentences like (19a), which is resolved in favor of the *would* interpretation, than they are with sentences like (19b), with a *had* resolution.

(19) a. He'd come to the house and paint the exterior.
      b. He'd come to the house and painted the exterior.
      c. He would come to the house and paint the exterior.
      d. He had come to the house and painted the exterior.

Subjects were required to read sentences like (19a-b)—together with control conditions (like (19c-d))—in a self-paced reading task. Reading times for the disambiguating display *and paint(ed)* confirmed that there were longer latencies in the (a) than in the (b) condition (982 ms vs. 893 ms, respectively) and that this was reliably different from the (reverse) effect in the control conditions (806 ms for (c); 929 ms for (d)).

TABLE 6.4
Percentages of High-Attachment Judgments at Different Ages

Year in School	% High-Attachment
2	59.1
3	72.7
4	74.9

The next set of predictions concerns tuning effects and parsing biases that are expected to change over time. According to the tuning hypothesis, in the absence of statistical evidence, there should be no a priori reason for choosing one resolution over any of its competitors. This means that prior to being exposed to the language in question, people should theoretically respond in an unbiased fashion: then, as contact with the language increases, their preferences should steadily asymptote toward the values represented in the corpus. In the case of Spanish two-site attachments, it follows that we can predict that preferences should begin by being unbiased (with 50% high- and 50% low-attachment), but gradually follow the corpus statistics and shift in the direction of high-attachment preference. Thus, we predicted that Spanish-speaking children should progressively favor high-attachment as they get older and are increasingly exposed to biased material. (English-speaking children, in contrast, should start in the same position and move in the opposite direction.) To test the Spanish part of this prediction, we carried out questionnaire studies with three groups of 24 children each, in their second, third, and fourth years of school attendance (7, 8, and 9 years old, respectively).

As expected, the results showed that there was a significant positive correlation between the children's chronological age and the percentage of high-attachment choices they made on the questionnaire ($r = 0.3789$, $p < .001$). The overall group averages are given in Table 6.4.

Another prediction that can be made from the short-term effects of the statistical tuning hypothesis is that, if it is really the frequency with which the structures appear that determines their structural choices, then if people are exposed to an artificial preponderance of one particular attachment, it should be possible to demonstrate that this has an effect on their preferences. To test this prediction, we carried out an intervention study in which we exposed Spanish children in second grade (7 years old) to a highly biased sample of attachment materials. One group was systematically exposed to high-attachment sentences, and the other was exposed to low-attachment materials. The study was carried out in three stages. First, a group of children was pretested, using an attachment questionnaire similar to those used by Cuetos and Mitchell (1988). On the basis of the results, children were divided into two groups of 24 each, matched closely for attachment bias. Over the next 2 weeks (10 school days), both groups of children were required each day to read three short stories that included two NP-PP-RC sentences each (i.e., each child read 60 two-site exposure sentences in all). In the high-attachment bias group, the RCs were always resolved as being attached to the first noun, whereas in the low-attachment bias group they always modified the second noun. After a one-week interval without any activity associated with the topic of research, the subjects were required to complete a second, matched form of the questionnaire. The results showed that the exposure regime had a reliable effect on the children's attachment preferences. Following the different experimental treatments, the two groups differed significantly in the proportion of high-attachment choices they made on the final (posttest) questionnaire, $F(1, 46) = 11.1$, $p < .005$) (see Table 6.5).

The effects of exposure to high- and low-attached materials was asymmetrical. The subjects exposed to a preponderance of high-attachment materials shifted in the direction of making a higher proportion of high-attachment choices, but there was no reliable change in the other direction in the second group. This is not the pattern we had expected, but a little thought shows that it is exactly the result that should have been anticipated on the basis of the tuning hypothesis. During the two-week period between the pretest and posttest, the children were not just exposed to the (artificially biased) experimental materials. They obviously continued to experience the biases that prevail outside the experiment and outside the school. By hypothesis, these external biases are assumed to favor high-attachment in both experimental groups. By combining these effects with the biases introduced by the experiment itself, the natural effect would be for the experimental bias to be enhanced in the high-attachment group, and reduced or even cancelled in the low-attachment condition. In short, the pattern of results, although unanticipated, is exactly what might have been expected on the basis of the tuning hypothesis.

TABLE 6.5
Percentages of High- and Low-attachment Judgments in Pretest and Posttest Conditions

	Pretest (matched)	Posttest
Group 1 (High-attachment bias)		
High-attachment preference	71.44	92.17
Low-attachment preference	28.56	7.83
Group 2 (Low-attachment bias)		
High-attachment preference	70.80	72.19
Low-attachment preference	29.20	27.81

These intervention data are difficult to explain on the basis of theories that postulate that parsing choices are governed by fixed, linguistically determined strategies that operate in the same way for all subjects in all languages.

As a general proposal, the tuning hypothesis is capable of providing a satisfactory account of all the observations concerning parsing preferences that occur in modifier-attachment ambiguities. (A strong case can be made for extending the application of the proposal to account for initial preferences in all other forms of structural ambiguity. However, this is beyond the scope of the present chapter.) Despite the positive support from corpus analyses and from intervention studies, however, this account of immediate decision making has been criticized.

One objection (expressed, e.g., by Carreiras & Clifton; 1993; Gibson et al., 1994) is that in its most general form, the hypothesis does not specify the precise level of detail at which statistical records are kept for later use in guiding parsing processes. Are two-site data stored (and consulted) separately from three-site data? Are the attachment tallies for complex NPs of the form NP-PP distinct from those for NP-RC complexes? Where the NP includes a PP are detailed statistics filed away for attachment patterns in different subclasses of prepositions? Are the records further subdivided when the NPs are modified by adjectives?

Clearly, a fully predictive account would have to make a commitment on each of these distinctions. The tuning hypothesis as it stands really represents a family of models whose individual members differ from one another with respect to the grain of analysis. Viewed from this perspective, it is an empirical question whether particular variants of the model are viable or not. Experimental findings already discussed indicate that the coarser grained versions of the model would not be capable of accounting for the data. A model that merged the statistical counts for NP-PP structures with those for attachments to NP-RC forms would not have any explanation for the different patterns of attachment that appear to characterize these two forms. Equally, existing data suggest that any viable version of the model would have to take account of preposition identity in subdividing its records.

The obvious danger in allowing the issue to be settled by empirical evidence in this way is that it may eventually prove to be impossible to falsify the hypothesis. Each new discovery might be used to justify a new form of record keeping, allowing the hypothesis itself to survive unscathed. However, it is unlikely to be a straightforward matter to keep the hypothesis on "life-support" in this way. If the proposal is to remain persuasive, it will always be necessary to find a level of detail or grain in which corpus statistics and behavioral evidence pattern in the same way, and there is no guarantee that this will inevitably prove to be possible. Moreover, to provide a convincing account of the data, rather than a mere redescription, there would have to be a clear restriction on the freedom to vary grain in providing explanations for different findings. Given these provisos there does not seem to be any case for viewing the hypothesis as less falsifiable than any of its existing competitors.

A second objection to the tuning hypothesis is that, by concentrating on statistical patterns in the language, it directs attention away from the underlying explanations for those patterns: the linguistic phenomena that may be the ultimate determinants of parsing preferences (see Carreiras & Clifton, 1993, for a version of this argument).[2] This observation presupposes that an account that "explains" the distribution of structures in the language is necessarily a better or more satisfactory account. However, it is not at all evident that this is the case. The relative merits of the different accounts depend on precisely which phenomena

---

[2]This criticism is comparable to objecting to DNA-based accounts of medical and biological phenomena on the grounds that they offer no explanation of the provenance of different distributions of DNA patterns. However, it is uncontroversial that DNA is the vehicle of genetic transmission and therefore perfectly respectable to formulate hypotheses in terms of DNA distinctions. Moreover, hypotheses formulated at this level can, and do, coexist with speculations about ultimate causes of DNA distributions. Like DNA, though with vastly more modest scope, the tuning hypothesis is concerned with providing a low-level molecular account of the immediate mechanism by which biases and tendencies are implemented.

they are trying to explain. In proposing a mechanism for using distributional information in parsing, the tuning hypothesis does not place any restrictions on the development of theories concerning the origins of the distributional patterns. The proposal can coexist readily with theories of this kind. For example, there may be some truth in the Gricean account of the preference for low-attachments to English structures of the form NP-*of*-NP. For the reasons discussed earlier, one resolution may be associated with the postnominal genitive, while the other is typically expressed by the prenominal form (e.g., *the colonel's daughter*). However, it is not necessary to propose that parsing biases occur because the Gricean computations are carried out "on the fly." Such factors may merely influence the statistical record of resolutions, and the real-time parser may then act very rapidly to convert this intermediate record into an appropriate parsing preference. The function of the statistically driven parser is to explain the rapid mechanisms employed in real-time parsing and not to go beyond that to account for the prevalence of different structures in the language. Of course, a theory that is capable of operating over both domains would rightly be seen as a better theory. However, such a theory would not be capable of accounting for statistical effects that are truly arbitrary or conventional, or for effects that are introduced at an experimenter's whim, such as the intervention findings discussed earlier. No explanation that concentrates exclusively on computational and linguistic effects (ignoring "unmotivated" statistical effects) will be able to explain results of this kind.

In short, we simply do not agree that the tuning hypothesis is any less adequate as a theoretical framework than most of its competitors. It is capable of generating testable predictions—as in the case of the developmental and intervention studies discussed earlier—and it is capable of providing a plausible account of most of the existing findings within its domain of application.

Evaluation of Data-Shaped Parsers

We limit ourselves to a very brief observation about the viability of models in this category, and that is that they do not provide a natural account of the fact that attachment preferences do not appear to be strongly influenced by semantic and discourse biases. As already indicated, Carreiras (1992) failed to show semantic effects and Zagar and Pynte (1992) found no evidence of discourse influences. In contrast to these findings, models in which parsing decisions are made by nonmodular neural nets should be subject to nonsyntactic influences of this kind. The absence of such effects suggests that there is a degree of modularization—a feature that is better captured by all of the accounts we have considered in more detail.

Overview of Evaluation

Although the evidence is sketchy and still covers only a minute proportion of the world's 6,000-plus languages, it is possible to use these investigations to draw some tentative conclusions about the nature of the parsing process. The results pose severe problems for theories that maintain that parsing is a completely universal process. The various forms of the garden path theory and the construal theory are undermined by evidence that ambiguity resolution procedures can be altered by experience and can vary from individual to individual. To accommodate such variation, these accounts need to be expanded or developed in some way. These models are also incomplete in their account of crosslinguistic differences and apparently show shortcomings in explaining attachment preferences in NP-RC-RC structures.

Parameterized accounts explicitly incorporate devices for simulating variation, and are therefore less challenged by evidence that attachment preferences vary between people and can be changed by exposure to language. However, these models encounter problems of their own. Modifier-straddling seems beyond salvaging, having made the wrong predictions for at least two of the six languages for which we have preliminary evidence. The recency/predicate proximity model has considerably greater potential, but faces severe problems in the accumulating evidence that some attachment preferences may be preposition-specific.

The tuning hypothesis provides a satisfactory account of the data, particularly the intervention and developmental findings. As indicated at several points in the discussion, statistical devices are perfectly capable of explaining most of the findings traditionally interpreted in terms of linguistic or computational simplicity. It only needs to be shown that ambiguity-resolution distributions in corpora are skewed in the same way as the processing biases in parsing studies. At present, positive support is restricted to the structures considered in the Construal Theory section. However, we are currently carrying out corpus studies on a wider range of structures in an attempt to establish whether the hypothesis continues to provide a plausible explanation of the data. These findings should allow us to be more specific about, for example, the grain of record keeping and we anticipate that this work will provide a basis for formulating the proposal as a fully predictive model of parsing choices.

CONCLUDING REMARKS

We can now return to the questions raised at the beginning of the chapter. Is the parsing mechanism essentially preconfigured or fixed for all languages, or do its internal workings vary either as a function of the language user's contact with linguistic material or on some other unrelated basis? If the parser's configuration is related to language contact, is it appropriate to view the parser for a particular language as a computational process in which grammar parameters set during acquisition are used to customize the parsing mechanism? Or, is the putative customization process unrelated to the acquisition of grammar and linked, instead, to more basic principles of efficiency?

Some of these questions can be addressed by the investigations of the way in which people process sentences that include modifiers that have to be attached to one of two or more sites within a complex NP. Our survey of the work in a number of different languages raises numerous problems for models that assume that the parser is a fixed, universal, generic mechanism (e.g., the garden path and construal theories). In contrast, it shows that the models that fare best are those that allow a degree of customization within the system. In principle, this tailoring of the parsing routine could be limited to setting the value of a single parameter, as in the recency/predicate proximity model. However, this particular model does not appear to be flexible enough to account for existing data, and it seems unlikely that a single-parameter account of this kind will ultimately prove to be viable. More plausible are multiparameter accounts in which contact with language is used to adjust the weights associated with a number of different combinations of linguistic units (as in the tuning hypothesis). Thus, the evidence argues against both completely universal parsers (e.g., Bever, 1970; Crocker, 1992; Frazier, 1987; Inoue & Fodor, 1995; Kimball, 1973; Pritchett, 1992) and parsers that are universal apart from variations that are parametrically linked to grammar settings (e.g., Frazier & Rayner, 1988; Mazuka & Lust, 1990).

In drawing these conclusions, we are making no claims about the universality of parsing processes other than those used to select the initial structural interpretation of linguistic material. Linguistic experience may or may not have an influence on the processes used to assemble structures, to check that they are internally consistent and compatible with what has gone before, and to reanalyze material following garden-pathing. The results reviewed here are compatible with the proposal that these decisions are determined entirely by language users' individual experiences—suggesting that parsing processes may be characterized by a considerable degree of adjustment or customization. At the same time, it is not yet feasible to rule out the possibility that a significant proportion of parsing operations other than those highlighted here are fixed and universal, or are parameterized within a universal framework. The fundamental questions with which we introduced the chapter therefore remain open to further debate. However, it is encouraging to note that empirical findings are beginning to place constraints on the kinds of answers that can reasonably be given to them.

ACKNOWLEDGMENTS

The research reported here was supported by grant DGICYT No. PB92-0656-C04-02 from the Spanish Government and by grant No. R0023 4062 from the Economic and Social Research Council (UK). We are grateful to Chuck Clifton, Neal Pearlmutter, and three anonymous referees for offering critical comments on an earlier draft of this chapter.

REFERENCES

Atkinson, M. (1992). *Children's syntax: Introduction to principles and parameters theory.* Oxford, England: Basil Blackwell.

Bates, E., & MacWhinney, B. (1987). Competition variation and language learning. In B. MacWhinney (Ed.), *Mechanisms of Language Acquisition* (pp. 157–193). Hillsdale, NJ: Lawrence Erlbaum Associates.

Bever, T.G. (1970). The cognitive basis for linguistic structures. In J.R. Hayes (Ed.), *Cognition and the development of language* (pp. 279–360). New York: Wiley.

Bickerton, D. (1990). *Language and species.* London: University of Chicago Press.

Bock, K., & Miller, C.A. (1991). Broken agreement. *Cognitive Psychology, 23,* 45–93.

Brysbaert, M., & Mitchell, D.C. (1993, December). *Sentence parsing in Dutch: Another departure from Late Closure.* Paper presented to the Dutch Psychonomic Society, Amsterdam.

Brysbaert, M., & Mitchell, D.C. (in press). Modifier attatchment in sentence parsing: Evidence from Dutch. *Quaterly Journal of Experimental Psychology.*

Carreiras, M. (1992). Estrategias de análisis sintáctico en el procesamiento de frases: Cierre temprano versus cierre último [Parsing strategies in sentence processing: Early versus late closure.] *Cognitiva, 4,* 3–27.

Carreiras, M., & Clifton, C. (1993). Relative clause interpretation preferences in Spanish and English. *Language and Speech, 36,* 353–372.

Chomsky, N. (1981). Principles and parameters in syntactic theory. In N. Horstein & D. Lightfoot (Eds.), *Explanations in linguistics.* London: Longman.

Chomsky, N. (1986). *Knowledge of language: Its nature, origin and use.* New York: Praeger.

Clifton, C. (1988, August). *Restrictions on Late Closure: Appearance and reality.* Paper presented at the 6th Australian Language and Speech conference, Sydney.

Clifton, C., & Ferreira, F. (1989). Ambiguity in context. *Language and Cognitive Processes, 4,* 77–103.

Cook, V.J. (1988). *Chomsky's Universal Grammar: An introduction.* Oxford, England: Basil Blackwell.

Corley M.M.B. (1995) *The Role of statistics in human sentence processing.* Manuscript. University of Exeter.

Corley, M.M.B., Mitchell, D.C., & Cuetos, F. (1993, September). *Parsing biases for non-structural differences: Evidence for the use of statistics in parsing.* Paper presented at the Conference on Psychology of Language and Communication, Glasgow, UK.

Crocker, M.W. (1992). *A logical model of competence and performance in the human sentence processor.* (Research Paper HCRC/RP-34). Glasgow, UK: Human Communication Research Centre.

Cuetos, F., & Mitchell, D. (1988). Cross-linguistic differences in parsing: Restrictions on the use of the Late Closure strategy in Spanish. *Cognition, 30,* 73–105.

de Vincenzi, M. & Job, R. (1993). Some observations on the universality of the Late Closure strategy. *Journal of Psycholinguistic Research, 22,* 189–206.

de Vincenzi, M. & Job, R. (in press). An investigation of Late Closure: The role of syntax, thematic structures, and pragmatics in initial and final interpretation. *Journal of Experimental Psychology: Learning, Memory, and Cognition.*

Ferreira, F., & Clifton, C. (1986). The independence of syntatic processing. *Journal of Memory and Language, 25,* 348–368.

Ferreira, F., & Henderson, J.M. (1991). Recovery from misanalysis of garden-path sentences. *Journal of Memory and Language, 30,* 725–745.

Flores d'Arcais, G.B. (1990). Parsing principles and language comprehension during reading. In D. Balota, G.B. Flores d'Arcais, & K. Rayner (Eds.), *Comprehension processes in reading* (pp. 345–357). Hillsdale, NJ: Lawrence Erlbaum Associates.

Frazier, L.(1979). *On comprehending sentences: Syntactic parsing strategies.* Bloomington: Indiana University Linguistics Club.

Frazier, L. (1987). Sentence processing. In M. Coltheart (Ed.), *Attention and performance XII: The Psychology of reading* (pp. 559–586). Hillsdale, NJ: Lawrence Erlbaum Associates.

Frazier, L. (1990a). Parsing modifiers: Special purpose strategies in the human sentence processing mechanism. In D. Balota, G.B. Flores d'Arcais, & K. Rayner (Eds.), *Comprehension Processes in Reading* (pp. 303–330). Hillsdale, NJ: Lawrence Erlbaum Associates.

Frazier, L. (1990b). Exploring the architecture of the language system. In G. Altmann (Ed.), *Cognitive models of speech processing: Psycholinguistics and computational perspectives* (pp. 409–433). Cambridge, MA: MIT Press.

Frazier, L., & Clifton, C., Jr. (in press). *Construal.* Cambridge, MA: MIT Press.

Frazier, L., Clifton, C., & Randall, J. (1983). Filling gaps: Decision principles and structure in sentence comprehension. *Cognition, 13,* 187–222.

Frazier, L., & Rayner, K. (1982). Making and correcting errors during sentence comprehension. *Cognitive Psychology, 14,* 178–210.

Frazier, L., & Rayner, K. (1988). Parameterizing the language processing system: Left-versus right-branching within and across languages. In J. Hawkins (Ed.), *Explaining language universals* (pp. 247–279). Oxford, England: Basil Blackwell.

Gibson, E., & Loomis, J. (1995). A corpus analysis of recency preference and predicate proximity. *Proceeding of the Sixteenth Annual Conference of the Cognitive Science Society* (pp. 351–362). Alabama, Georgia.

Gibson, E., & Pearlmutter, N.C. (in press). A corpus-based analysis of psycholinguistic constraints on prepositional phrase attachment. In C. Clifton, L. Frazier & K. Rayner (Eds.), *Perspectives insentence processing* (pp. 181–198). Hillsdale, NJ: Lawrence Erlbaum Associates.

Gibson, E., Pearlmutter, N., Canseco-Gonzales, E., & Hickok, G. (1995). *Cross-linguistic attachment preferences: Evidence from English and Spanish.* Manuscript submitted for publication.

Gilboy, E., Sopena, J.M., Clifton, C., Jr., & Frazier, L. (1995). Argument structure and association preferences in Spanish and English compound NPs. *Cognition, 54,* 131–167

Hemforth, B., Konieczny, L., & Scheepers, C. (1994). Principle-based and probabilistic approaches to human parsing: How universal is the human language processor? In H. Trost (Ed.), *Tagungsband Konvens'94* (pp. 161–170). Berlin: Springer.

Inoue, A., & Fodor, J.D. (1995). Information-paced parsing of Japanese. In R. Mazuka & N. Nagai (Eds.), *Japanese sentence processing,* (pp. 9–63). Hillsdale, NJ: Lawrence Erlbaum Associates.

Kimball, J. (1973). Seven principles of surface structure parsing in natural language. *Cognition, 2,* 15–47.

MacDonald, M.C. (1994). Probabilistic constraints and syntactic ambiguity resolution. *Language and Cognitive Processes, 9,* 157–201.

MacWhinney, B. (1987). The competition model. In B. MacWhinney (Ed.), *Mechanisms of language acquisition* (pp. 249–308). Hillsdale, NJ: Lawrence Erlbaum Associates.

Mazuka, R., & Lust, B. (1990). On parameter setting and parsing: Predictions for crosslinguistic differences in adult and child processing. In L. Frazier & J. de Villiers (Eds.), *Language processing and language Acquisition* (pp. 163–205). Dordrecht: Kluwer.

McClelland, J.L., & Rumelhart, D.E. (1981). The interactive activation model of context effects in letter perception: Part I. An account of basic findings. *Psychological Review, 88,* 375–407.

Mitchell, D.C. (1987a). Lexical guidance in human parsing: Locus and processing characteristics. In M. Coltheart (Ed.), *Attention and Performance Xll: The psychology of reading* (pp. 601–618). Hillsdale, NJ: Lawrence Erlbaum Associates.

Mitchell, D.C. (1987b). Reading and syntactic analysis. In J. Beech & A. Colley (Eds.), *Cognitive approaches to reading* (pp. 87–112). Chichester, Wiley.

Mitchell, D.C. (1988). Natural language processing: A psychological perspective. *Institute of Electrical Engineers Computing and Control Division Digest, No. 1988/118.*

Mitchell, D.C. (1994). Sentence parsing. In M. Gernsbacher (Ed.), *Handbook of Psycholinguistics* (pp. 375–409). New York: Academic Press.

Mitchell, D.C., & Cuetos, F. (1991a). The origins of parsing strategies. In C. Smith (Ed.), *Current issues in natural language processing* (pp. 1–12). Austin, TX: University of Austin Press.

Mitchell, D.C., & Cuetos, F. (1991b). *Restrictions on Late Closure: The computational underpinnings of parsing strategies in Spanish and English.* Unpublished manuscript, University of Exeter, UK.

Mitchell, D.C., Cuetos, F., & Brysbaert, M. (1994, May). *Modifier attachment in Dutch and Spanish: Evidence favoring statistical rather than universal "linguistic" accounts.* Paper presented at the Fourth Workshop of Language Comprehension, Giens, France.

Mitchell, D.C., Cuetos, F., & Corley, M.M.B. (1992, March). *Statistical versus linguistic determinants of parsing bias: Crosslinguistic evidence.* Paper presented at the Fifth Annual CUNY Conference on Human Sentence Processing, New York.

Mitchell, D.C., Cuetos, F., & Zagar, D. (1990). Reading in different languages: Is there a universal mechanism for parsing sentences? In D. Balota, G.B. Flores d'Arcais, & K. Rayner (Eds.), *Comprehension processes in reading* (pp. 285–302). Hillsdale, NJ: Lawrence Erlbaum Associates.

Pinker, S. (1994). *The language instinct: The new science of language and mind.* London: Allen Lane.

Pritchett, B.L. (1992). *Grammatical competence and parsing performance.* Chicago: University of Chicago Press.

Radford, A. (1990). *Syntactic theory and the acquisition of English syntax.* Oxford, England: Basil Blackwell.

Rayner, K., Carlson, M., & Frazier, L. (1983). The interaction of syntax and semantics during sentence processing: Eye movements in the analysis of semantically biased sentences. *Journal of Verbal Learning and Verbal Behavior, 22,* 358–374.

Seidenberg, M.S., & McClelland, J.L. (1989). A distributed developmental model of visual word recognition and naming. *Psychological Review, 96,* 523–568.

St. John, M.F., & McClelland, J.L. (1990). Learning and applying contextual constraints in sentence comprehension. *Artificial Intelligence, 46,* 217–257.

Tabossi, P., Spivey-Knowlton, M.J., McRae, K., & Tanenhaus, M.K. (in press). Semantic effects on syntactic ambiguity resolution: Evidence for a constraint-based resolution process. In C. Umilta & and M. Moscovitch (Eds.) *Attention and performance, XV* (pp. 589–616). Cambridge, MA: MIT Press.

Trueswell, J.C., Tanenhaus, M.K., & Garnsey, S.M. (1994). Semantic influences on parsing: Use of thematic role information in syntactic disambiguation. *Journal of Memory and Language, 33,* 285–318.

Trueswell, J.C., Tanenhaus, M.K., & Kello, C. (1993). Verb-specific constraints in sentence processing: Separating effects of lexical preference from garden-paths. *Journal of Experimental Psychology: Learning, Memory, and Cognition, 19,* 528–553.

Valle, F., Cuetos, F., Igoa, J.M., & del Viso, S. (1990). *Lecturas de psicolingüística: 1. Comprehensión y Producción del Lenguaje* [Lectures in psycholinguistics: Language comprehension and production]. Madrid: Alianza Editorial.

Zagar, D., & Pynte, J. (1992, September). *The role of semantic information and of attention in processing syntactic ambiguity: Eye-movement study.* Paper presented at the fifth conference of the European Society for Cognitive Psychology, Paris, France.

7

Segmentation Effects in the Processing of Complex NPs with Relative Clauses

Elizabeth Gilboy and Josep M. Sopena
Universitat de Barcelona
Barcelona, Spain

Crosslinguistic approaches to language comprehension are not only useful, but essential if we are interested in understanding how people comprehend sentences. Among other things, they help us to avoid the risk of considering models that are language-specific as universal models of the language comprehension system. Restricting ourselves to the area of syntactic parsing, a great deal of empirical data based on English is available, but less is known about other languages. The aim of this chapter is to contribute to the body of knowledge of the human parsing system with some empirical data from Spanish.

When comprehending a sentence (either orally expressed or written) subjects must engage themselves in a range of processes, one of which is syntactic parsing. To comprehend a sentence, one must compute a syntactic analysis in order to determine "who did what and to whom", to quote Cuetos, Mitchell and Corley (this volume; chap. 6, p. 146). In comprehension it is important to know what sources of information are available to the parsing system and when they come into play.

Although it is generally acknowledged that all sources of information influence the final outcome of the comprehension system, when exactly these different pieces of information influence the decisions of the human language comprehension system is a much-debated issue.

Several models of the human parsing system have been proposed, ranging from universal accounts of the parsing system to frequency based accounts. Those we accept should be able to account for the fact that such a system exhibits some preferences when reading a sentence, such as, for example, the well-known:

(1)   The horse raced past the barn fell. (Bever, 1970)

The verb (V) *raced* is ambiguous between a main V and a past participle. There is a consistent preference to interpret it as a main V; On encountering *fell,* however, subjects experience a difficulty, because what was required was the past participle interpretation. The existence of this kind of preference is well-documented in English (e.g., Bever, 1970; Frazier, 1979; Frazier & J.D. Fodor, 1978; Kimball, 1973); it is also present in other languages, such as Spanish. Spanish subjects are also led down the garden-path when they read a sentence like:

(2)   El hombre le dijo a la mujer que tenía dos hijas que la invitaba a cenar.
       The man told the woman who had two daughters that (he) would invite her
       for dinner

When reading this sentence, native speakers of Spanish take the fragment *que tenía dos hijas* as a sentential complement subcategorized by the verb *dijo* (tell); hence, they experience difficulty on encountering the second *que*, which requires the interpretation of the first *que* as a wh-word, and the whole fragment *que tenía dos hijas* as a relative clause (RC).

As we have said, different models have been proposed to explain the existence of these preferences. Some postulate the existence of purely structurally based strategies (Frazier, 1987, 1990a), some rely on the importance of the context (Altmann & Steedman, 1988; Crain & Steedman, 1985); some understand the parsing process as a constraint-satisfaction process (MacDonald, Pearlmutter, & Seidenberg, 1994); and, finally, others postulate frequency based strategies (Cuetos et al., this volume, chap. 6). In this chapter, we offer some evidence in favor of a universal account of a parsing system. The chapter is organized in the following manner: We begin by reviewing a theory, the tuning hypothesis, that has been developed primarily on the basis of Spanish data, and we express some concerns about it; then, we present our own explanation of some of the data that seem to give support to the tuning hypothesis, and discuss some findings from our laboratory.

THE TUNING HYPOTHESIS

Since the initial work by Cuetos and Mitchell (1988), several papers have appeared on the attachment problems for a relative clause within a complex noun phrase (NP; Carreiras, 1992; Carreiras & Clifton, 1993; Clifton, 1988; de Vicenzi & Job, 1993; Frazier, 1990b; Frazier & Clifton, in press; Gibson, Pearlmutter, Canseco-González, & Hickok, 1994; Gilboy, Sopena, Clifton, & Frazier, 1995; Mitchell, Cuetos, & Zagar, 1990. For an extensive review, see Cuetos et al., this volume, chap. 6).

Cuetos, Mitchell, and their colleagues have presented evidence based on NP-PP-RC (noun phrase-prepositional phrase-relative clause) ambiguities to support what they call the *tuning hypothesis*. At the core of the tuning hypothesis is the idea that parsing principles should best be understood as frequency-based strategies. For each language, each particular system (or, in its more extreme formulation, each individual) computes the frequency of each syntactic ambiguity and presumably ranks them. When faced with an ambiguity, the parser chooses the solution that has priority over the rest because it is the one that has given the best results in the past.

This being the case, the tuning hypothesis predicts that in cases of temporary ambiguity, there should be agreement between corpus data and behaviorial measures (off- and on-line) in all languages and for all constructions. On-line data must show that the most frequent solution for a specific structural ambiguity is easier to process than less frequent solutions. It is also claimed that the tuning hypothesis explains not only crosslanguage differences, but also individual differences. Further, it is hypothesized that one can modify subjects' preferences by exposing them to biased corpora.

We would like to raise some issues concerning the predictions of the tuning hypothesis that we believe the theory has to sort out. The first is that the theory should specify what has to be counted. Restricting ourselves to the type of ambiguity studied by Cuetos, Mitchell, and their colleagues, should we count: the possible attachment site for a RC in a NP-*of*-NP complex NP; or in a NP-PP complex, ignoring the type of preposition? Should we analyze the relation between the two NPs in a complex NP, distinguishing between deverbal nouns (Ns) that assign a theta-role and Ns that do not assign a theta-role? (for similar arguments, see Carreiras & Clifton, 1993; Carreiras, Frazier, & Clifton, 1995).

Several studies have shown that some on-line effects might be modulated by linguistic factors, such as the type of preposition in a NP-PP-RC ambiguity (de Vicenzi & Job, 1993; Gilboy et al., 1995), and the relation between the two NPs in a complex NP (Gilboy et al., 1995). Gilboy et al. (1995) ran a questionnaire study where they studied the preferences for ambiguous RCs to attach to the first NP (from now on N1) of a complex NP or to the second NP (from now on N2); (e.g., *Yesterday they gave me the sweater of cotton that was illegally imported*). Results showed differences between the types of NP studied, indicating that the relation between the two Ns in the complex NP was relevant: for example, Substance NPs (*Yesterday they gave me the sweater of cotton that was illegally imported*) versus Animate possessives (*The professor read the book of the student that was in the living room*), the former showing significantly fewer N2 preferences than the latter. Among other things, our conclusion was that the relation held by the two Ns in a complex NP was relevant when deciding the most plausible host for the ambiguous RC.

A second issue that arises with an account such as the one advocated by the tuning hypothesis is this: What sort of relation do we expect between a frequency-based strategy and behaviorial measures? Assuming we are talking about self-paced reading experiments (which the majority of the experiments run up until now on the topic of NP-PP-RC structures are), the most parsimonious one would be the one which assumes which the more frequent a solution is in the corpus, the less time it takes to read a sentence that is disambiguated toward this solution. However, studying another type of ambiguity in the corpus, such as PP-attachment ambiguities (i.e., ambiguities that arise in a sequence like V-NP-PP, where the PP could modify either the verb or the NP; Brill & Resnik, (1994); (see also Hindle & Rooth, 1991), show that in English the PP tends to modify the preceding NP 64% of the time (at least for the sentences that conform to this pattern in the *Penn Treebank Wall Street Journal*). However, several studies using this type of material have shown a preference in reading times for a PP to modify a V, which would imply that the human processing system follows a strategy that contrasts with corpus statistics (Clifton & Ferreira, 1989; Clifton, Speer, & Abney, 1991; Rayner, Carlson and Frazier, 1983; for opposite results, see Altmann & Steedman, 1988; Taraban & McClelland, 1988).

Associated with this is the relation between the frequency in a corpus study of a given solution and the magnitude of the effect in reanalysis, when the sentence is disambiguated toward the less favored option. If each alternative is assigned a preference value, low values would be associated with some of them, because they seldom appear in a corpus. This seems to imply that there would be a penalty associated with these alternatives, analogous to a penalty associated with an infrequent word, for example. We can find some evidence that directly bears on this issue in the study of Juliano and Tanenhaus (1993). In the Brown

Corpus, these authors found that after a V the particle *that* is a complementizer 93% of the time and a determiner only 6% of the time, whereas at the beginning of the sentence, it is a complementizer 11% of the time and a determiner 35% of the time. In a subsequent word-by-word self-paced reading experiment, they focused on the complementizer versus determiner ambiguity at the beginning of the sentence and after a V, and, surprisingly, the magnitude of the reanalysis effect in the *that*-after-V condition (93% vs. 6%) was only 59 ms, wheras in the initial-*that* condition (35% vs. 11%), the magnitude of the reanalysis effect was is 125 ms.[1]

Finally, we think that a word of caution is needed when talking about corpus statistics. Merely showing that there is a correlation between a well-known effect (such as the main clause/reduced relative case) and frequency in a corpus does not help to adjudicate between alternatives. This implies that the study cited in Cuetos et al. (this volume, chap. 6) showing that subjects are led down the garden-path when reading a sentence like *He'd come to the house and paint the exterior* simply indicates that there is a preference that correlates with corpus statistics, but it says nothing about a structurally based model, like the gardenpath model. It is necessary to show on-line that a given structure is resolved toward the most frequent solution in the corpus, which, in turn, is not the outcome predicted by a structural strategy based theory.

THE CONSTRUAL HYPOTHESIS

The construal hypothesis (Frazier & Clifton, in press) is a major revision of the well-known garden path model (for a complete description of the model see Frazier, 1987, 1990a). It is an extension of the model that tries to accommodate evidence that did not fit well with previous versions. The key concept of this version is the distinction between two sorts of structures present in the language: primary relations and nonprimary relations. *Primary relations* and phrases include:

. The subject and main predicate of any (+ or -) finite clause.
. Complements and obligatory constituents of primary phrases.

---

[1]The authors explain the result by assuming that the reanalysis is more costly in the initial-*that* case, because the whole structure of the sentence has to be revised. Although this is certainly true, it remains to be shown that the *that*-after-V condition is capable of producing a comparable reanalysis effect in a context similar to the initial-*that* condition.

Primary phrases are immediately assigned to a tree structure by minimal attachment and late closure and, thus, are interpreted as honoring the constraints imposed by the grammar. For example, the ambiguity that arises on encountering the sequence V-NP-PP, where the PP could be attached as a sister of the V (*The man saw the woman with a telescope*) or attached to the NP, creating a complex NP (*The man saw the woman with a handbag*), is an example of an ambiguity that arises with primary phrases because *with a telescope* can be the complement of the main V. This structural ambiguity is resolved via minimal attachment, which implies that there is a preference for the PP to attach to the tree as a complement of the V (for a complete list of structural attachment ambiguities see Frazier & Clifton, in press).

In contrast, *nonprimary phrases* are not immediately assigned to a tree structure, but *associated* to a certain domain. The construal principle:

. Associates a phrase XP that cannot be analyzed as instantiating a primary relation into the current thematic processing domain.
. Interprets an XP within that domain using structural and nonstructural (interpretive) principles.

The current thematic processing domain   is the extended maximal projection of the last theta-assigner.[2] Complex NPs with RCs are an example of nonprimary phrases and, thus, are construally processed. When reading a sentence like (3), the processor will identify the RC as a nonprimary phrase and will associate it to the last thematic domain, which in our example is the NP including both, *the daughter and the colonel*. Nonstructural principles, including semantics and world knowledge, will choose the best candidate as host of the relative clause.

(3)   El periodista entrevistó a la hija del coronel que tuvo el accidente.
       The journalist interviewed the daughter of the colonel who had the accident

One of the ambiguities that arises with nonprimary phrases is RCs with complex NPs, but see Frazier and Clifton (in press) for an extensive review an empirical data about the processing of nonprimary relations and Gilboy et al., 1995, for RCs with complex NPs).

---

[2]*Extended maximal projection* defines a domain that includes one and only one θ-assigner (e.g., Vs, prepositions, Ns) and any projection dominating it that is compatible in terms of syntactic features. Thus V, I(nflection), and C(omplementizer) are compatible with a Verb as a θ-assigner (for a detailed discussion, see Frazier & Clifton, in press)

Why should the parser distinguish between primary and nonprimary phrases? In a phrase structure based model like the garden path model, phrase structure rules allow the parser to impose a quick analysis on the incoming lexical items to sort out limitations of human short-term memory. Phrase structure rules make it possible to assign a coherent syntactic analysis to each lexical item: Primary phrases are phrases that interact with the syntactic properties of previously analyzed items and, thus, should be analyzed in a manner that is globally consistent with the analysis carried out before. On the other hand, nonprimary phrases do not interact with any syntactic property of previous lexical items, and there is less pressure to make a decision, so it could be the case that no option needs to be chosen in the absence of more information.

THE PROCESSING OF RCS WITH COMPLEX NPs

As we have already said, the tuning hypothesis was elaborated primarily on the basis of Spanish data. Very briefly, in their original paper, Cuetos and Mitchell (1988) found that Spanish subjects attached a RC to the first NP in a complex NP of the form NP1-*of*-NP2.

(4)   El periodista entrevistó a la hija del coronel que tuvo el accidente.
        The journalist interviewed the daughter of the colonel who had the accident

The authors interpreted this result as a violation of the late closure principle in Spanish for this specific construction. More recently, they explored the hypothesis that this early attachment reflected the bias obtained in the Spanish corpus, where high-attachment was more frequent than low-attachment (Mitchell, Cuetos, & Corley, 1992). Since the original 1988 paper, different studies have addressed the problem of the processing of RCs with complex NPs in different languages (mostly Spanish and English, but also Italian, de Vicenzi & Job; 1993), and Dutch, Mitchell, Cuetos, & Brysbaert, 1994). For the moment, we restrict ourselves to the Spanish and English results.

The studies published on Spanish to date show an overwhelming preference for N1 in constructions of the type NP of NP RC in self paced reading experiments (Carreiras, 1992; Carreiras & Clifton, 1993; Cuetos & Mitchell, 1988; Mitchell & Cuetos, 1991). The results in English show a nonpreference when the exact translation of the Spanish versions are used (Carreiras & Clifton, 1993; Cuetos et al., this volume, chap. 6).

Gilboy et al. (1995) argued that in the case of RCs structural principles like minimal attachment and late closure are not at work. The principle involved in the processing of this construction is the construal principle. The construal principle predicts no difference in reading times for sentences like:

(5)   a. La policía arrestó a la hermana del criado que dió a luz recientemente dos gemelos.[3]
The police arrested the sister of the handyman who recently gave birth to twins

b. La policía arrestó al hermano de la criada que dió a luz recientemente dos gemelos.
The police arrested the brother of the handywoman who recently gave birth to twins

The RC will be associated with the extended maximal projection of the last theta-assigner, and this includes both Ns, *hermana* and *criado*. Nonstructural interpretive principles will help to choose the best host for the RC from among the candidates. Those principles include semantic or real-world plausibility.

In contrast, the tuning hypothesis predicts a N1 preference in Spanish, and a N2 preference in English. As we have already said, one of the predictions of the tuning hypothesis is that corpus bias and on-line effects should be the same; that is, a N1 bias in a Spanish corpus should produce an on-line N1 preference effect, whereas a N2 bias in an English corpus should produce an on-line N2 effect. The Spanish results conform to the hypothesis, but the English results do not: According to Mitchell's corpus studies (Mitchell, et al., 1992), there was a 62% bias toward N2 in an English corpus study, and consequently a N2 preference should be found in on-line experiments, at least when using the exact translations of the Spanish versions.[4]

Our aim in the rest of this chapter is to offer an explanation of the contradictory results obtained in Spanish and English in the processing of complex NPs with RCs. We hope to show that the differences between English and Spanish in the early versus late closure experiments previously cited are due not to frequency effects, but to segmentation effects in self-paced reading experiments, which, in turn, might be related to differences in prosodic patterns in the two languages.

---

[3]Sentences are from Carreiras and Clifton (1993).

[4]Frazier and Clifton found a N2 preference when using material slightly different from that normally studied: They included a reflexive in the RC. This is the only known experiment where an advantage of N2 over N1 was found in English.

SEGMENTATION EFFECTS

It has been established that segmentation affects reading times in self-paced reading experiments (Mitchell, 1987), so we would like to explore the possibility that segmentation is responsible for the apparent preference for the RC to be attached to the first NP in a complex NP (e.g., *hermana* in example (5a)). To explore this idea, we chose two different types of segmentation that were used in other experiments:

Large segmentation: This is the standard segmentation used in the majority of experiments published on Spanish. In this segmentation, the whole sentence, including the complex NP, is presented in one segment; the second segment contains the RC with the disambiguation.

(6)   La policía arrestó a la hermana del criado / que dió a luz recientemente dos gemelos.
       The police arrested the sister of the handyman / who recently gave birth to twins

Small segmentation: In this segmentation, the complex NP is further subdivided into two groups, so after the V we have the first NP in one segment, followed by the second NP in the second segment, and the RC at the end.

(7)   La policía arrestó / a la hermana / del criado / que dio a luz recientemente dos gemelos.
       The police arrested / the sister / of the handyman / who recently gave birth to twins

We designed an experiment using both types of segmentation. With large segmentation, we expected to replicate the N1 preference already found in the literature. On the other hand, if segmentation affects the outcome of a self-paced reading experiment, we expected small segmentation to behave differently; in particular, we expected there to be no preference for either N1 or N2.

Method

Forty-four Spanish-speaking undergraduates from the University of Barcelona participated for course credit. Twenty-four sentences were used, 16 from Carreiras and Clifton (1993), plus 8 more. Each sentence had a complex NP in postverbal position of the form N1-*de*-N2-RC, disambiguated with gender information that was conveyed semantically. One version of each pair was disambiguated towards a reading in which the RC modified N1 (early closure) and the other was disambiguated toward N2 (late closure). Disambiguation was effected by reversing the gender of N1 and N2 (by changing the gender markings). In half the sentences, the RC required a feminine host, and in half a masculine host. In addition, large and small segmentation were used. In the large segmentation, the whole sentence up to NP2 was presented in one frame, and the second frame included the RC. In the small segmentation, the sentence was divided in four frames: The first frame was from the beginning to the main V, the second included the first NP of the complex NP, the third included the *of*-NP part of the complex NP, and the fourth was the RC.

Each subject read 24 experimental sentences mixed with 90 filler sentences. All sentences were followed by a question. The questions for the experimental sentences asked about the content and host of the RC. The filler questions were either true/false statements or questions about the content of the sentences. Subjects were instructed to read at a normal rate and to answer as quickly and accurately as possible. A self paced moving window procedure was used, with underline preview of where letters would appear. Before each sentence a message was presented: APRIETA UNA TECLA CUANDO ESTES LISTO PARA EL SIGUIENTE ITEM, instructing subjects to press a specific key marked on the keyboard with their dominant hand when they were ready. Each successive pressing of the same key brought up the next segment of the sentence. Once the subject had read the whole sentence, a question appeared in the middle of the screen. Then, another press of the same key brought up the answers, again in the middle of the screen. Subjects had to press one of two specific keys to decide which was the correct answer. Each sentence was seen by one fourth of the subjects in each condition, and no subject saw more than one version of each sentence.

There were 20 practice trials to familiarize subjects with the self-paced reading procedure.

Results

Mean reading times for the RC segment appear in Table 7.1. A 2×2 analysis of variance, (ANOVA; disambiguation by segmentation) was performed. The main effect of disambiguation was reliable by subjects, $F_s(1, 43) = 25.13$, $p < .001$, and by items, $F_i(1, 23) = 14.12$, $p = .001$, indicating that RCs were read faster when disambiguating toward N1 than toward N2. The interaction Closure

× Segmentation was also significant, $F_s(1, 43) = 5.05$, $p < .05$, $F_i(1, 23) = 4.87$, $p < .05$. Planned comparisons indicated that RCs were read faster when they were disambiguated toward N1 only when subjects could read the whole sentence up to N2 in one frame (large segmentation), $F_s(1, 43) = 16.56$, $p < .001$, $F_i(1, 23) = 19.26$, $p < .001$), but not when the sentence was broken down into small segments (small segmentation), $F_s(1, 43) < 1$, $F_i(1, 23) < 1$.

TABLE 7.1
Mean Reading Times (in ms) for the RCs

Disambiguation	Segmentation	
	Large	Small
N1	2160	2241
N2	2704	2340

DISCUSSION AND CONCLUDING REMARKS

Our explanation of the segmentation effects found in our experiment relies on the prosodic information available in English and Spanish. Because differences in intonational patterns are of central importance in the discussion of our results, we offer here a description of the intonational patterns in English and Spanish.

English

Basically, it seems that what constitutes an intonative contour in English is a combination of pitch accents, phrasal stress, and boundary tone (Pierrehumbert, 1980). Phrasal stress and boundary tone are fixed, in the sense that a boundary tone comes at the end of an intonational contour, and phrasal stress comes right after the nuclear accent (Pierrehumbert, 1980). In English, the position of the nuclear accent is variable, because it is the primary way for English speakers to focus on any element, and, in principle, any word in a sentence is a candidate for nuclear stress.

Spanish

In Spanish, an intonational contour is defined as a combination of stress accent, phrasal accent, and boundary tone. Stress accent conforms to what are called the *accentual units,* a concept that can be equated to the concept of phonological word, as developed in the area of prosodic phonology. With respect to phrasal accent, what seems to be relevant in Spanish for its assignment is the position of the syllable in a sequence: It should be the last stressed syllable of the sentence (Martí, 1993; Navarro Tomás, 1982). Studies on the pronunciation of Spanish have emphasized that Spanish has a fixed invariable contour from the first stressed syllable to the last stressed syllable (called the *body* in Spanish), which is characterized by an overall decreasing tendency (Martí, 1993).

From the previous exposition, we highlight that Spanish has a fixed invariable contour and places prominence on the clause-final position. This implies that when native speakers of Spanish want to focus on an element of the sentence, they cannot use the same prosodic devices as English speakers; they must use syntactic devices, such as left-detachment and topicalization. In English, on the other hand, the position of phrase accent is variable; it follows nuclear stress whose position is variable, because almost any word in an English sentence can bear nuclear stress, depending on whether it is focused or not.

Turning now to a slightly different matter, many studies have shown that subvocalization is important in reading comprehension (Hardyck & Petrinovich, 1970; McGuigan & Shepperson, 1971). Slowiaczek and Clifton (1980) hypothesized that subvocalization allows a prosodic structure to be created. Like them, we hypothesize that subjects try to build the prosodic structure of a sentence while reading, and we also hypothetize that the prosodic structure will have information about the evolution of the intonative curve. In reading, information about which syllable will be the last one in an intonational phrase may come from different sources—for example, from punctuation marks (as Carreiras, 1992, has shown)—so it might also come from segmentation in a self-paced reading task.

If we assume that Spanish subjects use information provided by segmentation to create an intonative contour in a self-paced reading task, we predict different patterns of results in Spanish as a function of variations in segmentation.

Turning to the different forms of segmentation we used, we look first at the large segmentation. Because Spanish has such a fixed intonative contour, the usual declining curve will be assigned to written material: in our experiment, the whole frame *la policía arrestó a la hermana del criado.* The phrasal accent will be placed on the last stressed syllable of the segment, in our example *ado* (from *criado*), and we assume a closure of the utterance will be forced, because, as we have said, phrasal accent signals clause-final position. If, as Slowiaczek and Clifton (1980) proposed, prosodic structure helps to reorganize the structure of the sentence and highlight important information, then we assume that N1 will be readily available as a candidate for the RC, because it forms the main assertion of the sentence. When the RC appears, it will be associated with the domain of the last theta-assigner, but information from prosody already available will bias the association toward NP1.

In small segmentation, there is no cue for prosodic boundaries. This segmentation does not allow the reader to assign an intonative contour to the sentence in the usual way. When the segment containing the RC appears, the construal principle applies, and the RC is associated with the domain of the last θ-assigner. The selection of the best host (N1 or N2) for the RC is made on real-world plausibility grounds, so no preference for either N1 or N2 should be shown.

On the other hand, we are assuming that English-speaking subjects do not behave in the same way. In English the position of phrasal accent is variable, and, as we have said, follows the nuclear stress. The position of the nuclear stress depends on several factors (including focus and pragmatic factors). What we are suggesting is that English subjects cannot decide where to place phrasal accents as easily as Spanish subjects, and because the information coming from segmentation is not as important as it is for Spanish subjects, it is probably not used. For this reason, small segmentation and large segmentation in English will probably behave in the same way. In fact, we have some evidence of this, because Carreiras and Clifton (1993) used large segmentation and found no preference for N1 or N2 in English. Unpublished data from Clifton at the University of Massachusetts at Amherst (C. Clifton, personal communication), where small segmentation was used, also showed no preference in English. Taken together, these results suggest that large segmentation and small segmentation behave the same way in English.

We think we have offered an explanation of the Spanish data. In all experiments on Spanish published to date, the complex NP was presented together with the beginning of the sentence. It seems uncontroversial that segmentation may have some effect in the processing of sentences. What our results show is that it affects the preference for N1 or N2 as hosts of the RC in Spanish.

We believe that there is no effect of early or late closure in Spanish, because these structures are processed by the construal principle, not by the late closure principle. The effect found in the experiments in Spanish is due to an interaction between the segmentation used in self-paced reading experiments and the characteristics of prosodic patterns in Spanish. When prosody is not allowed to come into play, Spanish-speaking subjects behave like English-speaking subjects and show preference for neither N1 nor N2.

Certainly, several issues remain unresolved: For example, how does our explanation accounts for the different results obtained in other languages? How does the account explain individual differences?. More work needs to be done before the issue will be resolved, but we hope to continue working, trying to seek answers for every question.

REFERENCES

Altmann, G., & Steedman, M.J. (1988). Interaction with context during human sentence processing. *Cognition, 30,* 191–238.

Bever, T.G. (1970). The cognitive basis for linguistic structures. In J.R. Hayes (Ed.), *Cognition and the development of language* (pp. 279–362). New York: Wiley.

Brill, E., & Resnik, P. (1994). *A rule-based approach to prepositional phrase attachment disambiguation.* Proceedings of the fifteenth international conference on computational linguistics (COLING 94).

Carreiras, M. (1992). Estrategias de análisis sintáctico en el procesamiento de frases: cierre temprano vs. cierre tardío [Strategies of syntactic analysis in the processing of phrases: Early closure vs. late closure]. *Cognitiva, 4,* 3–27.

Carreiras, M., & Clifton, C. (1993). Relative clause interpretation preferences in Spanish and English. *Language and Speech, 36,* 353–372.

Clifton, C. (1988, August). *Restrictions on late closure: Appearance and reality.* Paper presented at the Sixth Australian Language and Speech Conference, University of New South Wales, Australia.

Clifton, C., & Ferreira, F. (1989). Ambiguity in context. *Language and Cognitive Processes, 4,* 77–104.

Clifton, C., Speer, S., & Abney, S.P. (1991). Parsing arguments: Phrase structure and argument structure as determinants of initial parsing decisions. *Journal of Memory and Language, 30,* 251–272.

Cuetos, F., & Mitchell, D.C. (1988). Crosslinguistic differences in parsing: Restrictions on the use of the late closure strategy in Spanish. *Cognition, 30,* 73–105.

Crain, S., & Steedman, M.J. (1985). On not being led up by the garden path: The use of context by the psychological parser. In D. Dowty, L. Kartunen, & A. Zwicky (Eds.), *Natural language parsing: Psychological, computational and theoretical perspectives* (pp. 320–358). Cambridge, England: Cambridge University Press.

de Vincenzi, M., & Job, R. (1993). Some observations on the universality of the late closure strategy. *Journal of Psycholinguistic Research, 22,* 189–206.

Frazier, L. (1978). *On comprehending sentences: Syntactic parsing strategies.* Doctoral dissertation, University of Connecticut. Distributed by Indiana University Linguistics Club.

Frazier, L. (1987). Sentence processing: A tutorial review. In M. Coltheart (Ed.), *Attention and performance XII: The psychology of reading* (pp. 559–586). Hillsdale, NJ: Lawrence Erlbaum Associates.

Frazier, L. (1990a). Exploring the architecture of the language system. In G. Altmann (Ed.). *Cognitive models of speech processing: Psycholinguistic and computational perspectives* (pp. 409–433). Cambridge, MA: MIT Press.

Frazier, L. (1990b). Parsing modifiers: Special purpose routines in the HSPM? In D. Balota, G.B. Flores d'Arcais, & K. Rayner (Eds.), *Comprehension processes in reading* (pp. 303–330). Hillsdale, NJ: Lawrence Erlbaum Associates.

Frazier, L., & Clifton, Ch. (in press). *Construal.* Cambridge, MA: MIT Press.

Frazier, L., & Fodor, J.D. (1978). The sausage machine: A new two-stage parsing model. *Cognition, 6,* 291–325.

Gibson, E., Pearlmutter, N., Canseco-González, E., & Hickok, G. (1995). *Cross-linguistic attachment preferences: evidence from English and Spanish.* Manuscript submitted for publication.

Gilboy, E., Sopena, J.M., Clifton, C., & Frazier, L. (1995). Argument structure and association preferences in the processing of Spanish and English complex NPs. *Cognition, 54,* 131–167.

Hardyck, C.D., & Petrinovich, L.R. (1970). Subvocal speech and comprehension level as a function of the difficulty level of reading material. *Journal of Verbal Learning and Verbal Behaviour, 9,* 647–652.

Hindle, D., & Rooth, M. (1991). Structural ambiguity and lexical relations. In *Proceedings of the 29th annual Meeting of the Association for Computational Linguistics,* Berkeley, CA.

Juliano, C., & Tanenhaus, M.K. (1993). *Contingent frequency effects in syntactic ambiguity resolution.* Proceedings of the 15th Annual Conference of the Cognitive Science Society.

Kimball, J. (1973). Seven principles of surface structure parsing in natural language. *Cognition, 2,* 15–47.

MacDonald, M., Pearlmutter, N., & Seidenberg, M. (1994). The lexical nature of syntactic ambiguity resolution. *Psychological Review, 101,* 676–703.

Marcus, M., Santorini, B, & Marcinkiewicz, M. (1993). Building a large annotated corpus of English: the Penn Treebank. *Computational Linguistics, 19 (2),* 103–103.

Martí, J. (1993, November). *Prosody as the global expression of the speech cognitive structure.* Paper presented at the Workshop on Language Cognition and Computation, Barcelona, Spain.

McGuigan, F.J., & Shepperson, M.H. (1971). The effect of remedial reading in covert oral behavior. *Journal of Clininal Psychology, 27,* 541–543.

Mitchell, D.C. (1987). Lexical guidance in human parsing: Locus and processing characteristics. In M. Coltheart (Ed.), *Attention and Performance XII: The psychology of reading* (pp. 601–618). Hillsdale, NJ: Lawrence Erlbaum Associates.

Mitchell, D.C., & Cuetos, F. (1991). *Restrictions on Late Closure: The computational underpinnings of parsing strategies in Spanish and English.* Unpublished manuscript.

Mitchell, D.C., Cuetos, F., & Brysbaert, M. (1994, May). *Modifier attachment in Dutch and Spanish: Evidence favoring statistical rather than universal "linguistic" accounts.* Paper presented at the Fourth Workshop of Language Comprehension, Giens, France.

Mitchell, D.C., Cuetos, F., & Corley, M.M.B. (1992, March). *Statistical versus linguistic determinants of parsing bias: Crosslinguistic evidence.* Paper presented at the Fifth Annual CUNY conference on Human Sentence Processing, New York.

Mitchell, D.C., Cuetos, F. & Zagar, D. (1990). Reading in different languages: Is there a universal mechanism for parsing sentences? In D. Balota, G.B. Flores D'Arcais, & K. Rayner (Eds.). *Comprehension processes in reading* (pp. 285–302). Hillsdale, NJ: Lawrence Erlbaum Associates.

Navarro Tomás, T. (1982). *Manual de pronunciación española* [Manual of Spanish pronunciation]. Madrid, Spain: Consejo Superior de Investigaciones Científicas.

Pierrehumbert, J. (1980). *The phonology and phonetics of English intonation.* Unpublished doctoral dissertation, Massachusetts Institute of Technology, Cambridge.

Rayner, K., Carlson, M., & Frazier, L. (1983). The interaction of syntax and semantics during sentence processing: Eye movements in the analysis of semantically biased sentences. *Journal of Verbal Learning and Verbal Behavior, 22,* 358–374.

Slowiaczek, M.L., & Clifton, C. (1980). Subvocalization and reading for meaning. *Journal of Verbal Learning and Verbal Behavior, 19,* 573–582.

Taraban, R., & McClelland, J.L. (1988). Constituent attachment and thematic role assignment in sentence processing: Influences of content-based expectations. *Journal of Memory and Language, 27,* 597–632.

8

Processing Empty Categories in Spanish

José E. García-Albea
Universitat Rovira i Virgili
Tarragona, Spain

Sheila Meltzer
Graduate Center of CUNY
New York, USA

THE MODULARITY ISSUE IN LANGUAGE PROCESSING

The ongoing debate about the best human language processing model has inspired a surge of experimental work designed to address issues of cognitive architecture. Much of this work has attempted to address specifically the question of whether the language processor operates in a modular or an interactionist manner. It is recognized that, although these are two idealized extremes, the possibility also exists that reality is not quite so ideal. Nevertheless, it is a useful, and perhaps necessary, exercise for the field, in these pioneering forays, to assume an extreme hypothesis, even if that leads to the conclusion that such a hypothesis must be rejected. Therefore, for introductory purposes at least, we speak in terms of strictly modular versus freely interactive models.

The mandate of formal linguistic theory, by virtue of the competence–performance distinction (Chomsky, 1965), is the study of a presumably autonomous domain, the contents of which are limited to conscious grammatical intuitions; the theory need not concern itself with phenomena located beyond these borders. The issue we address here, broadly put, is whether the autonomous domain defined by linguistic competence has, in fact, some correlate in an empirically valid psychological model of language processing.

A modular model of the human language processor is one in which part of the cognitive system is specifically assigned to the processing of syntactic information, enjoying a cognitive autonomy that might be thought of as mirroring the informational autonomy of a linguistic competence model. J.A. Fodor (1983) presented a strong defense of such a modularity thesis, providing the schema for a cognitive architecture composed of two inherently distinct types of processes. One set is composed of the central, or global, cognitive processes, such as the ones involved in belief fixation, analogical reasoning, and nondemonstrative inference—the sort of processes that are sensitive to the subject's expectations, utilities, and general world knowledge. The other set is comprised of the input systems, or vertical faculties, related to eccentric processing domains, such as musical ability, visuomotor coordination, face recognition, and spatial relations. This latter is the set in which language processing would constitute yet another eccentric domain, a genuine module unto itself. In contrast with central cognitive processes, each of the modular input systems is characterized by speed, mandatory application, domain specificity, shallow output, and, crucially, informational encapsulation. The mechanism, once it has been automatically triggered by a stimulus relevant to its domain, is impenetrable, its operations impervious to influence from other cognitive systems. In this sense, language processing is strictly bottom–up, so that syntactic principles, where applicable, are always the first to operate. This does not imply that there is never any influence of extralinguistic information on sentence comprehension, but that syntactic principles, where applicable, always operate first and independently.

Although the attribution of remarkable speed and mandatoriness to the language processor is, effectively, universally accepted by researchers in this field, the same cannot be said of the strict informational encapsulation that is at the core of J.A. Fodor's model. Alternative models, with a certain intuitive appeal, feature a so-called *interactive processor,* unfettered by the rigid constraints of modularity. A model of such a processor need ascribe neither autonomy nor priority to a syntactic, or any other, component of the machine. Such an opportunistic parsing machine is free, at least in instances of ambiguity in the input string, to appeal to clues inferred from the discourse context, without particular deference to any structural levels. Guided instead by the search for the quickest route to a comprehensive interpretation of the stimulus, such a language processor will access a wide variety of clues, syntactic as well as contextual, in order to get the job done.

If there is to be any discussion at all about whether the human mind processes syntax in an encapsulated module, we must begin with some clarification of what belongs inside that capsule. The most likely definition of that can be borrowed from syntactic theory, and we assume here some fairly well-established tenets of the government and binding (GB)[1] theory framework of generative grammar (Chomsky, 1981). An ongoing debate throughout the history of psycholinguistic experimentation has considered the degree to which the real-time language processing mechanism makes reference to the linguistic competence that is described by generative linguistic theory (see J.D. Fodor, 1993). We return later to discussion of some of the relevant evidence. It should be said from the start, nonetheless, that this chapter is informed by and built on the hypothesis that the human processor does, in fact, have access to, and makes use of, a knowledge of syntax.

Nicol (1988) distinguished between the tree-parsing and the coreference-processing activities of the processor. Whereas the former takes charge of the structural relations between constituents, the business of the latter is the interpretation of referentially dependent elements—often called, in a loose, atheoretic sense, *anaphora*—instances of which abound in any sampling of language data. Reflexives (e.g., *herself, himself*), reciprocals (e.g., *each other*) and pronouns (e.g., *she, he*) require an antecedent in the previous discourse in order to be interpretable. The process of antecedent assignment to such anaphoric elements is one area where pragmatics might plausibly influence the processor.

Syntax distinguishes among several classes of these elements. Some have their antecedents clearly determined by the syntax: the binding theory does this for reflexives, the empty category principle (ECP) does it for syntactic movement traces, and control theory does it for the implicit subjects of nonfinite (i.e., uninflected) verbs. For others, such as pronouns and the implicit subjects of finite (i.e., inflected) verbs, there is little in the grammar that actually serves to fully disambiguate their antecedents. In these latter cases, it is clear that pragmatics will eventually come into play. The question can then be asked: When, and under

---

[1]GB theory is a cover term for the whole Chomskian framework (after Chomsky, 1981), sometimes called principles and parameters theory. BT (binding theory), and GT (government theory), are two subcomponents of GB. The former is concerned with the realations of anaphors and pronominals to their antecedents (binding principles); the latter introduces the central notions of government and governing category, which are crucial for establishing the domains and conditions of application of other principles (binding, theta-role and case assignment, empty category principle).

what circumstances?

The identification and interpretation of anaphoric elements, a prominent topic throughout the development of modern syntactic theory, is a likely focus of interest in the development of a processing theory. Effectively, every discourse includes these elements, so it is essential that some mechanism for their processing be provided by any model of the human language processor. Given an interactive model, assignment of a referent to an anaphor will be made at least as quickly as conscious awareness of the referent's identity exists. This can be achieved in a completely opportunistic manner, taking equal advantage of all available clues, be they syntactic (i.e., inflexible) or pragmatic (i.e., dependent on one's common sense). Given a modular model, the default hypothesis would be that anaphora, like all other syntactic units, must at least get a stamp of approval from the language module before being passed along to the more creative faculties. Each element of a sentence must satisfy the constraints of Universal Grammar (UG; as defined by a given theory of syntax), as well as the rules of the language-specific grammar; processing of all referentially dependent elements, then, at least to this extent, falls within the jurisdiction of the syntactic module.

Counterevidence

Marslen-Wilson and Tyler (1987) reported experimental data that suggest that pragmatic implications drawn from the discourse are used parallel with, and equally as fast as, syntactic clues in the assignment of an antecedent to the pronominal subject of a verb.

Following the aural presentation of an incomplete discourse as in (1), subjects responded to a visually presented object pronoun.

(1)   As Philip was walking back from the shop he saw an old woman trip and fall flat on her face in the street. She seemed unable to get up again. Running toward ... HIM/HER

Naming latency to *him* was slower than to *her.* The reason for this difference, according to the authors, is that as soon as you hear *running,* you make use of the pragmatic implications of the verb and the context to assign *Philip* as the subject of the gerund. This makes *him* an inappropriate continuation of the fragment (under the most plausible assumption that this is not a presentation sentence introducing a new character into the context, or a statement about the feasibility of her running).

Furthermore, the effect was not significantly greater when fragments were presented with overt subject pronouns, as in (2).

(2)   He ran toward ... HIM/HER

The conclusion drawn from this pattern of results is that the effect of pragmatic inference is effectively equivalent to that of the gender disambiguation provided by overt pronouns. This demonstrates the use of pragmatic inference and top–down control of the parser, prohibited by the modularity hypothesis.

These data, at face value, go a long way toward undermining the modularity hypothesis. However, there are several serious flaws in the materials and design of the study. For instance, fully half of the experimental items presented only one human (or otherwise animate) referent in the introductory sentence. Consider (3):

(3)   As John was walking home, he realized that he didn't have his door-key. Searching through ... HIS/HER

In an item like this, the pragmatically inappropriate completion (*her*) is in fact an ungrammatical one, irrespective of any subject assignment, because there is no gender-matched antecedent available for the possessive pronoun (again assuming that this will not turn out to be a presentation clause, such as *Searching through her bag was a neighbor...*).

Furthermore, *her* is lexically ambiguous in some contexts. In (3), for example, the experimental assumption is that *her* will be parsed as a possessive pronoun. Consider, then, (4).

(4)   As they were walking home through the wood, Clare noticed with alarm that a large rotten branch was about to fall onto Sam's head. She realized that she had to act quickly.
Shouting loudly at ... HIM/HER

Assume for a moment that the processor has indeed selected Clare as the shouter. Whom would she be shouting at? One perfectly plausible object would be *her companion* (friend, brother, etc.). The existence of this grammatical option (against the predicted advantage for *him*) casts doubt on the interpretation, supposing the need for reanalysis. An alternative proposal (J.A. Fodor, Garrett, & Swinney, 1994) suggests that the search for an antecedent is normally triggered by encountering an overt anaphoric element in the speech stream. In this experiment, the probe itself is a pronoun that must be integrated into the ongoing sentence. The effect, then, would be a consequence of not having used a task that could tap the on-line comprehension processes more subtly.

Apart from the flaws in the materials, there are other limitations inherent to these experiments that, at the very least, make the results far from conclusive. On the one hand, the distance (time interval) between the verb and the probe varies substantially, without having any effect on the naming times. This favors an interpretation involving the triggering role of the anaphoric probe and casts some doubt on the rapid and opportunistic processes assumed by the interactive model. On the other hand, Marslen-Wilson and Tyler (1987) did not use baseline controls in their experiments, comparing the congruent probes directly with incongruent probes. This makes it especially difficult to decide between an excitatory or an inhibitory interpretation of the experimental effects.

In conclusion, it is clear that Marslen-Wilson and Tyler's results show contextual/interactive effects on the naming task, but important questions can be asked about the nature and *locus* of those effects along the course of sentence processing. There is not sufficient evidence to show whether pragmatic factors intervened in the syntactic module or, in fact, occurred only after the syntax had done its work.

Positive Evidence: Some Preliminary Considerations

Regardless of any methodological weaknesses of the Marslen-Wilson and Tyler study, it is incumbent on the proponents of the modularity hypothesis to respond to its claims. Although a simple failure to replicate results would supply ammunition, it would also fail, obviously, to improve on the methodological problems inherent in the experimental approach, leaving us no better informed at all. Even if the counterevidence to the modularity hypothesis were shown to be questionable, that is far from tantamount to providing support for the existence of modularity itself.

How, then, can modularity be proven, or at least supported, experimentally? One doesn't have to be long at this exercise to realize that, although it is relatively easy to design an experiment that would demonstrate the violation of modularity where it is expected, the same is not true of the contrary design. An instance of interaction could be identified and quantified, thus compromising a theory of autonomous processing. Any given instance of autonomous processing, on the other hand, would not compromise a theory allowing for interaction.

We want to emphasize that the modularity thesis as proposed by J.A. Fodor (1983) most specifically does not claim that all mental processes are performed within the autonomous modular systems. There are a number of perceptual modules or input systems, and the language processor is one of them. These input systems function to get information into the central processors; the flow of information is one-way. Language data, once encoded by the language module, are served to the central cognitive mechanisms for further processing. Thus, we would expect that language comprehension will demonstrate, in the end, effects of higher level cognition; this kind of effect will then be more easily reflected in the output of the whole system. But a demonstration of plausibility effects on the output of comprehension does not imply that all factors have operated in the same way and at the same time. The challenging task for experimental psycholinguistics, guided by the modularity hypothesis, is to discover which factors are involved and to what extent their effects can be dissociated, mostly by being sensitive to different temporal constraints.

One approach, then, to facing this challenge is to highlight the contrast between operations on two specific bits of linguistic data, one of which we expect the language module to take greater proprietary interest in than the other. Generative linguistic theory draws distinctions among syntactic elements (e.g., different classes of words) and the nature and extent of syntactic operations on each one. Two different elements that appear in otherwise identical input strings can have greater or lesser obligations to the syntactic module. We can rely on these theoretical distinctions to provide a gauge for where we expect greater or lesser modular versus central cognitive activity. We can then plot the time course closely enough to detect the pattern of dissociations that follow from the processing of the sentence.

In addition to the referentially dependent elements that are phonologically overt (i.e., can be heard in the speech stream and, not coincidentally, are graphically represented by writing systems and listed in dictionaries), there is a parallel set of covert elements that, though not perceivable by the ear, should arguably be present in an abstract representation of sentence structure. Chomsky (1981, 1982, 1986b) distinguished two such phonologically empty pronominals, *PRO* (also known as *big pro*) and *pro* (also known as *little pro*). These two elements are licensed and controlled by different, though intricately interwoven, mechanisms of the theory; in fact, explanation of their distinction has been a driving motivation in much of the theory's formal development. Their definition, even their uniqueness, remains a matter of considerable debate among theorists. If the processor makes the same distinction as GB grammar, and if the processor is a modular one, then we would expect to see a difference in the on-line treatment of these two elements.

This is the approach that we have taken in the experimental research we present here. Before we do that, however, we need to outline some fundamentals of the relevant linguistic properties.

EMPTY CATEGORIES IN LINGUISTIC THEORY

An empty category (EC) is an abstract entity, void of phonological content, that fills a node in a syntactic constituent tree. The ECs that have drawn the interest of psycholinguists are exclusively noun phrases (NPs). Although they lack semantic content, they serve the grammatical function of nominals, and fill NP nodes in syntactic trees. Parallel to the set of different types of audible NPs—lexical nouns and expressions, pronouns, reflexives—is a set of types of inaudible ones. Each NP must be licensed in its position through observance of the principles of UG, and each must have content in order to be interpretable. In order to have content, an EC must be identifiable, and this is accomplished through association with another referential element in the tree.

This grammatical association can be examined by observing its effects on antecedent activation during sentence processing. One of the major areas of examination in psycholinguistics has been the processing of these elements, often referred to as *gaps,* or *implicit arguments* (see J.D. Fodor, 1989, for a review). A profitable evaluation of the experimental data relies crucially on a clarification of the descriptive characteristics of these elements and a reasonable understanding of their theoretical role. The remainder of this section is devoted to outlining, in an accessible way, the minimum relevant aspects of GB theory needed to make such an evaluation.

The Projection Principle

Each verb discharges a certain number of prespecified thematic roles, or arguments, inherent in the meaning of the verb. If a given verb subcategorizes for an object with a patient role, then a clause headed by that verb cannot be understood without at least an implicit understanding of a nominal representing that role; the use of the verb *fill* in example (5) requires that some X be understood as filled.

(5)   a. Which node does the patient fill?
　　　　b. The patient fills the node of the object NP.
　　　　c. *The patient fills.[2]

---

[2]The asterisk indicates an ungrammatical expression.

D-structure[3] is a "pure" representation of these thematically relevant relationships as grammatical functions. Some arguments are moved at S-stucture to satisfy other principles of the grammar, such as the case filter, but guided, as well, by the theta-criterion, which says essentially that each chain must have one and only one theta role. The Logical Form (LF) representation of a clause expresses, in a particular formal notation, the argument relationships inherent to the verb. It is possible to avoid redundancy in the grammar by stipulating that representations at each syntactic level are projected from the lexicon. This generalization is captured by the *projection principle* (Chomsky, 1981), which states that the thematic properties of a tree remain constant throughout the syntactic derivation. In other words, all the arguments of a verb must be present at each level. If the rule Move α applies and a NP is moved, as in, for example, the derivation of a *wh*-question, such as (5a), at S-structure an abstract trace is left in the D-structure object position, enabling the identification of the argument via a chain, and satisfying the projection principle. As a configuration of the grammatical functions of a clause, every D-structure requires a subject in addition to any lexically specified complements. The extended projection principle (Chomsky, 1982) stipulates that, because there is a subject position at D-structure, there must also be one present at every level of grammatical representation.

To illustrate these configurational relationships, let us assume a tree representing the major expansions shown in (6).

The subject NP is generated in the Spec(ifier) node of the inflectional projection Agr(eement). Finite and nonfinite clauses are distinguished by a feature of Tense [+/- finite]. Infinitivals and gerunds are [-finite], and do not have explicit subjects. On the other hand, in all [+finite] clauses in English, the subject is a lexical NP. Spanish, like all the Romance languages (with the exception of French), and unlike English, is a null-subject language: Its grammar allows for a gap in the subject position of a finite verb as well. Following the projection principle, there must be an EC in each of these subject positions. The

---

[3]The notions D-structure and S-structure are reminiscent of the previous notions of deep structure and surface structure, respectively. The new expressions are not only intended to avoid some misunderstandings evoked by the former ones, but they also stand for some changes in content that correspond to the developments of generative grammar in the last fifteen years. Briefly, D-structure is the level that encodes the lexical properties of the constituents of the sentence and represents the basic argument relations between those constituents; S-structure represents the more superficial properties of the sentence, the actual ordering of the constituents in the surface string, and the traces of all elements that have been moved from their base positions via syntactic transformations. D-structure is thus related to S-structure by the transformational component, whereas S-structure provides input to the interpretative components, the phonetic form (PF) and the logical form (LF).

earlier, *PRO,* is defined as a pronominal anaphor (Chomsky, 1981); the later, *pro,* is a pure pronoun (Chomsky, 1982).

(6)   C''

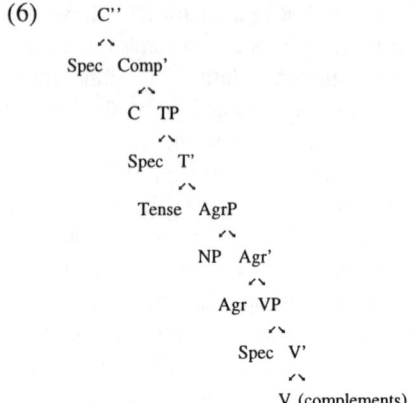

Lacking lexical content, a null subject, like other ECs, must be linked to some other element from which it inherits a referential index and identifying Phi (agreement) features (person, number, and gender). A discussion of the properties of *PRO* and *pro,* and the mechanisms by which they are licensed and identified, necessitates first a brief outline of the theory of binding.

Binding Theory: Anaphors Versus Pronouns

The standard BT evolved through several different formal definitions of anaphors and pronouns during its development by Chomsky in various works over two decades (Chomsky, 1973, 1980, 1981, 1982, 1986a, 1986b). This component of the grammar explains the distribution of the different NP types in terms of their structural dependence on, or independence from, coreferential elements in the same sentence.

In common usage outside of theoretical linguistics, the terms *anaphor* and *pronoun* overlap. Any substantive to which a word occurring later in the sentence refers back is an *antecedent;* the word that refers back to this antecedent is usually called a *pronoun.* The process is often referred to as *anaphora.* In fact, there are two distinct subclasses of such semantically deficient NPs, and they fall into (a near, but not totally perfect) complementary distribution. The categories are defined by their values (+ or -) for the abstract syntactic features [pronominal] and [anaphor]. The formulation, as standardly given (Chomsky, 1981), consists of the following three principles:

(7)   a. An anaphor is A(rgument)-bound in its governing category.[4]
           b. A pronominal is A-free in its governing category.
           c. An Referring-expression is A-free everywhere.

In other words, an anaphor (i.e., any NP that has the value [+anaphoric] in its feature representation) must be preceded by a referentially coindexed antecedent in the same domain. Hence, a reflexive, which is anaphoric, cannot appear in subject position in example (8). Wherever an anaphor may appear, a pronoun (i.e., any NP bearing the feature value [+pronominal]) enters into obligatory disjoint reference with the potential antecedent. Hence, a pronoun in object position may not be coreferential with the subject of the same clause (example (9)). A R-expression does not bear a positive value for either of the relevant features, and must always be free, as illustrated by the unacceptability of (10) with the given indexing.

(8)   *Himself saw him.

(9)   *John$_i$ saw him$_i$.

(10)   *John$_i$ saw John$_i$.

The Distribution of ECs

Chomsky (1981) assumed that there is actually only one EC, which appears with different feature combinations distributed according to functional use. Every EC must have an index and a means by which it inherits content. Some are created by virtue of the rule *Move* α. When a NP moves from one argument position to another, it leaves behind a NP-trace [+anaphoric, -pronominal]. When a NP moves to Comp position in question formation, it leaves behind a [-anaphoric, -pronominal] *wh*-trace. An EC created by movement is coindexed (bound) and chain-linked to its moved antecedent, from which it inherits its content.

---

[4]Obviously, Government Theory (GT) is crucial to BT, because the binding relations hold in a certain domain that is defined under government. The relevant concepts can be defined informally as follows:
  Government: α governs β if the first maximal projection dominating α is also the first maximal projection dominating β, and α is a lexical category.
  Governing category: α is the governing category for β if α is the first maximal projection dominating the governor of β that also has a subject accessible to β. (For a more formal discussion of the concepts, cf. Chomsky, 1986b).

An EC may also be base-generated. The subject of nonfinite verbs, for one, may not be explicitly stated, as shown in the well-formed cases of (11).

(11)   a. *Mary doesn't know what Mary to do.
         b. Mary doesn't know what to do.
         c. *John admitted John eating all the chocolate.
         d. John admitted eating all the chocolate.

Rather, the subject of the nonfinite verb is understood. It is coreferent with an antecedent in the matrix clause, even though there is no syntactic movement chain linking them. The empty category *PRO,* defined by the features [+anaphoric, +pronominal], stands for this implicit subject and gets its referential index via control theory, which relates it to an antecedent NP in a higher clause.[5]

Chomsky (1982) completed the paradigm with the introduction of *pro,* defined as [-anaphoric, +pronominal]. It is licensed in subject position in languages that have "strong agreement." It inherits its agreement features from the subject agreement node at S-structure, in the Spec position of this node. Like overt pronouns, and unlike *PRO, pro* is freely linked to an antecedent outside its local domain (for a more extended treatment, see also Fernández Soriano, 1989; Rizzi, 1982, 1986; Torrego, 1981).

---

[5]This coreference is thus achieved by a relationship known as control. In the core case of complement clauses, the controller may be either the subject or the object of the matrix clause, depending on the matrix verb. This is illustrated by the following examples:

(a) John$_i$ promised Bill *PRO$_i$* to go on a diet.
(b) John persuaded Bill$_i$ *PRO$_i$* to go on a diet.

Chomsky (1981) introduced the base-generated category *PRO* and derived its distribution via BT in what is known as the *PRO Theorem,* which stipulates that *PRO* does not have a governing category. This prevents the simultaneous application of the principles designated as (7a) and (7b) of BT, which would otherwise yield a paradoxical situation. An element has a governing category only if it is governed by a lexical item. An element in subject position of a nonfinite verb has no governor, and, hence, no governing category. It follows from this that there is no domain in which *PRO* must be both bound and free, hence, leaving no paradox. The question of when PRO is actually bound or free, behaving like an anaphor or a pronoun, respectively, is also undertaken by control theory. We are obviously interested in the former case, as developed in the experimental work presented in the next section.

THE CONTRAST BETWEEN PRONOUNS AND *PRO* AS A CASE STUDY FOR MODULARITY

Although English is standardly analyzed (at least within this theoretical framework) to license the occurrence of *PRO* as a subject of a nonfinite (i.e., uninflected) sentential clause, it is commonly assumed that English grammar does not license the occurrence of *pro* in any position. Spanish, on the other hand, although evidencing a usage of *PRO* similar to that of English, is a null-subject language, licensing the use of *pro* as grammatical subject of a finite verb. Because it is a null subject language, Spanish offers an opportunity to compare the on-line treatment of two abstract elements with different syntactic statuses that appear in otherwise comparable surface strings.

Accordingly, we present here data from original experimental research conducted in Spanish with native Spanish-speaking subjects. This research aims to elucidate the psychological reality of empty categories by discerning whether the processor treats *PRO* and *pro* in identical or distinctive manners. The research asks to what extent people appeal to discourse context in their unconscious processing of these two elements. If there is evidence that they are in fact treated differently, then it will be interesting to ask whether that difference can be predicted by syntactic theory.

Tangential to the stated methodological efficacy of studying a language that licenses both of the null pronominals, there lies a more general interest, for what should be obvious reasons, in contributing to the extension of the realm of processing studies beyond the boundaries of the English language. The experiments we present here employ a slightly revised version of the crossmodal priming (CMP) paradigm. Although the methodology is by now a familiar one in the psycholinguistic literature, this study is one of the first to have extended it to materials in a language other than English. Any significant results yielded by these efforts, then, will attest, at the least, to the applicability of this technique to a wider examination of the human language processor, not simply the English language processor. Let us start, however, by briefly discussing the main applications of this technique to English, to provide the necessary background for a better justification of our experiments.

Empirical Evidence from CMP Experiments: English Results

The CMP paradigm (Swinney, 1979) has been extended in several recent studies to the interpretation of referentially dependent elements; a review of this work can be found in Nicol and Swinney (1989). The combined results of these studies suggest that when an antecedent for a referentially dependent NP is uniquely selected by the syntax, there is priming for that NP and only that NP (Swinney, Ford, Frauenfelder, & Bresnan, 1988, for *wh*-traces; Nicol, 1988, for reflexives). When there is syntactic ambiguity as to the referent, then all potential referents are reaccessed, without regard to real-world knowledge (Nicol, 1988, for object pronouns).

Subjects watch a CRT monitor while listening through a headset to prerecorded sentences. At some point during each item—crucially predetermined, but unknown to the subject—a word is flashed briefly on the screen. The task can be either to make a yes/no lexical decision, or to say the word aloud (the naming task), while the aural stimulus continues on to some experimentally irrelevant but contextually sound completion of the sentence. The interval between presentation of the visual target and onset of subject's response is measured. When the visual target is a high associate of a potential antecedent in the sentence (or the same repeated antecedent), shorter reaction times (RTs; with respect to a control condition) will indicate priming and, in consequence, some kind of antecedent reactivation.

As discussed in the introduction, one of the weaknesses inherent in the fragment completion task employed by Marslen-Wilson and Tyler (1989) is the inability to precisely determine the basis for the RT difference. The CMP paradigm provides a way to more closely track the course of antecedent priming. With this task, there is no need to wait for a resolution point at which to look for overload. If referential assignment is made immediately on encountering a pragmatic clue, then at that point—immediately after the biasing verb—there should be priming for only the pragmatically preferred subject.

J.A. Fodor, et al., (1994) ran a CMP experiment, using materials closely modeled on Marslen-Wilson and Tyler's. After replicating the original results with a completion task, they proceeded to use CMP to examine processing of *PRO* while avoiding the effects of object pronouns. Their study presented items like those in (12):

(12)   The fireman carried a rope toward the little girl who was trapped on the ledge, immobilized with fear. He moved very careful/[1]ly.

       a.   He crawled cautiously/[2] toward her/[3] so he could hand her the rope and save her.
       b.   Crawling cautiously/[2] toward her/[3] so that he could hand her the rope, he managed to save her.

In the overt pronoun condition (12a), naming of *fireman* (but not of *girl*) was significantly faster at test point 2 when compared with test point 1. In the

PRO condition (12b), there was no such change in the RTs. The authors attributed this to a parsing strategy by which antecedent assignment to a zero pronoun is delayed until the appearance of some kind of sentential trigger, (e.g., an overt anaphoric element). In fact, when comparing test point 3 with test point 2, there was priming only in the *PRO* condition, but it occurred for both the appropriate (*fireman*) and the inappropriate (*girl*) antecedents.

These results are clearly incompatible with the interactive model proposed by Marslen-Wilson and Tyler. They suggest that semantic/pragmatic influences from the previous discourse are submitted to the dicta of the grammatical information. In the only case that shows contextual facilitation, this is confounded with the potential effect of the overt pronoun and its agreement features of gender, number, and person (and also with the possible influence of the discourse focus). The critical condition, for Marslen-Wilson and Tyler's argumentation, that of *PRO,* did not show any separate (and/or differential) contextual effect.

Processing differences between *PRO* and overt pronouns might be due to their acoustic reality (empty vs. full elements) or to the syntactic constraints to which they are subject (A-bound vs. A-free pronominals). The possibility of testing the behavior of an empty category that is also a free pronominal, such as *pro,* provides us with an opportunity to disentangle those two potential factors. The main question addressed in the experiments that follow can now be formulated in this way: Does *pro* behave like *PRO* or like an overt pronoun? The answer to this question should be most pertinent to testing the modular extent of sentence processing.

Two Empty Categories in Parallel Structures: Spanish Results

Spanish has a set of overt subject pronouns, similar to the English paradigm, overtly specified for gender and for number in the third person, as shown in (13).

(13)   *él:* masculine, singular, third person
          ella: feminine, singular, third person
          ellos: masculine, plural, third person
          ellas: feminine, plural, third person

Contrary to English, Spanish is a null-subject (or *pro*-drop) language, and, as such, also licenses a phonologically empty counterpart to the overt pronouns as the subject of a finite verb, which is designated *pro.*

Principle (7b) of the BT states that a pronoun must be free in its governing category. For all relevant purposes, this means simply that a pronoun cannot have an antecedent within the same clause. The theory makes this negative statement about the referential indexing of any pronoun, limiting the set of possible antecedents, but has no business in the actual selection process. Where licensed, *pro* inherits its Phi features from the Agreement node. Like any other pronoun, as long as it remains unbound in its governing category, it is syntactically free to pick any discourse referent with appropriate Phi features. Whatever procedure is involved in the interpretation of pronouns, there is, at least, no sentence grammar rule of coreference involved. *PRO,* on the other hand, is not a pure pronoun but an anaphoric element. It inherits its Phi features from its controller, another NP with which it is coindexed, and it must be coreferential with that NP.

According to the extended projection principle examined before, every clause must have a subject. Nonfinite verbs, namely gerunds and infinitives, may not have lexical NP subjects because this is not a position in which a NP can receive syntactic Case. The subject of a nonfinite verb, in Spanish as in English, is the phonologically empty element *PRO*. Like *pro, PRO* is an abstract syntactic element with no phonological content. Unlike *pro, PRO* is controlled by a NP in a higher clause.

Because *PRO* as the subject of a nonfinite verb in a simple sentence can only have arbitrary reference (e.g., PRO_{arb} *Voting twice is illegal*), and the studies presented examine the search for antecedents of null subjects, two-clause sentences were required. In the sentence items composed for these studies, the null subjects appeared in subordinate adverbial clauses. When *PRO* is the subject of a subordinate adverbial clause, it was antecedent-controlled by, and coindexed with, the subject NP of the main clause. This was true even if the adverbial was preposed, as in the experimental sentences we have used, so that *PRO* linearly precedes its antecedent.[6]

Assuming that the standard syntactic theory is correct in its characterization of referentially dependent elements, we would expect a modular processor to respect the distinctions it makes. If encapsulation of processing is contingent on structure, then we would expect to see differential treatment of these two different null subjects. Given the same discourse and parallel sentence structures, a processor that respects the encapsulation of syntax would treat *PRO* and *pro* in distinct manners, since one has a syntactic controller, whereas the other can

---

[6]The obligatory character of this controlling relation is illustrated by the contrast in acceptability between (a) and (b) in the following context:

- Mary and John held hands in the delivery room.
(a) While <u>PRO_i</u> squeezing her hand, he$_i$ kissed her.
(b) While <u>PRO_i</u> giving birth, he$_i$ kissed her. (?)

be freely coindexed with any discourse antecedent outside its governing category.

Two experiments are now reported. They were run with different subject samples (from the same population), but the materials, design, and procedure were the same. The only relevant variation affected the stimulus onset asymmetry (SOA; i.e., the temporal interval between the onsets of two consecutive stimuli) for the naming target with respect to a contextually based priming clue (a subordinate verb). In Experiment 1, the visual probe appeared immediately after that clue; in Experiment 2, it was displayed 300 ms later.

Experiment 1

Seventy-two students at the Universidad Complutense de Madrid were paid for their participation in the experiment. All were native Spanish speakers with normal or corrected vision and no hearing loss. Subjects were informed that the experiment was part of a study of normal language processing.

Experimental items consist of 48 two-sentence paragraphs. The first sentence (S1) provided the context, introducing one male and one female, each referred to by a common noun identifying either an occupation (e.g., *professor*) or a relationship term (e.g., *uncle*). They were, like every common noun in Spanish, marked for gender (feminine or masculine) by the definite article. The two nouns formed the conjoined subject of S1 in order to eliminate any possible discourse topic effects.[7] An example of S1 is given in (14).

---

[7]There is reason to believe that the conscious choice of referential antecedent for *pro* would not necessarily be based entirely—or even mostly—on pragmatics. It might be, as planned, due to pragmatics, such that, for example, all things being equal, one would expect the subject of *ran* to be a youth rather than an old woman. There is, however, every likelihood that the selection of referent for the subject is influenced by the discourse focus, based on the expectation that the subject will continue to be the same as the current focused referent. So, if we ask readers to name the referent for *pro*, we don't know which of the two factors—focus and/or pragmatics—motivates their choice.

Marslen-Wilson and Tyler (1987) reported an experiment designed to covary the discourse focus with the pragmatics of the verb (as well as with the lexical specificity of anaphors). They did find an appropriateness effect based on discourse focus, but this effect was the weakest of the three; it was outweighed by the availability of either a disambiguating syntactic clue (a lexical subject pronoun) or, crucially, pragmatic implications.

Nonetheless, there is a distinct possibility that discourse focus in Spanish (or in all null-subject languages) plays a significant role in the relative distributions of *pro* and overt pronouns. When native informants were asked to informally evaluate revised materials where a clear focus was covaried with a strong pragmatic bias, their responses suggested that the effects of discourse focus consistently outweigh the pragmatic bias, at least on a conscious level. This we take to imply that the antecedent for *pro* is assigned systematically by discourse rules. We should expect, therefore, antecedent priming for *pro* in Spanish to be constrained by the discourse focus. If this is the correct analysis of the facts of Spanish, then it is important for us to distinguish pragmatic from discourse

(14)   La arrogante millonaria y el huérfano abandonado llegaron al mismo
         tiempo a la puerta del restaurante.
         The arrogant millionaire(f) and the abandoned orphan(m) arrived at the
         same time at the door of the restaurant

In the second sentence, (S2), the verb was pragmatically loaded so as to
select either the male or the female (equally rotated through items) as its agent
and subject.

There were three different versions of S2, corresponding to the three distinct
pronominal types that can appear in subject position in Spanish: *PRO, pro,* and
overt pronoun. The completions for (14) are shown in (15a-c):

(15)   a. Mendigando lastimeramente una comida caliente, se desmayó.
         Begging sorrowfully for a hot meal, *(pro)* fainted

         b. Mientras mendigaba lastimeramente una comida caliente, se desmayó.
         While *(pro)* was begging sorrowfully for a hot meal, *(pro)* fainted

         c. Mientras él mendigaba lastimeramente una comida caliente, se
         desmayó.
         While he was begging sorrowfully for a hot meal, *(pro)* fainted

The *PRO* sentences included instances of verbs in both gerund and infinitive
form. This split corresponds to a split, in the finite conditions, between imperfect
and simple past.

We verified the existence of a clear plausibility bias toward one or the other
of the discourse referents as antecedent of the subject with a conscious judgment
task. We presented high school seniors in Madrid with printed questionnaires. For
each item, S1 appeared as it does in (14) and S2 appeared as one of the three
fragments given in (16).

(16)   a. Mendigando...   _____
         b. Mientras mendigaba...   _____
         c. Mendigando lastimeramente una comida...   _____

---

focus influence on priming, because the latter might be considered a grammatical constraint and
therefore ought not be considered a top–down influence on linguistic processing.

   With this in mind, we decided to create materials without any clear discourse focus. In this way,
we could avoid the possible confounding of the pragmatic bias with the focus factor. The only way
we could see to create this condition was to have both characters as conjoined subject in the context,
perhaps reciprocally, but not necessarily (as in (14)).

Participants were instructed to indicate who was the subject of the verb by writing in either the masculine or feminine subject pronoun, as appropriate. They were also given the option of choosing *both, someone else,* or *I don't know.*

Based on the results of this pretest, we rejected any materials that had over 10% total incorrect responses, where incorrect was anything other than the "appropriate" pronoun. Thus, we were assured that for each of the discourses used in the main experiment, there was one clearly preferred antecedent, at least to the conscious mind, for each of the null pronominals.

For each paragraph, there were four corresponding probe words: plausible experimental (e.g., *huérfano,* orphan), plausible control (e.g., *orificio,* orifice), implausible experimental (e.g., *millonaria,* millionaire), and implausible control (e.g., *medicación,* medication). The experimental probes were the human identity nouns heard in S1 (without articles or adjectives). The control probes were inanimate nouns that did not appear anywhere in the discourse and were not semantically related to either the context or the experimental probe. Each control probe was matched with its respective experimental probe for gender and number of graphemes. Onset phones were, when not identical, at least of the same phonological class; this was done to remove any effect of acoustic differences on the triggering of the voice-activated device providing the RT measurement. Probe words were visually presented right after the verb of the adverbial clause, coinciding with the first syllable of the following word (in the case, e.g., of (15a-c), coinciding with the audition of *las* from *lastimeramente*).

Given the limitations of the published Spanish word frequency counts with respect to our materials, experimental probes and their controls were not strictly matched for frequency. Instead, we matched these word pairs in a two-step process. The first was a far-from-definitive intuitive rating by six native speakers, which we used to narrow our selection. Next we acquired what we believed to be an even more precise source of baseline information about lexical items by running a word list naming task. Twenty subjects read the words aloud as they were presented on a CRT monitor one after the other, in a random ordered list format. Naming times were measured in milliseconds; for each probe word, we then took a mean baseline RT, that is, the naming latency for each of the critical items in isolation $(4 \times 48 = 192)$. Then we constructed an adjustment for each item, namely its deviation from the grand mean for all 192 items, which was 506 ms. That is, for an item uttered in isolation, we calculated the difference of its naming latency from that of the mean for all items, getting a deviation score for each word. For example, *millonaria,* because of its item-intrinsic traits (frequency, length, and acoustic and graphemic features) has an average naming latency, in isolation, of 512 ms, or a deviation score of $(512-506 = 6 \text{ ms})$. So, before analyzing the cross-modal data, we subtracted a constant of 6 from each

RT for *millonaria,* and similarly for each word. We dubbed these corrected RTs *baseline-adjusted reaction times,* or BARTs. A BART represents the latency, for each word, directly linked to the experimental conditions. All analyses reported here were performed directly on BARTs.

Other aspects of the procedure used in this experiment can be summarized as follows.

The three versions of S2 were counterbalanced across three tape-recorded scripts, so that each tape contained one version of each of the discourse materials and 12 tokens of each S2 version. In this way, each subject heard tokens of each S2 version, but only one version of each discourse.

Cuing tones were manually inserted at the syllable peak following the initial verb of S2. These tones controlled the presentation of the visual probes (exposed for 300 ms) and were not heard by the subjects. The four probe words were rotated through four word lists, such that each subject read all four classes of probe words, but read only one of each for any given discourse.

The three within-subject factors (pronominal type, plausible vs. implausible, antecedent, and experimental vs. control probe) yielded a 3 × 2 × 2 design with 12 groups. Experimental items were padded with 54 filler items of similar length and style. Tones were inserted at random positions in the filler items; probe words were randomly chosen nouns, some of which had appeared in the filler discourse.

Subjects were seated before a video display terminal that they monitored while listening to a recording through a headset. Prerecorded instructions explained that their main task would be to listen attentively to a series of unrelated paragraphs. Simultaneously, they were to watch the monitor in front of them. At some point during each paragraph, a word would flash briefly on the screen and they were to say the word aloud as quickly as they could, while continuing to listen to the paragraph. There were five practice items. The experiment ran for approximately 30 minutes, with a 5 minute break in the middle. The interval between visual presentation of the probe and onset of naming were measured and recorded by a computer program.

Predictions. If encapsulation of processing is contingent on structure, then we would expect to see differential treatment of these two phonologically empty subject pronominals. Given the same discourse and parallel sentence stuctures, a processor that respects the encapsulation of syntax should treat *PRO* and *pro* in distinct manners, because the former, but not the latter, has a syntactic controller. On encountering *PRO,* the processor should look first to the syntactic controller to identify the antecedent, whereas the antecedent for *pro,* just as any other pronoun, has to be found in the discourse.

Spanish *pro* is a syntactically free pronoun. Because the ambiguity of its referent cannot be resolved by the syntax, we would not be surprised if pragmatic clues were engaged immediately; hence we predicted the likelihood of a plausibility effect, (i.e., a significant difference between RTs for the plausible and implausible probes). Because the overt pronoun was always gender-specific, there was only one human in the discourse that could be its antecedent. The morphological gender marking and the contextual plausibility selected the same antecedent; hence, we expected to see a significant effect of plausibility (confounded with the effect of grammatical agreement) in the overt pronoun condition.

PRO is a syntactically controlled element. In adverbial clauses (like the ones we used in our materials), it must be coindexed and coreferential with the subject of the root clause. Because the adverbial phrase was preposed in these sentences, *PRO* actually preceded its antecedent. If the processor recognizes that this subject of a nonfinite verb is a syntactically bound element, then the strongest modular prediction would be that the processor waits until it actually reaches the subject of the root clause to assign a referent to *PRO*.

This being a strikingly counterintuitive probability, we made the weaker prediction that the processor might take note of the syntactic dependency of *PRO,* recognize that the antecedent would not appear until the following clause, and possibly then entertain candidates from the set of discourse antecedents. In other words, although we predicted that there would not be an instantaneous selection of antecedent for *PRO* based purely on pragmatic inference, we allowed for the possibility of such activation, but at a slower pace expected than expected for the pronouns.[8]

We have seen that at the probe position, the processor has heard both the pragmatic clue as well as evidence for a silent, if not overt, subject pronominal. If referential assignment is made immediately on encountering a pragmatic clue, then naming times immediately after the verb should reflect activation for only the pragmatically plausible antecedent. On the other hand, we expected that a repetition effect would make BARTs for the experimental probes faster than those for the control probes, which are unrelated to anything in the discourse. Hence, our planned measure of antecedent activation was a comparison of the BARTs for plausible versus implausible experimental probes, after they have

---

[8]What information is available to the processor at the presentation of the probe? One, it has passed the pragmatic clue as to the plausible agent of the verb. Two, it has evidence of a subject. In the case of an overt pronoun, this is obvious. But, what about in the case of implicit subjects? It is well known that Spanish allows the possibility of postverbal subjects. Nonetheless, there is evidence in Italian (De Vincenzi, 1989) that the the parser prefers the canonical subject-verb-object order, and Spanish is similar to Italian in all relevant details.

been subtracted from the BARTs for the respective control probes. This interaction would reveal the pure effect of plausible versus implausible antecedents.

Results. Of the original 72 subjects, 12 were excluded from the final analysis, because of technical problems or because more than 10% (>5) of the responses to the experimental items were missing. Therefore, the data reported here are from 60 subjects, evenly divided among the 12 subject groups.

Prior to analysis, any data points that were either missing or greater than 2000 ms were replaced with the subjects' mean RT to all targets, including the fillers. All remaining extreme RTs were then normalized to ±2 standard deviations from the subject's mean.

Table 8.1 summarizes the main results of the experiment, by showing the mean BARTs for probe and antecedent type for each pronominal type.

TABLE 8.1
Mean BARTs (in ms) for Probe and Antecedent Type by Pronominal Type

	Experimental	Control	Difference
PRO			
Plausible	628	663	35
Implausible	640	675	35
pro			
Plausible	632	688	56
Implausible	645	659	14
Overt Pronoun			
Plausible	638	684	46
Implausible	636	653	17

Analyses of variance (ANOVAs), by subjects and by items, were performed separately for each pronominal type, with antecedents (plausible/implausible) and probes (experimental/control) as within-subjects/items factors. Only the latter induced a significant main effect, *PRO*: $minF'(1, 83) = 11.27$, $p < .01$; *pro*: $minF'(1, 71) = 8.33$, $p < .01$; overt pronoun: $minF'(1, 78) = 6.64$, $p < .025$, the experimental probes being faster than the control probes in all cases. This was an entirely predictable and (relatively) uninteresting result, because the experimental probes were nouns that had been heard in the same discourse, whereas the controls had not been previously encountered in the materials. With respect to the interactions, the ANOVA for the *PRO* condition showed virtually no interaction of antecedent by probe (F<1 in all cases). The same test in the *pro* condition revealed a significant interaction of antecedent by probe, $F_1(1, 48) = 8.89$, $p < .005$; $F_2(1, 36) = 5.00$, $p < .05$. In the overt pronoun condition, the interaction of antecedent by probe only reached significance in the subject analysis, $F_1(1, 48) = 4.06$, $p < .05$; $F_2(1, 36) = 2.35$, $p > .10$.

Individual tests of particular differences within conditions show that in *PRO* cases, the advantage of experimental over control (35 ms) was significant in both plausible and implausible antecedents. By contrast, in the two other pronominal cases (*pro* and overt pronoun), that advantage was only significant with respect to the plausible antecedents (56 and 46 ms, respectively), and not with respect to the implausible ones (14 and 17 ms, respectively). Given this pattern of results, we further analyzed differences across pronominal types, comparing *PRO* with *pro,* on one side, and *pro* with overt pronoun, on the other. What is critical here is the three-term interaction ($2 \times 2 \times 2$) of pronominal type, antecedent, and probe, which tests the different patterns of experimental effects. The joint analysis of *PRO* and *pro* showed that the 35:35 difference pattern of the former was significantly different from the 56:14 pattern of the latter, $F_1(1, 48) = 4.90$, $p < .05$; $F_2(1, 36) = 5.36$, $p < .05$. By contrast, in the joint analysis of *pro* and overt pronoun, no interaction was found ($F < 1$ in all cases), which means that the 56:14 pattern of the former did not significantly differ from the 46:17 pattern of the latter.

Finally, to identify the cause of the variation across all three pronominal types, we analyzed the control and experimental conditions separately. The only significant effect was the interaction between pronominal type and antecedent (plausible vs. implausible) in the control condition, $F_1(2, 96) = 4.35$, $p < .025$; $F_2(2,72) = 4.95$, $p < .025$. Differences between plausible and implausible antecedent types were only significant in the control cases for *pro* and overt pronoun, where RT for the control of the plausible antecedent was much slower than RT for the control of the implausible antecedent. No significant differences were found between the plausible and implausible antecedents themselves for any pronominal type.

Discussion. The interesting analyses examine the plausibility effects within each pronominal type. Our planned measure of antecedent activation was a comparison of the BARTs for plausible versus implausible experimental probes, after they had been subtracted from the BARTs for the respective control probes. That is, we expected activation of the plausible antecedent, where it occurs, to be reflected in a greater difference between the plausible antecedent and its control than for the implausible antecedent and its control. The significance of this difference of differences is shown by the ANOVA with antecedents (plausible vs. implausible) and probes (experimental vs. control) as within-subjects/items factors.

The ANOVA for the *PRO* condition showed virtually no interaction of antecedent and probe. The same test in the *pro* condition revealed a significant interaction of antecedent and probe. Although the predicted interaction did not reach significance for the overt pronouns, there was a clear trend in this direction.

For the *PRO* condition, where the verb in the first clause of S2 was nonfinite, we saw no significant effect of plausibility. This contrasts directly with the *pro* condition, where there was a significant effect of the interaction between antecedent and probe word, as predicted. This differential treatment of these two phonologically null pronominals suggests an architecture in which the processor recognizes the difference in status between the subject of a finite and the subject of a nonfinite verb. The former, which is syntactically free, proceeds immediately to access its antecedent in the discourse and employs pragmatic clues available in the discourse to that end. The latter is syntactically linked to a controller in the same sentence, even if that controller is yet to appear in the string; despite the presence of pragmatic clues in the discourse, these clues are—at least temporarily—not employed in the search for an antecedent for *PRO*.

Further examination of the data led us to the initially surprising discovery that the significant interaction we saw in the *pro* condition was due, largely, to an inhibition of the plausible control word, rather than to an activation of the plausible experimental probe. In fact, statistical tests comparing the plausible experimental probes directly with the implausible experimental probes showed no significant effect in any of the pronoun conditions; it is the difference between plausible and implausible controls (to the detriment of the former) that seems to be relevant. This inhibition effect, we propose, is due to the similarity between the experimental and control words. That is, an excitation of the plausible antecedent results in an inhibition of the control word that is phonologically and graphemically similar (and is also matched in gender). A pilot study examining this hypothesis has been run and will be discussed further on.

Experiment 2

One of the specific advantages of the CMP task is that it allows us to examine the effect in question at whatever point in the input we may choose. Past investigations have shown that a modest change in test position can lead to highly significant changes in output.

It may be that the only way to know the complete and precise course of activation is to probe at an infinite number of discrete points. Given the impossibility of that approach, we chose to examine a position 300 ms downstream from the sentence position tested in Experiment 1 (immediately after the verb of S2). The goal of this experiment was twofold: first, to examine whether the effect observed in Experiment 1 for *pro* and overt pronouns is observable but delayed for *PRO;* and second, to determine how quickly the observed effect deteriorates for the pronouns.

For this experiment, we used the identical recorded tapes and word lists as those used in Experiment 1. Subjects were 75 individuals from the same subject pool as those in Experiment 1, but all were different individuals. The only novelty in the procedure was a 300 ms computer-timed delay between the postverbal cueing tone and the visual presentation of the target word. All other procedures were identical to Experiment 1.

Predictions. There is a growing body of evidence that antecedent activation decreases rather rapidly after it peaks. Although it is obvious that the effect we saw for *pro* and overt pronouns in Experiment 1 eventually declines, we did not know how long this would take. The sentence position we tested was a modest 300 ms downstream from the test position in Experiment 1. We would not have been surprised to see this effect begin to decrease or even dissipate entirely by this point. Conversely, as already discussed, it is highly counterintuitive to expect that the processor would completely ignore consciously available pragmatic clues while waiting during an indeterminate period for the appearance of the controller of *PRO* in the subsequent matrix clause. Therefore, we would not be surprised if the effect observed for the pronouns were evidenced in the *PRO* condition.

Results and Discussion. By the same criteria as in Experiment 1, the sample was reduced to 60 subjects, evenly divided among 12 subject groups, and the analyses were based on data that were filtered according to cutoff points placed at ±2 standard deviations from each subject's mean.

Table 8.2 summarizes the main results of the experiment, showing the mean BARTs for probe and antecedent type for each pronominal type.

The corresponding ANOVAs were performed separately for each pronominal type, under the same factorial design as in Experiment 1. There was, again, a significant effect of probe type (experimental probes faster than controls), although it was less pronounced than before: For *PRO,* minF' was only significant at $p < .10$, $F_1(1, 48) = 8.18$, $p < .005$; $F_2(1, 36) = 6.85$, $p < .025$; for *pro*, it was significant, min$F'(1, 80) = 4.53$, $p < .05$; and for overt pronoun, the effect only reached significance in the subject analysis, $F_1(1, 48) = 4.81$, $p < .05$; $F_2(1, 36) = 2.44$, $p > .10$. Other than for probe type, there were no further significant main effects revealed by either the subject or the item analyses. With respect to the antecedent by probe interactions, the pattern changed dramatically.

The only case in which the interaction approached significance was the *PRO* condition, $F_1(1, 48) = 2.90$, $p < .10$; $F_2(1, 36) = 3.85$, $p < .10$, whereas it dissipated entirely for the null and overt pronouns ($F < 1$ in all cases). Following these negative results, we dispensed with further statistical comparisons.

TABLE 8.2
Mean BARTs (in ms) for Probe and Antecedent Type by Pronominal Type

	Experimental	Control	Difference
PRO			
Plausible	629	670	41
Implausible	631	646	15
pro			
Plausible	630	661	31
Implausible	632	651	19
Overt Pronoun			
Plausible	635	653	18
Implausible	638	646	8

A closer inspection of the data shows, just at a descriptive level, that the advantage of experimental over control probes for plausible targets exceeded the one for implausible targets in all three pronominal conditions. However, the magnitude of this difference of differences was now more conspicuous in the *PRO* condition than in the other two pronominal cases, the reverse of Experiment 1. It looks as if the 300 ms delay was sufficient for the pragmatic influences to begin to emerge in the *PRO* constructions, coinciding with the decline of those same influences over the *pro* and overt pronoun constructions. Again, *PRO* and *pro* seemed to fall apart, the behavior of the latter being more in correspondence with the behavior of overt pronouns.

On the other hand, we can also see now that the putative effects were more inhibitory than facilitatory. Differences in RT between plausible and implausible antecedents were negligible, whereas their controls bore the main weight of the contrast, in accordance with the global pattern of results. This means that the inhibitory effect in this experiment shows mainly in the *PRO* condition (plausible controls were 24 ms slower than implausible controls), having almost disappeared in the other two pronominal conditions (10 and 7 ms for *pro* and overt pronoun, respectively). We maintain our proposal that the similarities of form between each antecedent and its control word might be responsible for this unexpected result.

PHONOLOGICAL INHIBITION THROUGH ANTECEDENT REACTIVATION: SOME CONSIDERATIONS ABOUT CMP EFFECTS

The foregoing examination of the data in the Spanish experiments revealed that the antecedent by probe interactions observed were largely driven by the action of control probes, rather than by the repetition (experimental) probes. When plausibility effects were detected, they manifested themselves more in the form of an inhibition of the control for the plausible antecedent than in facilitation of the plausible antecedent by itself. This is consistent with the pattern of results across the two experiments. In Experiment 1, where the probe appeared immediately after the biasing verb, plausibility only affected the syntactically free pronouns (*pro* and overt), the only conditions in which the alleged inhibition holds; in Experiment 2, with the probe presented 300 ms later, the graduation in the tendency toward plausibility effects (mostly shown in the *PRO* condition) was correlated with a corresponding graduation of the inhibitory trends.

There are at least two questions that can now be posed. First, why don't we obtain the standard facilitation effects in the pertinent cases? And second, what is the actual basis of the presumed inhibitory effects?

With regard to the first question, it is important to remember that the standard facilitation effects obtained in most CMP studies (Nicol & Swinney, 1989; J.A. Fodor, et al., 1994) have been interpreted as being the result of a reactivation of the permissible antecedent on encountering the referentially dependent element (trace, anaphor, or pronoun).[9] That reactivated antecedent is what primes the naming (or lexical decision) of the very same word (or of a close associate in meaning) when presented shortly after the referentially dependent element. In using the very same word as a probe, as we did in our experiments, there is a risk of inducing a priming ceiling that might confound reactivation with a merely episodic repetition effect. The overall significance of the probe type factor we have obtained shows that the repetition effect pervaded both the plausible and the implausible conditions, preventing reactivation from being more clearly manifested. A different design, like the one used by J.A. Fodor, et al., might have avoided that risk, by using a baseline position for the

---

[9]Nicol (1993) put forward the alternative interpretation that, rather than the trace, it is the verb and the demands of its argument structure that trigger the reactivation of the antecedent. We remain neutral on this issue, because our probe position was always after the biasing verb, which was immediately preceded by the referentially dependent element; therefore, we cannot distinguish which of them drives reactivation.

probes earlier in the discourse (before the critical reactivating element) as a control for pure repetition effects. We used instead control probes for each antecedent type, which were presented at the same critical testing points. The fact that these controls were differentially sensitive to the antecedent manipulation can provide an alternative, and quite indirect, way of assessing the pragmatic influences on anaphoric resolutions. In this sense, the cost in naming times that affects the controls of the plausible antecedents is contingent on the bias introduced by the verb (given the previous context) toward this kind of antecedent. Their expected reactivation, probably concealed by the repetition effect, was finally shown through the higher unexpected inhibition we obtained.

We are now left with the second question, which is about the basis for those inhibitory effects. The only relation between each antecedent and its control that was explicitly considered concerned the form of the words: They had similar length, phonemic onset, and grammatical gender (frequency was indirectly controlled through our baseline estimates). With respect to their meaning, controls were always inanimate nouns without any associative link with their animate (human) antecedents. This led us to hypothesize that inhibitory effects may have been due to the formal similarities between the experimental and control words.

In a preliminary attempt to give further support to this hypothesis, we ran a pilot study in English, using a CMP naming task. We looked for cases in which previous studies had found clear facilitatory effects due to the reactivation of the antecedent. Reflexive constructions (overt anaphors) were chosen; because they had been widely and positively tested (Nicol, 1988), their coreferential relations are maximally constrained by syntactic principles, and they were well suited for the manipulations required by the experimental design. In this study, we concentrated on the role played by the similarity of form between the binding antecedent and the probe of the naming task, using more refined criteria to establish that similarity.

For each auditorily presented sentence, the same word was used as a visual probe under each of four conditions. These were created by making one or two changes in that sentence: a change in the antecedent (to make it similar or dissimilar to the probe) and/or a change in the object of the transitive verb (for contrasting the reflexive with a neutral and referentially free NP expression). We thus had a double control, and the probes always appeared immediately after the direct object (reflexive or not) of the main verb. According to the hypothesis derived from our previous results, we expected that naming latencies for the same probe word should be longer when it was similar to the antecedent, which implies that this would occur only in the reflexive constructions.

Fifty undergraduate students at Rutgers University participated in this experiment for extra credit in a psychology course. All were native speakers of

English. Subjects with more than 10% erroneous or missing responses were disregarded, so that the sample was finally reduced to 40 subjects, evenly divided into four groups. A between-within-group design was used and both data analyses, by subjects and by items, were performed.

Thirty-two experimental items were constructed. Each constituted a set of four versions of one sentence with a single corresponding naming target word. In each sentence, a common noun identifying a human by occupation (*secretary, technician*), similar activity (*tourist, swimmer*), or recognizable feature (*adolescent, orphan*) was the subject of a transitive verb. In two versions, the object of the verb was reflexive (in half the items this was *himself* and in the other half, *herself*). These two versions differed in that the subjects were different nouns, unrelated to each other, either of which was an equally plausible subject of the sentence. In one version, the subject shared several specific graphemic and phonological features with the naming target, whereas in the other version, it did not. The shared features were: number of letters, initial letter, initial phoneme, number of syllables, stress pattern, and at least one vowel in common. In the other two versions of each sentence, the object of the verb was another unrelated common noun, equally as plausible as the reflexive object. An example of the experimental items is given in (17).

(17)   Annoyingly, the *technician/representative* from the customer service department at the computer company contradicted *himself/the boss* during a discussion of hardware installation.
Naming target: *temptation*

Naming targets were always inanimate nouns also unrelated in meaning or associative force to the subject of the sentence. Four tapes of the materials were prepared, such that each included one of the four versions of each of the sentences. Thirty-nine filler sentences were also prepared; five of these were used as practice items and the rest were interspersed with the experimental items in a pseudorandom order. Half of the naming targets for the filler sentences were words that had appeared in the corresponding sentence, and the other half were new words.

Table 8.3 summarizes the main results of the experiment, showing the mean RTs for each condition.

ANOVAs performed over subjects and itema showed a marginally significant effect of structural type (reflexive vs. neutral) $F_1(1, 36) = 3.99$, $p < .10$; $F_2(1, 28) = 5.20$, $p < .05$. No effects of similarity and interactions were found ($F < 1$ in all cases). The advantage in RT of the neutral condition over the reflexive could be attributed to the extra load imposed by the resolution of the anaphora, suggesting that the antecedent may have been reactivated by the reflexive. However, this assumed reactivation had no influence on the naming latencies of the similar probes. We failed to get any inhibitory effect.

TABLE 8.3
Mean RTs (in ms) for Naming Targets Under Four Different Sentence Conditions

	Direct Object	
Sentence Subject	Reflexive	Neutral
Similar	644	632
Dissimilar	649	635

There were several ways of dealing with that failure. We could simply have considered that the interpretation of our previous results in terms of inhibition through antecedent reactivation did not hold, and look elsewhere for an explanation. Assuming that those results were not spurious, because there was a consistent pattern of interactions across the two Spanish experiments, we thought about other possibilities. It might be said, for example, that the shared features on which we chose to match the naming targets with the antecedents were not sufficient to produce the desired effects. In fact, those features refer mainly to the global characteristics of the word form, and not so much to the segmental content; so, perhaps a wider overlap in the form of each word pair would have been required. Notice, however, that in the English experiment we used more exigent criteria than in the Spanish ones and a more constrained case for antecedent reactivation.

One further possibility is that phonological (and/or graphemic) similarity was not the main source responsible of the RT differences between the controls in the Spanish experiments. Apart from the phonological/graphemic similarity (which, after all, was not that strict), the other thing that the experimental and control items always had in common was their grammatical gender. At the same time, it was grammatical gender (usually marked in Spanish by suffixes -o and -a and by the article) that systematically distinguished between the two potential antecedents in our S1 sentences. So, it may well have happened that when the plausible antecedent was reactivated, the other similar word with the same gender was inhibited. If gender was so crucial, that would explain why we did not obtain the inhibitory effect in English, where grammatical gender for nouns is virtually nonexistent.

Recent studies have shown that Spanish gender is lexically specified by features that can operate at three different representational levels: phono-morphological, syntactic, and semantic (Elías-Cintrón, 1994; Harris, 1991; Klein,

1989; Roca, 1989). These features would be recovered when the lexical entry is accessed, and used for establishing agreement relations between words of the same sentence. The impact of this information on sentence parsing has been illustrated through a series of priming experiments with a probe recognition task and NP-traces (Elías-Cintrón, 1994; Elías-Cintrón, Kurtzman & Montalbetti, 1994). Given differences in task, materials, and purpose in our study, their precise results do not concern us here. What is more to the point is the wide open possibility that gender information would also contribute to coreference processing. One way of making sense of this very tentative proposal, in the context of CMP research, might be summarized as follows.

Perhaps what triggers the so-called "reactivation" effect is not the pronominal itself, but the agreement node. Following current GB theory, there is an Agr node dominating every verb phrase. In fact, at S-structure, the finite verb has actually moved into the head position in that node, from which it inherits its Phi features. The subject NP is in the Spec position of that phrase, where it gets nominative Case from this Spec/Head relation. The crucial point is that this only applies to finite verbs, and hence to subject pronouns (and other lexical NPs); nonfinite verbs are not in this relation with Agr, and do not receive nominative Case, and hence can have only *PRO* as their subjects. Appealing to the Agr node amounts to the same thing as appealing to the verb, which is its surface manifestation. Once the verb of the subordinate sentence has been encountered, information about argument structure and agreement (in the case of finite verbs) might become available. Naming latencies for the immediately presented plausible antecedents would then be aided only in finite verb conditions (overt pronouns and *pro*); controls that shared gender (and also global similarity in form) with the plausible antecedents would be inhibited in those same conditions. This rough outline of the proposal requires much more elaboration, probably following the recent claims made by Nicol (1993) that we commented on in footnote 9.

All these considerations remain speculative for the moment, but they suggest new lines for further research in this field. They also imply the necessity for a better understanding of the nature of the effects typically associated with the use of CMP tasks.

CONCLUDING REMARKS

One of the main morals of this study has been that psycholinguistic research across different languages turns out to be highly productive. It contributes not only by adding validity and generality to previous results obtained in a particular language, but, most important, it also allows an examination of new contrasts and data that can deepen our understanding of the general properties of the language processing system.

The research presented here has taken advantage of a distinctive characteristic of Spanish as a *pro*-drop language: the licensing in subject position of pronouns that are void of phonological content, but that share all relevant syntactic features with fully realized pronouns. At the same time, these "empty" pronouns *(pro)* contrast with another class of null subjects, *PRO,* precisely in the same set of syntactic features. These features have to do with the class of verbs they are subjects of (finite/nonfinite), the type of relation they have with their antecedents (control/free coindexing), and the constraints imposed on their binding domains (principles (7a) and (7b) of BT).

The question we have addressed all along is to what extent real-time language processing respects (and reflects) those contrasts, mainly derived from a theory of grammar. After all, this is a way to frame the oldest and deepest question in psycholinguistics, the one about the relations between competence and performance (grammars and processors). In recent research, responses to this kind of question have rested on issues of cognitive architecture (J.A. Fodor, 1983; Pylyshyn, 1984). In this respect, the distinction between modular and interactive components has been mainly based on the combined action of these two criteria: domain specificity and informational encapsulation. The development of experimental technology has allowed for the possibility of testing the degree of accomplishment of both criteria in typical psycholinguistic tasks.

The CMP technique has been used in our experiments to detect differences in performance associated with the linguistically relevant contrasts between pure pronouns and anaphoric pronominals. It has also allowed the possibility of dissociating linguistic and extralinguistic influences by tapping different moments of the temporal course of sentence processing. The results of the Spanish experiments we have reported coincide with results obtained in English (J.A. Fodor, et al., 1994) in that the influence of extralinguistic information on sentence processing is severely restricted. In both languages, the anaphoric pronominal *PRO,* which is syntactically controlled by the subject of the main clause (which has not yet appeared in the speech stream), does not show any clear contextually driven priming effect. When these effects are obtained, it is only in cases in which pragmatics might have taken advantage of the lack of syntactic constraints (e.g., about antecedent assignment). But, even in these cases (mostly in the case of overt pronouns), the potential influence of pragmatic variables is confounded with the influence of linguistic variables (e.g., gender agreement).

The study of the Spanish null subject *pro* has given extra support to the idea that interactive processes have to wait until the syntactic modular ones have done their job. Our results clearly attest that the two empty categories, *pro* and *PRO,* fall apart, according to the predictions of linguistic theory. The inclusion of *pro* in the class of pure pronouns seems, therefore, entirely justified on psycholinguistic grounds. In spite of the acoustic nonexistence of the two empty categories, subjects seem to take account of the linguistic information conveyed by the verb (inflected/noninflected) to distinguish between them, and behave in consequence. On the other hand, *pro* allows more room than the overt pronoun for isolating contextual effects, because in the former case, the agreement information conveyed by the verb does not include gender. Even so, the difference between these two conditions was not significant.

Before closing, we would like to make a final point. In the discussion of our English experiment, we pointed out the possibility that gender information may have an important role in the kind of effects we obtained in Spanish (but not in English). To the extent that our interaction effects, when significant, were mainly driven by the inhibition of the control words, this seems to be the only place to look for an explanation compatible with our results in both languages. Furthermore, this explanation ought to be based just on grammatical gender, not on semantic gender (controls were always inanimate nouns). In summarizing, we proposed a rationale for the plausibility of this claim, and for pursuing this kind of research. Testing modularity of sentence processing (against interactionist accounts) is important, but it is at least as important to advance toward a better understanding of the elements and principles of the language module.

ACKNOWLEDGMENTS

This research was supported, in part, by an exchange grant (BE91-303) and by a project grant (PB93-0363) from the DGICYT (Ministry of Education and Science of Spain) to J.E. García-Albea. The authors are very grateful to Janet Fodor, Jerry Fodor, and David Swinney for advice and assistance. Our thanks also to Dianne Bradley for her help in data analysis and interpretation, and to Chiung Chen Yu, Luis López Bascuas, Teófilo García Chico, and Lola Roldán for their assistance in running the experiments.

REFERENCES

Chomsky, N. (1965). *Aspects of the theory of syntax.* Cambridge, MA: MIT Press.
Chomsky, N. (1973). Conditions on transformations. In S. Anderson & P.Kiparsky (Eds.). *A*

240   GARCIA-ALBEA AND MELTZER

festschrift for Morris Halle (pp. 232–286). New York: Holt, Rinehart & Winston.

Chomsky, N. (1980). On binding. *Linguistic Inquiry, 11,* 1–46.

Chomsky, N. (1981). *Lectures on government and binding.* Dordrecht: Foris.

Chomsky, N. (1982). *Some concepts and consequences of the theory of government and binding.* Cambridge, MA: MIT Press.

Chomsky, N. (1986a). *Barriers.* Cambridge, MA: MIT Press.

Chomsky, N. (1986b). *Knowledge of language: Its nature, origin, and use.* New York: Praeger.

de Vincenzi, M. (1989). *Syntactic parsing strategies in a null subject language.* Unpublished doctoral dissertation, University of Massachusetts, Amherst.

Elías-Cintrón, R. (1994). *Towards a general theory of agreement: A psycholinguistic study of Spanish gender.* Unpublished doctoral dissertation, Cornell University, Ithaca, NY.

Elías-Cintrón, R., Kurtzman, H.S. & Montalbetti, R. (1994). *Processing consequences of NP-trace and agreement morphology.* Unpublished manuscript, Cornell University, Ithaca, NY.

Fernández-Soriano, O. (1989). Strong pronouns in null-subject languages and the Avoid Pronoun Principle. *MIT Working Papers in Linguistics, 11.*

Fodor, J.A. (1983). *The modularity of mind.* Cambridge, MA: MIT Press.

Fodor, J.A., Garrett, M.F., & Swinney, D. (1994). *A modular effect in parsing.* Unpublished manuscript, CUNY Graduate Center, New York.

Fodor, J.D. (1989). Empty categories in sentence processing. *Language and Cognitive Processes, 4,* 155–209.

Fodor, J.D. (1993). Processing empty categories: A question of visibility. In G. Altmann & R. Shillcock (Eds.), *Cognitive models of speech processing: The second Sperlonga meeting.* (pp. 351–400). Hillsdale, NJ: Lawrence Erlbaum Associates.

Harris, J.W. (1991). The exponence of gender in Spanish. *Linguistic Inquiry, 22,* 27–62.

Klein, P.W. (1989). Spanish "gender" vowels and lexical representation. *Hispanic Linguistics, 3,* 147–162.

Marslen-Wilson, W., & Tyler, L.K. (1987). Against modularity. In J.L. Garfield (Ed.). *Modularity in knowledge representation and natural-language understanding* (pp. 37–62). Cambridge, MA: MIT Press.

Nicol, J. (1988). *Coreference processing during sentence comprehension.* Unpublished doctoral dissertation, Massachusetts Institute of Technology, Cambridge.

Nicol, J. (1993). Reconsidering reactivation. In G. Altmann & R. Shillcock (Eds.), *Cognitive models of speech processing: The second Sperlonga meeting* (pp. 321–347). Hillsdale, NJ: Lawrence Erlbaum Associates.

Nicol, J., & Swinney, D. (1989). The role of structure in coreference assignment during sentence comprehension. *Journal of Psycholinguistic Research, 18,* 5–19.

Pylyshyn, Z.W. (1984). *Computation and cognition: Toward a foundation for cognitive science.* Cambridge, MA: MIT Press.

Rizzi, L. (1982). *Issues in Italian syntax.* Dordrecht: Foris.

Rizzi, L. (1986). Null objects in Italian and the theory of pro. *Linguistic Inquiry, 17,* 501–557.

Roca, I.M. (1989). The organization of grammatical gender. *Transactions of the Philological Society, 87,* 1–32.

Swinney, D. (1979). Lexical access during sentence comprehension: (Re)consideration of context effects. *Journal of Verbal Learning and Verbal Behavior, 18,* 645–659.

Swinney, D., Ford, M., Frauenfelder, U., & Bresnan, J. (1988). *On the temporal course of gap-filling and antecedent assignment during sentence comprehension.* Unpublished manuscript.

Torrego, E. (1981). *Spanish as a "pro-drop" language.* Umpublished manuscript, University of Massachusetts, Boston.

9
Understanding Anaphora: The Role of Superficial and Conceptual Information

Manuel Carreiras
Universidad de La Laguna
Tenerife, Spain

Alan Garnham
University of Sussex
Brighton, UK

Jane Oakhill
University of Sussex
Brighton, UK

In most cases, the goal, or one of the goals, of language processing is to extract information from what one is reading or listening to. This information is about the real world or an imaginary world, and not about the linguistic forms that are used to convey that information. The process of converting linguistic inputs into representations of parts of the real world, or of an imaginary world, is a complex process. In this chapter, we focus on one aspect of that process: the understanding of anaphoric expressions and, in particular the case of definite pronouns.

THE MENTAL MODELS THEORY AS A FRAMEWORK FOR A THEORY OF ANAPHOR INTERPRETATION

Understanding one's native language is something that comes so naturally to people that it can be difficult to stand back from this process and characterize it properly, in order to study it scientifically. Similarly, the mechanism underlying our ability to recognize everyday objects is something we do not usually worry about in our ordinary lives. Partly for this reason, Marr (1982) suggested that the study of a cognitive system should start with a task analysis: What does the system do and why? As we have already suggested, in comprehending discourse, readers and listeners are typically aiming to construct a representation of a situation, or a set of ideas, that the discourse is about. This claim leads directly to the notion of a *mental model,* a mental representation of part of the real or imaginary world (see, e.g., Garnham, 1987; Johnson-Laird, 1983). The structure of such a model should parallel the structure of the part of the world it represents, and not the structure of the text in which it is described or the structure of the sentences of that text. Thus, a mental model is different from the kind of propositional representation of text meaning that was postulated in the early 1970s (e.g., Kintsch, 1974). Johnson-Laird (1983) distinguished between a propositional representation of a text as being "close to the surface form of the sentence" and "a mental model whose structure is analogous to the state of affairs described by the discourse" p. 244).

A particularly vivid demonstration of the difference between model-like representations and ones more closely tied to the surface form of a text was provided by Mani and Johnson-Laird (1982). They showed that memory for the meaning of determinate spatial descriptions (those consistent with only one layout) was better than that for indeterminate descriptions (those consistent with more than one layout), but that verbatim memory was superior for the indeterminate descriptions. So, people might make use of the two kinds of representation, and the theory of mental models—provided that it allows for an interaction between superficial and content-based representation—is an appropriate framework for developing a more detailed account of how people understand texts.

A situation or a set of ideas can be described in many ways, but the model extracted from each description should be the same. Furthermore, we would expect that the representations extracted from (linguistic) descriptions of the world would be broadly similar to those derived from perceiving the world and those used in thinking about the world. The components of mental models must, therefore, be representations of the kinds of things that we take the world to be made up of: individuals (including people, animals, objects, places, and ideas), events, and properties. These components of mental models are bound together, because individuals and events have properties, and individuals have roles in events.

Each person has an overall model of the world, although it may be somewhat fragmented and not entirely consistent. However, understanding a discourse requires a model specific to that discourse. This model represents just the bit of the world, or the set of ideas, that the discourse is about. The existence of these discourse-specific models explains why expressions that would otherwise be referentially indeterminate, such as *el gato* (the cat; think how many cats there are in the real world, and add to that the many fictional ones), will be taken, in the context of a properly constructed discourse, to refer to a particular individual.

The process of constructing the model corresponding to a particular text is an incremental one for the reader or listener. Information in the sentence or clause currently being processed is integrated with the representation of the discourse that has been constructed up to that point. Each clause typically introduces one new event (in the broad sense, which includes acts, actions, states, and processes), and maybe a small number of new individuals and properties. Compared with a model of the world, a mental model of a discourse contains relatively few items, and it is this fact that constrains the interpretation of terms that refer back to things that have already been mentioned. The new, incremented, representation that results from the processing of the current clause then becomes part of the context for understanding the next clause. In addition, focusing mechanisms, which are by no means fully understood, tend to give priority, in this integration process, to information from the immediately preceding discourse, although the structure of these *focus spaces* may also depend on the structure of what is being described (Grosz, 1981). So, the linguistic expressions that carry the least information by themselves (e.g., definite pronouns) have an even more restricted range of possible referents. Indeed, an important role that pronouns play is maintaining continuity in discourse. They are typically used to make assertions about a previously introduced topic (Fletcher, 1984; Givón, 1983; Vonk, Hustinx, & Simons, 1992).

The immediately preceding sentence or clause may have a special status for another reason: It is usually the only part of the preceding text for which the reader or listener has an accurate representation of the surface form (e.g., Caplan,

1972; Chang, 1980; Jarvella, 1979). We discuss the role of this representation in the interpretation of pronouns further on in this chapter.

In addition to maintaining representations of the content of the discourse so far and of the surface form of the immediately preceding part of the discourse, readers and listeners can use both general and specific knowledge about the world to help them understand what they are reading or hearing. The text itself is somehow able to help in accessing potentially relevant pieces of information from the huge amount of knowledge that any individual has, but, again, the mechanisms by which this occurs are not fully understood.

The mental models theory explains how information from a text and relevant background information can be put together. Both are representations of part of the real or an imaginary world, so their formats are compatible. Coherent texts refer to the same individuals over and over again. However, the fact that the linguistic referring expression used to denote a particular individual may vary from mention to mention poses a problem in formulating theories of comprehension. In particular, reduced forms, such as pronouns, are commonly used for second and subsequent mentions. These expressions must be interpreted on the basis of the context in which they are encountered, using world knowledge, if necessary, to help out. Anaphoric definite pronouns are one of the most important devices that indicate links between information in different parts of the text. In their most typical uses, they reintroduce a previously mentioned person or object without repeating the name or a fuller description. That person or thing will be represented in the mental model of the text so far, but the question is, how is the correct referent identified? A mental model may represent a limited set of individuals, but it will rarely represent only one.

Spanish pronouns are marked for gender, number, and case. Of these, gender and number may help to determine who or what the pronoun refers to. Case is fixed by the grammatical role of the pronoun in its own clause, but gender and number often do not provide enough constraints to identify a referent uniquely. In such cases, other factors need to be taken into account. Syntax is one. Within a single sentence, there are constraints on the structural relations between anaphors and their antecedents, particularly when the anaphor precedes the antecedent (cases of *backward anaphora* or *cataphora*). Focusing is another. Indeed, some theorists have claimed that in well-written texts there should, at each point, be only one obvious candidate for pronominal reference. However, this claim is clearly falsified by sentences such as:

(1)   a. Max confessed to Bill because he wanted a reduced sentence.
       b. Max confessed to Bill because he offered a reduced sentence.

In cases of this kind, and in many others, the most important factor in determining the referent of a pronoun is knowledge of general and specific facts about the world (in this case about confessing; its relation to sentence length; and whether confessors or confessees might want, or be in a position to offer, reduced sentences).

PSYCHOLOGICAL STUDIES OF PRONOUN INTERPRETATION

On the view we have presented, the process of pronoun interpretation is somewhat akin to problem solving. Once a pronoun has been identified, which is relatively straightforward in Spanish (and English), the various sources of knowledge are used to identify a set of potential antecedents and, if the set contains more than one, to "search" through them to find the actual antecedent (Clark & Sengul, 1979; Ehrlich & Rayner, 1983). Once the antecedent has been identified, a meaning can be assigned to the pronoun on the basis of the meaning of the antecedent. In the mental models theory, the most obvious conception of this process is a search in (the focused part of) the model of the text so far, and, in the case of definite pronouns, the meaning of the pronoun is that it refers to the object identified in the search process. Definite pronouns are, therefore, sometimes referred to as *identity of reference* anaphors, because they refer to the same things as their linguistic antecedents. That is, a definite pronoun refers to the person or thing that the linguistic antecedent caused to be represented in the mental model.

This general conception of pronoun interpretation raises many questions. The most general one is whether the representation of the superficial form of the text is unimportant in pronoun resolution, so that the mental model is all-important. This idea was suggested by Sag and Hankamer (1984), but we argue further on that it is incorrect, and that the superficial representation does play a role in pronoun interpretation. More specifically, assuming that many factors play a role in pronoun comprehension, there are empirical questions to be answered about where, in the overall process, each factor plays a role, and about how strong an effect each one has.

There have been many psychological studies of the factors that help readers to determine the referents of anaphoric pronouns, in particular, in cases of potential referential indeterminacy. One set of features that is obviously readily available to processing mechanisms are the morphosyntactic features of the pronouns themselves, such as gender and number. Pronouns typically match their antecedents in number and gender. So, in cases where there is more than one candidate antecedent, mismatches on these features provide potentially disambiguating information. And indeed, it is found that pronouns are interpreted more quickly when they can be resolved on the basis of their morphological form (Carreiras, Garnham, & Oakhill, 1993; Corbett & Chang, 1983; Garnham & Oakhill, 1985).

There are also many demonstrations that antecedents of one kind are favored over those of another kind. These demonstrations may reflect the focusing mechanisms that are believed to operate within mental models, although no general account of these focusing mechanisms has yet emerged. For example, some authors (e.g., Grober, Beardsley, & Caramazza, 1978) have suggested that a pronoun will be easier to understand if it plays the same role in its clause as the antecedent plays in its clause (the *parallel function hypothesis*). Other studies suggest a preference for antecedents in subject position (Stevenson, 1986), and point out that Grober et al.'s data is consistent with this view, because they only studied pronouns in subject position. Gernsbacher (1989) suggested that the effective variable is not grammatical position, but whether the antecedent is the first-mentioned person or thing in its clause.

Another probable reflex of focusing effects is the fact that close antecedents are preferred to ones that are further away (Clark & Sengul, 1979; Daneman & Carpenter, 1980; Ehrlich & Rayner, 1983). However, if mental models are important in pronoun resolution, it is unlikely that distance in the text, per se, is the controlling factor, because text distance is not necessarily reflected in distance in the model. Distance between an antecedent and a pronoun provides an opportunity for the object introduced into the model by the antecedent to go out of focus. Thus, the nature of the material between the pronoun and the antecedent and, in particular, whether it shifts attention from the antecedent, is likely to affect how easy the pronoun is to understand. The comparatively small number of studies that have manipulated distance and focusing independently have shown that focusing is the crucial variable (Lesgold, Roth, & Curtis, 1979; Whitehead, 1982).

There are many reasons why a person or object can go out of focus. For example, some characters are tied to specific episodes in stories—a waiter who serves the main character in a restaurant, for instance. When the restaurant episode ends, the main character will remain in focus, but the waiter will not. Readers have difficulty interpreting pronominal references to such episode-bound characters if a time change indicates the episode is over, for example, "Six hours later, he..." (Anderson, Garrod, & Sanford, 1983). Likewise, changes of focusing and therefore in information accesibility are observed by manipulating tense and aspects of verbs (Carreiras, Carriedo, Alonso, & Fernandez, 1995). Thus, focus plays an important role in the interpretation of anaphoric expressions, although no complete account has yet been given of how items mentioned in a text are maintained in focus or how they go out of focus.

Another factor that might affect pronoun interpretation through a focusing mechanism is *implicit verb causality* (Garvey & Caramazza, 1974). A verb like *confess* suggests an event initiated by the confessor (the subject of an active sentence containing the verb), whereas a verb like a *blame* suggests an event for which the person who got blamed (the grammatical object in an active sentence) was probably the cause (because he or she did something wrong). Often, a description of an event with an implicit cause is followed by a *because* clause that gives an explicit cause. The *because* clause may contain a subject pronoun, and this pronoun is preferentially linked to the implicit cause, although this assignment can be overridden by the content of the *because* clause, as in *Max confessed to Bill because he offered a reduced sentence* (e.g., Caramazza, Grober, Garvey, & Tates, 1977; Garnham, Oakhill, & Cruttenden, 1992). However, recent work (Garnham, Traxler, Oakhill, & Gernsbacher, 1995) suggests that this effect is not one of focusing on the implicit clause, but it arises from backward inferencing when the *because* clause is read.

The research we have outlined confirms that a variety of factors—including structural information in the text, morphosyntactic cues, and knowledge about the world—play a role in the comprehension of pronouns. In the rest of this chapter, we describe some of the work on pronoun resolution that has been carried out in Spanish and try to draw out its implications for a general theory of anaphor resolution in the mental models framework.

DEEP AND SURFACE ANAPHORS

Hankamer and Sag (1976) proposed that anaphors be divided into two categories, *deep* anaphors and *surface* anaphors. In a later paper, Sag and Hankamer (1984) suggested that this distinction could be mapped onto a processing distinction in the way the two types of anaphor are interpreted. *Ellipses*, as they now renamed surface anaphors, are interpreted by first copying over a piece of the superficial representation of the preceding text, and then interpreting the full form as if it had occurred at that point in the discourse. This dependence on the superficial representation explains why surface anaphors should have a form parallel to that of their antecedents and why they need to be close to them: because of the relatively short-lived nature of superficial representations. *Model-interpretative* (formerly deep) anaphors, on the other hand, take their meaning directly from elements in mental models, according to Sag and Hankamer. Definite pronouns are the prototypical example of model-interpretative anaphors.

Most accounts of pronoun assignment have assumed that a pronoun triggers a search through the memory representation formed from previous text (e.g., Clark & Sengul, 1979; Ehrlich & Rayner, 1983), although they have not always been specific about the nature of that memory representation. Once a suitable antecedent is found, the pronoun is linked to or replaced by the antecedent or by a conceptual entity related to the antecedent. This antecedent determines the meaning of the anaphor, typically by a relation of coreference. Thus, the comprehension of a pronoun requires that it ultimately be associated with a representation of an entity in a mental model, and Hankamer and Sag's suggestion is that the search for the antecedent takes place in the mental model itself, and not in a representation of the text. On this view, no specifically linguistic representation is involved in the interpretation of pronouns at all.

Although this view is plausible, it is by no means necessarily true. An anaphor may access the conceptual aspects of the antecedent representation directly. Alternatively, it may initially access the antecedent representation at a surface/linguistic level, insofar as it is available, and gain access to the conceptual content only indirectly. Nevertheless, it is quite difficult to find conclusive evidence against the former view. For example, we have already seen that in English, the language of most experiments on pronoun interpretation, the morphological properties of a pronoun can help in deciding what it refers to, but, pronoun morphology in English is reflected in pronoun semantics. So, feminine gender on a pronoun could be used merely to specify that the search in the model is to be for an entity that is female. Similarly, although the effect of distance on pronoun interpretation might at first suggest the use of a superficial representation, distance often corresponds to focus and, hence, to properties of mental models.

There is also some evidence in favor of the *direct access hypothesis*. For example, Clifton and Ferreira (1987) argued that antecedents for pronouns are found by consulting a representation that captures referential identity, rather than by consulting a syntactic representation. They compared reading time for the segment containing the word *they* in sentences like (2a) with reading time for the same segment in sentences like (2b).

(2)   a. John and Mary pushed toward the head of the line, but suddenly / they discovered / that all their money was missing.
        b. John pushed Mary to the head of the line, but suddenly / they discovered / that all their money was missing.

Clifton and Ferreira reasoned that if a reader first examines a syntactic representation in search of the antecedent for a pronoun, he or she should be slower in the second version of the sentence, where the antecedent of the pronoun (*they*) does not form a single syntactic constituent of the preceding clause. In fact, they found no difference between the two sentences in a self-paced segment-by-segment reading task. This result implies that a pronoun does not take a surface structure constituent as an antecedent, but instead must find its antecedent in a more abstract representation: a discourse representation or a mental model. However, they also pointed out, given that they report a null result, that their task may not have been sufficiently sensitive to detect a difference.

Although the two antecedents in Clifton and Ferreira's sentences played the same syntactic role in one case and different syntactic roles in the other, they were always in the same clause. Moreover, Ferreira and Clifton did not find any positive evidence for the involvement of an abstract representation in pronoun resolution. Another way of looking at surface effects on pronoun resolution is by manipulating the superficial distance between antecedents. Alonso and Carreiras (1994) manipulated both the superficial distance and the representational distance between the two antecedents of a plural pronoun. They used texts such as those in (3), that mentioned three people and then the Spanish plural feminine pronoun (*ellas*), which can only be use to refer to females. So, in each of the four passages, the plural pronoun *ellas* could only refer to Mary and Eve. In (3a) and (3b), both female antecedents are in the same sentence (superficially close), whereas in (3c) and (3d) they are in different sentences (superficially distant). Moreover, in sentences (3a) and (3c) they are located in the same physical place (spatially close), whereas in sentences (3b) and (3d) they are in two different locations (spatially distant).

(3)   a.   María y Eva compiten en un campeonato de atletismo en Barcelona./
            Jaime compite en un campeonato de Judo en Madrid./
            Ellas han pasado a la final.

            Mary and Eve compete in athletic trials in Barcelona/
            James competes in a Judo tournament in Madrid/
            They (FEM) have qualified for the final

    b.   María y Eva compiten en campeonatos de atletismo en Barcelona y Sevilla respectivamente./
            Jaime compite en un campeonato de Judo en Madrid./
            Ellas han pasado a la final.

            Mary and Eve compete in athletic trials in Barcelona and Seville respectively/
            James competes in a Judo tournament in Madrid/
            They (FEM) have qualified for the final

    c. María y Jaime compiten en un campeonato de atletismo en Barcelona./
       Eva corre por la calle sexta./
       Ellas han pasado a la final.

       Mary and James compete in athletic trials in Barcelona/
       Eve is running in the sixth lane/
       They (FEM) have qualified for the final

    d. María y Jaime compiten en un campeonato de atletismo en Barcelona./
       Eva compite en un campeonato de Judo en Madrid./
       Ellas han pasado a la final.

       Mary and James compete in athletic trials in Barcelona/
       Eve competes in a Judo tournament in Madrid/
       They (FEM) have qualified for the final

If subjects have to link elements of a superficial representation to produce an antecedent for a plural pronoun, it should take longer to read the sentence that contains the pronoun in (3c) and (3d), than that in (3a) and (3b). However, if they are grouping elements in a conceptual representation, it should take longer to read the pronoun in sentences (3b) and (3d), than that in (3a) and (3c).

Reading times for the sentence that contained the pronoun *ellas* are presented in Table 9.1. Only the superficial distance between antecedents offered a reliable effect. Reading times were faster when the two feminine antecedents were in the same sentence than when they were in different sentences.

TABLE 9.1
Mean Reading Times (in ms) for the Sentence Containing the Pronoun as a Function Superficial Distance and Distance in Physical Space (Semantic Distance) in the First Experiment in Alonso and Carreiras (1994)

	Superficially close	Superficially distant
Spatially close	1,878	1,973
Spatially distant	1,850	1,974

The results suggest that, notwithstanding Sag and Hankamer's claims, a superficial representation plays an important role in the comprehension of definite pronouns, that are deep anaphors. However, the lack of an effect of the spatial separation of the two antecedents suggests that a conceptual representation, or mental model, is not important. This idea is implausible. Furthermore, there is an alternative explanation of the results. In these passages, subjects could have realized that they needed to interpret plural pronouns, and they could have followed a simple strategy of attending to the gender of the characters to carry out this task, without processing the texts' content more deeply. Shallow processing would produce an effect of surface distance, but would be unlikely to produce an effect of physical distance. Alonso and Carreiras therefore ran another experiment using the same passages but with a speeded continuation task that required deeper text processing. Subjects were presented the first two displays of each passage. Immediately after they had read the second display, the pronoun *ellas* appeared in the center of the screen. Subjects were asked to produce a sensible continuation of the text as quickly as possible. The mean times from the presentation of the pronoun until the subjects started speaking appear in Table 9.2.

TABLE 9.2

Mean Times (in ms) From the Presentation of the Pronoun Until the Beginning of Speaking as a Function of Superficial Distance and Physical Space (Semantic Distance) in the Second Experiment by Alonso and Carreiras (1994)

	Superficially close	*Superficially distant*
Spatially close	2,557	2,644
Spatially distant	2,536	3,107

In this experiment, the interaction between superficial and physical distance was reliable. If the antecedents were superficially or spatially close, or both, the subjects began to speak sooner than when they were both superficially and spatially distant. Therefore, these results suggest that both superficial and conceptual representations play a role in the comprehension of pronouns. The results remain inconsistent with Sag and Hankamer's suggestion that deep anaphors are always interpreted directly from mental models.

Other authors have used less direct methods for determining the type of representation used to interpret pronouns and have claimed to find support for Sag and Hankamer's thesis that antecedent assignment for pronouns is mediated by a discourse model. Cloitre and Bever (1988) and Lucas, Tanenhaus, and Carlson (1990) used tasks in which subjects had to respond in various ways (lexical decision, category naming, probe recognition, and naming) to words presented immediately after passages containing anaphors. The validity of using different tasks rests on the assumption that they tap different processes. For instance, Lucas et al. (1990), who used lexical decision and naming, assumed that lexical decision is sensitive to both lexical and discourse-level representations, whereas naming is primarily sensitive to lexical representations. Both sets of authors concluded that English pronouns are interpreted from mental models. However, whereas Cloitre and Bever argued that definite noun phrase anaphors are interpreted indirectly, using a superficial representation to access a discourse model, Lucas et al argue that they are interpreted directly from a discourse model, as Sag and Hankamer's theory would predict. Carreiras, et al. (1993) have suggested that these different conclusions are best explained by differences between the materials in the two sets of studies and by the different ways that Cloitre and Bever and Lucas et al. interpreted data from their lexical decision tasks.

Carreiras et al. (1993) suggested a different way to investigate the involvement of superficial representations in the interpretation of pronouns. In English, pronouns are marked for gender and number, and when they are resolved on the basis of these morphological markings they are understood more quickly. For instance, Garnham and Oakhill (1985) showed that the second clause of :

(4)   Alan lent a pen to Jill because she wanted to write a letter.

was read more quickly than the same second clause in:

(5)   Sally lent a pen to Jill because she wanted to write a letter.

However, in almost all cases in English, agreement between a pronoun and its antecedent at the morphological level goes hand in hand with agreement at the semantic level. For example, if a person is introduced into a mental model using a female proper name, that person can subsequently be referred to by the pronoun *she*. This pronoun matches both the gender of the name and the gender of the person. So, the fact that such a match aids comprehension does not provide evidence for the use of superficial representation in the interpretation of English pronouns. The findings are compatible with the use of either a superficial representation or a mental model. In contrast, in many languages other than English, nouns (and, hence, noun phrase antecedents for pronouns) have genders that have no semantic counterpart. *Table,* for example, is feminine in Spanish, *la mesa,* and French, *la table,* and masculine in German, *der Tisch,* although tables themselves are neither male nor female. Because Spanish nouns referring to objects have arbitrary genders, it is possible to compare cases in which the referential determinacy provided by morphological markings on pronouns might operate via a semantic mechanism (in many references to people), with those where it could only be morphologically based (e.g., in many references to objects in Spanish). This comparison can be used to establish the type of representation—superficial or content-based—that is used to interpret the pronouns. Carreiras et al. (1993) argued that if pronoun resolution was speeded by a gender cue, even though the genders of the antecedent noun phrases were purely formal (and arbitrary, from a semantic point of view), such an effect could not readily be explained by a theory that claimed that only a representation of content was important in resolving pronouns.

In an initial on-line experiment, Carreiras et al. (1993, Exp. 1) presented sentences such as (6a) and (6b) with two people of either the same or different gender in the first clause, and a pronoun (*el/ella*) referring to one of them in the second clause. They also presented sentences such as (7a) and (7b) with two things of either the same or different gender in a first clause and a pronoun (*éste/ésta*) referring to one of them in the second clause. They compared reading times for the subordinate clauses of (6a) and (6b) sentences and for the subordinate clauses of (7a) and (7b).

(6) a. Isabel le dio su viejo puzzle a Pamela
         porque ella había comprado uno nuevo.
         Betty gave her old jigsaw to Pam
         because she had bought a new one

     b. Isabel le dio su viejo puzzle a David
         porque ella había comprado uno nuevo.
         Betty gave her old jigsaw to David
         because she had bought a new one

(7) a. El neumático perdió el aire
         porque éste pinchó.
         The tire (MASC) lost air (MASC)
         because it-MASC had a puncture

     b. El neumático perdió la presión
         porque éste pinchó.
         The tire (MASC) lost air (FEM)
         because it-MASC had a puncture

The mean reading times for the subordinate clauses are displayed in Table 9.3. In the sentences about people, the second clauses were read more quickly when there was a gender cue; however, the gender cue had no effect in the sentences about things.

These effects suggested that gender cuing was restricted to sentences in which the pronouns referred to people and, hence, that purely morphological cues were not used in determining the referents of pronouns. Because Spanish is a *pro*-drop language, in which subject pronouns are usually omitted, having all the sentences contain subject pronouns was unnatural. Furthermore, the sentences about people used different pronouns (*el/ella*) from the sentences about things (*éste/ésta*), and a second experiment (Carreiras et al., 1993, Exp. 2) showed that these pronouns were interpreted differently.

TABLE 9.3

Mean Reading Times (in ms) for Subordinate Clauses as a Function of Type of Sentence and Gender Cue in Experiment 1 by Carreiras, et al. (1993)

	Sentences about people	Sentences about things
Cue	2,355	2,423
No cue	2,949	2,464

In addition, the sentences about things were less ambiguous than the sentences about people. For example, a tire (*el neumático*) can have a puncture, but air (*el aire*) cannot. So, although both are masculine, a masculine subject pronoun *éste* would certainly refer to the tire. Given this strong pragmatic cue, it was unlikely that an additional gender cue would further speed pronoun interpretation. However, sentences about people are quite different. Because people were always referred to by arbitrary proper names, the predicates in the second clauses of the sentences were inevitably potentially applicable to either person. A predicate such as *had bought a new one,* can apply equally to someone called Betty or to someone called Pam or to someone called David.

A second on-line experiment (Carreiras et al., 1993, Exp. 3) used second clauses with omitted subjects and accusative pronouns (*lo/la,* him/her), which are more natural in Spanish. The pragmatic constraints in some of the predicates were also reduced. Sentences such as (8a) and (8b) were presented, each mentioning two things with the same or different gender in the first clause and referring back to one of them using an accusative pronoun in the subordinate clause.

(8)   a.   El polvo se pegó al helado
           porque lo arrojaron al suelo.
           The dust (MASC) stuck to the ice-cream (MASC)
           because [OMITTED SUBJECT] it-ACCUSATIVE (MASC) threw onto the ground
           (because it was thrown onto the ground)

      b.   La arena se pegó al helado
           porque lo arrojaron al suelo.

The sand (FEM) stuck to the ice-cream (MASC)
because [OMITTED SUBJECT] it-ACCUSATIVE (MASC) threw onto the ground
(because it was thrown onto the ground)

Mean reading times for subordinate clauses were 2,346 ms in the gender cue condition (8b) and 2,453 ms. in the no-cue condition (8a). Thus, the subordinate clauses were read more quickly when there was a gender cue to the pronoun's antecedent than when there was none. So, this experiment, with more natural Spanish sentences, provided preliminary support for the idea that gender cuing can speed the interpretation of pronouns that refer to things. However, it did not include sentences about people, so it was not possible to make a direct comparison between effects in sentences about things and effects in sentences about people. Such a comparison is crucial for establishing what representations are used, and when they are used, in understanding anaphoric pronouns, because the relative sizes of the effects in the two types of sentence indicate the extent to which the effects depend on the use of content-based representations.

In order to compare the relative sizes of the effects of gender cuing for sentences about people and sentences about things, Garnham, Oakhill, Ehrlich, and Carreiras (1995) carried out several self-paced reading experiments. In an experiment in Spanish, similar to the experiment just described except that it also contained sentences about people, Garnham et al. (1995, Exp. 1) presented sentences such as (9) and (10), followed by questions. All the sentences had accusative pronouns in their second clauses. As in the experiments previously described, in the version in which the protagonists or things were of different genders, the pronoun could be resolved on the basis of gender alone. In the other version, more complex inferential processes were required.

(9)   a. Alicia/Ricardo arrestó a Pablo
         porque lo descubrió robando un coche.
         Alice/Richard arrested Paul
         because (OMITTED SUBJECT) him-ACCUSATIVE found stealing a car
         (because he/she found him stealing a car)

       b. ¿Descubrió Ricardo/Alicia a Pablo robando un coche?
          Did Richard/Alice see Paul stealing a car?

       c. ¿Descubrió Pablo a Ricardo/Alicia robando un coche?
          Did Paul see Richard/Alice stealing a car

(10) a. La grúa (FEM)/El camión (MASC) remolcó al autobús (MASC)
         porque lo inmovilizó la nieve.
         The tow truck/lorry towed the bus

because   [OMITTED   SUBJECT]   it-ACCUSATIVE   immobilized   the
snow-NOMINATIVE
(because it was stuck in the snow)

b. ¿Inmovilizó la nieve al autobús?
Was the bus stuck in the snow

c. ¿Inmovilizó la nieve a la grúa/al camión?
Was the lorry/tow truck stuck in the snow

The mean reading times and question answering times are shown in Table
9.4. Reading times for the subordinate clauses showed a gender cue effect for
both types of sentences, those about people and those about things. Furthermore,
there was no interaction between gender cue and type of sentence.

TABLE 9.4

Mean Reading Times for Subordinate Clauses and Question Answering Times (in ms) as a
Function of Type of Sentence and Gender Cue in Exp. 1 by Garnham, et al. (1995)

	Sentences about people	*Sentences about things*
Reading times		
Cue	1,889	1,724
No cue	1,977	1,783
Question answering times		
Cue	2,347	2,288
No cue	3,020	2,393

The strong effects of cue in the reading times of both types of sentences and
the lack of interaction between cue and type of sentence suggest that pronouns
are resolved in the same way in the two types of sentence. Furthermore, because
the effect of cuing must arise at a superficial level in the sentences about things,
the results suggest that it arises at this level in the sentences about people, too.
Cuing also had an effect on the question answering times for both types of
sentence. However, in this case there was an interaction between type of sentence
and cuing: The effect was considerably stronger for sentences about people. This
finding is consistent with the fact that representations of the superficial form of
texts decay rapidly. In the sentences about people, the different genders of the
people are reflected in the longer lasting model-based representation. However,
in the sentences about things, gender is only encoded at a superficial level, and,
therefore, it becomes unavailable as a cue to help in distinguishing between the

entities that the text is about (whether for subsequent pronoun resolution or, in this case, for answering a "Who did what?" question). This experiment, therefore, provides considerably clearer evidence for the involvement of a representation that includes formal (superficial) gender information in the interpretation of definite pronouns, even though those pronouns are deep anaphors.

The idea that superficial information is used in the resolution of definite pronouns in languages with formal gender, and that effects of gender cuing should, therefore, be reduced with distance between a pronoun and its potential antecedents, was further supported in another experiment (Garnham et al., 1995, Exp. 3). In the passages used in this experiment, an extra phrase and a sentence boundary were inserted between the pronoun and its potential antecedents. The experiment was performed in French, again using sentences about people and sentences about things. It was predicted that, where the morphosyntactic information was more superficial (formal gender of nouns referring to inanimate things), the effect of gender cue would be smaller, given this separation between the pronoun and its potential antecedents. This prediction was made in light of the results of a previous French experiment (Garnham et al., 1995, Exp. 2), in which, as in Spanish, the effects of cuieng had been the same for sentences about people and sentences about things. The mean reading times and the mean question answering times for the experiment in which the pronoun and its potential antecedents were separated are displayed in Table 9.5.

As predicted, there was a smaller effect of cuieng when the genders of the potential antecedents were purely formal (sentences about things) than when they reflected semantic facts about their referents (sentences about people). This effect was obtained in both reading times and question answering times.

TABLE 9.5

Mean Reading Times for Subordinate Clauses and Question Answering Times (in ms) as a Function of Type of Sentence and Gender cue in Garnham et al. (1995), Experiment 3

	Sentences about people	Sentences about things
Reading times		
Cue	2,368	2,417
No cue	2,786	2,541
Question answering times		
Cue	1,892	1,892
No cue	2,247	2,069

Taken together, the results of Garnham et al. (1995) provide a strong case for the conclusion that the use of morphosyntactic cues is an integral part of the pronoun resolution process, even when those cues have no semantic counterpart. The data are clearly incompatible with Sag and Hankamer's (1984) suggestion that pronouns, being deep anaphors, are interpreted directly from a representation of content. Both types of representation, superficial and content-based, are implicated in the interpretation of pronouns. Alternatively, one might conclude that a mental model is not just a representation of the content, but also contains information about superficial aspects of the text. However, on this formulation, one would have to claim that different aspects of mental models decay at different rates.

We have described a series of experimental results showing that pronominal reference is governed by superficial information. Pronouns are devoid of semantic content except for specifications of number and gender, and they normally match their antecedents with respect to these features. Where there is more than one candidate antecedent, mismatches in gender marking provide clear disambiguating information, as demonstrated in some of the experiments described. Gender marking is a highly salient aspect of a pronoun, one that is presumably extracted with little or no observable effort under normal circumstances. We expect that number is treated in the same way, although there are some obvious differences between number and gender. Gender, for example, plays a role in noun–adjective agreement, whereas number is important in both subject–verb agreement and noun–adjective agreement. However, in both English and Spanish, it is difficult to distinguish between the formal number of nouns and their semantic or conceptual number, except in a few cases. And even then, it is not entirely arbitrary, from a conceptual perspective, that *scissors* and *trousers* are plural in English (although trousers can be either singular, *pantalón,* or plural, *pantalones,* in Spanish). Another interesting case is that of singular nouns used to denote collective sets (e.g., *band*). Here, the singular item is the set itself, but because it is a set of individuals, it is also in some sense plural. We discuss the use of definite pronouns that refer back to collective sets in the next section, on conceptual pronouns. Interestingly, in American English, a verb following a collective noun is almost always singular, and hence agrees with the morphosyntactic form of the noun. In British English, both singular and plural verbs are common. In Spanish, a language in which morphology plays a more prominent role, morphological agreement is obligatory: A singular collective subject noun phrase must agree with a singular verb. However, as we show, once the text moves on to a new sentence, agreement (of a pronoun or other anaphor) is preferably at the conceptual, rather than the morphological, level.

CONCEPTUAL ANAPHORS

The term *conceptual pronoun* was introduced by Gernsbacher (1991) to designate a range of cases (in English) in which the normal agreement in number between a pronoun and its antecedent appears to be broken. In the three types of case that Gernsbacher identified, a plural pronoun follows what appears to be a singular antecedent. These cases raise both linguistic and psycholinguistic questions. Why is the plural form preferred, when the most obvious *antecedent* is singular? How are such pronouns understood, and what are they taken to refer to?

In normal cases, plural pronouns have plural noun phrases as their antecedents (e.g., *The students were talking about the math lesson. They...*). The pronoun then refers to the set of things (*students,* in this case) that the plural noun phrase introduced into the mental model. Alternatively, as in the passages used by Alonso and Carreiras (1994), plural pronouns can refer to people or things introduced into the model by several different noun phrases, singular or plural (e.g., *The student(s) and the teacher(s) were talking about the math lesson. They...*). In both types of example, the pronoun *they* refers to several people: more than one student in the first case, and one or more students and one or more teachers in the other case. In these examples, number agreement between the pronoun and its antecedent occurs at both the semantic and the morphosyntactic level (*the student and the teacher* has no morphological marking for number, but it is syntactically plural, because it must take a plural verb: *the student and the teacher are...,* not *the student and the teacher is...*). However, in some of the passages used by Clifton and Ferreira (1987) there was number agreement at the semantic or conceptual level, but not at the morphosyntactic level (e.g., *John pushed Mary to the head of the line, but suddenly they...*). Those authors reported no effect of a lack of match at the morphosyntactic level, but found it difficult to draw a strong conclusion from a null result. In terms of mental models, we could conclude that, when two closely related individuals are represented in a model, either they are already grouped in the model, or it is very easy to group them so that they can act as referents for a plural pronoun.

Any collection of individuals can be thought of as a set, which is a single *higher order entity.* Because plural noun phrases in Spanish and English take plural verbs, the primary referent of the noun phrase must be considered to be the individuals and not the set itself. However, with collective noun phrases (e.g., *the band*), an emphasis on the set itself is possible. As already mentioned, singular verbs are obligatory with collective noun phrases in Spanish, almost obligatory in American English, and permissible but optional in British English. Similarly, subsequent pronouns may be either singular or plural, with the choice being determined partly by whether the collection is acting as a whole or as individuals (e.g., *the committee...it decided...* vs. *the committee...they disagreed...*). A plural pronoun following a singular collective noun is one of the three types of conceptual pronoun that Gernsbacher identified. The name *conceptual pronoun* is based on the idea that the primary referent of the collective noun phrase, the one that determines its singular form, is the set. The referent of the pronoun, the individuals that comprise the set, is based on a concept related to the one that determines the primary referent. This idea is clearer in the other two types of example. One is generic reference. Following a reference to a specific individual, it is often possible to make a generic reference to individuals of the same type. Generic references often use plural pronouns. For example, if we change the passage about students and math lessons to (11a), the most plausible reading is that math lessons, in general, are very difficult to understand, although it could also mean that students are difficult to understand! In any case, both noun phrases in the first sentence are singular, so that whichever is conceptually related to the intended referent of *they,* it does not match that pronoun in gender.

(11)　a.　The student was talking about the math lesson.
　　　　　They are very difficult to understand.

In the corresponding passage, (11b), there is an ordinary reference to the particular math lesson that the student was talking about.

(11)　b.　The student was talking about the math lesson.
　　　　　It was very difficult to understand.

In English (and in Spanish), the most natural tenses in the second sentences of these two examples are different. Generic references are typically, but not always, followed by a timeless use of the present tense, as in (11a).

　　　The third type of conceptual pronoun identified by Gernsbacher is more complex. Sometimes a singular reference, often a nonspecific one, suggests a context in which many items of the kind referred to are likely to exist. So, someone who says, *I want a shirt,* may not have a particular shirt in mind, but he or she is likely to be either at home or in a store that sells shirts. In either case, there will actually be many shirts. So an appropriate response might be, *They are all in your chest of drawers* or *They are on the third floor, at the rear.* In both cases, the referent of *they* is a particular set of shirts, which is somehow evoked by the nonspecific reference; in experiments in which these passages are presented with no context, an inference is made about the probable context.

　　　Gernsbacher (1991) investigated the comprehension of these three types of conceptual pronoun and compared them with closely matched cases of ordinary pronominal reference, in which the number of the antecedent matched that of the pronoun (reference to specific individuals, rather than sets of individuals; to specific tokens, rather than to generic types; and to items of which there was only likely to be one in the most readily constructed context, rather than many, (e.g., a vacuum cleaner in a home). Gernsbacher found that when an "illegal" plural pronoun (i.e., one that mismatched the only plausible linguistic antecedent's morphosyntactic number) had an obvious conceptual interpretation (i.e., it referred to the members of a collective set, or to a generic type, or to multiple items, such as shirts, that could be inferred to exist in the most likely context), those pronouns were rated as more natural, and were understood more rapidly than singular pronouns (i.e., pronouns that matched the only plausible antecedent's morphosyntactic number) in the same sentences. However, in the control sentences, in which the conceptual readings for the anaphors were not plausible, the reverse pattern of results was found, with the linguistically "correct" pronouns being preferred.

These results were replicated and extended in English by Oakhill, Garnham, Gernsbacher, and Cain (1992), and in Spanish by Carreiras and Gernsbacher (1992). In their first experiment, Carreiras and Gernsbacher (1992) asked subjects to rate the naturalness of passages like those in (12), (13), and (14). In each case, the (c) sentence has a natural conceptual reading when it follows the (a) sentence, but not when it follows the (b) sentence. Because subject pronouns are usually omitted in Spanish, whether the subject of the (c) sentence is singular or plural is indicated by the ending of the verb.

Collective sets versus individual members

(12) a. Tengo que llamar de nuevo a Telefónica.
         I have to call the telephone company again

      b. Tengo que llamar de nuevo al técnico que me arregló el teléfono.
         I have to call the engineer who mended my telephone

      c. Se equivocaron/equivocó en el importe de la factura.
         They/he or she made a mistake in the amount of the bill

Generic types versus specific tokens

(13) a. Mi padre me ha regalado una novela.
         My father gave me a novel as a present

      b. Mi padre me ha regalado El Quijote.
         My father gave me Don Quixote as a present

      c. Te transportan/transporta a un mundo de fantasía.
        They transport/it transports you to a world of fantasy

Multiple items/events versus unique items/events

   (14)   a. ¿Buscas una camisa limpia?
          Are you looking for a clean shirt?

         b. ¿Buscas la guía telefónica?
          Are you looking for the telephone directory?

         c. Están/Está en el cajón de arriba.
          They are/It is in the top drawer

The results of this study paralleled those of Gernsbacher's (1991) rating study. In particular, the plural forms of verbs, and hence the implied plural subjects, were preferred when they could be taken to refer to the members of a collective set, the exemplars of a generic type, or multiple items or events whose existence was implied by the mention of a single item or event of the same kind.

In subsequent on-line experiments, Carreiras and Gernsbacher, (1992), investigated the comprehension of plural verbs (Exp. 2) and explicit plural subject pronouns (Exp. 4) in passages of the kind shown in (12), (13), and (14), using a self-paced reading task. The passages were presented in two displays. The first contained the (a) or the (b) version of the first sentence, and the second contained a version of the (c) sentence, with a singular or plural verb form (Exp. 2) or with an explicit plural or singular subject pronoun added (Exp. 4). The results of the two experiments were essentially the same, and the pooled mean reading times for the second displays are shown in Table 9.6.

The results indicated that plural verbs alone (Exp. 2) or plural verbs in conjunction with plural pronouns (Exp. 4) were understood more quickly than singular verbs, with or without singular pronouns, when they could be construed as referring to the members of collective sets or to exemplars of generic types. However, this effect was not found for the third class of conceptual pronouns, those referring to suggested multiple sets of items or events. In all cases, the singular verbs, with or without the singular pronouns, were easier to understand than the plural verbs and plural pronouns when they referred to single members of sets, to specific tokens of a generic type, or to unique items or events. These results suggest that with two of the three types of conceptual anaphor (collectives and generics), it is easier to construct a plural referent for the anaphor than a singular one, despite the fact that the noun phrase most closely associated with the antecedent is singular. Furthermore, in the third case, difference between the two conditions was only 11 ms. There is no evidence that singular antecedents are easier to construct in these cases.

TABLE 9.6

Mean Reading Times (in ms) for Second Sentences in Experiments 2 and 4 of Carreiras and Gernsbacher (1992)

	Plural	Singular
Collective sets	2,500	2,850
Individual members	2,586	2,484
Generic types	2,479	2,644
Specific tokens	2,606	2,432
Multiple items/events	2,095	2,084
Unique items/events	2,230	2,003

The experiments reported so far show that conceptual anaphors can be understood readily, but they do not answer the question of when the referents for those anaphors are entered into the mental model. If the referents are already there before the conceptual anaphors are encountered, those anaphors may not only be easy to understand; they may be no more difficult than ordinary, linguistically correct, anaphors that refer to the antecedent introduced directly into the model by their antecedents. On the other hand, if the referent for a conceptual anaphor has to be constructed when the anaphor is read (from the related material that is already in the model), such anaphors should be somewhat more difficult to understand than anaphors used in a more standard way. In the first case, plural anaphors (pronouns or zero anaphors whose number is indicated by the marking on the following verb) should be at least as easy to understand when they are preceded by an explicit plural antecedent as when they are conceptual and, hence, preceded by an implicit plural antecedent (the members of a collective set or the exemplars of a generic type).

In a further experiment, Carreiras and Gernsbacher (1992, Exp. 3) compared the reading times for sentences containing a plural anaphor (null subject with plural verb form) that was most naturally construed as a conceptual anaphor, with those for the same sentences following an explicit plural antecedent. The mean reading times for the second sentences that were preceded by an explicit plural or an implicit plural antecedent (a collective set and generic type) are presented in Table 9.7. We omit the data for the multiple items or events condition, because it produced weaker effects in the experiments reported earlier.

Plural anaphors were as easy to interpret when they followed implicit plural antecedents (collective sets and generic types) as when they followed explicit plural antecedents. Also, both implicit plural and explicit plural antecedents were more naturally followed by a plural verb than by a singular verb. This result replicates earlier findings for conceptual anaphors. For the passages with explicit plural antecedents, the result is not surprising, because the singular pronouns were both linguistically and conceptually anomalous in these passages.

TABLE 9.7

Mean Reading Times (in ms) for Second Sentences of the Collective Set and Generic Type Passages in Experiment 3 Carreiras and Gernsbacher (1992)

	Plural anaphor	Singular anaphor
Collective sets	2,870	3,165
Several members	2,899	3,284
Generic types	2,398	2,423
Several tokens	2,325	2,684

These results are compatible with the suggestion that when a passage mentions a collective set or a generic type, the members of the set or the exemplars of the type are introduced directly into the mental model and are available for subsequent anaphoric reference. An anaphor referring to these entities will naturally be plural. Similar results were obtained in English by Oakhill et al (1992) for collective set antecedents, but not for generic types. In Spanish, too, the results were stronger for collective sets, probably because it is more difficult to think of a set without thinking of its members than to think of an individual item without thinking of the other tokens of generic type to which it belongs.

In the previous section, we showed that morphosyntactic marking plays an important role in guiding anaphor resolution, and not just because it maps onto the semantic content of the antecedent. Not only semantic gender but also arbitrary gender is included in the discourse representation to which processes that resolve deep anaphors have access. However, morphosyntactic marking is not the only information used to resolve pronouns. In this section, we have shown that anaphors that do not agree in morphological number with their putative antecedents can still be readily understood. Indeed, in some cases they may be understood with no more difficulty than matched anaphors that do agree in number with their antecedents. It appears that semantic and pragmatic cues can operate successfully and quickly when morphological cues are not available.

STEREOTYPES

Readers can construct a mental representation of events reported in a newspaper article by interpreting it in relation to what they know about the real world. They can also construct models of events in a science fiction story by relating those events to what they know about the imaginary world in which the story is set. In general, when readers understand a text, they are able to evaluate how the information in the text is related to the world that the text is about. In particular, they can judge whether the events in the text are probable or plausible in that world. The representation that readers construct in understanding a discourse contains information that is expressed by the text, and also information that is not explicit in the text, but that can be derived or assumed on the basis of what is in the text, together with background knowledge. The process that puts the latter information into the model is inference making. Inferences not only depend on the use of knowledge about the world knowledge, they are controlled by it (Noordman & Vonk, 1992). In this section, we discuss the use of background knowledge in constructing a mental representation of a text or discourse. In particular, we discuss the incorporation of one kind of information (gender stereotyping) into a mental model and attempt to discover when the relevant world knowledge is used to make an inference.

Inferences about the gender of one or more characters in a text, when gender is not explicitly given, are one class of inferences that can be made on the basis of world knowledge. Characters are sometimes introduced into the discourse by role names that are not marked for gender (e.g., *taxi driver*). In such cases, when the text does not provide explicit information about the gender of a participant, prior knowledge in the form of a gender stereotype could be used to provide a default gender. If a character is referred to as *the taxi driver,* a reader might infer that this character is a male. However, as the text unfolds, that character might subsequently be referred to by a masculine or a feminine pronoun, which might or might not match the stereotypical default gender of the role name. It is not impossible for a taxi driver to be female, although a reader would probably expect to find that someone described only as *the taxi driver* was male.

The violation of gender expectations that is produced by role names is particularly interesting for a theory of discourse comprehension. Because role names in English do not always provide explicit information about gender, the gender of the character introduced into the mental model may be inferred using knowledge of the stereotypical gender of that person's profession. But if, as the text continues (e.g., when a pronoun is encountered), the gender of the character is shown to be different from the gender provided by the social stereotype, the mental model will need to be revised. In addition, if gender stereotype information is used immediately to encode gender, it is being used to make a knowledge-based inference. This inference would be, for example, from the fact that a particular person is a footballer (a soccer player, in UK english) to the inference that that person is (probably) male, or from the fact that a person is a nurse to the inference that it is probably a female. If the inference is made immediately, it is elaborative, because it is not necessary for establishing coherence at the point when it is made, even if it is used for this purpose later. However, it is also possible that readers do not encode the gender of a person described using a role name when that role name appears in the text for the first time, but only when gender information is explicitly provided by the text, as, for instance, when a pronoun is used to refer to the person.

Carreiras, Garnham, Oakhill, and Cain (1995) investigated how and when world knowledge about social stereotypes of occupations is incorporated into a mental model by measuring reading times for sentences in English and in Spanish, such as (15), (16) and (17). The first sentence of each text introduced a stereotypically masculine or feminine participant (e.g., *footballer, nurse*) or one that was not stereotyped for gender (e.g., *student*). The last sentence included a pronoun (*he/she*) that was intended to refer back to that participant, and that could match or mismatch the gender of the referent, if it had already been assigned a gender either from a definite article (in Spanish), or from a social stereotype (in English). Many role names are not clearly marked for gender in English and are subject to the influence of stereotypes. Therefore, when a pronoun is employed later in the text to refer to a character introduced by a role name, the gender of the pronoun could either match or mismatch the stereotypical gender of the role name, as in (15b) and (15c) respectively. In contrast to English, the gender of the participants will often be explicitly instantiated by the preceding article (*el/la*) in Spanish, as in sentences (16a) and (17a).

Carreiras et al. reasoned that if default gender information from social stereotypes is activated when a role name is read and is used to set up a representation of a particular person, longer reading times for the second sentence would be expected in English when the pronoun mismatches the stereotype. Because *footballer* is a stereotypically male role name, it should take longer to read sentence (15c) than sentence (15b). However, no differences would be expected in second sentences when the pronominal reference was to a character not stereotyped for gender (e.g., *student*). On the same assumption, longer reading times would be expected for the first sentence in Spanish, when the gender of the article mismatched the stereotype. Thus, it should take longer to read (17a) than (16a), because *futbolista* is a stereotypically male role name. As in English, no differences in reading times were expected with names not stereotyped for gender (e.g., *estudiante,* student).

(15)   a. The footballer wanted to play in the match.
        b. He had been training very hard during the week.
        c. She had been training very hard during the week.

(16)   a. El futbolista quería jugar el partido.
        b. El había estado entrenando mucho durante la semana.

(17)   a. La futbolista quería jugar el partido.
        b. Ella había estado entrenando mucho durante la semana.

The mean reading times for the second sentences in Carreiras et al.'s (1995) Experiment 1, with English texts, are shown in Table 9.8. When the first sentences contained a stereotyped role name, biased to either a male profession or a female profession, second sentences reading times were slower in the mismatch condition than in the match condition. However, when the first sentence contained a neutral role name, second sentences with a masculine pronoun were read as fast as second sentences with a feminine pronoun.

TABLE 9.8

Mean Reading Times (in ms) for the Second Sentences in Carreiras et al.'s (1995) Experiment 1 (English texts).

	Stereotyped characters		Neutral characters	
	Match	Mismatch	Masculine	Feminine
Reading time for second sentence	1,641	1,771	1,708	1,708

The match/mismatch effect in the sentences that contained the pronoun suggests that when the role name (e.g., *the footballer*) is read, its stereotyped gender is activated and initially encoded in the mental model of the text. Later on, if the pronoun disconfirms the gender indicated by the stereotype, the mental model has to be updated, resulting in longer reading times for those sentences. However, as we mentioned earlier, another possible explanation is that the stereotype information is not activated by the encoding of the noun phrase, but only when the morphologically marked pronoun has to be linked to the referent of that noun phrase. In this case, the information about the stereotyped gender of the protagonist is not included in the mental model when the token representing that protagonist and his or her occupation is incorporated into the mental model.

These two alternative hypotheses were tested in the experiments that

Carreiras et al. (1995) carried out in Spanish. If an early inference is found in Spanish, an early inference probably occurred in the English experiment, because it is unlikely that English and Spanish readers activate stereotypical information in different ways. In Spanish, the gender of the characters identified by role names can readily be determined by an accompanying article and incorporated into the mental model. However, if the stereotypical information of the role name is also activated and used to construct a representation of the character in a mental model at this point, the first sentences of the Spanish passages should show longer reading times when there is a mismatch, rather than a match, between the morphological gender of the article and the stereotypical gender of the role name. In contrast, no differences should appear in the sentence with the pronoun, because the mismatch between the stereotypical gender and the actual gender will already have been resolved. For instance, reading times should be longer for (17a) than for (16a), because the morphological gender of the article matches the stereotypical gender of the role name in (16a) but not in (17a). However, reading times for sentences (16b) and (17b) should not differ, although the stereotypical gender of the role name matches the gender of the pronoun in (16b) but not in (17b).

On the other hand, if the English findings are explained by backward inference, then, in Spanish, gender will be encoded in the first sentence from the morphological information on the definite article alone, but stereotype information should not be activated. Therefore, a late effect would be expected to occur in Spanish as it does in English—when the stereotype information is activated on linking the pronoun to its referent. In particular, no differences should appear in the first sentences (e.g. (16a) as opposed to (17a)), but reading times should be longer for the sentence containing the pronoun in the stereotype mismatch condition (17b) than in the stereotype match condition (16b).

The mean reading times for the first and third sentences of Carreiras et al.'s (1995) Experiment 3 are displayed in Table 9.9. In the Spanish experiments, the sentence that contained the pronoun was the third sentence in the text. A second sentence was included to catch any spillover effects from the first sentence. When a stereotyped role name was used, first sentence reading times were slower in the mismatch condition than in the match condition. However, when a neutral role name was used, first sentence reading times did not differ when the neutral character was preceded by a masculine or a feminine article. Third sentence reading times for texts that contained stereotyped characters showed no reliable difference between the match and mismatch conditions. In addition, no differences were found in the third sentence reading times of texts that contained neutral role names.

The results suggest that world knowledge about social stereotypes is activated at the earliest possible point, which, in the Spanish texts, is when the character's role name or occupational title first appears. The token representing the character in the mental model includes information about the person's gender. Reading is slower when the stereotypical gender fails to match the morphological gender of the definite article than when the two genders are the same.

TABLE 9.9
Mean Reading Times (in ms) for the First and Third Sentences in Carreiras et al.'s (1995) Experiment 3.

| | Stereotyped characters | | Neutral characters | |
	Match	Mismatch	Masculine	Feminine
Sentence 1	2,929	3,154	2,793	2,837
Sentence 3	2,141	2,151	2,450	2,447

However, once the real gender is encoded into the mental model, the stereotypical gender does not affect the reading of the pronoun-containing sentence. If the gender of the pronoun is the same as that of the definite article in the first sentence, readers do not slow down, even if the gender of the pronoun does not match the stereotypical gender of the character mentioned in the first sentence.

In order to test whether the disagreement between the morphological gender of the definite article and the stereotypical gender associated with the role name is sufficient, by itself, to produce the effect obtained in Spanish, Carreiras et. al. (1995, Exp. 4) presented the first sentences of the Spanish texts in two displays. The first display contained only the article and the noun, and the rest of the sentence appeared in a second display. The mean reading times for the first and second displays in the match and mismatch conditions are shown in Table 9.10. Reading times were slower in the mismatch than in the match condition, in both the first and the second display. So, although the match/mismatch effect occurs in the second display, it also occurs in the first display, where it is both numerically larger and statistically more reliable. Therefore, these results indicate that, although the scenario created by the whole sentence might contribute to the effects found in the previous experiments, a mismatch between the gender of the definite article and the stereotypical gender of the role name is sufficient to produce the effect.

The results of these experiments show that stereotypical gender is included in the representation of characters introduced by role names and revised, if necessary, in the light of other information. The English noun phrase *the footballer,* signals that a representation of a person who is a footballer should be included in the current mental model. Because this noun phrase is not morphologically marked for gender, the person will be assumed to be male because the stereotypical gender of footballers is male. If a subsequent pronoun refers to this person, it will indicate the actual gender of the person, and it may match or mismatch the stereotypical gender. In the case of a match, referential assignment is easy. However, in the case of a mismatch, the model must be updated, a process that is time-consuming. On this view, an inference is made when a character introduced by a role name is represented in a mental model: Footballers are stereotypically male, so this person is probably male. However, an alternative explanation of the English data is that the stereotype information is not used to make an early elaborative inference, but that all the inferential work happens when the pronoun is read.

TABLE 9.10

Mean Reading Times (in ms) for the First and Second Displays of Sentences in the Match and Mismatch Conditions of Carreiras et al. (1995), Experiment 4

	Match	Mismatch
Display 1	924	1,011
Display 2	1,669	1,737

In the Spanish texts, the pronoun never called for a revision of the mental model, because the gender of the person was always explicitly signaled by the definite article in the first sentence. However, the Spanish data show that, when el/la futbolista is read, the stereotypical gender is compared with, and if necessary overridden by, the gender of the article. Stereotype information is activated when the noun phrase is interpreted, and it affects the assignment of gender to the referent of the noun phrase: Readers do not simply encode the fact that someone is male or female from the morphological information. In addition, the effect cannot be explained merely in terms of the activation of stereotype information. That information must be brought to bear on the gender of the individual that the passage is about. Therefore, the results of these experiments lead us to conclude that an elaborative, and probably *nonminimal* inference—an inference not needed for local coherence (cf. McKoon & Ratcliff, 1992)—is made to incorporate stereotypical information in the mental model of the discourse when the role name is first encountered.

CONCLUDING REMARKS

In this chapter, we have described the results of a number of experiments on anaphor interpretation in Spanish. The results of these experiments show that both superficial and conceptual information is used in the interpretation of pronouns, and related types of anaphor, such as null subjects in Spanish. The first set of experiments established, contrary to the hypothesis of Sag and Hankamer (1984), that a superficial level of representation is used to interpret pronouns. Although we did not probe the time course of this effect in fine detail, it occurs when the clause containing the pronoun is read. Furthermore, because superficial representations tend to decay rapidly, the use of superficial information tends to be superceded by the use of conceptual information after one or two clauses. When both types of information are available, they appear to be used in parallel. In the experiments of Garnham et al. (1995), a gender cue was as effective when it was purely morphological as when it was also semantically based. Furthermore, the results of Alonso and Carreiras (1994) second experiment showed that either superficial proximity or proximity in a mental model was sufficient to produce rapid pronoun resolution.

We also reported two sets of experiments that primarily examined the use of conceptual information in anaphor resolution. In both cases, we obtained evidence for early elaboration of a mental model, although under highly constrained circumstances. In the experiments on conceptual anaphors, we found evidence that the mention of a collective set led immediately to the representation of its members, which could then be referred to by a plural anaphor. The Spanish data also suggested that reference to a particular individual made other tokens of that individual's generic type available for generic reference. However, this data has to be reconciled with contradictory data from English (Oakhill et al., 1992), which suggests that generic referents take time to construct.

From our studies of stereotypes, we argued that stereotype information is also used early. In English, it is used to make an elaborative inference about the probable gender of a character introduced by a role name—an inference that may be shown later to be incorrect, if the morphological form of the pronoun used to refer to the character does not match the character's stereotypical gender. In Spanish, stereotype information is also activated, even though it may interfere with gender assignment from morphological marking, (e.g., of a definite article). Again, our clause-by-clause reading time data do not allow us to track the detailed time course of these effects, although self-paced reading experiments with smaller displays are of some help in resolving this matter. However, to make a detailed examination of the time course of anaphor interpretation, it will probably be necessary to turn to other methodologies, such as eye-movement monitoring. Future work in the new eye-movement monitoring laboratory in La Laguna, will bring us nearer to providing answers to these questions.

ACKNOWLEDGMENTS

Our collaboration was made possible by a NATO collaborative research grant (CRG.890527) and by an Acción Integrada grant (HB93-212) from the British Council and the Spanish Ministry of Education and Science. The research reported in this chapter was also supported by grants 91/103 from the Dirección General de Universidades del Gobierno Autónomo de Canarias and PB93-0562 from the DGICYT awarded to Manuel Carreiras, and grant RC00232439, Mental Models and the Interpretation of Anaphora, from the Economic and Social Research Council (UK) awarded to Alan Garnham and Jane Oakhill.

REFERENCES

Alonso, M.A., & Carreiras, M. (1994, September). *Syntactic and semantic cues in plural anaphora resolution.* Paper presented at the Seventh Conference of the European Society for Cognitive Psychology, Lisbon, Portugal 1994.

Anderson, A., Garrod, S.C., & Sanford, A.J. (1983). The accessibility of pronominal antecedents as a function of episode shifts in narrative text. *Quarterly Journal of Experimental Psychology, 35A,* 427–440.

Caplan, D. (1972). Clause boundaries and recognition latencies for words in sentences. *Perception & Psychophysics, 12,* 73–76.

Caramazza, A., Grober, E., Garvey, C., & Yates, J. (1977). Comprehension of anaphoric pronouns. *Journal of Verbal Learning and Verbal Behavior, 16,* 601–609.

Carreiras, M., Carriedo, N., Alonso, M.A., & Fernandez, A. (1995). *The role of verbal tense and verbal aspect in the foregrounding of information during reading.* Manuscript submitted for publication.

Carreiras, M., Garnham, A., & Oakhill, J.V. (1993). The use of superficial and meaning-based representations in interpreting pronouns: Evidence from Spanish. *European Journal of Cognitive Psychology, 5,* 93–116.

Carreiras, M., Garnham, A., Oakhill, J.V., & Cain, K. (in press). The use of stereotypical gender information in constructing a mental model: Evidence from English and Spanish. *Quaterly Journal of Experimental Psychology.*

Carreiras, M., & Gernsbacher, M.A. (1992). Comprehending conceptual anaphors in Spanish. *Language and Cognitive Processes, 7,* 281–299.

Chang, F.R. (1980). Active memory processes in visual sentence comprehension: Clause effects and pronominal reference. *Memory and Cognition, 8,* 58–64.

Clark, H.H., & Sengul, C.J. (1979). In search of referents for nouns and pronouns. *Memory and Cognition, 7,* 35–41.

Clifton, C., & Ferreira, F. (1987). Discourse structure and anaphora: Some experimental results. In M. Coltheart (Ed.), *Attention and performance XII: The psychology of reading* (pp. 635–654). Hillsdale, NJ: Lawrence Erlbaum Associates.

Cloitre, M., & Bever, T.G. (1988). Linguistic anaphors: Levels of representation and discourse. *Language and Cognitive Processes, 3,* 293–322.

Corbett, A.T., & Chang, F.R. (1983). Pronoun disambiguation: Accessing potential antecedents. *Memory and Cognition, 11,* 283–294.

Daneman, M., & Carpenter, P. (1980). Individual differences in working memory and reading. *Journal of Verbal Learning and Verbal Behavior, 19,* 450–466.

Ehrlich, K., & Rayner, K. (1983). Pronoun assignment and semantic integration during reading: Eye movements and immediacy of processing. *Journal of Verbal Learning and Verbal Behavior, 22,* 75–87.

Fletcher, C.R. (1984). Markedness and topic continuity in discourse processing. *Journal of Verbal Learning and Verbal Behavior, 23,* 487–493.

Garnham, A. (1987). *Mental models as representations of discourse and text.* Chichester, West Sussex: Ellis Horwood.

Garnham, A., Traxler, M., Oakhill, J.V., & Gernsbacher, M.A. (in press). The locus of implicit causality effects in comprehension. *Journal of Memory and Language.*

Garnham, A., & Oakhill, J.V. (1985). On-line resolution of anaphoric pronouns: Effects of inference making and verb semantics. *British Journal of Psychology, 76,* 385–393.

Garnham, A., Oakhill, J.V., & Cruttenden, H. (1992). The role of implicit causality and gender cue in the interpretation of pronouns. *Language and Cognitive Processes, 7,* 231–255.

Garnham, A., Oakhill, J.V., Ehrlich, M.F., & Carreiras, M. (1995). Representations and processes in the interpretation of pronouns: New evidence from Spanish and French. *Journal of Memory and Language, 34,* 41–62.

Garvey, C., & Caramazza, A. (1974). Implicit causality in verbs. *Linguistic Inquiry, 5,* 459–464.

Gernsbacher, M.A. (1989). Mechanisms that improve referential access. *Cognition, 32,* 99–156.

Gernsbacher, M.A. (1991). Comprehending conceptual anaphors. *Language and Cognitive Processes, 6,* 81–105.

Givón, T. (Ed.). (1983). *Topic continuity in discourse: A quantitative cross-language study.* Amsterdam: John Benjamins.

Grober, E.H., Beardsley, W., & Caramazza, A. (1978). Parallel function in pronoun assignment. *Cognition, 6,* 117–133.

Grosz, B. (1981). Focusing and description in natural language dialogues. In A. K. Joshi, B.L. Webber & I.A. Sag (Eds.), *Elements of discourse understanding.* Cambridge, England: Cambridge University Press.

Hankamer, J., & Sag, I.A. (1976). Deep and surface anaphora. *Linguistic Inquiry, 7,* 391–428.

Jarvella, R.J. (1979). Immediate memory and discourse processing. In G. H. Bower (Ed.), *The psychology of learning and motivation* (Vol. 13). New York: Academic Press

Johnson-Laird, P.N. (1983). *Mental models: Towards a cognitive science of language, inference, and consciousness.* Cambridge, England: Cambridge University Press.

Kintsch, W. (1974). *The representation of meaning in memory.* Hillsdale, NJ: Lawrence Erlbaum Associates.

Lesgold, A., Roth, S., & Curtis, M. (1979). Foregrounding effects in discourse comprehension. *Journal of Verbal Learning and Verbal Behavior, 18,* 291–308

Lucas, M.M., Tanenhaus, M., & Carlson, G. (1990). Levels of representation in the interpretation of anaphoric reference and instrument inference. *Memory and Cognition, 18,* 611–631

Mani, K., & Johnson-Laird, P.N. (1982). The mental representation of spatial descriptions. *Memory and Cognition, 10,* 181–187.

Marr, D. (1982). *Vision: A computational investigation into the human representation and procesing of visual information.* San Francisco: Freeman.

McKoon, G., & Ratcliff, R. (1992). Inference during reading. *Psychological Review, 99,* 440–466.

Noordman, L.G.M., & Vonk, W. (1992). Readers' knowledge and the control of inferences in reading. *Language and Cognitive Processes, 7,* 373–391.

Oakhill, J.V., Garnham, A., Gernsbacher, M.A., & Cain, K. (1992). How natural are conceptual anaphors? *Language and Cognitive Processes, 7,* 257–280.

Sag, I.A., & Hankamer, J. (1984). Toward a theory of anaphoric processing. *Linguistics and Philosophy, 7,* 325–345.

Stevenson, R.J. (1986). The time course of pronoun comprehension. In C. Clifton (Ed.), *Proceedings of the Eighth Annual Conference of the Cognitive Science Society* (pp. 102–109). Lawrence Erlbaum Associates.

Vonk, W., Hustinx, L.G.M., & Simons, W.H.G. (1992). The use of referential expressions in structuring discourse. *Language and Cognitive Processes, 7,* 301–333.

Whitehead, E.L. (1982). *Distance and foregrounding effects on pronoun interpretation.* Paper presented to the Experimental Psychological Society, Cambridge.

10

Spatial and Interpersonal Models in the Comprehension of Narratives

Manuel de Vega
Universidad de La Laguna
Tenerife, Spain

This chapter addresses the nature of the representation of reference in narratives, using the constructionist notion of mental models. The main assumption of the mental models approach is that readers build representations of situations referred to by narrative (the objects, characters, events, and processes described), in addition to representations of the text itself (Bower & Morrow, 1990; Garnham, 1987; Glenberg, Meyer and Lindem, 1987; Mani & Johnson-Laird, 1982; Sanford & Garrod, 1981). The representation of a situation has some functional consequences that can be empirically explored. For instance, situation models govern the selective activation *foregrounding* of some pieces of information in working memory, guide readers' inferences, and contribute to building the coherence of the text.

Some early experiments supported the notion of mental models in comprehension. For instance, Mani and Johnson-Laird (1982) presented subjects with either determinate or indeterminate descriptions of layouts. A determinate description was consistent with a single layout, whereas an indeterminate description was consistent with two different layouts. The two versions differed, however, by only a single word, and their propositional textbases were of identical complexity. Table 10.1 shows an example of the materials.

TABLE 10.1
Materials From the Experiment of Mani and Johnson-Laird (1982)

Determinate description:
        The spoon is to the left of the knife.
        The plate is to the right of the knife.
        The fork is in front of the spoon.
        The cup is in front of the knife.

Consistent layout:
        spoon   knife   plate
        fork   cup

Indeterminate description:
        The spoon is to the left of the knife.
        The plate is to the right of the spoon.
        The fork is in front of the spoon.
        The cup is in front of the knife.

Consistent layouts:
        spoon   knife   plate
        fork   cup

        spoon   plate   knife
        fork   cup

After subjects had listened to a given description, they had to decide whether it was true or false with respect to a diagram of a layout. After all of the truth judgments, subjects were given an unexpected recognition task that include the actual description, an equivalent description of the same layout that used different sentences, and two foil descriptions. Subjects recognized determinate descriptons better than indeterminate ones. However, for determinate descriptions subjects did not discriminate between the actual description and the equivalent description of the layout, whereas for indeterminate descriptions they did. The results suggest that mental models—built for determinate descriptions—preserve the structure of the layout, but not the verbatim details, whereas propositional representations—built for indeterminate descriptions—lead to good retention of the text, but not the layout.

Many experiments on mental models are carried out for demonstrative purposes (e.g., to show that readers' spatial representations are "life-like"), while the nature of mental models remains vague. This chapter reviews the mental model notion in the light of some recent experiments and tries to provide some information about the nature of mental models.

WHY ARE MENTAL MODELS NECESSARY?

Most theories of text comprehension assume that readers parse sentences into a text-based propositional structure (Johnson-Laird, 1983; Kintsch & van Dijk, 1978; van Dijk and Kintsch, 1983). According to this view, the superficial text is encoded into a set of micropropositions that represent the concepts and relations underlying individual sentences and groups of sentences. The propositional encoding preserves the formal coherence of text by means of *coreference* (argument overlap) and the co-occurrence of propositions in working memory (Fletcher & Bloom, 1988; Kintsch & van Dijk, 1978).

Despite their merits, text-based propositions are not sufficient to explain full comprehension. Some phenomena in text comprehension are not appropriately reflected in the propositional textbase (Mani & Johnson-Laird, 1982; van Dijk & Kintsch, 1983). I focus in the next section on some limitations of propositional textbase representations—in particular, on their inability to explain the processing of coherence and as some kinds of inferences.

Coherence and Inferences

Standard propositional theories do not account appropriately for how text coherence is processed. It has been argued that coreference (among consecutive clauses and sentences) is important for building text coherence. However, although coreference usually correlates with coherence, it cannot be identified with it. Sometimes coreference is marked in the text by means of anaphoric devices (e.g., *Maria and John married. They are on their honeymoon*). In other cases, the coreference is not marked, as when a text uses several words with different conceptual meaning to refer to the same individual in the world. In this case, only the reader's world knowledge can guarantee the coreference. For instance, in the following sentences—*Peter has his office in downtown. The architect is now working on a project,* both *Peter* and *the architect* can refer to the same person, assuming a particular world knowledge. It is possible, also, to write a text with coreference that is not coherent at all (e.g., *John went to the theater. Arthur Miller wrote theater plays in America. New York is in America).*

Thus, coherence is related to the model of the situation, which involves the interpretive activity of the reader, rather than a simple encoding of the text words. To put it another way, coherence is something in the mind, rather than in the text (Hobbs, 1979; Sanford & Garrod, 1994; Givón, 1992). Certainly, texts provide some cohesion markers, such as anaphors and connectives, that indicate which sentences (and their underlying meanings) are related. However, the relation between cohesion markers (in the text) and coherence (in the mind) is rather complex, as we see further on.

Anaphors and Connectives

Anaphors and connectives are text devices that contribute to the building of integrated and coherent representations. Anaphors indicate to the reader that a concept found in a previous sentence (the *antecedent*) must be included in the representation of the current sentence. In addition, connectives like *because* and *therefore* signal a certain conceptual relation (i.e., causal) between the content of adjacent sentences (e.g., Millis & Just, 1994). Anaphors and connectives play similar roles in comprehension. Firs, anaphors and connectives govern the activation of certain pieces of discourse. Anaphors maintain the activation of the antecedent concept and inhibit nonantecedent concepts (e.g., Gernsbacher, 1989). For their part, connectives placed between two clauses reactivate the first clause and sometimes the second one (Millis & Just, 1994). Second, anaphors and connectives increase the probability of integrating clauses into a coherent representation. Thus, when two adjacent clauses include a *because,* rather than being coordinated, it is more likely that the reader will integrate them by inferring a causal relation (e.g., Millis & Just, 1994).

Notice that in all the experiments discussed, the functional relation among markers, activation, and integration is not clear. One possibility is that markers directly cause concepts to be integrated (and, eventually, inferences to be made), and, as a consequence, some concepts become more activated. An alternative is that markers initially increase the activation of concepts and this makes it more likely that integration and inferences will take place.

On the other hand, the correspondence between markers and coherence cannot be taken for granted. In some cases, the cohesion markers and the coherence elaborated by the reader diverge. First, readers can generate *bridging inferences,* relying on their semantic and pragmatic knowledge, even in the absence of the relevant syntactic marker (e.g., Haviland & Clark, 1974; Singer, Revlin, & Halldorson, 1990). For instance, people who read, *The sun was warm.*

The snowman melted, very likely infer that the cause of the snowman melting was the heat produced by the sun. This causal link allows the reader to integrate the two sentences, which would otherwise remain unrelated, into a coherent representation of meaning.

Second, the situation model allows the reader to process text markers that are formally anomalous. For instance, in conceptual anaphors, subjects solve the referent of a pronoun despite a morphological mismatch between the pronoun and its text antecedent. Thus, in the sentences, *I need a plate. Where do you keep them / it,* subjects who read the anaphor *them* are faster and rate it as more natural that those who read *it,* and this occurs despite the fact that the latter—but not the former—matches the antecedent syntactically (Carreiras & Gernsbacher, 1992; Gernsbacher, 1991). The reader's model of the situation (in houses, there are many plates stored together) explains this linguistic anomaly.

Finally, on some occasions, a relation marked by grammar is not encoded by readers. Thus, in some experiments by Noordman, Vonk, and Kempff (1992), readers of expository texts did not establish a causal relation, although it was explicitly marked by the word *because* in the text and it was necessary for local coherence. Consider the sentence, *Chlorine compounds are frequently used as propellants because they do not react with other substances.* In their experiments, Noordman et al. found that the inference necessary for local coherence (that good propellants do not react with other substances) was not established on-line. Apparently, subjects did not have the appropriate knowledge to "fill in" the marked causal relation. Therefore, the content of inferences cannot be identified with the encoding of superficial text markers.

Conclusions

Although there is a correlation between text markers and the integrated, coherent structure built by the reader, the correspondence is not perfect. Sometimes, the reader establishes bridging inferences that go beyond the nominal information provided by the text; in other cases, the reader disregards the rules of grammatical concordance in order to fit anaphors to an implicit situation model; and finally, on occasion, the reader fails to activate an inference necessary for coherence, despite the appropriate relation being signaled by the text. Cohesion markers in the text are important: They can be considered as "processing instructions" (Givón, 1992) with two important functions: to indicate which concepts must be activated (or inhibited) and to prompt the reader to integrate some concepts into a coherent trace. However, the markers themselves do not automatically produce a coherent representation. Readers must be able to activate their semantic and pragmatic knowledge in order to elaborate the coherence promoted by the text markers. Consequently, most theories of text comprehension postulate mental models or situation models in addition to textbase propositions (Johnson-Laird, 1983; Kintsch & van Dijk, 1978; van Dijk & Kintsch, 1983).

The consensus on the necessity of mental models for a theory of comprehension is quite general. More controversial is the nature of these mental structures. Some authors claim that mental models are isomorphic (or at least homomorphic) to real-world experience (Franklin & Tversky, 1990; Glenberg et al., 1987; Morrow, Bower, & Greenspan, 1989): Namely, mental models are held to involve a structural similarity to our experience, rather than being encoded in the symbols of a "mental language" with an arbitrary syntax. Others assume that mental models are built into the mental language of propositions, the same format responsible for representing the textbase (e.g., van Dijk & Kintsch, 1983). I return to the representational issue later.

SPATIAL MODELS

Most experiments on mental models have explored spatial representations built from texts. This bias is a matter of methodological convenience. It is relatively easy to demonstrate that the structure of spatial models (visuospatial, Euclidian) differs from the structure of the propositional textbase (linear and with an arbitrary syntax).

Experiments With Learned Descriptions

Some experiments on spatial models involve tasks that require the initial learning of a layout (from either a description or a picture), followed by some sort of spatial judgments whose reaction times are recorded. These experiments have shown that readers are able to elaborate perspective-based models of the situation, which differ remarkably from the textbase representations. For instance, in the experiments of Franklin and Tversky (1990), subjects initially learned a narrative describing an environment with several objects located around the reader (mentioned as the second-person pronoun *you*). Later on, subjects were given other portions of the narrative that reoriented their point of view each time so that they were facing particular objects. For each orientation, subjects were asked to name the object in any direction described by one of the locative words: *front, back, above, below, left,* or *right.* The response times showed a dimensional pattern: *above–below* faster than *front–back* faster than *right–left*, regardless of the orientation prompted by the text. In addition, there was a within-dimension effect: the *front* locations were faster than the *back* ones. Therefore, the accessibility of objects in a described layout depends on their position in an egocentric framework, just as it does in real world experience.

Readers are also able to keep track of the perspective of two characters with different points of view of the same described environment, as was demonstrated by de Vega (1994), with a slightly different paradigm. Subjects were given verbal descriptions, in the second person, of an environment like the one illustrated in Fig. 10.1.

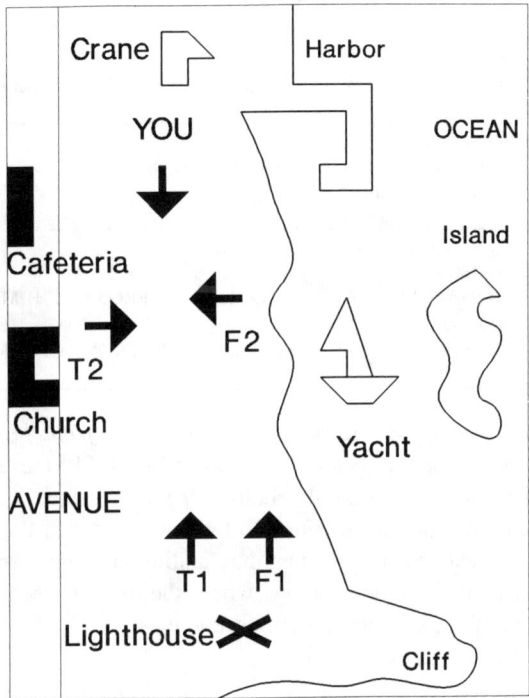

FIG. 10.1.   Illustration of scene described in the experiments of de Vega (1994), showing the landmarks; the *you* perspective; and the tourist (T) and the fisherman (F), either sharing (T1 and F1) or differing in (T2 and F2) perspective.

After learning the described environment, subjects read a text that introduced two characters (e.g., the fisherman and the tourist) who either shared a similar perspective (e.g., they were walking in the same direction) or had an opposite perspective (they were facing each other), although neither of them had the same perspective as that initially described for *you*. In this way, the spatial relations among the landmarks and characters were not directly described at any point, but had to be inferred by the subjects.

Afterwards, subjects were given blocks of three sentences to read at their own pace. The first two sentences guided the reader's attention to one character, and the third sentence described a spatial relation between a landmark and a character (either the one introduced by the previous sentences or the other). Subjects had to verify whether the relation was true or false. Table 10.2 illustrates the verification materials of one experiment.

TABLE 10.2
Verification Material From de Vega (1994; Translated From Spanish)

Introduction sentences:
The tourist stops for a while and puts on his coat.
It is mid-afternoon and the temperature is cool.
Verification sentence:
One character:
Afterward he looks at the lighthouse IN FRONT OF HIM.
Two characters:
The fisherman looks at the lighthouse IN FRONT OF HIM.

The results showed the standard dimension effect (*front–back* is faster than *right–left*) replicating some of Franklin and Tversky's (1995) results. In addition, subjects were able to verify spatial relations from any character's perspective, although verification times were about 340 ms slower when the two characters had opposite perspectives, suggesting that additional cognitive resources are necessary to instantiate a perspective when the reader keeps in mind two alternative points of view of the described layout.

Continuous Reading Experiments

Experiments with learning paradigms have generally shown that subjects can elaborate quite detailed models of a situation, which allows them to compute or *infer* implicit spatial relations. This means that the accessibility of some tokens is governed by the spatial structure of the situation, rather than by the superficial features of the text. In addition, mental models are updated (and the accessibility of tokens are modified) as the text describes a change in the situation (e.g., a change of perspective). However, we cannot establish firm conclusions about text comprehension from these experiments, because they depart considerably from ordinary comprehension demands (de Vega, 1995). Thus, learning the description of a layout probably makes the spatial representation more accurate and accessible than reading this description just once. In addition, the experimental procedures explicitly demanded a judgment about spatial relations, whereas in ordinary reading (e.g., of a narrative) this is not the case.

Some experiments have explored the nature of spatial models in more naturalistic reading tasks (de Vega, 1995; Glenberg et al., 1987; O'Brien & Albrecht, 1992). The study of Glenberg et al. (1987) is a good illustration of the continuous reading paradigm. Subjects in that study read short texts in which a target object was described early in the text as spatially associated to the protagonist (e.g., *John put on his sweatshirt*) or as spatially dissociated from the protagonist (e.g., *John took off his sweatshirt*). Later in the text, when the protagonist was described as moving to a different location, subjects were tested with an identification probe in which they judged whether the target word (*sweatshirt*) had been included in the text. The results showed faster responses after reading the associated version than after reading the dissociated version of the text, indicating that in the former condition the target was more accessible in the reader's memory. This greater accessibility was attributed to the represented structure of the situation rather than to the surface features of the text (which was identical in the two versions, except for a single verb) or their propositional encoding (although see McKoon & Ratcliff, 1992, for an alternative explanation).

Readers of narratives also keep track of the protagonist's location, as was shown by O'Brien and Albrecht (1992). In their experiments, subjects read passages in a sentence-by-sentence paradigm. The first sentence of each passage contained information about the location of the protagonist (e.g., *Kim stood inside / outside the health club*. After reading some filler sentences, subjects were given a critical sentence describing the protagonist as leaving the original location, (e.g., "She decided to go outside the health club". This sentence was either consistent with the initial protagonist's position (*Kim was inside... and she decided to go outside.*) or inconsistent (*Kim was outside... and she decided to go outside.*). The results showed that subjects read the critical sentence in the inconsistent condition more slowly, suggesting that they were sensitive to the location of the protagonist. This was the case even though the filler sentences ruled out the possibility that the initial spatial information was still available in working memory. In another experiment, however, O'Brien and Albrecht failed to show the reader's sensitivity to the protagonist's perspective when a secondary character's motion was either consistent or inconsistent with the protagonist's position. Only when subjects were explicitly instructed to imagine themselves as taking the protagonist's perspective did the consistent–inconsistent pattern emerge again.

These studies show that readers update a character's location, but are they sensitive to the protagonist's implicit surroundings? Some recent experiments by de Vega (1995) explored this issue by testing the accessibility of objects spatially related to the protagonist's position. Subjects were given short stories describing a character moving through an environment. Two topological relations were included in the stories. Some stories described two target objects, situated *inside* and *outside* a building. After describing the layout, each story described the protagonist as entering or leaving the building. Other stories described the target objects as situated at the *top* and the *bottom* of a place (e.g., a tower) and the protagonist as moving *up* or *down*. All the experiments tested, with different procedures, whether a target object becomes more accessible when it is consistent with the protagonist's location. In Experiment 1, subjects read, sentence-by-sentence at their own pace, short narratives like the one illustrated in Table 10.3, and the computer recorded the reading time of the final critical sentence. This sentence described the protagonist as interacting with one target object that was either consistent or inconsistent with his or her position. The reading times were about 185 ms faster for the consistent critical sentence than for the inconsistent one, demonstrating that readers were sensitive to the implicit surroundings of a protagonist who was described as moving in the environment.

TABLE 10.3
Illustration of a Narrative Used by de Vega (1995; Translated From Spanish)

Introductory sentence:
    Carmen likes to walk around in the museum area.
Layout description:
    Entrance to the museum is free so that people can explore the past. The museum has a famous room with very well preserved Egyptian mummies. In the street, just in front of the museum, many pigeons came, because people feed them.
Biasing sentence:
    Carmen went into (went out of) the museum
Filler:
    and she walked a few steps.
Last sentence:
    She approached the mummies (pigeons) quietly.

The readers' performance in this experiment raises a question. Do readers update their situation model on line or backward? According to the on-line updating hypothesis, readers update their representation, focusing on the consistent object, as soon as they read about the protagonist's motion (e.g., *Carmen went into the Museum*). By contrast, the backward updating hypothesis claims that subjects only focus on the protagonist's surroundings when they read a sentence that explicitly or implicitly mentions the target object (e.g., *She approached the mummies quietly*). At this time, subjects would try to integrate the new information with their previous model of the environment and find the new information spatially consistent or inconsistent.

In Experiments 2 and 3, the final sentence did not mention a target (e.g., *She looked around with admiration*), and one of the target words (e.g., *mummies / pigeons*) was introduced as an identification probe immediately after the last sentence (de Vega, 1995). The reaction time for consistent and inconsistent probes did not differ significantly, indicating that both targets were equally activated and subjects did not update their situation model on line. Finally, in the last sentence, Experiments 4 and 5 included an implicit mention of the target by means of an ambiguous pronoun (e.g., *She looked at them with admiration.*), followed by the identification probe. In this case, the consistency effect emerged again: Consistent probes were verified about 100 ms faster than inconsistent ones. The effect cannot be attributed to a grammar-based resolution of the pronoun, because the pronoun *them* was compatible with both targets (e.g., *mummies / pigeons*). In addition, the consistency effect was obtained both at the end of the critical sentence (Experiment 4) and immediately after reading the ambiguous pronoun (Experiment 5), suggesting that the pronoun triggers the updating of the spatial model.

The overall results of these experiments indicate that subjects can update relatively complex mental models (involving two places, two potential objects, and one moving protagonist). However, the updating process is subject to some qualifications. The description of the protagonist's motion (e.g., entering or leaving a building) is not sufficient to produce an immediate update of his or her surrounding objects. In order to keep an updating (consistency effect), it is necessary that the narrative explicitly or implicitly mention (by means of an ambiguous pronoun) a target object, after the protagonist's motion has been described. Consequently, updating seems to be a backward process, consisting of mapping a relevant piece of spatial information against the previous model of the situation.

The results I have described seem to be at odds with the classic results of Glenberg et al.'s (1987) experiments. They found that target objects described as spatially associated with the protagonist were more accessible than those that were dissociated from the protagonist. The effect was robust, despite the fact that the target object was not mentioned, either explicitly or implicitly, after describing the protagonist's motion. Several features of Glenberg et al.'s experiments might contribute to making the updating of a mental model easier than it is in de Vega's (1995) experiments. First, in Glenberg et al., the spatial association between the protagonist and the target was very close, involving relations of *attachment* and *portability,* whereas in my experiments, the spatial relation was, most of the time, a distant "perceptual" interaction between the protagonist and the object. Second, in Glenberg et al., there was just one target object in each narrative, whereas in my experiments the situation model was more complex, involving two competing target objects associated with two different places. Finally, the critical relation between the protagonist and the target was explicit in Glenberg et al.'s narratives, whereas it had to be inferred in my experiments. In other words, when Glenberg et al. mentioned that the protagonist *put on* or *take off* the sweatshirt, the corresponding association and dissociation could be immediately encoded, regardless of the nature of the incoming information. By contrast, in my experiments, the choice of a target for foregrounding had to be derived from understanding the whole set of topological relations of the layout (where the objects were) as well as the protagonist's motion (where he or she was coming from). Further experiments are necessary to explore how the complexity of situations and the kinds of spatial relations modulate the updating of spatial models.

Conclusions

The experiments I have described indicate that building and updating situation models is a demanding, nonautomatic process. The clearest perspective effects were obtained in those experiments in which the subjects were asked to learn a description of the layout. However, when subjects read descriptions continuously, the updating of spatial relations could not be taken for granted unless the implicit spatial relations were very simple (e.g., Glenberg et al., 1987) or the relevance of updating was signaled by text markers (e.g., de Vega, 1995). In the latter case, the updating seems to be a backward process rather than an anticipatory or predictive process. Therefore, situation models do not represent all the implicit spatial details. This is hardly surprising, because a complete spatial representation would be very demanding, and situation models are constrained by the limited resources of working memory.

Another property of spatial models that emerges from these experiments is that models are organized around a few body-centered or object-centered categories, that correspond to common topological labels: *front, back, right, left,* and so on. The topological categories determine the different accessibility of objects, as we have seen. This hierarchical organization of spatial models is probably related to the way people organize their world experience around their bodies (e.g., Lakoff, 1987).

INTERPERSONAL MODELS

It is intuitively obvious that outside the spatial domain, readers of narratives represent the characters' psychological perspective, which includes the characters' features, their interpersonal relations, and their mental states. This contention does not seem controversial; after all, stories explicitly provide abundant information about interpersonal and mental states. The critical point is whether readers of narratives build such representations beyond the propositional textbase, actively using their general knowledge, as well as the text-based knowledge of characters, to derive nonexplicit consequences of the described events, such as the characters' mood, emotions, intentions, and so on. In this section, I focus on experiments that explore how readers understand characters' emotions and beliefs.

Representing Emotions

A few studies have demonstrated that readers are able to represent accurately the implicit emotional states of protagonists, as a consequence of understanding their actions, their goals, and their relationships with other characters (de Vega, León, & Díaz, in press; Gernsbacher, Goldsmith, & Robertson, 1992). Thus, in Gernsbacher et al.'s experiments, subjects read a story in which a main character stole money from a store where his best friend worked, and later learned that his friend had been fired. At the end of the story subjects read a critical sentence that described the protagonist as feeling either guilt (matching the implicit emotion) or pride (mismatching the implicit emotion). Subjects read the sentences with the word that matched the emotion induced by the story faster than sentences with the mismatching emotion word.

Emotions are sometimes transitory states. For an appropriate understanding of stories, readers must be able to track protagonists' implicit emotions, updating their representations as emotionally relevant information is provided by the text. De Vega, León, & Díaz (in press) have shown that readers are capable of updating the protagonist's implicit emotion as new emotionally significant events are read. In their study, subjects were asked to read short stories with a shifting emotion context, like the one illustrated in Table 10.4.

TABLE 10.4

Illustration of a Story With a Shifting Emotion Context from de Vega, León, et al. (in press, Exp. 1 Translated From Spanish)

First part:

> Arthur thought about it once more. The most beautiful girl in the class had asked him to teach her to play tennis in the afternoons. He had many doubts about it. He couldn't believe that she was interested in him. Probably she was looking for an excuse to get into the club and to meet another boy. He had an appointment with her that afternoon. Everything depended on whether she came or not; and, if she came, what her attitude would be toward him. Then he would know if she was really interested in him.

Target sentences at the first locus:

> Arthur felt quite insecure. (<u>consistent</u> with first part)
>
> or
>
> Arthur felt quite flattered. (<u>inconsistent</u> with first part)

Second part:

> He saw her with her short skirt. She was talking with other classmates. Arthur noticed that she immediately left the others and joined him. All afternoon she was interested only in him.

Target sentences at the second locus:

> Arthur felt quite insecure. (<u>consistent</u> with first part)
>
> or
>
> Arthur felt quite flattered. (<u>inconsistent</u> with first part)

Final sentence:

> Arthur couldn't believe it.

The first part of the story induced one emotion (insecurity), whereas the second part suggested a different one (flattered). A target sentence describing an emotion (e.g., *Arthur felt quite insecure/flattered*) was placed immediately after the first or the second part of the story and was either consistent or inconsistent with the first part of the story. The results in Fig. 10.2 showed that the reading times for the target sentences were slower for the inconsistent than the consistent condition in the first locus, and the pattern reversed in the second locus, indicating that readers had updated the emotion representation.

An alternative explanation for this result, however, is that inferred emotions are governed by the local context (the three or four immediately preceding sentences). Thus, sentences in the second part of the story (the shifting portion) may simply cause the previous representations to drop out of working memory, including the initial emotion (e.g., *insecure*). Then the second part of the story suggests an emotion (e.g. *flattered*) independently of the previous emotion representation, which has been "lost." This hypothetical mechanism identifies the phenomenon observed in the experiment as a passive side effect of working memory limitation, rather than as an active process of updating the emotion parameters of the situation.

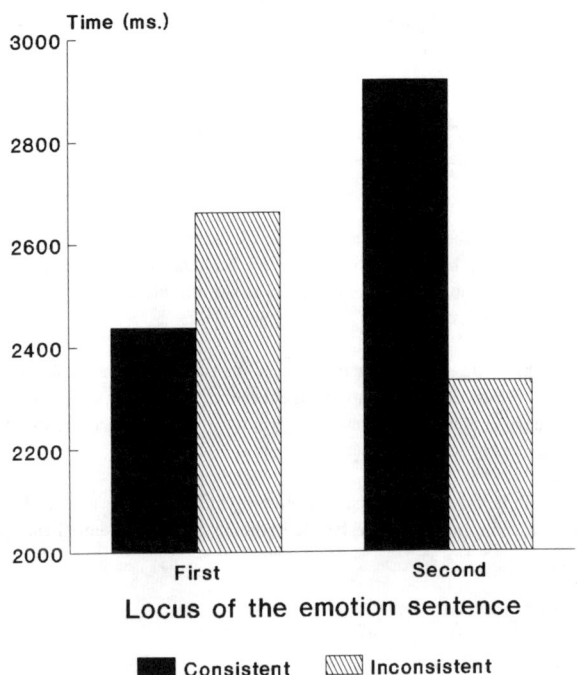

FIG. 10.2.   Reading times for sentences consistent and inconsistent with the first part of the story using two loci in a shifting emotion context (de Vega, León, et al., in press).

In order to rule out the local context hypothesis, another experiment was run. The stories were rewritten with some modifications: (a) The first part of each story (the emotion context) had two versions aimed at suggesting opposite emotions; (b) the second part of each story (the local context) was always emotionally neutral, describing environments and characters' routine actions; and (c) The target sentence was always placed at the end of the stories, immediately after the neutral sentences. An illustration of the materials is shown in Table 10.5.

As was expected, reading times were faster for consistent targets (2,498 ms) than for inconsistent targets (2,848 ms), even though both were preceded by the same local context. In other words, the emotion activated by the first part of the story remained available when the local context did not convey additional emotion clues.

TABLE 10.5
Illustration of a Story Used in de Vega, León, et al. (in press, Exp. 2;
Translated From Spanish)

First part:
>   Arthur thought about it once more. The most beautiful girl in the class had asked him to teach her to play tennis in the afternoons.

Biasing emotion 1:
>   He had many doubts about it. Probably she was looking for an excuse to get into the club and meet another boy. He had an appointment with her that afternoon. Everything depended on whether she came or not; and if she came, what her attitude would be toward him. He might know if she was interested in him.

Biasing emotion 2:
>   He smiled to himself. It was clear that, rather than learning tennis, she was looking for an excuse to talk to him. He had an appointment with her that afternoon. He went to the court ready for an easy conquest. He knew that girls were always interested in him.

Second part (fillers):
>   He saw her with her short skirt. She was pitching the ball on the court. The tennis court was the one closest to the entrance door; beside it, there were the basketball and volleyball courts.

Target sentences:
>   Arthur felt quite insecure / flattered.
Final sentences:
>   She saw him and ran to him.
>   This kind of thing does not happen every day.

In the previous experiments, subjects received emotion labels at the end of each story, supposedly after they had already built their emotion representation. However, it is possible that the presence of emotion labels induced subjects to use a particular sort of strategy. They may have realized that most stories ended with a description of protagonists' emotions and, consequently, they activated emotion representations in order to fit the task demands. This explanation, however, was ruled out in de Vega, León, et al.'s (in press) Experiment 3, which aimed to test whether the consistency effects found in the previous experiment also appear in the absence of explicit emotion terms. So, the stories like the one in Table 10.5 were modified: The sentence containing the emotion word (e.g., *Arthur felt quite flattered*) was replaced by a sentence describing the behavior (*Arthur smiled and winked while approaching her*) that reflected the protagonist's emotion. The results showed that the target sentence was read faster when it was consistent with the protagonist's implicit emotion, suggesting that readers represent emotions even in the absence of any emotional label.

Representing Beliefs

An important feature of human interpersonal cognition is that people try to understand and predict others' beliefs, even if these beliefs are false or do not fit with their own beliefs. Narratives frequently exploit this complex modeling capability, providing the reader with information about an event, while the protagonist in the narrative is ignorant of it. This may produce an interesting representation problem, because the reader must keep two situation models in mind: the objective state of the world (after the event) and the protagonist's false belief. Even 6-year-old children are able to cope with these representational complexities. Thus, in Wimmer and Perner's (1983) experiments, children were told stories, with the aid of figurative materials, in which a sequence of events occurred while the protagonist was absent (e.g., the chocolate was moved by the protagonist's mother to a different cupboard). Following the experimenter's instructions, the children were able to point to the cupboard in which the chocolate really was, as well as to the cupboard in which the protagonist believed the chocolate to be. Other experiments suggest that adult readers can also represent both the objective situation and the protagonist's belief about the situation (Barquero, Schnotz, & Rivière, 1994; Rivière, Barquero & Sarriá, 1994). Some texts used by Barquero et al. described a protagonist who left a person at a particular place after leaving that place to accomplish an action (e.g., *Michael left Laura at the entrance of the faculty building, while he went to ask a teacher a question*). The text then described the other character moving to another place, and the protagonist either as finding out about the location change or not (e.g., *Michael saw [didn't see] that Laura went to the cafeteria*). Finally, subjects were given a verification sentence describing the protagonist as going to meet the other character either in the initial location (*the entrance*) or the present location (*the cafeteria*). The results partially supported the idea that readers represent both the situation and the protagonist's beliefs. Thus, it took longer to verify *Michael will go to meet Laura at the entrance* when the protagonist had been described as being ignorant of the fact that Laura had moved to the cafeteria, that is, when there was a conflict between the objective situation model (*Laura is in the cafeteria*) and the protagonist's belief (*Laura is at the entrance*).

These experiments suggest that subjects can represent both the situation described in a text and the protagonist's beliefs. However, the experimental procedures involved, to some extent, a problem solving demand, because subjects were explicitly asked to estimate or verify the protagonist's future actions. In some recent experiments, the representation of the protagonist's beliefs was explored under ordinary reading demands (de Vega, Díaz, & León, 1995). Subjects read the emotional stories of de Vega, León, et al. (in press) with some modifications, as Table 10.6 illustrates. The initial paragraph introduced the protagonist and biased a given emotion (e.g., insecurity); then, new sentences described a critical event that might induce a change in the protagonist's emotion (e.g., being flattered). In the informed version of the story, the protagonist knew the critical event, whereas in the noninformed version, he or she did not. Finally, a sentence including the emotion associated either to the initial context or to the critical event was given.

TABLE 10.6
Illustration of a Story Used by de Vega, et al. (1995, Exp. 1)
Translated From Spanish)

Initial context (biasing *insecure*):
> Arthur thought about it once more. Betty, the most beautiful girl in the class, had asked him to teach her to play tennis in the afternoons. He had many doubts about it. Probably she was looking for an excuse to get into the club and to meet another boy. He had an appointment with her that afternoon.

Protagonist's knowledge state:
> Someone / Nobody told Arthur
Critical information (biasing *flattered*):
> that Betty talked about nobody but him,
> and she was in love with him.
Target sentence:
> When Arthur entered the tennis court,
> he felt quite insecure / flattered.
Filler:
> She saw him and ran to him.

The reading times for the emotion clause were recorded. The main results are illustrated in Fig. 10.3. Subjects read the target clause with the initial emotion (*insecure*) faster when they had read that the protagonist did not know the critical event, whereas they read the clause with the new emotion (*flattered*) faster when they had read that the protagonist knew the event.

This experiment demonstrates not only that readers represent the protagonist's beliefs, but also that they can derive emotional representations from those beliefs. This experiment, however, does not show us a clear picture of the time course of these processes. The on-line updating hypothesis and the backward updating hypothesis mentioned in the research on spatial mental models are also two options for the updating of interpersonal models.

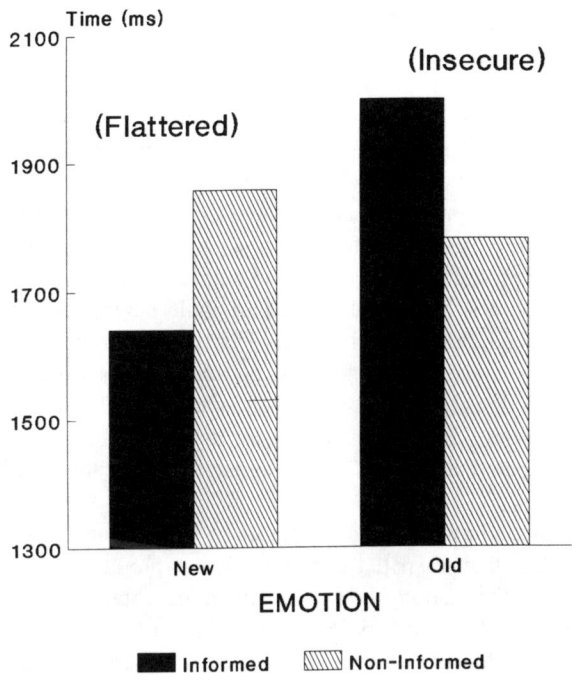

FIG. 10.3. Reading times for emotion sentences when the protagonist was informed or ignorant of a critical event (de Vega, et al., 1995).

In a second experiment, de Vega, et al. (1995) analyzed whether readers represent the protagonist's beliefs and their associated emotions immediately. Subjects read the stories of the previous experiment, with the same manipulation of the protagonist's knowledge. The only modification was that the target sentence did not include any emotion word. For instance, in the example in Table 10.6 the new version of the sentence was, *When Arthur entered the tennis court, he waved to Betty in the distance.* Immediately after this sentence was read, a target word for lexical decision was given. The target for the experimental stories was always the emotion label related to the initial context (e.g., *insecure*), and the reaction time was intended to measure the activation of the corresponding emotional representation. The main effect of protagonists knowledge was significant: Subjects spent an additional 60 ms with the emotion word when they had read that the protagonist knew the critical event, supporting an on-line updating of protagonist's beliefs and belief-based emotions.

Conclusions

The results of the experiments reported in this section indicate that readers are immediately sensitive to characters' implicit emotions and beliefs. The representation of emotions and beliefs requires the reader to use his or her pragmatic knowledge as part of the comprehension processes. The reader may be able to compute some pieces of information explicit in the text (e.g., the events in the story and the protagonist's actions) and build an interpersonal model of the characters that includes both explicit and implicit parameters (goals, status, emotions, personal relations, beliefs, etc.). The representation of mental states cannot be reduced to a text-based encoding, because readers seem to actively use their general knowledge about human interaction and mental states, going beyond the information explicit in the text. At least for the comprehension of narratives, the notion of interpersonal models seems as necessary as the notion of spatial models.

We must realize, however, that the nature of interpersonal cognition is even more enigmatic than that of spatial cognition. The exploration of spatial models has been guided by the analogy between these representations and visuospatial perception (e.g., de Vega, Intons-Peterson, Johnson-Laird, & Marschark, in press). The visuospatial guideline has shown many differences between mental models built from verbal sources and those drawn from direct perception, but still has been useful for generating hypotheses. Interpersonal representations (even in their perceptual aspect) are less well understood, although there is a growing emphasis in developmental psychology (e.g., Perner, 1991; Rivière, 1991) and cognitive psychology (e.g., Cosmides, 1989; Neisser, 1994) on the importance and singularity of interpersonal cognition.

MENTAL MODELS AS REPRESENTATIONS

This section outlines a theoretical approach to the representational nature of mental models. I contrast mental models with three other kinds of mental representation: propositions, mental images, and schemas.

Propositions and Rules Versus Mental Models

Perhaps the most obvious way to conceive of mental models is in terms of a propositional format. This position is defended by Kintsch, who postulated the necessity of situation models, although, according to him, these situation models can be reduced in some cases to sets of propositions derived from the text or retrieved from memory (e.g., Kintsch, 1988; van Dijk & Kintsch, 1983). One general problem with propositions is their *circularity* or *symbolic fallacy* (de Vega, 1981; Johnson-Laird, 1983). Propositions and meaning postulates do not convey meaning themselves, but only relate symbols to other symbols, without any reference to entities in the world. Mental models try to explain precisely the referential aspect of comprehension: how subjects represent possible states of the world when they process linguistic inputs. If we reduce mental models to the simple addition of more propositions retrieved from memory, the symbolic fallacy is not resolved.

Consider the more specific issue of spatial inferences. A propositional account needs some rule-based machinery to explain the inferential properties of mental models. The complete process of inference may involve: the encoding of the text as a list of propositions, the retrieval of meaning postulates or rules concerning the "logical" properties of spatial terms, and the application of procedures to draw conclusions from the propositions (premises) and meaning postulates (see Johnson-Laird, 1983; de Vega, 1995, for critical discussions on proposition-based inferences). Thus, when subjects read a story like the one in Table 10.3 (de Vega, 1995, Exp. 4) with the biasing sentence, *Carmen went into the museum from the street,* they can encode the relevant information of the layout as follows:

p1:   (inside, museum, mummies)
p2:   (inside, museum, Carmen)

Tthe critical sentence, *She looked at them with admiration* would be encoded:

p3:   (looks-at, X, Carmen)

In order to fill the empty slot X, some meaning postulates must be retrieved:

m1:   For any x, y, and z, if x is inside z and y is inside z, then x and y are close to each other.

m2:   for any x and y, if x looks forward and y is in front of x, and y is close to x, then x looks at y.

From propositions p1, p2, and the meaning postulates, m1 and m2, p3 may be completed by filling the empty slot of the pronoun:

p3':   (looks-at, mummies, Carmen)

The idea has some drawbacks. First, meaning postulates m1 and m2 are insufficient sources from which to draw correct inferences in every possible case. Let us consider, for instance, the following variant of the text: *Inside the museum there was a collection of mummies, the ball went into the museum and looked at them.* In this case, the proposed system would resolve the pronoun reference by using m1 and m2, without noticing that the inference is nonsense. New meaning postulates should be added in order to grasp the "logical" properties of animate and inanimate objects. The problem is that the number of meaning postulates necessary to capture people's topological (or interpersonal) knowledge is unknown and presumably very high. On the other hand, it would involve a considerable amount of information to be processed on-line (i.e., while subjects read the pronoun), which may result in working memory overload.

Mental Images Versus Mental Models

The statement that mental models preserve the "structure of the situation," along with the fact that many experiments on mental models are devoted to spatial representations, may suggest that mental models and mental images are alike. Thus, mental models could be conceived of as Euclidian representations that preserve the metric and kinematic properties of visuospatial perception. Glenberg and Langston (1992) proposed a view akin to this one when they suggested that mental models make use of the visuospatial scratch pad of working memory (Baddeley, 1986). However, there are arguments for not identifying mental models with mental images (Denis & de Vega, 1993; de Vega, Intons-Peterson, et al., in press).

First, mental images and mental models differ in spatial resolution. Mental images are usually thought of as fine-grained Euclidian representations that preserve perceptual properties, such as the metric distances, orientations, and kinematic transformations of depicted objects. However, according to the data reviewed in this chapter, spatial mental models are usually reduced representations that, given working memory limitations, rarely instantiate more than a few implicit spatial relations. In fluent reading, implicit relations are only updated when the described situation is quite simple or the text marks the relevance of spatial updating. Even when subjects deal with overlearned descriptions, their spatial models differ considerably from a continuous Euclidian representation. By contrast, the structure of situation models is organized around discrete topological categories.

Another reason for rejecting the identification of mental models and mental images is that mental models—unlike mental images—can also represent nonspatial information. As we have seen in this chapter, subjects show inferential capabilities related to some nonvisualizable information, such as characters' goals, beliefs, emotions, and so on. One way to explore these inferences is by postulating that subjects build and update interpersonal models. It is, in principle, more parsimonious to explain all kinds of inferences—spatial and nonspatial—within a single theoretical framework. For instance, Glenberg and Langston (1992) suggest that abstract nonspatial information describing sequential procedures could be successfully represented in terms of visuospatial models. However, it seems unlikely that interpersonal knowledge can be systematically encoded in spatial terms (with the exception, perhaps, of the "embodied" spatial metaphors described by Lakoff, 1987). The interpretation of characters' actions seems to be governed by primitive categories (intentions and goals, emotions and affects, and personal links) that belong to the basic human "theory of mind" (see, e.g., Cosmides, 1989; Rivière, 1991).

Schemas Versus Mental Models

Both the mental models approach and the schema theory are members of the same constructivist family (Graesser, Singer, & Trabasso, 1994; McKoon & Ratcliff, 1992). Schemas (or scripts) consist of long-term memory structures of stereotyped information about particular domains. By contrast, mental models are episodic structures built on line in the working memory. However, there may be functional relations between schemas and mental models. Thus, scripted knowledged is sometimes retrieved from long-term memory and inserted into the episodic trace of a mental model. Sanford and Garrod (1981) proposed, for instance, that on-line structures built for narratives involve an explicit focus (a protagonist-based representation of the individuals in the current episode) and an implicit focus, corresponding to scripted information about the scenario. Walker and Yekovich (1987) have shown, in addition, that some script-based information is integrated on line in the discourse model during reading. In particular, when a text describes a conventional situation (e.g., a restaurant), the central concepts of the script (e.g., tables) are immediately incorporated into the episodic representation, even when they are not explicitly mentioned, facilitating the comprehension of an incoming anaphoric sentence (e.g., *the table was near the window*). By contrast, peripheral concepts of the script are only activated when they have been explicitly mentioned in the text. Thus, scripts govern slot filling, but only for central, highly accessible information. Finally, script-based knowledge produces activation of related words, which differs from ordinary lexical priming. Therefore, script-based priming is associated with large linguistic contexts, instead of a single word, and it is a long-lived effect, that persists over several sentences, as compared with the rapid decay of lexical priming (Sharkey & Mitchell 1985).

The ability of mental models to use scripted information does not mean, however, that mental models are reducible to a process of schema instantiation. Scripts and schemas are representations of stereotyped knowledge that do not exhaust the contents of stories. In fact, stories usually attempt to describe singular (nonconventional) sequences of events and actions, organized around characters, that hold the reader's interest more efficiently than scripted contents. In addition, both script-based and singular information must be activated and packed into episodic structures or mental models during comprehension. The focus on developing mental models rather than on static schemas, generates important issues for research that otherwise would not be addressed.

Conclusions

The representational properties of mental models are still unclear. The representational theories available in cognitive psychology do not grasp entirely the functional properties of mental models. Propositions and rules are powerful formalisms, although they usually involve many ad hoc rules, introduced, top–down by the scientist, to explain the semantic computations people do in the spatial and interpersonal domains. Mental images are spatial representations that preserve the metric and kinematics of visuospatial information. However, spatial mental models are non-Euclidian representations that reduce spatial information to a few topological relations. In addition, there are mental models that are not spatial at all, like the representation of emotions and beliefs. Finally, schemas (and scripts), like mental models, are representations that operate in a constructivist manner. There are functional relations between schemas and mental models, although they differ in some respects. Mental models are episodic structures built and updated on-line, whereas schemas are stereotyped and relatively fixed structures stored in the long-term memory.

CONCLUDING REMARKS

Because their dynamic properties, mental models are elusive structures. However, it is necessary to develop our understanding of them in order to get a complete picture of language comprehension. This chapter has tried to extend the mental models framework to nonspatial domains—in particular, to interpersonal contents that form a substantial part of narratives. The structure of spatial and interpersonal mental models may differ considerably, and they may even be computed by different "modules" in the brain. However, there are some properties they share.

1. *Models are Reduced Representations.* A situation (either described or real) can, potentially, be modeled with an arbitrary degree of detail. However, mental models use the limited resources of working memory, and, consequently, they should be reduced representations in which only a few tokens are activated or foregrounded at any time, in order not to overload working memory. Some concepts are more likely to be foregrounded than others. For instance, main characters are usually foregrounded, and those pieces of information related to main characters (e.g., their emotions and their surrounding environment) become more available in reading. The inferential power of mental models—their capacity to activate implicit information—is also constrained by working memory resources, at least in ordinary reading. For instance, when a described environment is relatively complex, subjects do not activate all the implicit spatial relations among objects in advance, unless there are anaphoric references to the target objects (de Vega, 1995).

2. *Models Involve Multiple Constraints.* Mental models are constructive representations that result from processing information from different sources in the text, in long-term memory, and in the mental model itself. Thus, models are sensitive to grammatical devices, such as anaphors, connectives, and adverbials. These markers can be considered as processing instructions to the reader on how to construct the model of the situation denoted by the text (e.g., Givón, 1992). One way grammatical markers contribute to shaping mental models is by signaling the concepts in the text that might be foregrounded, inhibited, or related: Pronouns prompt the reader to keep the activation of their antecedents (e.g., Gernsbacher, 1989), negations reduce the activation of the negated concepts (e.g., MacDonald, & Just, 1989), add connectives (like *because*) signal the relation between two events (e.g., Millis & Just, 1994). Furthermore, mental models require the instantiation of schematic or scripted information retrieved from long-term memory, as I have shown. Finally, a mental model at a given time, T_n, depends on its previous state at time T_{n-1}. This means that mental models have temporal constraints, because the order of activation of the

represented entities determines the future states of the model. All three sources—the text, the scripted knowledge, and the previous model states—are combined to produce an updatable model of the referent.

3. *Models are Embodied Representations.* A recurrent statement in the literature is that mental models—unlike propositional representations for instance—are life-like representations. A more specific claim is that mental models are shaped by our bodily experience. Thus, spatial models may be organized and accessed according to our bodies' morphological and functional features. Some experiments described in this chapter show that the accessibility of object names in a described environment depends on their relative position with respect to the protagonist's body (de Vega, 1994; Franklin & Tversky, 1990). The same principle of embodiment may govern our representation of protagonists' emotions. The updating of emotional states of fictional characters probably demands a computation of interpersonal cues that parallels the computations that lead to emotions in real life. The embodiment principle does not mean that readers of stories "perceive" environments or "feel" emotions. Instead, they use their bodies and interpersonal experience as a framework in which to compute spatial and emotional representations.

An important feature of embodied representations is that they are *perspectivist:* The information provided by the text produces different mental model states, depending on the particular perspective. For instance, the accessibility of objects and places in a described layout changes dramatically as the fictional character is described as moving or turning around in the environment. In the same vein, there is a *psychological perspective.* The protagonist's beliefs, instead of *objective* events, tell the reader whether to update an emotional representation (de Vega, Díaz, & León, 1995).

4. *Models are Discrete Structures.* Mental models allow people to organize the continuous flow of information into discrete packages or *chucks.* Following Gernsbacher's (1990) structure-building framework, readers build mental structures (or models), mapping new segments of the text onto the ongoing mental structure. This corresponds to a continuous phase in the development of a mental model. However, this mapping process is interrupted periodically when the text describes a change in certain parameters of the situation, such as location, temporal setting, perspective, the presence of new protagonists, a change in the emotional valence of events, and so on. In these cases, a new mental structure is initiated, and the information that belongs to the old structure becomes less accessible. The discontinuity in mental structures is generally marked by grammatical devices, such as adverbials (*then, next year, outside,* etc.), but the process of shifting and initiating mental structures mimics the way people segment their real-world experience into episodes according to parameters of time, location, characters, and so on. It is likely that grammatical devices

instruct the reader to start a new episodic structure; rather, the reader has to apply his or her modeling capabilities in order to perform the appropriate segmentation in the developing structure.

ACKOWLEDGMENTS

This work was supported by grant PB92-0656-C04-01 from the Ministerio de Educación y Ciencia, Spain.

REFERENCES

Baddeley, A.D. (1986). *Working memory*. Oxford, England: Oxford University Press.

Barquero, B., Schnotz, W. & Rivière, A. (1994, June). *Analyzing mental models of belief situations by sentence verification*. Paper presented at the Conference on Construction of Knowledge in Verbal and Pictorial Environments, University of Helsinki, Finland.

Bower, G. H., & Morrow, D.G. (1990). Mental models in narrative comprehension. *Science, 247,* 44–48.

Carreiras, M., & Gernsbacher, M.A. (1992). Comprehending conceptual anaphors in Spanish. *Language and Cognitive Processes, 7,* 281–299.

Cosmides, L. (1989). The logic of social exchange: Has natural selection shaped how humans reason? Studies with the Wason selection task. *Cognition, 31,* 187–276.

Denis, M., & de Vega, M. (1993). Modéles mentaux et imagerie mentale [Mental models and mental imagery]. In M.F. Ehrlich, H. Tardieu, & M. Cavazza (Eds.), *Les modèles mentaux: Approache cognitive des représentations* (pp. 79–100). Paris: Masson.

de Vega, M. (1981). Una exploración de los metapostulados de la psicología contemporánea: el logicismo [An exploration of the metapostulates of contemporany psychology: The Logicism]. *Análisis y Modificación de Conducta, 7,* 345–376.

de Vega, M. (1994). Characters and their perspectives in narratives describing spatial environments. *Psychological Research, 56,* 116–126.

de Vega, M. (1995). Backward updating of mental models during continuous reading of narratives. *Journal of Experimental Psychology: Learning, Memory, and Cognition, 21,* 373–385.

de Vega, M., Díaz, J.M., & León, I. (1995). *Do readers represent protagonist's beliefs and belief-based emotions?* Paper presented at the VI Conference of the European Society for Cognitive Psychology, Rome, Italy.

de Vega, M., Intons-Peterson, M., Johnson-Laird, P., Denis, M., & Marschark, M. (Eds.). (in press). *Models of visuospatial cognition*. Oxford, England: Oxford University Press.

de Vega, M., León, I., & Díaz, J.M. (in press). The representation of changing emotions in reading comprehension. *Cognition and Emotion.*

Fletcher, C.R., & Bloom, C.P. (1988). Causal reasoning in the comprehension of simple narrative texts. *Journal of Memory and Language, 27,* 235–244.

Franklin, N., & Tversky, B. (1990). Searching imagined environments. *Journal of Experimental Psychology: General, 119,* 63–76.

Garnham, A. (1987). *Mental Models as Representations of discourse and text.* New York: Wiley.

Gernsbacher, M.A. (1989). Mechanisms that improve referential access. *Cognition, 32,* 99–156.

Gernsbacher, M.A. (1990). *Language comprehension as structure building.* Hillsdale: Erlbaum.

Gernsbacher, M.A. (1991). Comprehending conceptual anaphors. *Language and Cognitive Processes, 6,* 81–105.

Gernsbacher, M.A., Goldsmith, H.H., & Robertson, R.R.W. (1992) Do readers mentally represent characters' emotional states? *Cognition and Emotion, 6, 2,* 89–111.

Givón, T. (1992). The grammar of referential coherence as mental processing instructions. *Linguistics, 30,* 5–55.

Glenberg, A.M., & Langston, W.E. (1992). Comprehension of illustrated text: Pictures help to build mental models. *Journal of Memory and Language, 31,* 129–151.

Glenberg, A.M., Meyer, M., & Lindem, K. (1987). Mental models contribute to foregrounding during text comprehension. *Journal of Memory and Language, 26,* 69–83.

Graesser, A.C., Singer, M., & Trabasso, T. (1994). Constructing inferences during narrative text comprehension. *Psychological Review, 101,* 371–396.

Haviland, S.E., & Clark, H.H. (1974). What's new? Acquiring new information as a process in comprehension. *Journal of Verbal Learning and Verbal Behavior, 13,* 512–521.

Hobbs, J.R. (1979). Coherence and coreference. *Cognitive Science, 3,* 67–90.

Johnson-Laird, P.N. (1983). *Mental models.* Cambridge, England: Cambridge University Press.

Kintsch, W. (1988). The role of knowledge in discourse comprehension: A construction-integration model. *Psychological Review, 95,* 163–182.

Kintsch, W., & van Dijk, T.A. (1978). Toward a model of text comprehension and production. *Psychological Review, 85,* 363–394.

Lakoff, G. (1987). *Woman, fire, and dangerous things.* Chicago: University of Chicago Press.

MacDonald, M.C., & Just, M.A. (1989). Changes in activation levels with negation. *Journal of Experimental Psychology: Learning, Memory, and Cognition, 15,* 633–643.

Mani, K., & Johnson-Laird, P. N. (1982). The mental representation of spatial descriptions. *Memory and Cognition, 10,* 181–187.

McKoon, G., & Ratcliff, R. (1992). Inferences during reading. *Psychological Review, 99,* 440–466.

Millis, K.K., & Just, M.A. (1994). The influence of connectives on sentence comprehension. *Journal of Memory and Language, 33,* 128–147.

Morrow, D.G., Bower, G.H., & Greenspan, S.L. (1989). Updating situation models during narrative comprehension. *Journal of Memory and Language, 28,* 292–312.

Neisser, U. (1994). Multiple systems: A new approach to cognitive theory. *European Journal of Cognitive Psychology, 6,* 225–241.

Noordman, L.G.M., Vonk, W., & Kempff, H.J. (1992). Causal inferences during the reading of expository texts. *Journal of Memory and Language, 31,* 573–591.

O'Brien, E.J., & Albrecht, J.E. (1992). Comprehension strategies in the development of a mental model. *Journal of Experimental Psychology: Learning, Memory, and Cognition, 18,* 777–785.

Perner, J. (1991). *Understanding the representational mind.* Cambridge, MA: MIT Press.

Rivière, A. (1991). *Objetos con mente* [Objects with mind]. Madrid: Alianza.

Rivière, A., Barquero, B., & Sarriá, E. (1994). La representación de estados mentales en la comprensión de textos [The representation of mental states in texts comprehension]. *Cognitiva, 6,* 175–188.

Sanford, A.J., & Garrod, S.C. (1981). *Understanding written language: Exploration of comprehension beyond the sentence.* Chichester: Wiley.

Sanford, A.J., & Garrod, S.C. (1994). Selective processing in text understanding. In M.A. Gernsbacher (Ed.): *Handbook of Psycholinguistics.* New York, Academic Press.

Sharkey, N.E., & Mitchell, D.C. (1985). Word recognition in a functional context: The use of scripts in reading. *Journal of Memory and Language, 24,* 253–270.

Singer, M., Revlin, R., & Halldorson, M. (1990). Bridging inferences and enthymemes. In A. C. Graesser & G.H. Bower (Eds.), *Inferences and text comprehension.* New York: Academic Press.

van Dijk, T.A., & Kintsch, W. (1983). *Strategies of discourse comprehension.* New York: Academic Press.

Walker, C.H., & Yekovich, F.R. (1987). Activation and use of script-based antecedents in anaphoric reference. *Journal of Memory and Language, 26,* 673–691.

Wimmer, H., & Perner, J. (1983). Beliefs about beliefs: Representation and constraining function of wrong beliefs in young children's understanding of deception. *Cognition, 13,* 103–128.

11

The Relationship Between Conceptualization and Formulation Processes in Sentence Production: Some Evidence From Spanish

José Manuel Igoa
Universidad Autónoma de Madrid
Madrid, Spain

Crosslinguistic research is becoming increasingly popular in both linguistics and psycholinguistics, especially since the advent of generative theories of language competence and the models of language acquisition and performance they inspired. There is a twofold interest in crosslinguistic comparisons from the perspective of language performance models. One is in their helping us to focus on a number of language-specific properties so that we may single out and refine particular details of the processing apparatus involved in language understanding and production. Here, the issue is to clarify the contribution of certain language particulars to the processes of speech perception, word recognition, sentence parsing, and sentence planning, to find out whether the reported processing differences among languages might be traced to differences in the structural properties of particular languages or language families. Alternatively, one may concentrate on a range of conceptual or structural characteristics shared by different languages, with the aim of exploring crosslinguistic commonalities in terms of the processing strategies employed in various performance domains. In either case, the major concern of crosslinguistic studies is to gather empirical evidence to validate hypotheses regarding the organization of linguistic knowledge and/or the mechanisms by which this knowledge is put to use in a diversity of linguistic tasks.

This chapter addresses a number of issues related to the processes involved in the formulation of linguistic utterances, with particular emphasis on the constraints set on these processes by various information sources. Specifically, my focus is on seeing how conceptual, lexical, and phonological representations guide and constrain the syntactic properties of linguistic messages during sentence formulation, and determining to what extent the processes of building the forms of utterances are insulated from their conceptual content and dependent on the structural properties of the language. This problem has been thoroughly investigated in the recent literature on sentence production carried out in English, but is still in need of crosslinguistic evidence.

In order to set the studies reported in this chapter in a broad perspective, I consider, first, a few paradoxical facts about language production research. The first fact is the relative importance of syntactic structure for sentence formulation, as compared to sentence interpretation. As Garrett (1980a) and Bock (1990), among others, have pointed out, "one of the most distinctive things about production is the relevance of syntactic patterning to the goals of the processing system" (Bock 1990, p. 1223). In other words, a major goal of sentence production processes is to provide a full structural representation of the sentence without missing any of its details, however irrelevant these may seem from the standpoint of meaning. In contrast, readers or listeners may have more chances to build the semantic representation of a sentence without the compulsory mediation of its syntactic structure. In fact, some authors claim that the structural properties of the language are but one source of information that subjects use to arrive at the interpretation of sentence meaning (see Bates & MacWhinney, 1982, 1989; McClelland, St. John, & Taraban, 1989). Surprisingly, however, much less attention has been paid to the role of syntax in sentence production than in sentence comprehension. And, as far as crosslinguistic research is concerned, to my knowledge, there are very few data on the subject on languages other than English.

This paradoxical asymmetry may be partly accounted for by two other well-attested facts about sentence production research. The first concerns what some authors claim to be a methodological pitfall of language production research, namely, the *opacity* of the language production system with regard to the conceptual representations that are fed into the sentence formulator. Inevitably, the evidence available for investigating sentence production mechanisms turns out to be flawed in many instances, because the researcher cannot establish control over this conceptual input. Hence, any claim about the causal relations between whatever variables are thought to be operative in sentence formulation can only, at best, be indirectly tested (see Garrett, 1980a). Another fact that may help us to understand the inaccesibility of structural variables to close scrutiny in sentence production is the relative stability of grammatical well-formedness that is usually found in the output of the formulator. That is, sentence production mechanisms appear to be well protected against gross failures in utterance form, but remain vulnerable to semantic ill-formedness (Garrett, 1991). As I show further on, this happens at the levels of both grammatical planning and phonological encoding, but it is particularly apparent in the paucity of spontaneous and experimentally elicited errors in the syntactic structure of sentences (see Bierwisch, 1982; Bock, 1990, 1991). Thus, it appears that sentence structure operates as a constraining, rather than a constrained, variable in the formulation process.

In this chapter, I pursue two of the research problems sketched by Bock, (1991) in a recent review on language production: the problem of regulating the flow of information between the components of the sentence production system and the so-called "coordination problem." With regard to the regulation of the information flow, there is, as Bock persuasively pointed out, a twofold problem: On the one hand, one must explain how the speaker frames and selects the relevant knowledge or conceptual structures he or she wishes to convey to the listener at a given time. It is as important to decide what to talk about as to decide what *not* to talk about. This is but one manifestation of the *frame problem* that all cognitive systems face (Fodor, 1983, 1987), the problem of selecting information that is relevant to the task at hand to convey a given communicative intent, while preventing any irrelevant information from intruding into the speech plans. Normal speakers seem to be very adept at solving the frame problem in language production, as evidenced by how few unintended messages are found in spoken discourse and conversation. On the other hand, the flow of information must also be regulated within the formulator itself, so as to ensure both the well-formedness of the message to be conveyed and its compliance with the communicative intention of the speaker. If we rely on the evidence supplied by speech errors, we find that, even though slips may occur at many different loci and affect a wide variety of linguistic units, they still obey powerful constraints on well-formedness. However, as pointed out earlier, the formulation devices seem to be more sensitive to the formal properties of words and sentences than to the semantic congruity of the message. This means that the influence of conceptual representations on sentence formulation is, at best, quite short-lived.

So, as far as the problem of information flow is concerned, there is some indication that some parts of the formulation processes are impervious to semantic influences, despite the obvious fact that sentence form is, of necessity, shaped by the semantic content of the message. However, just as there might be reasons to think that the formulator is partly encapsulated from top–down influences from the conceptualizer, we may also wonder whether the processes of message generation are subject to a bottom–up influence from certain formal properties of linguistic materials. In principle, we cannot dismiss the possibility that the inner workings of the formulator may impinge on the construal of conceptual plans or the selection of semantic components of the message. Just as there is evidence that the lexical nature of the output of phonological encoding increases the likelihood of sound errors (Dell & Reich, 1981), it might be the case that the misselection of a given concept at the message level is prompted by the phonological similarity of the word forms by which two competing concepts are expressed. In summary, restrictions on the flow of information among components of the language production system might be operative not only between the major components of the system (i.e., the conceptualizer and the formulator), but also between subsystems within each major component (i.e., grammatical encoding, lexical retrieval, and phonological encoding). Also, the regulation of the flow of information must be performed, and tested, in all possible directions within and between the language production components.

The second problem I deal with is the coordination problem. Here, also, we find two different versions of the notion of *coordination:* One is the coordination of words in sentence structure, and the other is the coordination of sound segments in phonological structure. Generally speaking, the problem lies in working out the organization and interplay of two different kinds of processes in sentence planning: the selection and retrieval of linguistic representations (i.e., words, morphemes, syllables, and segments), on the one hand, and the construction of sentence frames (i.e., clauses and phrases), on the other. Simply stated, the issue is to test what sources of information come into play in each of these components of the formulation process and to clarify their time course and the alleged autonomy of each of them. As with the problem of the flow of information, three different sources of information seem to be relevant to this problem: One is the set of conceptual representations that are input to the formulator. As we see later on, these representations range from the argument structure of the message (i.e., the thematic roles and their relations) to the semantic features of the elements that comprise it (e.g., animacy, concreteness, category membership). Another source of information is the set of lexical representations that the concepts included in the message are mapped on to, at the levels of both lemmas and lexemes (Bierwisch & Schreuder, 1992; Roelofs,

1992), with regard to the semantic, syntactic, and phonological properties of the lexical entries to be retrieved during sentence formulation. The third source of information is internal to the structure-building process and refers to the representations that give rise to the syntactic structure of the sentence, irrespective of whether such representations are computed by rules or are retrieved in a precompiled form. Thus, the coordination problem at the level of syntactic structure is focused on the relationships among message meaning, word retrieval, and sentence form.

The issues just reviewed are tackled in the rest of this chapter via a set of studies that used two different methodologies employed in sentence production research. First, I report a study on the analysis of a broad sample of speech errors from the Spanish corpus collected by del Viso, Igoa, and García-Albea (1987); then, I present some results from a few experiments run in Spanish on the effect on syntactic planning of lexical priming under conceptual constraints. As I mentioned before, my aim is to use Spanish data to provide converging evidence of the relationship between conceptual planning and sentence formulation in general, and, at the same time, to point out, where relevant, certain characteristics of the Spanish language that may contribute to illuminating some details of the formulation processes for which English is not suited.

OUTLINE OF THE LANGUAGE PRODUCTION SYSTEM

Most current theories of language production assume that the processing system for sentence production is organized in three broad components. Levelt's (1989) delination of the *conceptualizer,* the *formulator,* and the *articulator* closely mirrors other distinctions made earlier by Bock (1982), Garrett (1984, 1988), and Blanken, Dittman, Haas, & Wallesh (1987), among others. Thus, Bock (1982) distinguished the *referential arena,* which encompasses conceptual planning processes, from the *lexico-syntactic processes,* which correspond to Levelt's formulation processes, and the *motor programming* or articulatory processes. Similarly, Blanken et al.'s (1987) production model is organized as the *pragmatic-conceptual* apparatus, the *formulation* apparatus, and the *articulatory* apparatus, whereas Garrett's (1984, 1988) proposal includes the *message-level* processes, the *sentence-level* processes and the *articulatory-level* processes.

Conceptualization involves the generation of a communicative intention on the part of the speaker, the selection of nonlinguistic information the speaker wishes to convey, and the comparison of the speaker's discourse model to the most relevant aspects of the extralinguistic context in which the communicative episode takes place. Conceptualization should be characterized as a *belief-selection* process (as opposed to the *belief-fixation* processes involved in language comprehension and reasoning), insofar as its main task is to select and retrieve a subset of the speaker's beliefs in order to convey them to the listener in a linguistic guise. For convenience, I assume that the *preverbal message* that results from these processes is encoded in an abstract propositional format whose constituent elements (concepts and thematic roles) are unordered (see Levelt, 1989).

The formulation processes, in turn, are intended to encode the preverbal message in a linguistic format, that encompasses no less than three different kinds of representations: the syntactic and phonological structures of the utterance and the utterance's lexical formatives. All models of sentence formulation assume that there are special-purpose mechanisms for the construction and retrieval of linguistic representations at each of these three levels, although they might disagree as to the degree of encapsulation each one of them enjoys (compare, e.g., Garrett's, 1984, autonomous and Stemberger's, 1985, interactive models of sentence production).

The main task of the articulator is to plan and execute the motor commands necessary for overt speech. Thus, the articulator is capable of two different types of processes: First, it must transform the string of phonetic segments given as output by the formulator (the phonetic plan) into an abstract representation of the sequence of motor commands to be executed by the organs of the vocal tract (the *motor plan*); and then, it must map this representation of the articulatory gestures to the appropriate neuromuscular entities for their physical execution—that is, it must perform a motor transduction function.

Given this general description of the major components of the language production system, I now examine some data concerning the two issues addressed in the introduction: the regulation of information flow and the coordination of linguistic units in speech plans. Most empirical evidence bearing on the problem of the regulation of the information flow between and within the components of the language production apparatus comes from the analysis of spontaneous speech errors. Notwithstanding the disadvantages of this methodology (Cutler, 1988; Garrett, 1980a), especially when compared with experimental procedures, there are also a number of advantages. Perhaps the most outstanding is that speech error data cover a wide variety of phenomena in language production, from the very conception of messages, at the top of the processing hierarchy, to the processes of phonological encoding, at the bottom of the formulation component. However, given the reconstructive nature of error interpretation research, the major conclusions that may be drawn from the analysis of these pieces of evidence concern the constraints of the functional architecture of the processing apparatus on the information structures that it manipulates. In contrast, the analysis of speech errors does not seem well suited for exploring the nature of the computations performed on such representations (Lapointe & Dell, 1989).

INFORMATION FLOW BETWEEN THE CONCEPTUALIZER AND THE FORMULATOR: A STUDY OF SPANISH SPEECH ERRORS AND REPAIRS

A good deal of research on language production based on the analysis of speech errors has taken for granted that the relationship between conceptualization and formulation processes proceeds in a strictly top–down fashion. Accordingly, it is thought that the decisions made at the sentence level (i.e., the formulation processes) are dependent either on properties of the message-level representations (i.e., the conceptualization processes) or on constraints set by the formulation processes themselves. Most error patterns reported in the literature are accounted for in terms of transient failures of the formulation apparatus, with no influence whatsoever from conceptual plans. These errors are said to be *plan-internal,* because they belong to a single linguistic plan.

However, it has been argued (Butterworth, 1982) that errors that are thought to be internal to the formulation of a single message might, in fact, arise as a result of the mutual interference of different messages or conceptual plans. In some cases, these plans are conceptually distinct—that is, they bear different meanings—whereas in others, they might convey similar or related meanings in different linguistic guises. Take, for instance, the word substitutions shown in (1).

(1)   a. A y veintisiete salía el *perro* [tren] de la estación.
          At twenty-seven past the *dog* [train] left the station.

       b. El estómago de las *uñas* [rumiantes].
          The *fingernails'* [ruminants'] stomach

       c. Se me cayó una *ensalada* [zapatilla] en la cueva.
          I lost one *salad* [shoe] in the cave

If we ask ourselves how these errors could have arisen, we might hypothesize that, for unknown reasons, a given concept from an unrelated and unintended message (e.g., dog, finger nails, or salad) had been attached to the message actually intended by the speaker, resulting in a kind of *cognitive intrusion* (Harley, 1984). In these cases, known as *competing plan* errors, the causes of the slip lie outside the formulator, but the mechanism whereby the slip comes into being are within. Alternatively, there are cases in which a single message has more than one linguistic medium through which it can be conveyed. In some word and phrase blends (see examples in (2)), and word exchanges and shifts, like those in (3), there seems to be a single message that the speaker had partly formulated in alternative ways. That is, the speaker appears to have been unable to suppress one of two alternative linguistic plans.

(2) a. Debe estar en el *bajón* de abajo [baúl/cajón].
It must be in the *drawnk* downstairs [drawer/trunk]

b. Es que vas con *la lengua al cuello* [la lengua fuera/el agua al cuello].
Your tongue's up to your neck [Your tongue's sticking out/The water's up to your neck; meaning "You're getting too stressed"]

(3) a. ¿Quieres ir al *coche* en *banco*? [al banco en coche/en coche al banco].
Wanna go to the *car* by *bank*? [to the bank by car/by car to the bank]

b. Merece *ser* la pena escuchado [merece ser escuchado/merece la pena ser escuchado].
This *should* be worth listened to [should be listened to/is worth listening to]

Now, what is the difference between errors described in strictly formulation terms and formulation errors induced by competing and alternative plans, as in examples (1-3)? Unlike the former, competing- and alternative-plan errors entail the display and mixture of at least two different linguistic formulae that cannot merge into a single well-formed utterance.

Importantly, however, there is a substantial difference between competing- and alternative-plan errors that should not be overlooked, for only in competing-plan cases is the conceptualizer actually involved in the generation of errors. When two different plans generated at the conceptual level are fed into the formulator, the resulting utterance is contaminated by spurious elements that belong to an unrelated message. This is not the case with alternative-plan or with plan-internal errors. In alternative-plan errors, the conceptualizer provides the formulator with one single message, for which the formulator displays more than one linguistic plan. This often makes alternative-plan errors quite indistinguishable in practice from plan-internal errors, because both originate from failures in formulation processes. Admittedly, we may set forth certain semantic and/or structural criteria to distinguish these two error categories, on the assumptions that (a) the semantic relationship between two alternative linguistic plans should be somewhat weaker than the elements involved in a plan-internal error; and/or (b) alternative-plan errors should involve incompatible syntactic structures, whereas plan-internal errors need not.

Based on these distinctions, we may conclude that cognitive intrusions arising from competing plans originate at the conceptual level and are carried over to the formulator, where they show up as slips of the tongue of different sorts. Alternative-plan errors are supposedly created at the interface between the conceptualizer and the formulator, either at the point at which concepts are lexicalized (i.e., at the level of lemma retrieval; cf. Roelofs, 1992), or when thematic roles are mapped onto syntactic constituents (i.e., at the functional-level representation; cf. Garrett, 1982, 1988). Plan-internal errors, in turn, may occur anywhere below these processing levels; that is, during the retrieval of linguistic units of various kinds, from words and morphemes to syllables and phonemes, when proceeding from the functional to the positional representation of the sentence, or at phonological encoding.

Interactive models of sentence production (e.g., Dell & Reich, 1981; Harley, 1984) claim that errors involving lexical formatives (i.e., words and stems or roots) are facilitated by certain low-level properties of the linguistic representations that contain them, regardless of their origin, that is, irrespective of whether they originate at the formulator or at the conceptualizer. In particular, the phonological similarity between the error source and the error target has been claimed to increase the likelihood of slips. This has proved to be the case in English plan-internal errors, such as word substitutions, blends, and exchanges (Dell & Reich, 1981; Levelt 1989; but see del Viso, Igoa, & García-Albea, 1991, for different results in a Spanish corpus). If this observation should also hold for slips of the competing- and alternative-plan types, we would have the following implications: First, this would show that conceptual representations can be activated by feedback from phonological representations that lie deep within the formulator, which would suggest that conceptual planning processes are not entirely autonomous with respect to linguistic planning processes; second, it would imply that formulation processes are not sequential in nature, although most autonomous models of sentence production claim they are (Fromkin, 1971; Garrett, 1975, 1980a), but operate in a parallel fashion (Butterworth, 1980, 1982; Stemberger, 1985). In contrast, if phonological information is found to influence only alternative-plan errors (and plan-internal errors), this would indicate that feedback from lower levels of representation is confined within the formulator, which would preserve the autonomy of the conceptualizer, at least with respect to the phonological specification of sentential constituents.

The main concern of this section is to examine whether the bottom–up flow of information from phonological to conceptual representations of messages actually occurs, as interactive models predict. To this end, I analyze a subset of spontaneous slips taken from the Spanish corpus collected by del Viso et al.

(1987), to find out to what extent there is above-chance phonological similarity between the source and target elements involved in these errors. The errors included in this subset had been previously classified as either alternative-plan or competing-plan errors, following the criteria laid down earlier. In a subsequent section, I turn to another piece of evidence concerning the autonomy of formulation processes. There, the issue is approached by exploring whether the processes that perform spontaneous repairs in utterances containing speech errors are sensitive to the conceptual well-formedness of otherwise anomalous utterances.

Phonological Influence on Alternative- and Competing-Plan Errors

If the claims of interactive models of sentence production as to the influence of phonological structure on conceptual planning and lexical retrieval turn out to be correct, this influence should eventually surface in slips involving words and even phrases, irrespective of whether they are brought about within a single linguistic plan (as in plan-internal errors) or by alternative or competing plans. Previous research with English slips (Dell 1986, 1988; Dell & Reich 1981) has shown this to be the case. Specifically, plan-internal lexical errors, such as substitutions, blends, and exchanges, were found to obey phonological similarity constraints.

By computing the percentage of cases in which source and target words share the same segments in serial positions 1 through 6 (see Table 10.1), Dell and Reich were able to demonstrate that the phonological similarity between the interacting words in errors is well above that expected by chance, and this happens in both retrieval errors (such as word substitutions and blends) and insertion errors (such as word exchanges). Admittedly, the former type has its locus at the functional level of processing, at the point where concepts are lexicalized, whereas the latter occurs at the interface between the functional and positional levels of representation, once the phrasal frames of the sentences have been already built (see Garrett, 1975, 1980a, for further details). Contrary to the claims of autonomous models of sentence production, Dell and Reich's data show that by the time words are retrieved from the lexicon and inserted into phrasal frames, they must have some specification of their segmental structure; otherwise, the errors stemming from such operations would have no special phonetic resemblance to the intended targets.

Further evidence of the interaction between phonological encoding and lexical retrieval processes has been supplied by Harley's (1984) analyses of *non–plan-internal* errors of the types discussed earlier. According to his findings, not only are lexical errors within the formulator subject to phonological constraints, but so are those caused by the intrusion of lexical material from a different conceptual plan. Harley's criteria for phonological similarity consisted of the correspondence between source and target words in terms of (a) the first consonant of the word's stressed syllable, (b) the number of syllables, and (c) the stress pattern of the words involved. The phonological similarity of source and target words applied to the two following error categories:

. *Cognitive intrusions*, such as contextual contaminations (4a), conversationally-induced slips (4b), and higher-level intrusions (4c).

. *Content-addressable errors*, which comprise word substitutions based on weak semantic ties. These seem to be halfway between plan-internal and non–plan-internal errors.

(4)   a. A mí no me gustan las *gaseosas* [empanadillas].
         I don't like *soda water* [turnover pies] (the speaker had a bottle of soda water in front of her)

      b. Yo también pedía el *huevo* [plato] número seis.
         I also asked for *egg* [dish] number six (the speaker's interlocutor was talking about the ingredients of one of the meals)

      c. ¿De qué quieres el *chorizo* [bocadillo]?
         What kind of *sausage* [sandwich] do you want? (the speaker claimed to be thinking about sausage sandwiches)

However, Harley did not include any alternative-plan errors per se, such as word blends (5a) or word exchanges (5b), that may be caused by blending two alternative phrase orders. We must note that Harley's category of content-addressable errors might be equated with Butterworth's category of alternative-plan errors, because both kinds of slips are characterized by a weak semantic relationship between source and target words.

(5)   a. Te voy a dejar la *hueca* en el cuello [huella/boca].
         I'll leave a *mourk* in your neck [mark/mouth]

      b. A María le tiraron el *río* al *bolso* [el bolso al río/al río el bolso].
         Maria's *river* was thrown into her *purse* [her purse into the river/into the river her purse]

In the analysis I report, the phonological similarity between source and target words was computed from a sample of Spanish slips of the tongue broken down into competing-plan and alternative-plan errors. Four criteria of phonological resemblance were employed: (a) shared phonemes in serial positions 1 through 6 of the source and target words, (b) shared vowels in serial positions 1 through 3 (in cases of polysyllabic words), (c) number of syllables, and (d) stress pattern. The first criterion was also employed by Dell and Reich, and the last two were used by Harley. (See examples of the analysis in Table 11.1). I also calculated, as a baseline measure, the likelihood that any two Spanish words taken at random would comply with the criteria just mentioned, following the same procedure as Dell and Reich (the details of this sampling procedure, together with the results obtained for Spanish materials, are reported in del Viso 1990). Only errors involving words as source and target were included in this analysis.

TABLE 11.1

Examples of Phonological Similarity Criteria Employed in the Analysis of Competing- and Alternative-Plan Errors

Source word	casa	disfrutado
Target word	calle	dictado
Phonemes in same serial positions		
Serial position	1 2 3 4	1 2 3 4 5 6
Source word	/k/ /a/ /s/ /a/	/d/ /i/ /s/ /f/ /r/ /u/
Target word	/k/ /a/ /j/ /e/	/d/ /i/ /k/ /t/ /a/ /d/
Correspondence	+ + - -	+ + - - - -
Vowels in same serial positions		
Serial position	1 2	1 2 3 4
Source word	/a/ /a/	/i/ /u/ /a/ /o/
Target word	/a/ /e/	/i/ /a/ /o/
Correspondence	+ -	+ - -
Syllable number		
Source word	#ka#sa#	#dis#fru#ta#do#
Target word	#ka#je#	#dik#ta#do#
Correspondence	+	-
Stress pattern		
Source word	#KA#sa#	#dis#fru#TA#do#
Target word	#KA#je#	#dik#TA#do#
Correspondence	+	-

The results for alternative-plan errors indicate that only in blending errors was there an overall above-chance phonological similarity between source and target words (in this case, the two words that were blended in the error; see example

(5a)). In addition, this similarity held across the first three segments of the words. However, no trace of an above-chance phonological similarity emerged for movement errors (mostly word exchanges, as (5b)). This pattern of results does not seem surprising, given that blending errors always result in a mixture of two competing lexical targets, whereas in the case of exchanges, the two words involved are part of the interacting plans from alternative utterances, and do not have to compete for a single lexical slot in the output phonetic representation.

As for the criterion of vowel correspondence, a similar pattern of results was obtained: Source and target words tended to share the same vowel segments in the same serial positions only in blends. The third and fourth criteria rendered a somewhat similar pattern: Source and target words in blends showed a highly significant correspondence in number of syllables, although not in stress pattern, whereas exchanges did not show any above-chance similarity in either of these two parameters.

The picture is somewhat different for competing-plan errors. In the first two criteria (phonemic segment and vowel correspondence), in particular, there was no indication that the source and target words of the errors analyzed shared their segments above chance expectations, and this applied to both competing-plan blends and competing-plan substitutions (refer to examples (6a) and (6b), respectively). However, there was a tendency for the first vowels to coincide in both error types, although this trend did not reach statistical significance.

(6)   a.   Si le *llegas* a Piera el libro... [llega/mandas]
           If you *get* Piera the book... [you send/he gets]

      b.   Me van a *traducir* [Me van a suspender].
           I'm going to be *translated* [I'm going to fail] (the speaker was talking about a translation test)

Regarding the number of syllables, the two error types behaved quite similarly: There was a significant similarity between the source and target words, in both blends and substitutions, in word length, as measured by the number of syllables. However, the pattern was reversed when we consider stress pattern, for in neither case was there a significant correspondence. Thus, the only indication of a phonological similarity constraint across competing-plan errors is the correspondence of lexical sources and targets in terms of their numbers of syllables. This result is even more unexpected, given the general trend of results on the other three criteria, and in view of the fact that the syllabic structures of words is a property far removed, in principle, from their conceptual representations. However, we might still argue that syllable length and stress pattern are coarse-grained features of the phonological representation of words when compared to their segmental specification, because the former two are linked to the metrical and melodic envelope of the words. Hence, such properties seem to be more associated to the phrasal frames into which content words are inserted during sentence planning, and therefore should emerge in earlier stages of the formulation processes (cf. Cutler, 1982). If we were to draw an implicational hierarchy of phonological constraints governing lexical retrieval processes in sentence production, we would predict that syllable length and stress pattern would emerge, before the segmental specification of words. Evidence from tip-of-the-tongue studies has shown this to be the case (Brown & McNeill 1966; Rubin, 1975). The results reported here do not contradict this prediction. On this assumption, metrical information about the syllabic structure of a lexical constituent could occasionally facilitate the misselection of lexical representations previously activated by an alternative or competing plan within the formulator.

In summary, the results reported in this section indicate that those linguistic errors that stem from the intrusion of an unintended alternative linguistic plan in the formulator do seem to be facilitated by the phonological properties of their lexical constituents. Because such properties are called for only at a later processing stage, we must conclude either that the phonological information of words to be retrieved is fed back to the level of lexical retrieval; or that the formulator is capable of generating different linguistic plans in parallel, but these plans may get tangled up during the phonological encoding of words (e.g., lexemes), thus giving rise to word blends (Butterworth, 1982). In contrast, errors induced by competing plans (and, hence, generated at the conceptual level) do not seem to be sensitive to just any kind of phonological constraint. This means that the feedback of phonological information is restricted within the formulator and applies only to sentence-planning processes, and not to the generation of messages. In conclusion, the evidence examined tends to support a modular view of the formulation apparatus and, at the same time, reveals an interaction between lexical and phonological processes within the formulator.

Independence of Grammatical Well-Formedness From Conceptual Constraints on Errors and Repairs

I now review some evidence from the Spanish corpus of slips of the tongue concerning the sensitivity of speech monitoring and repair processes to the syntactic and semantic well-formedness of speech errors.

As mentioned earlier, grammatical well-formedness appears to be the rule, rather than the exception, in spontaneous speech errors. There is some evidence that speakers devote time and effort to scanning and controlling their linguistic outputs, and quite often they detect and repair their own speech errors. According to Levelt (1983, 1989), error scanning and repair may be independently applied to the various information structures involved in sentence planning. This means that these activities are most likely carried out at different processing stages. The most obvious case is when speakers monitor, and eventually repair, their utterances for conceptual and pragmatic anomalies. Perhaps the most usual experience of linguistic monitoring and repair occurs through overt speech, that is, when we pick up some conceptual, linguistic, or articulatory mistake by hearing and understanding our own speech. However, we monitor not only our overt speech, but also the preverbal message we are generating at a given time or the phonetic plan we are about to articulate, as happens when we interrupt ourselves just before uttering a message that, for some reason, we suddenly find to be misconstructed.

Intuitively speaking, each of the three major components of the sentence production apparatus may be subject to separate conscious control and monitoring. However, conscious detection, the editing and repair of slips through overt speech, is not the only means of preserving the well-formedness of the speech output. There is, indeed, a subtler way to keep the form of utterances under the constraints of grammatical well-formedness. The unconscious repair operation that speakers perform on-line on their faulty utterances to preserve their grammatical well-formedness is known as *accommodation.* When a speaker makes a speech error at a given processing level, accommodation processes come into play to preserve the well-formedness of the utterance at subsequent processing levels (Berg, 1987; Fromkin, 1971; Garrett, 1980b). For example, in many substitutions and exchanges of stems and open-class words, the modifiers and determiners of the target elements are accommodated in gender, number, and case marking to the source elements to which they are attached, as is the case in (7): (7a) is a gender accommodation and (7b) is a number accommodation.

(7) a. Se ha salido la *lavadora* del *agua* [el agua de la lavadora].
        The (feminine) *washing machine*'s leaking out of the *water* (masculine) [The water's leaking out of the washing machine]

     b. Las *chicas* de la *cara* [La cara de las chicas].
        The (plural) *girls* of the (singular) *face* [The face of the girls]

Accommodations may also affect the linguistic unit involved in an error, instead of its morphological environment. This occurs every time the phonological structure of a morphologically irregular lexical formative undergoes a morphological variation as a result of a change in its grammatical function. The roots of Spanish irregular verbs are found to follow this pattern when they are moved from a position in the sentence where they are in a finite form to a different one that requires a nonfinite form, as in (8), where the root of the irregular verb *sentarse* (to sit) is moved from the past participle position (*sentada*) in a subordinate clause to a third-person, present-tense position in the main clause (*sienta*):

(8)   Se *sient*a muy bien *planch*ada [Se plancha muy bien sentada].
      You *sit* very well when you're *iron*ed [You iron very well when you're seated]

Aside from the morphological accommodations just cited, there are also cases of phonological accommodations, where either the phonological environment or the phonological structure of the element involved in a slip gets accommodated (9).

(9)   a.   Un globo g/**r**/osa [Un globo /rr/osa].
           A pink palloon [A pink balloon]

      b.   ¿Cuándo vais a hacer las ka/**m**/partas [pa/ŋ/kartas]?
           When are you going to make the klapards [placards]?

In (9a), the word-initial, rolled /rr/ of the target word *rosa* turns into a postinitial cluster /r/ in *grosa,* which is no longer rolled when pronounced. In (9b), the velar nasal /ŋ/, which is coarticulated with the velar stop /k/ in *pancartas* is turned into a bilabial nasal stop /m/ to be coarticulated with the bilabial stop /p/.

What is the relevance of accommodatory processes to the autonomy of formulation processes in sentence production? According to a well-known hypothesis (cf. Garrett, 1980b), morphological accommodation is one of the most persuasive indications that phrasal building and lexical insertion processes are independent of one another; likewise, phonological accommodation provides evidence that lexical selection at the level of lexemes and phonological encoding processes do not interact. In addition, morphological accommodation seems to show that grammatical morphemes are represented in an abstract format during sentence planning, and that their segmental specification takes place at a stage subsequent to their retrieval. There is some evidence that accommodatory processes are mandatory whenever a speech error is made (Butterworth, 1980; Fromkin, 1971; Garrett, 1980b; MacKay, 1972). However, on closer inspection, it appears that the patterns of accommodation are different for each specific kind of grammatical information involved in slips. For instance, Berg (1987) found that grammatical accommodation to case in German speech errors is less frequent than to gender or person. Recall that German has case marking in both personal pronouns and adjectives. Also, accommodation is more likely to occur when the error source has a modifier (which is the element that gets accommodated) than when it does not.

Thus, there seems to be a greater likelihood of accommodation by contextual influences; as Berg has noted, morphological accommodation of determiners is much more frequent when the error source has a determiner (as in (10a)) than when it does not (as in (10b)).

(10) a. Con el *atasco* va a haber una *lluvia* tremenda
          [Con la lluvia va a haber un atasco tremendo].
          There'll be a big (feminine) *rain* with the (masculine) *traffic jam* [There'll be a big (masculine) traffic jam with the (feminine) rain]

      b. Te voy a llenar el *agua* de *cantimplora* [la cantimplora de agua].
          I'll fill the (masculine) *water* with *canteen* [the canteen (feminine) with water]

TABLE 11.2

Frequency and Distribution of Morphological Accommodations in Spanish Errors, According to Accommodation Type, Grammatical Information Involved, and Morphological Structure of the Error Source

Context Accommodation Grammatical information	*Error-source*								
	With modifier			*Without modifier*			*Overall*		
	Gender	Number	Both	Gender	Number	Both	Gender	Number	Both
Accommodations									
Frequency	25	9	1	8	4	1	33	13	2
Percentages	71	82	100	89	80	100	75	81	100

Error Accommodation

	Grammatical Category	
	Verbs	Nouns
Frequency	14	6
Percentages	78	67

Similar analyses to those performed by Berg (1987) with a German corpus of speech errors and Garrett (1980b) with an English corpus were carried out with our Spanish corpus. It should be stressed that the Spanish inflectional morphology allows, in principle, for gender and number accommodations, in contrast to English, which basically permits only number accommodations (with the possible exception of a few remnants of gender and case marking in personal pronouns); and German, which provides a richer inflectional morphology with gender, number, and case marking. As may be seen in Table 11.2, our data reveal that accommodations of the morphological context (which mainly involve determiners of noun phrases and gender and number suffixes of adjectives) affect gender and number morphemes and suffixes to a similar extent, which amount to 76.7 % of all possible cases. Moreover, there is no indication that the presence of a modifier in the source element increases the likelihood of accommodations, despite the limited number of cases found in errors without modifiers.

As for error accommodations, the cases analyzed belong to two different categories: (a) roots of irregular verbs that change their grammatical function as a consequence of their being misplaced (see example (10)); and (b) adjectives that undergo a change in gender assignment when they are moved from their original position in the sentence, as in (11).

11.   Castigo a tu *justa* perversidad [Justo castigo a tu perversidad].
      Punishment to your fair (feminine) perversity [Fair (masculine) punishment to your perversity]

Of the 27 errors analyzed from our corpus, we found that morphological adjustments in word misplacements took place in 74 % of cases. In all, the evidence reported from the analysis of the Spanish corpus of slips indicates that accommodations take place in three out of four speech errors that allow or require it to happen, irrespective of the type of grammatical information that is subject to accommodation and the environment in which the accommodation occurs. Therefore, at least for Spanish data, it is not the case that the frequency of accommodation depends on the type of accommodation: The figures for context and error accommodations were found to be practically the same. In addition, the likelihood of accommodation occurring in Spanish errors is not a function of the kind of grammatical information to be accommodated, for both gender and number marking of determiners and adjectives are accommodated to a similar degree. However, I must acknowledge that no detailed analysis has yet been performed in Spanish investigating the relative probability of accommodations across different gender and number word classes (for a recent analysis and theoretical account of the gender and number systems for Spanish, see Elías-Cintrón, 1994).

I turn now to another piece of evidence concerning the autonomy of the formulator with respect to the conceptualizer, and explore the sensitivity of conscious repair mechanisms of speech to the conceptual well-formedness of messages containing speech errors. The literature on speech error analysis shows that well-formedness constraints on errors are not only internal to the formulator and, thus, carried out through the on-line grammatical adjustments that speakers perform on linguistically ill-formed utterances, but also come about through the speaker's monitoring of overt speech in an attempt to detect and repair those utterances when the output message is at cross-purposes with the speaker's communicative intention. In the latter case, we may focus on the form of repairs, with the aim of finding out whether the patterns of interruption, editing, and repair, and the grammatical properties of the repair utterances themselves, depend on conceptual or pragmatic anomalies the speaker incurs when making a speech error. In so doing, we might see to what extent the monitoring processes associated with the formulation of sentences are responsive to the pragmatic and conceptual properties of otherwise ill-formed utterances.

I present the results of an analysis of 913 repairs of sublexical errors and 806 repairs of lexical errors that were transcribed verbatim in the corpus of Spanish slips of the tongue. Following Levelt's (1983) model of repair analysis, the well-formedness of these two sets of repairs was put to the test by analyzing the following features: (a) the patterns of interruption shown by speakers in their repairs; (b) the contextual restrictions that guide the choice of the site for restart; and (c) the relationship between the locus of interruption and the locus of repair (Levelt, 1983; Nooteboom, 1980). In addition, the patterns of interruption and restart were compared across two subsets of lexical errors: those that resulted in a semantically congruent message (however removed from the speaker's original intention) and those that showed some semantic ill-formedness.

According to several authors (Kempen & Hoenkamp 1987; Levelt, 1983; Nooteboom, 1980; van Wijk & Kempen, 1987), the form of repairs in fluent speech is governed by principles of grammatical well-formedness that relate the repair (target) utterance with the error utterance in such a way as to preserve speech fluency and discourse coherence. More specifically, Levelt (1983) proposed the following well-formedness criteria for spontaneous repairs: (a) the locus of interruption, the locus of repair or both should preserve the constituent structure of the string, that is, the site of the interruption and/or the site of the repair should fall on boundaries between sentence constituents; and/or (b) the error utterance and its repair should be related by a well-formedness rule that may be stated as follows: "A repair $<\alpha\gamma>$ is well-formed if and only if there is a string β such that the string $<\alpha\beta$ and* $\gamma>$ is well-formed, where β is a completion of the constituent directly dominating the last element of α. ($^*and$ to be deleted if γ's first element is itself a sentence connective" (p. 78). According to these criteria, the repairs in (12) are well-formed, whereas those in (13) are not.

(12) a. Dolores decía que ella se tomaba la *galleta* / la gallina cocida.
Dolores said that she ate the *cookie* / the chicken boiled

  b. He tenido que *apunt*ar muchos / acortar muchos puntos.
I had to *point* many / cut many points

(13) a. Yo he visto caerse mucha gente de *ruedas* con *motos* / gente de motos con ruedas.
I've seen many people fall from *wheels* with *motorcycles* / people fall from motorcycles with wheels like those

  b. Ahora que ya se me ha *pic*ado el / me ha pasado el picor.
Literally: Now that already it me has *itch*ed the / me has passed the itch ...
intention: Now that the itch is already over ...)

In (12a), α is the erroneous utterance *la galleta,* γ is the repair utterance *la gallina,* and the adjective *cocida* is postulated as the β sequence that is attached to α in order to preserve the well-formedness of the complete sequence $<\alpha\text{-}\beta\text{-}\gamma>$. A similar result obtains in (12b), although here the interruption falls in the middle of the phrase that is adjacent to the error utterance. Therefore, it becomes necessary to postulate a β sequence (i.e., *puntos*) so as to complete the α error utterance (*apuntar muchos*) and keep the well-formedness of the entire $<\alpha\text{-}\beta\text{-}\gamma>$ sequence. In contrast, the repairs in (13) are ill-formed, because they depart from the well-formedness criteria. Examples (14) and (15) show the results of the application of the rule to the repairs in (12) and (13), respectively.

(14) a. Ella se tomaba <[la galleta]$_\alpha$[cocida]$_\beta$/(y)[la gallina]$_\gamma$> cocida.
  b. He tenido que <[apuntar muchos]$_\alpha$[puntos]$_\beta$/(y)[acortar]$_\gamma$> muchos puntos.

(15) a. A mucha gente de <[ruedas con motos]$_\alpha$[Ø]$_\beta$/(y)[gente de motos con ruedas]$_\gamma$>.
  b. Ahora que ya se me ha <[picado]$_\alpha$[el picor]$_\beta$/(y)[me ha pasado el picor]$_\gamma$>.

In summary, the well-formedness of repairs is defined in terms of the structural relation that holds between error and repair utterances, and not merely in terms of the structural constraints set by the constituent boundaries in either of these two utterances taken separately (Levelt, 1983). Now let us see the results of the analysis of repairs from the Spanish corpus of speech errors.

Two subsets of errors were analyzed in this study: sublexical errors and lexical errors. The sublexical subset included single segment errors and was further divided into two categories: phonological errors that resulted in words (lexically biased output) and phonological errors whose output imcluded a nonword. The locus of interruption for sublexical errors was computed with two independent measures: the number of syllables between the error segment and the site of the interruption, and the kind of constituent boundary between the two sites (with the values within-word, across adjacent words belonging to the same phrase, and across adjacent phrases). The locus of interruption for lexical errors was limited to the last measure. As for the locus of restart, for both error types, I computed the distance from the error element (either phoneme or word) back to the point of restart, which yielded five different values: onset of current clause, onset of current phrase, two or more words within the current phrase, onset of current word and immediate restart (i.e., within the current word).

The results for locus of interruption were as follows: Lexically biased sublexical errors (16a) yielded longer spans of interruption than nonlexically biased ones (16b), as measured by number of syllables; this difference fell short of statistical significance, however. Nonetheless, the same trend turned out to be significant when measured by constituent boundaries; that is, immediate interruptions rose to 38 % in nonlexically biased sound errors (as in 16b), whereas they only reached 5,5 % in lexically biased sound errors. Conversely, the interruptions at the end of the current word showed the opposite trend: 57 % for nonlexically biased sound errors and 85 % for lexically biased ones (see (16a)). This seems to imply that the lexical status of the error output has an influence either on the rate at which the speaker spots the error in the first place or on his or her choice of the point at which to make hisor her intention clear to the listener. In this connection, the pattern of interruption of lexical errors (16c) closely resembles that of lexically biased sound errors. The only difference between these two error types concerns the greater proportion of late interruptions (i.e., across adjacent phrases) in lexical errors (14 %), when compared to lexically biased sound errors (5.5 %).

(16) a. Mamá es un poco rara para los ho*rrores*/ [olores]
          Mom's a little bit strange about horrors/ [smells]

      b. ...colaboración en las consu*s*/ [consultas]
          ...collaboration in the consus/ [consultations]

      c. Siempre tengo más largas las *manos*/ [las uñas de esta mano]
          I always have longer hands/ [nails on this hand]

The pattern of results for *restarts* is quite similar. Overall, lexically biased sound errors (17a) showed longer distance values from error site to restart site than nonlexically biased ones (17b), although the difference was only marginally significant. However, word errors (17c) showed the longest distance values, especially when compared with nonlexically biased sound errors. In turn, the difference between lexical errors and lexically biased sound errors in this respect was negligible. An interesting point to make here is that in most lexical and lexically biased sound errors, speakers choose the onset of the current phrase as the locus for restart (60 % and 51 %, respectively), whereas in nonlexically biased sound errors, this choice is split between the onset of the current phrase (43 %) and the onset of the current word (45 %). However, given the results of the locus of interruption for this error category, we might have expected a clearer trend toward the choice of the onset of the current word as a more appropriate site for restart in nonlexically biased sound errors.

(17) a. Me he *reído/* me he leído el resumen.
           I've laughed/ I've read the summary

      b. Le han dado una *feca/* una beca para Francia
           He's been given a folarship/ a scholarship in France

      c. Como si llevara toda la vida con el *hombro/* con el bolso en el hombro.
           As if I'd always been carrying my shoulder/ my bag in my shoulder

A further remark worth making is that the pattern of repairs in both lexical and sublexical errors satisfies Levelt's (1983) criteria of well-formedness in 91.7 % of the cases analyzed. Of the remaining 8.3 % of ill-formed repairs, 7.7 % were due to immediate interruptions, while only .6 % were found to actually violate the well-formedness rule, most of them because of an inadequate choice of restart sites.

The last analysis of speech error data I report on in this section concerns the influence of semantic well-formedness on the patterns of repairs. For this purpose, the subset of 806 lexical errors with repairs used in the previous analysis was broken down into two categories, and each error was assigned to one of those categories on the basis of the judgments of three independent judges (the rate of agreement among them was .86): An error was classified as *conceptually anomalous* if it violated the semantic restrictions among the concepts or entities mentioned in the message; otherwise, it was considered *conceptually adequate*. As classification criterion *conceptual congruity* was preferred to *conceptual plausibility,* given the need to dichotomize the pool of errors into two distinct subclasses. Thus, semantically anomalous utterances were also highly implausible by definition, whereas semantically congruent utterances could vary in their degree of plausibility. Altogether, 279 errors fell under the category *conceptually anomalous* (see example (18)), and 527 were classified as *conceptually correct* (see example (19)).

(18) He visto un *lavabo* en el *mosquito* [un mosquito en el lavabo].
       I've seen a *basin* in the *mosquito* [a mosquito in the basin]

(19) El *pato* parecía un *perro* [el perro parecía un pato].
       The *duck* looked like a *dog* [the dog looked like a duck]

Following this, the patterns of interruption and restart were compared across the two error types. If the conceptual characteristics of errors influenced the form of repairs, we would expect faster or more immediate interruptions in conceptually anomalous errors than in conceptually congruent errors, on the assumption that the conceptualizer should spot and filter out this kind of error more quickly than congruent ones. Similarly, the distance between error and restart sites should be broader for conceptually anomalous errors, provided that this gave the listener more chances to understand the repair and, consequently, the speaker's true intention.

However, the results do not square with these expectations. In fact, the interruption data indicate exactly the opposite trend. Interruption loci were significantly different across the two error types, with faster interruptions in conceptually anomalous errors than in conceptually congruent ones. Interruptions at the end of the current word were 61 % in the former group and 78 % in the latter, whereas interruptions at the end of the current phrase were 22 % in the semantically anomalous category and only 10 % in the semantically congruent. A possible explanation of this pattern of results is that the monitoring of speech output does not operate simultaneously on all levels of representation in which the speech signal can be decoded, and that monitoring at the conceptual level is delayed with respect to other hierarchically lower processing levels. This hypothesis is consistent with the observation that sound errors that produce nonword outputs (where conceptual representation is unaffected) tend to be interrupted more rapidly than lexically biased sound errors.

The patterns of restarts for the conceptually anomalous and conceptually congruent errors did not differ. Speakers tended to choose the onset of the current phrase as the restart site in 60 % of cases, and the onset of the current clause in 16 to 20 % of cases, regardless of the conceptual consequences of the error.

Conclusion

In this section, I have discussed some issues concerning the flow of information between the conceptualization and formulation components in sentence production by reviewing some evidence from studies on spontaneous speech errors and repairs in Spanish. The results allow us to conclude that a substantial part of the formulation processes subserving sentence planning are spared the influences of conceptualization processes involved in the generation of preverbal messages. The preservation of linguistic well-formedness in error repairs, irrespective of the conceptual congruency of the messages, as well as the use of unconscious accommodatory processes in most utterances containing slips, seem to demonstrate that the processes in charge of keeping the details of sentence form right are largely oblivious to the conceptual characteristics of the messages. In other words, our results suggest that the properties of the conceptual input with which the formulator is fed have limited consequences for the operations of the linguistic component of sentence planning.

Moreover, the studies presented in this section show that the processes of phonological encoding of sentences do not exert any bottom–up influence on message generation. There is, however, evidence of a positive feedback from the segmental and suprasegmental structure of words to the processes of lexical retrieval within the formulator, as attested to by the above-chance phonological similarity of error sources and targets in the alternative-plan lexical errors examined in the first study.

The evidence reviewed thus far seems to be compatible with the claim that sentence-planning processes show at least some of the properties that are typically associated with cognitive modules (Fodor, 1983): First, they are *informationally encapsulated*, inasmuch as they are insensitive to nonlinguistic representations supplied from other components of the production apparatus; second, the central systems they are connected to (i.e., the conceptualizer) have limited access to the representations they compute; and third, they seem to operate at considerable speed. Nevertheless, as pointed out earlier, evidence from speech errors and repairs seems insufficient to draw conclusions regarding other significant properties of the formulation component as a linguistic module. For instance, it remains unclear whether formulation processes are obligatory, because the well-formedness constraints examined earlier are still far from foolproof. In addition, the issue of the domain specificity of the formulation processes does not seem easy to articulate in the field of sentence production, for it may be defined either in terms of the output representations generated by the formulation system or in terms of the input conceptual representations it receives from higher order processing levels (see, however, a similar construal of the problem of domain specificity in parsing in Linebarger, 1990).

In the next section, I examine the coordination problem in sentence formulation by reporting a set of experiments carried out in Spanish on the relationship between lexical retrieval and syntactic planning processes. The main concern of this section is to sort out the relative contributions of conceptual, lexical, and syntactic information to the processes of building the underlying syntactic representation of sentences.

THE COORDINATION PROBLEM IN SENTENCE PRODUCTION: CONCEPTUAL, LEXICAL, AND SYNTACTIC FACTORS IN SENTENCE FORMULATION

All processing models of sentence production make a logical distinction between word retrieval and syntactic planning processes as two different operations involved in the formulation of sentences. Autonomous models, such as Fromkin's (1971) or Garrett's (1975, 1976), make the further claim that the processes underlying word retrieval and those subserving phrasal construction operate independently of each other. However, this claim has not been widely accepted (see, e.g., Levelt 1989), on the assumption that syntactic encoding is always lexically mediated, that is, that the activation of lexical representations from concepts drives the assignment of semantic roles at the message level, to syntactic constituents at the sentence level and, hence contributes to the ordering of constituents in the sentence plan.

According to the evidence gathered from the analysis of spontaneous speech errors and from the study of language-specific impairments in adults (i.e., acquired aphasias), lexical and syntactic processes in sentence formulation seem to be subserved by two distinct components or modules of linguistic knowledge. However, it is no less true that lexical retrieval and syntactic planning do not form two homogeneous sets of computations neatly confined in bounded regions of the functional architecture of the language processing system. Each of them spreads, so to speak, across different processing levels and carries out relatively specific tasks at each of these levels. For instance, lexicalization processes are thought to be organized in two autonomous subcomponents that operate in a serial fashion: a *semantic lexicon,* from which lexical representations are retrieved on the basis of their conceptual properties; and a *phonological lexicon,* from which the retrieval of word forms takes place (Kempen & Huijbers, 1983; Schriefers, Meyer, & Levelt, 1990; Levelt et al., 1991). Syntactic processes are also claimed to be organized in two separate processing levels: a more abstract *functional level,* where the thematic roles of the message representation are mapped onto the syntactic constituents of the sentence and the syntactic dependencies between constituents are established, thereby creating a representation of the logical relations among the sentence's syntactic constituents; and a *positional level,* which embodies other syntactic features, such as constituent order and agreement relations, that belong to a more superficial kind of syntactic representation (Garrett, 1975, 1980a, 1984, 1988).

Given this picture, the major components of lexical and syntactic processes in sentence production might be displayed according to the scheme in Fig. 11.1.

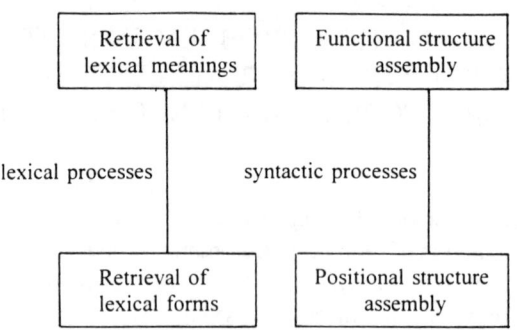

FIG. 11.1. Levels of processing and processing components sentence formulation.

This scheme serves as a starting point for testing hypotheses concerning the functional relations between subcomponents of the formulation apparatus and, eventually, their informational encapsulation. The experiment reported in this section focus on the contributions of lexical retrieval, at both lemma and word form levels, to the construction of a sentence's functional representation. Specifically, this experiment was intended to test the extent to which the availability of lexical representations determines the choice of the sentence's syntactic structure. This issue lies at the very core of the coordination problem in sentence production.

From the standpoint of crosslinguistic research, there is great diversity across languages in the solutions provided by different grammars to the coordination problem. There seems to be a continuum, from languages that make use of constituent order as the major syntactic device, to signal dependencies among sentence constituents and thematic relationships among discourse entities, to those that use inflectional morphology. As Bock (1987a) and Levelt (1989), among others, have noted, languages that exhibit complex inflectional systems (with gender, number, and case marking for determiners, pronouns, adjectives and nouns, and tense, aspect, and person marking for verbs) to signal grammatical relations among constituents (such as Slavic languages or Latin) do not usually prescribe fixed word orders; in contrast, languages with poor inflectional systems (such as English) are highly restrictive in terms of constituent order. This difference among language types has implications for the coordination problem in sentence processing, for it might turn out that those languages (such as Spanish) in which word order is not highly constrained by the grammar should show, *mutatis mutandis,* a greater influence of lexical retrieval operations on real-time syntactic planning than languages with a fixed word order (such as English). Thus, Spanish might shed some light on the coordination problem as seen from a crosslinguistic perspective.

Some psycholinguistic models of sentence production, assume that "the lexicon is an essential mediator between conceptualization and grammatical encoding" (Levelt, 1989, p. 181). This means that the passage from the conceptual representation of the message to the functional representation of the sentence entails, at least, the activation of certain lexical representations at the level of lemmas: for instance, the predicate of the message may be lexicalized as a finite verb, and the agent, experiencer, and patient may be lexicalized as nouns. Of course, this leaves open many possibilities regarding the interplay of conceptual, lexical, and syntactic factors in syntactic planning. First, it might be the case that lemmas are selected and retrieved in parallel to the syntactic routines that build the sentence functional representation. On this assumption, the choice of a sentence frame should not be influenced by lexicalization processes. Alternatively, the activation of certain lemma representations from concepts could guide the choice of a given syntactic frame. Thus, the greater availability of a given lexical item would privilege the assignment of a syntactic function (say, subjecthood) to the corresponding concept's thematic role (agent or patient) and, hence, its being mentioned earlier in the sentence. If a lexical item so activated (say, *car*) corresponded to a concept bearing the thematic role of agent, this would result in a canonical active structure (as (20a)), whereas if it corresponded to a concept with a thematic role of patient, it would originate in either a passive structure (20b) or a structure with a topicalized, left-dislocated argument (20c).

(20) a. The car bumped the street-lamp.
      b. The street-lamp was bumped by the car.
      c. It was the street-lamp that the car bumped.

However, as mentioned earlier on, the activation of lexical representations in sentence planning might take place at the levels of lemmas and word forms. Given this, we cannot, in principle, dismiss the possibility that the spurious activation of phonological representations of words might also influence the choice of a sentence's syntactic structure. In short, there are four possible sources of syntactic planning at the functional representation level:

. The conceptual properties of the message entities (i.e., its predicate and arguments)
. The lemma representations of these entities
. The word forms of the lexical items corresponding to these entities
. The choice of syntactic frames provided by the phrase-structure rules of the grammar.

I now review some experimental studies, mainly carried out in English, concerning the coordination of lexical representations in syntactic plans during sentence formulation.

Conceptual, Lexical, and Syntactic Variables in Sentence Planning: Background

According to different investigators, there are a number of conceptual factors that appear to have a direct bearing in syntactic planning. Levelt (1989) emphasized the *principle of natural order,* which states that the contents of a message shall be expressed according to the natural spatio-temporal sequence of events in the natural world, and the *principle of minimal load,* according to which any transitions or continuations in discourse or conversation shall make the least memory demands on the listener. According to Osgood and Bock (1977), the most outstanding conceptual criterion in constituent ordering in sentences is the relative *saliency* of the elements depicted in verbal messages. A given element or concept is said to be more salient whenever it bears a greater perceptual or affective vividness for the speaker or receives from the speaker a particular subjective significance. In addition, there are a number of conceptual factors that contribute to enhance the accessibility of lexical representations, namely, animacy, concreteness, imaginability, and prototypicality. Bock and her colleagues (Bock & Warren 1985; Kelly, Bock, & Keil, 1986) have carried out several studies to test the influence of these factors on sentence formulation. They found, for instance, that animate entities tend to be mentioned earlier in sentences than inanimate ones, and are usually found to occupy more relevant grammatical roles in the sentence (e.g., topic or subject). Similarly, concrete objects and events, as well as imageable ones, appear to be more privileged, relative to abstract or less imageable objects and events, in the sense just mentioned.

These observations should come as no surprise. They simply confirm the assumption that speakers have a variety of linguistic devices at their disposal when they need to single out some discourse entity and make it the topic or focus of a sentence. These linguistic devices range from syntactic procedures, such as topicalization by means of passive structures or cleft sentences (21a), to lexical procedures, as when a lexical anaphor is used to bring some noun phrase mentioned earlier into focus (21b), or even the use of prosodic cues, such as contrastive stress (21c). In any case, it seems clear that the conceptual and pragmatic characteristics of messages determine, at least to some extent, the structural choices available to the speaker at a given point (see Jarvella & Engelkamp, 1983, for a more detailed account of the pragmatic influences in language perception and production).

(21) a. *It was John* who did the cheating.
      b. *That little rascal* cheated all of us.
      c. *JOHN* did the cheating, not me!
          John was *CHEA*ting, not playing properly!

A different source of influence on syntactic structures during sentence planning is the activation of lexical representations of concepts, either at the level of lemmas or at the level of word forms. A number of studies on picture description (Levelt & Maassen 1981; van Wijk & Kempen, 1987) have found that the choice of syntactic structures is mainly guided by conceptual factors, whereas lexical retrieval processes appear to be subordinate to both conceptual and sentence planning processes. However, syntactic planning may also be altered on the basis of lexical factors; for instance, whenever the retrieval of a word form fails for some reason, subjects are often led to reformulate the sentence syntax. Thus, it seems that syntactic structure can be modified during sentence production on different grounds. What is not so clear, however, is that the factors that produce this modification directly influence the grammatical encoding processes or, rather, the execution of these processes, because they are instantiated once lexical retrieval and phonological encoding have taken place. Given the time-dependent nature of the evidence reported, it might just as well be the case that syntactic processes in sentence planning enjoy an informational encapsulation partially at the input end, while they are being computed from the propositional representation of the message, but are subject to interruption and reformulation at the output end, when they come in contact with phonological encoding processes by the time the phonetic plan is ready to be executed. The observation that sentence-planning operations proceed in a step-by-step incremental fashion makes this claim fairly plausible (see Kempen & Hoenkamp, 1987).

Perhaps the most thorough investigation of the effects of lexical activation on syntactic planning is a series of studies carried out by Bock (1986, 1987b), in which a picture description task was employed together with a lexical priming technique. In these studies, subjects saw pictures depicting scenes with two entities or protagonists that required different sorts of verbal descriptions: transitive clauses (*The dog is chasing the cat.*), dative constructions (*The man is reading a book to the girl.*), and coordinate noun phrases in sentences (*The cat and the dog are sleeping under the table.*), among others. Shortly before the picture was displayed on the screen, subjects heard or saw a word they had to read silently or aloud. This word could be related to either of the entities shown in the picture that followed in one of two ways: semantically or phonologically. The purpose of this experimental setting was to record the possible influences of lexical activation through priming on the order of mention of the picture's entities under different syntactic constructions, on the assumption that primed entities would normally be mentioned prior to unprimed entities. This, in turn, could entail changes in the syntactic frames of the utterances produced as descriptions of the pictures. For example, if a word semantically related to the name of the patient of a given picture (say, the word *worship* presented just before a scene showing a church struck by lightning) produced a greater proportion of responses in which the word *church* was mentioned first (e.g., *The church was struck by lightning*), this would be taken as an indication that lemma retrieval guides the choice of a syntactic frame for the utterance. A similar effect could also be tested under phonological priming conditions (e.g., with a word like *search* to prime the concept church, in the above example), this time through the activation of word forms instead of lemmas.

In the first of these studies (Bock, 1986), where transitive structures were tested, Bock obtained a reliable semantic priming effect and a nonsignificant phonological priming effect in the opposite direction: That is, semantic relations between word primes and conceptual targets produced a significant tendency to mention the primed entity first (if this was the patient, it resulted in passive constructions), whereas phonological relations induced a nonsignificant tendency to mention the primed entity last. Thus, word accessibility at the lemma level largely determines syntactic planning processes. In contrast, the accessibility of word forms does not substantially influence syntactic processing. The inhibitory effect Bock found for phonological priming, however tenuous, squares with similar results obtained in priming studies on word perception and production (see, e.g., O'Sheaghdha, Dell, Peterson, & Juliano, 1992; Peterson, O'Sheaghdha, & Dell, 1989).

In a subsequent study, Bock (1987b) tested this phonological inhibitory effect with the same priming technique, using two kinds of syntactic structures: transitive constructions and complex noun phrases. This time, however, she was able to find reliable inhibitory effects across the board. Leaving aside the precise locus and nature of the inhibitory priming effect found by Bock in this study (whether it was caused by a lexical suppression mechanism during the processing of the prime word, or by phonological competition during the retrieval of the target word), it seems beyond doubt that this effect leaves the autonomy of syntactic processes in jeopardy, because it shows that the computation of the functional representation of the sentence is susceptible to influences not only from the processes of lemma retrieval, but also from the activation of word forms at the positional level.

There are, to be sure, several methodological problems with Bock's studies that should be pointed out. One problem is the lack of a neutral condition with which to compare the results of semantic and phonological priming. Admittedly, it is extremely difficult to find a purely neutral condition in which no priming effects could ensue whatsoever. Previous studies employing the word–picture interference paradigm have tested several possibilities (such as unrelated words, no prime words at all, unpronounceable nonwords, or even a row of Xs), each with its pros and cons (see Glaser, 1992, for a review). In the Spanish study descibed further on, we decided to use an unrelated prime as a baseline condition for comparison. A second problem in Bock's studies is that she combined the data of priming effects for agents and patients, which makes it impossible to see whether the priming effects obtained accrue over agent and patient word targets to a similar degree. In our own study, we kept the data for agent and patient priming separate and found that there was a remarkable difference. The third problem is more a matter of choice: Bock did not manipulate any conceptual variables in her studies on lexical priming, whereas we decided that it would be quite informative to combine conceptual and lexical variables together in the same experimental design.

To summarize, in my view, of all the possible functional relations that can hold among conceptual, lexical, and syntactic factors in sentence planning, the only ones that would uphold a modular picture of syntactic processing at the functional level are the following: a feedforward influence from conceptual to lexical representations at the level of lemmas, and a cross-influence from the activation of lemmas to the building of the functional syntactic representation of the sentence. This amounts to admitting that grammatical encoding and lexical retrieval are not mutually independent processes, but interact at the point where thematic structures are mapped onto syntactic frames. However, the finding that activated word forms can modify the sentence functional representation would certainly be incompatible with any version of a nontrivial modular characterization of the formulator.

Conceptual and Lexical Variables in Sentence Planning: Spanish Data

Using the lexical priming procedure employed by Bock (1986, 1987b), I carried out an investigation with Spanish materials and subjects, using animacy and type of lexical priming as independent variables (see Igoa, 1991, for a detailed description of the design, materials, and procedure of these experiments). The purpose of these experiments was to test the role of lexical activation at both lemma and word form levels on sentence structure. A lexical priming procedure was used with a picture description task. Subjects sat in front of a screen while they listened to a tape. On each trial, they heard a word that they had to repeat out loud, saw a line drawing of a scene involving two entities or participants (objects, animals, or human beings) they had to describe, or experimental both events, in that order. For the description task, subjects were instructed to use a single sentence with no personal pronouns and to respond as quickly as possible. Following Bock's procedure, to conceal the actual purpose of the experiment, I told subjects that they would have to pass a recognition test with the words they had heard and the pictures they had seen at the end of the trials.

Besides lexical priming, two additional conceptual variables, animacy and agency, were taken into account. The animacy variable was manipulated by distributing the animacy of the agents and patients of the pictures in four different conditions: (a) animate agents and patients, (b) inanimate agents and patients, (c) animate agents and inanimate patients, and (d) inanimate agents and animate patients.[1] The role of agency was tested by computing separately the lexical priming effects on agents and patients. In this way, I could find out whether agents and patients are similarly influenced by the activation of lexical representations related to their corresponding names. As in Bock's experiments, lexical accessibility was induced by using semantically and phonologically related words as primes for the target concepts (i.e., agents and patients) depicted in each scene. The examples in (23) show the semantic and phonological word primes (in lower case) for eight different intended word targets (in upper case), associated to four different pictures (a neutral verbal description of the picture is provided in each case): (23a) the animate–animate" condition, (23b) the

---

[1]Strictly speaking, the role of agent and patient can only be ascribed to animate entities. Thus, inanimate agents should be best categorized as *instruments,* and inanimate patients should be considered *objects.* Likewise, in many instances, an animate patient in a scene with an inanimate agent should rather be taken as an *experiencers.* However, these thematic role reassignments are not relevant to the purposes of the experiments.

inanimate–inanimate condition, (23c) of the animate–inanimate condition, and (23d) of the inanimate–animate condition.[2] The words in italics are the intended names of the agent and patient in each picture description.

(23) a. A *thief* is stealing something from a *photographer*'s bag.
         LADRÓN (THIEF) - robo (robbery) - patrón (chief)
         FOTÓGRAFO (PHOTOGRAPHER) - cámara (camera) fonógrafo (phonograph)

      b. A *bottle* is pouring a black fluid over a white *shirt*.
         BOTELLA (BOTTLE) - vaso (glass) - batalla (battle)
         CAMISA (SHIRT) - traje (suit) - sumisa (sharp)

      c. An *Indian* is cutting a *palm-tree* with an axe.
         INDIO (INDIAN) - flecha (arrow) - lindo (injure)
         PALMERA (PALM-TREE) - oasis (oasis) - pantera (pantry)

      d. A *spear* wounds a *lion*.
         LANZA (SPEAR) - guerrero (warrior) - danza (spire)
         LEÓN (LION) - safari (safari) - limón (lying)

Thus, each critical picture showed two entities or participants related by an action and was supposed to be described by using a transitive construction. Despite the fact that Spanish, like English, is a Subject–Verb–Object (SVO) language, it admits, in principle, a wider variety of constituent orders than English. However, verb-final (SOV or OSV) and verb-initial (VSO or VOS) transitive constructions are quite rare, if not altogether anomalous (see Hernanz & Brucart, 1987, for a review). Accordingly, when using a two-place predicate–argument structure to encode and describe the kinds of pictures employed in these experiments, our Spanish-speaking subjects could resort to any of the following sentence structures (note that the English versions of the examples are literal translations):

(24) a. Un tenista persigue a un fotógrafo.
         A tennis-player chases to a photographer

      b. Un fotógrafo es perseguido por un tenista.
         A photographer is chased by a tennis-player

---

[2]The English versions of the phonological primes are not translations of the corresponding Spanish words, but possible phonological primes of the target words.

c. A un fotógrafo le persigue un tenista.
To a photographer him chases a tennis-player

d. Un tenista que persigue a un fotógrafo.
A tennis-player who chases to a photographer

e. Un fotógrafo que es perseguido por un tenista.
A photographer who is chased by a tennis-player

f. Un fotógrafo al que le persigue un tenista.
A photographer who him chases a tennis-player

Examples (24a) and ((24b)) are cases of active and passive structures, respectively; (24c) is a topicalized, left-dislocated structure quite commonly used in Spanish to signal the patient as the sentence focus; (24d), (24e), and (24f), in turn, are variants of (24a), (24b), and (24c), respectively, with a relative clause modifying the sentence focus. Responses using any of the structures illustrated were classified as *standard responses.*[3] Standard responses ranged from 64 to 97 % of all the responses given across different experimental conditions, with a mean of 84 %. A major contrast found in these sentence types is the order of mention of the agent and patient of the scene, which results in variations in the syntactic structure of the sentence at the functional representation level. Therefore, it is important to bear in mind that the choice among these structure types involves a specific mapping of thematic roles onto syntactic functions.

It is important to stress that each priming condition (semantic and phonological) was compared to a baseline condition where an unrelated word was presented as the prime. Responses containing errors (either in the identification of participants or in the assignment of thematic roles) were eliminated. All correct responses within each experimental condition were labeled according to the criterion *primed element mentioned first,* and the mean proportion of this kind of response was computed for each of the experimental conditions.

Based on the distribution of animacy between agents and patients (see earlier comments), the study was divided into four subexperiments. The results on

---

[3]*Nonstandard responses* include the following: (a) omissions of any of the three major elements of the message, that is, the agent, the action or the patient, which might result in complex noun phrases (e.g., *There's a policeman and a thief*), reduced passives, (e.g., *The thief is being shot*), or incomplete actives (e.g., *The policeman's shooting*); (b) a failure to identify any of the participants in the scene; for example, *Someone's shooting a thief, The policeman's shooting this guy here,* or *He's shooting the man;* and (c) complex subordinate structures, such as *A policeman's shooting while the thief tries to escape,* or sentences with instrument prepositional phrases, like *A policeman's shooting a thief with his gun.*

semantic priming are reported first for all four subexperiments, and the results on phonological priming follow. For convenience, the results of the animate–animate and inanimate–inanimate conditions have been collapsed, and are presented jointly.

The results of semantic priming rendered the following pattern: In those conditions where agent and patient share the same animacy value (animate or inanimate; Subexperiments 1 and 2), there were significant facilitatory priming effects only for patients. This means that in these conditions, priming the agents did not increase the likelihood that they would be mentioned first in the sentence. In contrast, when the patient was primed, it was almost twice as likely to be mentioned first than in the unrelated priming condition (33 vs. 17 % in the baseline condition; see Fig. 11.2, upper panel). The inefficiency of the priming procedure for agents can be better understood if we consider the fact that under neutral priming conditions, the agent is mentioned first on 82 % of the occasions. Thus, there appears to be a ceiling effect in the assignment of subjecthood to agents (or instruments) involved in actions directed toward a patient or object of the same animacy, such that the greater availability of lexical representations for agents does not enhance their likelihood of being given a prominent syntactic role in the sentence. We might call this the conceptual contraint of agency on sentence formulation.

Semantic priming was extremely inefficient in the animate–inanimate subexperiment; that is, there were no effects of lexical priming on the order of mention for either agents or patients. The same ceiling effect referred to earlier applies here in an even more pronounced way. As much as 97 % of the responses were given with the animate agent in subject position in the unrelated priming condition. We might hypothesize that the agency constraint postulated for the former two subexperiments (animate–animate and inanimate–inanimate) was supplemented in this case with an animacy constraint that drives speakers to assign subjecthood to animate entities whenever there is an asymmetry between thematic roles in terms of animacy (Dewart, 1979; Harris, 1978). This surely represents the most unmarked case of thematic-to-syntactic mapping, given a hypothetical hierarchy of markedness in the assignment of syntactic functions to thematic roles.

Finally, in the inanimate–animate subexperiment, the trend found in Subexperiments 1 and 2 was reversed, for there were only significant facilitatory effects of lexical priming in the agent priming condition (see Fig. 11.2, left part of lower panel). In this subexperiment, there was a limited tendency for subjects to assign subjecthood to the (animate) experiencer of the picture at the expense of the inanimate instrument (51 % of responses). However, with semantic priming of the instrument role, the instrument was reliably promoted to a subject position in 66 % of cases. Conversely, and surprisingly, semantic priming of the experiencer did not serve to increase its promotion to subject, but, if anything, reduced it.

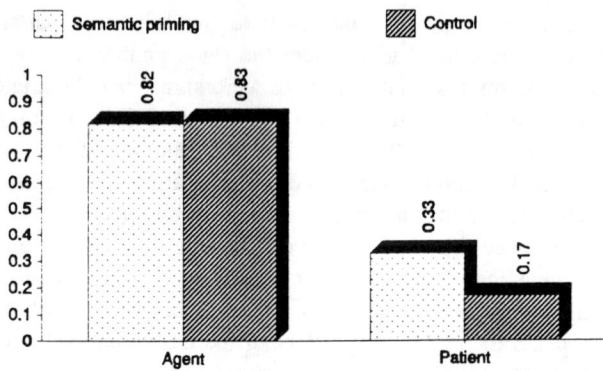

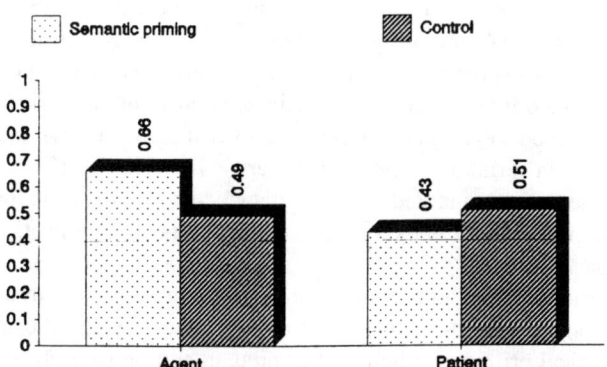

FIG. 11.2. Proportion of responses with primed element mentioned first across phonological priming conditions. Upper panel: Collapsed data from Subexperiments 1 (animate agent and animate patient) and 2 (inanimate agent and inanimate patient). Lower panel: Data from subexperiment 4 (inanimate agent and animate patient).

Altogether, the effects of semantic priming on the order of mention of participants appear to be limited and, at any rate, subordinated to other conceptual variables, such as animacy and agency. Semantic priming effects of a facilitatory nature apply to inanimate agents (instruments) when these are accompanied by animate patients (experiencers; Subexp. 4), and to both animate and inanimate patients that are related to agents of the same animacy value (Subexps. 1 and 2). This pattern of results seems to be in accordance with a hierarchy of markedness in conceptual-to-syntactic mapping, operating at the functional level representation of the syntactic structure of the sentence. Comparatively marked cases, such as those presenting inanimate agents acting over animate patients, allow for a greater effect of lexical availability at the level of lemmas on the order of mention of the entities involved, thus enhancing the subjecthood of the inanimate objects. As for animate and inanimate agents acting over entities of the same animacy type, the same principle of semantic priming for marked cases accounts for the greater effect of lexical availability at the lemma level on patients, as compared to agents. Finally, in the most unmarked case, an animate agent acting over an inanimate object, animacy and agency act together to prevent any effect of lexical availability on syntactic structure.

The results on phonological priming exhibit a completely different pattern. Fig. 11.3 displays the results of Subexperiments 1 and 2 (upper panel) and Subexperiment 4 (lower panel). With the exception of patient priming in Subexperiments 1 and 2, there is an obvious trend for phonological priming to induce inhibitory effects. However, this trend did not reach statistical significance in any of the conditions examined (refer to Igoa, 1991, for a detailed account of the results). Therefore, the possible inhibitory effect of phonological competitors of target words is negligible, as far as syntactic planning at the functional level is concerned. These negative results are quite similar to those reported by Bock in her 1986 study on lexical priming and, like all negative results, must be handled with extreme caution.

There are two tentative (and compatible) explanations for the lack of phonological effects found in this study. First, it might be the case that the phonological representation of words (i.e., the lexemes or word forms) of the target concepts is not fully specified by the time the syntactic frame of the sentence is being planned at the functional level. If this is so, the activation of competing word forms should have no influence on the mapping of thematic roles to syntactic functions at this level. Previous studies on the time course of lemma and lexeme activation in word production (Levelt et al., 1991; Meyer & Schriefers, 1991; Schriefers et al., 1990) have shown that lexical priming effects from lexemes to word targets happen at a comparatively late stage during word retrieval (i.e., at null or even positive stimulus onset asynchronies; SOAs). In contrast, the word-to-picture time lag in our experiment was always negative (i.e., word primes were presented 2 seconds before the onset of the picture).

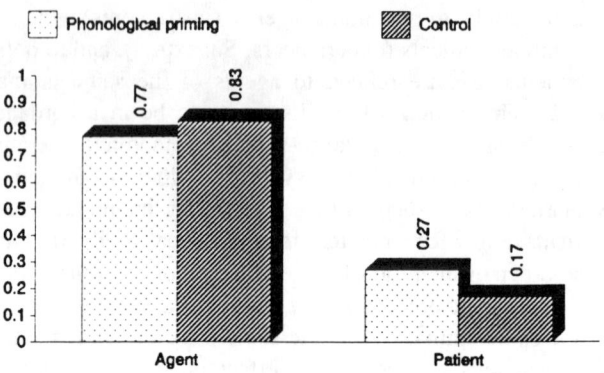

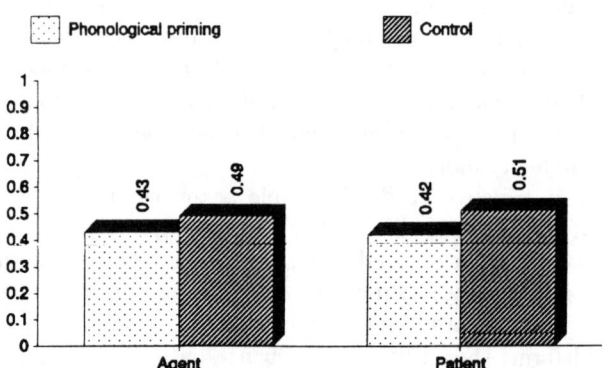

FIG. 11.3. Proportion of responses with primed element mentioned first across phonological priming conditions. <u>Upper panel</u>: Collapsed data for Subexperiments 1 (animate agent and animate patient) and 2 (inanimate agent and inanimate patient). <u>Lower panel</u>: Data from Subexperiment 4 (inanimate agent and animate patient).

A second possible explanation for the lack of phonological priming effects in our experiments is that this effect is not robust enough to alter the syntactic structure as it is being computed from the thematic structure of the message. If this is the case, and as Bock has repeatedly argued, there should be a substantially different pattern of hesitations and lexical errors at the beginnings of sentences in which the phonologically primed entity is mentioned first. The logic runs as follows: If phonological primes produce a partial inhibitory effect, this effect might surface as a transient failure to recover the word form of the first-mentioned entity of the picture. This would show up in the form of more hesitations and straightforward lexical errors when the primed element is mentioned first than in cases in which the primed element is mentioned last.

On this assumption, the frequencies of hesitations (upper panel of Fig. 11.4) and lexical errors (lower panel of Fig. 11.4) following phonological priming of the entity that was mentioned first in the sentence were computed and compared to those of the corresponding baseline conditions (i.e., unrelated priming). The overall pattern of results did not reach statistical significance; however, pairwise comparisons showed a significantly higher frequency of hesitations and errors when the first-mentioned primed element was an inanimate object (see second and fourth pairs of bars of both panels in Fig. 11.4). A similar computation for semantic priming revealed an entirely different pattern of results, with no trace of inhibition in any of the four subexperiments.

The overall lack of phonological effects in our experiment is congruent with the evidence available in the literature on sentence production. This evidence underscores the fact that semantic (lemma) and phonological (word form) representations of words are retrieved at different points in the production process, and that the former are retrieved within the domain of clausal planning units, whereas the latter are retrieved within the domain of phrasal planning units. Recall that the clause is the planning domain of the functional representation, whereas the phrase is the planning domain of the positional representation of the sentence (see Dell & O'Sheaghdha, 1992, and O'Sheaghdha, Dell, & Marin 1992, for recent experimental evidence). Because the planning task in my experiment was intended to tap the functional representations of sentences, it seems natural that no significant phonological effects emerged.[4]

---

[4]I have not dwelled on the precise nature of the priming effects, either excitatory or inhibitory, because there does not seem to be a straightforward interpretation of these effects. The usual effects found in studies of word priming using the picture–word interference paradigm is excitatory for semantic priming and inhibitory for phonological priming. However, recent studies on word priming (Dell & O'Sheaghdha, 1992; O'Sheaghdha, et al., 1992) have shown that phonological priming can be both excitatory and inhibitory, depending on the position of the target word in the sentence. Thus, early targets tend to be inhibited, and late targets tend to be facilitated. To complicate the issue

Two main issues have been addressed in this chapter: The first was the direction of the flow of information between two major components of the language production apparatus, the conceptualizer and the formulator; the second was the coordination of words in the syntactic frame of the sentence and the major determinants of this process. I have shown here that the distributional patterns of Spanish speech errors and repairs, and particularly the constraints on syntactic well-formedness they are found to obey, are largely oblivious to the conceptual consequences of the slips. Similarly, errors that are claimed to arise at the message level (i.e., competing-plan errors) receive no substantial influences from the phonological properties of the elements involved in them. As I argued before, these observations are compatible with a modular characterization of the formulator with respect to the conceptualizer.

On the other hand, the coordination process that lies at the interface between the conceptualizer and the formulator appears to be fundamentally driven by conceptual properties of the message and the entities represented therein. The last experiment described shows that the conceptual variables of animacy and agency seem to govern the assignment of the thematic roles of the message (i.e., agent, patient) to syntactic functions of the sentence (i.e., subject, object) at the level of the functional representation. Accordingly, the activation of linguistically encoded representations (e.g., lemmas) is usually not sufficient to alter the conceptually driven syntactic relations: Agents are systematically assigned the subject function, and patients the object function. The lexicalization of conceptual entities may only influence the conceptual-to-syntactic mapping process at the functional level provided that the conceptual constraints of the message representation are not heavy enough. This may occur when the message construes some state of affairs that is comparatively uncommon or marked, as when inanimate entities assume an agentive role or the animacy of the entities represented in the message is balanced. However, this limited influence of the activation of lexical representations on the construction of the functional syntactic structure is only brought about by semantic properties of words (i.e., lemmas), and never by their phonological properties (i.e., word forms).

---

further, the inhibitory effect for early targets found in sentence planning tasks turned facilitatory when the planning units were phrases. In these studies, excitatory phonological priming was interpreted as showing that the phonological form of the target words was not fully specified at the moment of testing. In turn, the excitatory semantic priming effects found by Bock (and me) in sentence planning tasks is interpreted in terms of a greater availability of lemmas at the point of conceptual-to-syntactic mapping. The reason for this discrepant account is that facilitatory and inhibitory effects are construed in different ways, and stem from different tasks, across the various experimental studies reviewed in this chapter.

HESITATIONS
Primed element mentioned first

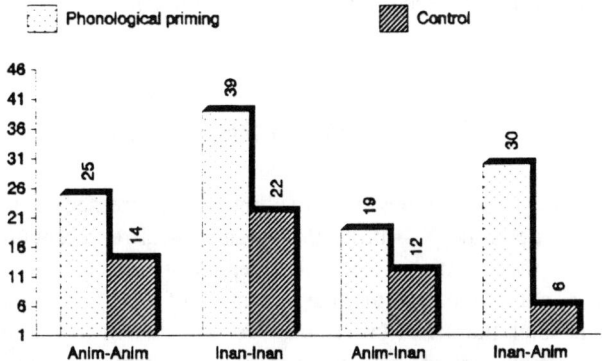

ERRORS
Primed element mentioned first

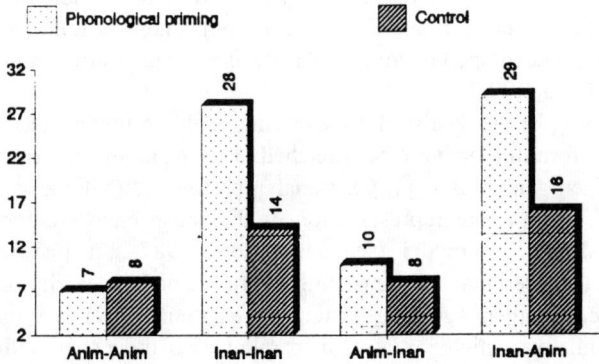

FIG. 11.4. Frequencies of hesitations and lexical errors across the four experiments under phonological priming when the printed element was mentioned first. Upper panel: Hesitation data. Lower Panel: Error data.

This results in patients being "upgraded" to become subjects in animate–animate or inanimate–inanimate thematic structures, and also in inanimate objects being assigned the subject role in inanimate–animate thematic structures (where the first member of the pair corresponds to the agent/instrument, and the second to the patient/object).

CONCLUDING REMARKS

There are two further issues that have not been addressed in the experiment reported here. One is the possibility that phonological representations of words may influence the positional syntactic representation of the sentence. In particular, it might be the case that the activation of word forms through lexical priming could alter the serial ordering of constituents in the sentence without affecting the assignment of syntactic functions to thematic roles. To test this possibility, it would be necessary to employ structures that allowed for a certain degree of freedom in the surface ordering of constituents, while keeping constant the underlying functional representation. This is something that Bock already found in some of her studies when she used coordinate noun phrases, but it could also be extended to other clausal structures. Spanish, being a language with relatively free word order, could offer a suitable opportunity to do so.

Another neglected issue is the precise time course of the activation of lexical representations and their insertion into syntactic frames during sentence production. As already stated, this problem has only been addressed with regard to phrasal units (see Schriefers, 1992), although new priming techniques are currently being developed to cover the analysis of clausal structures, as well (Dell & O'Sheaghdha, 1992).

On the basis of the results of our experiment, the following descriptive model of sentence formulation may be sketched: For a picture description task, the conceptualizer generates a propositional representation of the message to be conveyed from a visual representation of the scene encoded, for instance, in terms of Marr's 3D model (see Jackendoff, 1987, for justification). This propositional representation (consisting, as for standard descriptions, of a two-place predicate with an agent/instrument and a patient/object as arguments) is fed to the formulator, which initiates, in parallel, two processes at the functional level: (a) a lexicalization process, based on the conceptual properties of the entities of the message; and (b) a syntactic planning process. The latter consists of a mapping from abstract thematic roles to syntactic functions. Animacy, however, should somehow be reflected at this level in the thematic structure representation. The mapping process is carried out in sequence from the most prominent role in the message (usually referred to as the *topic*) to the others. This role, usually the agent, is given the subject function. However, if, for some reason, another thematic role acquires more prominence or gets more activated, then it is categorized as the *theme* before the agent has the chance to be, and thereby receives the subject function. This usually occurs when agency or animacy are not conceptually primed (i.e., in marked cases) and/or when the lemma representation associated to the most prominent thematic role happens to be more activated (as in the semantic priming conditions of my experiment). On the contrary, the activation of phonological representations of words induces a competition of word forms at the point where the positional representation of the sentence is being built, but does not interfere with syntactic planning at the functional level.

From this general picture of the first stages of the formulation process, a few implications may be drawn concerning the modular character of the operations carried out at this level. On the lexical side, the results reported here support a two-stage model of lexical retrieval in sentence production, that claims that the semantic and phonological properties of words are represented and retrieved on separate base. Thus, the two lexicalization processes appear to be both domain-specific and informationally encapsulated with respect to each other. On the syntactic side, the evidence appears to show that the building of the functional representation of the sentence is sensitive to conceptual constraints and, most importantly, to the availability of lexical representations. Consequently, we may argue that the processes leading to the functional representation of the sentence are more of an "integrative" type than of a "translation" type, following Jackendoff's (1987) terminology; that is, these processes serve to integrate conceptual information into a unified syntactic structure, rather than to transform, in an automatic and mandatory fashion, an information structure at one representation level into another information structure at a different representation level. In contrast, there is compelling evidence that the processes leading to the positional representation of the sentence might fall under the category of translation processes. As an illustration of this claim, it has been argued that most structural constraints operating on speech errors, such as morphological accommodation or suffix-stranding, are located at the positional representation level. This is, at the same time, consistent with the observation that the activation of word forms does intrude in the phrasal integration operations that take place at this processing level.

REFERENCES

Bates, E., & MacWhinney, B. (1982). Functionalist approaches to grammar. In E. Wanner & L. Gleitman (Eds.), *Language acquisition: The state of the art* (pp. 173–218). New York: Cambridge University Press.

Bates, E., & MacWhinney, B. (1989). Functionalism and the competition model. In B. MacWhinney & E. Bates (Eds.), *The cross-linguistic study of sentence processing* (pp. 1–73). Cambridge: Cambridge, England: Cambridge University Press.

Berg, T. (1987). The case against accommodation: Evidence from German speech error data. *Journal of Memory and Language, 26,* 277–299.

Bierwisch, M. (1982). Linguistics and language error. In A. Cutler (Ed.), *Slips of the tongue* (pp. 583–627). The Hague: Mouton.

Bierwisch, M., & Schreuder, R. (1992). From concepts to lexical items. *Cognition, 42,* 23–60.

Blanken, G., Dittman, J., Haas, J. C., & Wallesch, C.W. (1987). Spontaneous speech in senile dementia and aphasia: Implications for a neurolinguistic model of language production. *Cognition, 27,* 247–274.

Bock, J.K. (1982). Toward a cognitive psychology of syntax: Information-processing contributions to sentence formulation. *Psychological Review, 89,* 1–47.

Bock, J.K. (1986). Meaning, sound and syntax: Lexical priming in sentence production. *Journal of Experimental Psychology: Learning, Memory, and Cognition, 12,* 575–586.

Bock, J.K. (1987a). Co-ordinating words and syntax in speech plans. In A.W. Ellis (Ed.), *Progress in the psychology of language* (Vol. 3, pp. 337–390). Hove, UK: Lawrence Erlbaum Associates.

Bock, J.K. (1987b). An effect of the accessibility of word forms on sentence structures. *Journal of Memory and Language, 26,* 119–137.

Bock, J.K. (1990). Structure in language: Creating form in talk. *American Psychologist, 45,* 1221–1236.

Bock, J.K. (1991). A sketchbook of production problems. *Journal of Psycholinguistic Research, 20,* 141–160.

Bock, J.K., & Warren, R.K. (1985). Conceptual accessibility and syntactic structure in sentence formulation. *Cognition, 21,* 47–67.

Brown, R.W., & McNeill, D. (1966). The tip-of-the-tongue phenomenon. *Journal of Verbal Learning and Verbal Behavior, 5,* 325–337.

Butterworth, B. (1980). Introduction. In B. Butterworth (Ed.), *Language production: Vol. 1. Speech and talk* (pp. 1–17). London: Academic Press.

Butterworth, B. (1982). Speech errors: Old data in search of new theories. In A. Cutler (Ed.), *Slips of the tongue* (pp. 73–108). The Hague: Mouton.

Cutler, A. (1982). The reliability of speech error data. In A. Cutler (Ed.), *Slips of the tongue.* The Hague: Mouton.

Cutler, A. (1988). The perfect speech error. In L. Hyman & C.S. Li (Eds.), *Language, speech and mind: A zeitschrift for Vicki Fromkin.* New York: Routledge.

Dell, G.S. (1986). A spreading activation theory of retrieval in language production. *Psychological Review, 93,* 283–321.

Dell, G.S. (1988). The retrieval of phonological forms in production: Tests of predictions from a connectionist model. *Journal of Memory and Language, 27,* 124–142.

Dell, G.S., & O'Sheaghdha, P.G. (1992). Stages of lexical access in language production. *Cognition, 42,* 287–314.

Dell, G.S., & Reich, P.A. (1981). Stages in sentence production: An analysis of speech error data. *Journal of Verbal Learning and Verbal Behavior, 20,* 611–629.

del Viso, S. (1990). *Errores espontáneos del habla y producción del lenguaje* [Spontaneus errors of speech and language production]. Unpublished doctoral dissertation, Universidad Complutense de Madrid, Madrid, Spain.

del Viso, S., Igoa, J.M., & García-Albea, J.E. (1987). *Corpus de errores espontáneos del español* [Corpus of spontaneus speech errors in Spanish]. Unpublished manuscript. Universidad de Oviedo, Oviedo, Spain.

del Viso, S., Igoa, J.M., & García-Albea, J.E. (1991). On the autonomy of phonological encoding: Evidence from slips of the tongue in Spanish. *Journal of Psycholinguistic Research, 20,* 161–185.

Dewart, M.H. (1979). Role of animate and inanimate nouns in determining sentence voice. *British Journal of Psychology, 70,* 135–141.

Elías-Cintrón, R. (1994). *Towards a general theory of agreement: A psycholinguistic study of Spanish gender.* Unpublished doctoral dissertation, Cornell University, Ithaca, NY.

Fodor, J.A. (1983). *The modularity of mind.* Cambridge, MA: MIT Press.

Fodor, J.A. (1987). Modules, frames, fridgeons, sleeping dogs and the music of the spheres.In J.L. Garfield (Ed.), *Modularity in knowledge representation and natural language processing* (pp. 25–36). Cambridge, MA: MIT Press.

Fromkin, V. (1971). The nonanomalous nature of anomalous utterances. *Language, 47,* 27–52.

Garrett, M.F. (1975). The analysis of sentence production. In G. Bower (Ed.), *The Psychology of learning and motivation: Advances in research and theory* (Vol. 9, pp. 133–177). New York: Academic Press.

Garrett, M.F. (1976). Syntactic processes in sentence production. In R.J. Wales & E.C.T. Walker (Eds.), *New approaches to language mechanisms* (pp. 231–256). Amsterdam: North-Holland.

Garrett, M.F. (1980a). Levels of processing in sentence production. In B. Butterworth (Ed.), *Language production: Vol. 1. Speech and talk* (pp. 177–220). London: Academic Press.

Garrett, M.F. (1980b). The limits of accommodation: Arguments for independent processing levels in sentence production. In V. Fromkin (Ed.), *Errors in linguistic performance* (pp. 263–271). New York: Academic Press.

Garrett, M.F. (1982). Production of speech: Observations from normal and pathological language use. In A.W. Ellis (Ed.), *Normality and pathology in cognitive functions* (pp. 19–76). London: Academic Press.

Garrett, M.F. (1984). The organization of processing structure for language production: Applications to aphasic speech. In D. Caplan, A. Lecours, & A. Smith (Eds.), *Biological perspectives on language* (pp. 172–193). Cambridge, MA: MIT Press.

Garrett, M.F. (1988). Processes in language production. In F.J. Newmeyer (Ed.), *Linguistics: The Cambridge Survey: Vol. III. Language: Psychological and biological aspects* (pp. 69–96). Cambridge, England: Cambridge University Press.

Garrett, M.F. (1991). Errors and their relevance for models of language production. In G. Blanken, J. Dittman, H. Grim, J. Marshall & C. Wallesch (Eds.), *Linguistic disorders and pathologies.* Berlin: Walter de Gruyter.

Glaser, R.W. (1992). Picture naming. *Cognition, 42,* 61–105.

Harley, T.A. (1984). A critique of top–down independent levels models of speech production: Evidence from non–plan-internal speech errors. *Cognitive Science, 8,* 191–219.

Harris, M. (1978). Noun animacy and the passive voice: A developmental approach. *Quarterly Journal of Experimental Psychology, 30,* 495–501.

Hernanz, M.L., & Brucart, J.M. (1987). *La sintaxis* [Syntax]. Barcelona: Crítica.

Igoa, J.M. (1991). *La producción del lenguaje como sistema modular* [Language production as a modular system]. Unpublished doctoral dissertation, Universidad Complutense de Madrid, Madrid, Spain.

Jackendoff, R. (1987). *Consciousness and the computational mind.* Cambridge, MA: MIT Press.

Jarvella, R.J., & Engelkamp, J. (1983). Pragmatic influences in producing and perceiving language: A critical and historical perspective. In G.B. Flores d'Arcais & R.J. Jarvella (Eds.), *The process of language understanding* (pp. 225–270). New York: Wiley.

Kelly, M.H., Bock, J.K., & Keil, F.C. (1986). Prototypicality in a linguistic context: Effects on sentence structure. *Journal of Memory and Language, 25,* 59–74.

Kempen, G., & Hoenkamp, E. (1987). An incremental procedural grammar for sentence formulation. *Cognitive Science, 11,* 201–258.

Kempen, G., & Huijbers, P. (1983). The lexicalization process in sentence production and naming: Indirect election of words. *Cognition, 14,* 185–209.

Lapointe, S.G & Dell, G.S. (1989). A synthesis of some recent work in sentence production. In G.N. Carlson & M.K. Tanenhaus (Eds.), *Linguistic structure in language processing* (pp. 107–156). Dordrecht: Kluwer.

Levelt, W.J.M. (1983). Monitoring and self-repair in speech. *Cognition, 14,* 41–104.

Levelt, W.J.M. (1989). *Speaking: From intention to articulation.* Cambridge, MA: MIT Press.

Levelt, W.J.M., & Maassen, B. (1981). Lexical search and order of mention in sentence production. In W. Klein & W.J.M. Levelt (Eds.), *Crossing the boundaries in linguistics* (pp. 221–252). Dordrecht: Reidel.

Levelt, W.J.M., Schriefers, H., Vorberg, D., Meyer, A.S., Pechmann, T., & Havinga, J. (1991). The time course of lexical access in speech production: A time study of picture naming. *Psychological Review, 98,* 122–142.

Linebarger, M.C. (1990). Neuropsychology of sentence parsing. In A. Caramazza (Ed.) *Cognitive neuropsychology and neurolinguistics* (pp. 55–122). Hove, England: Lawrence Erlbaum Associates.

MacKay, D.G. (1972). The structure of words and syllables: Evidence from errors in speech. *Cognitive Psychology, 3,* 210–227.

McClelland, J.L., St. John, M., & Taraban, R. (1989). Sentence comprehension: A parallel distributed processing approach. In G. Altmann (Ed.), *Parsing and interpretation* (pp. 287–335). Hove, UK: Lawrence Erlbaum Associates.

Meyer, A.S., & Schriefers, H. (1991). Phonological facilitation in picture–word interference experiments: Effects of stimulus onset asynchrony and types of interfering stimuli. *Journal of Experimental Psychology: Learning, Memory and Cognition, 17,* 1146–1160.

Nooteboom, S. (1980). Speaking and unspeaking: Detection and correction of phonological and lexical errors in spontaneous speech. In V.A. Fromkin (Ed.), *Errors in linguistic performance* (pp. 87–96). New York: Academic Press.

Osgood, C.E., & Bock, J.K. (1977). Salience and sentencing: Some production principles. In S.Rosenberg (Ed.), *Sentence production: Developments in research and theory* (pp. 89–140). Hillsdale, NJ: Lawrence Erlbaum Associates.

O'Sheaghdha, P.G., Dell, G.S., & Marin, J.W. (1992, July). *Form activation in language production.* Poster presented at the 25th International Conference on Psychology. Brussels, Belgium.

O'Sheaghdha, P.G., Dell, G.S., Peterson, R.R., & Juliano, C. (1992). Models of form-related priming in comprehension and production. In R. Reilly & N.E. Sharkey (Eds.), *Connectionist approaches to language processing* (pp. 373–408). Hove, UK: Lawrence Erlbaum Associates.

Peterson, R.R., O'Sheaghdha, P.G., & Dell, G.S. (1989). *Phonological competition in form-related priming.* Paper presented at the 13th Annual Meeting of the Psychonomic Society, Atlanta, Georgia.

Roelofs, A. (1992). A spreading-activation theory of lemma retrieval in speaking. *Cognition, 42,* 107–142.

Rubin, D.S. (1975). Within word structure in the tip-of-the-tongue phenomenon. *Journal of Verbal Learning and Verbal Behavior, 14,* 392–397.

Schriefers, H. (1992). Lexical access in the production of noun phrases. *Cognition, 45,* 33–54.

Schriefers, H., Meyer, A.S., & Levelt, W.J.M. (1990). Exploring the time course of lexical access in language production: Picture–word interference tasks. *Journal of Memory and Language, 29,* 86–102.

Stemberger, J.P. (1985). An interactive activation model of language production. In A.W. Ellis (Ed.), *Progress in the psychology of language,* (Vol. 1, pp. 143–186). Hillsdale, NJ: Lawrence Erlbaum Associates.

van Wijk, C., & Kempen, G. (1987). A dual system for producing self-repairs in spontaneous speech: Evidence from experimentally-elicited corrections. *Cognitive Psychology, 19,* 403–440.

Author Index

Subject Index

W